ginal · Danbi Original · Danbi Original · Danbi Original · Danbi Original · Danbi Original · Da

One thousand and one nights

vol.2

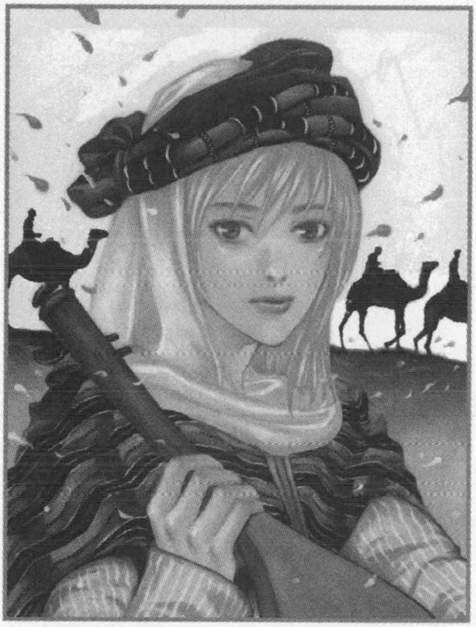

Han SeungHee · Jeon JinSeok

ice
Kunion

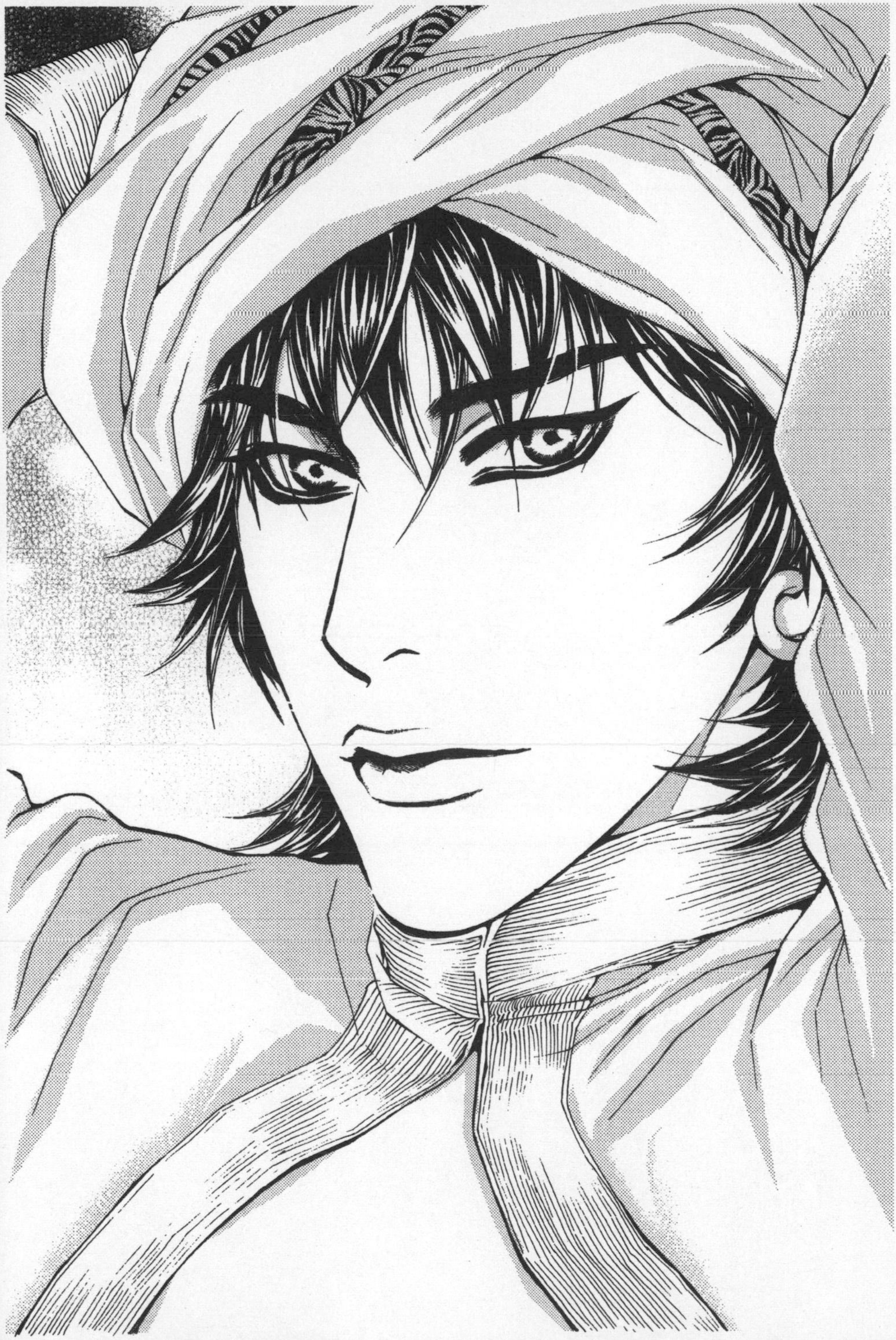

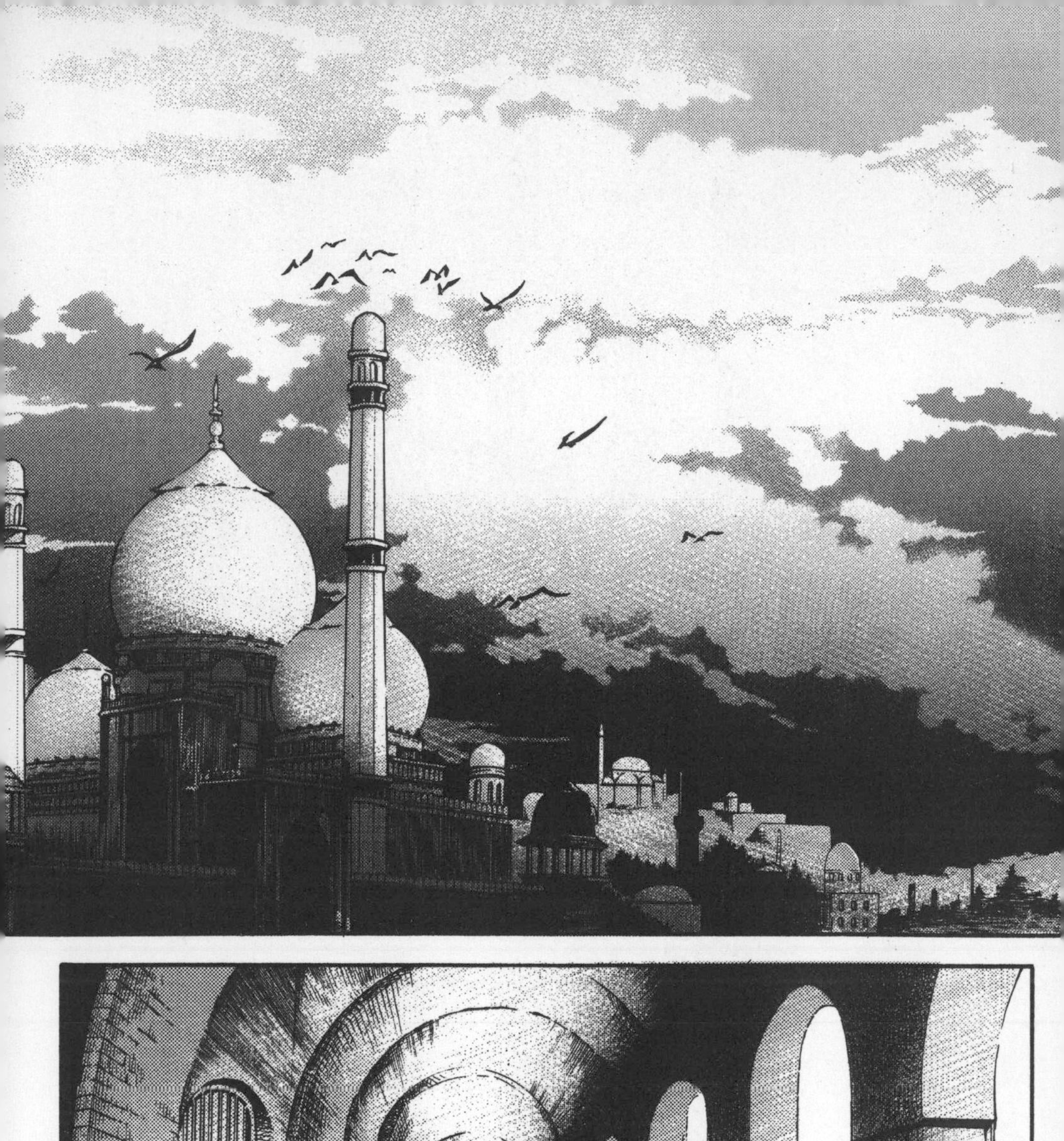
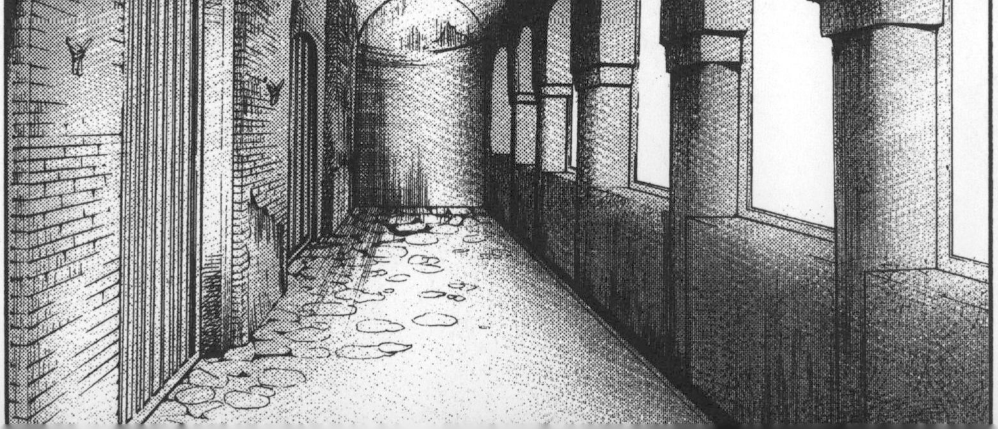

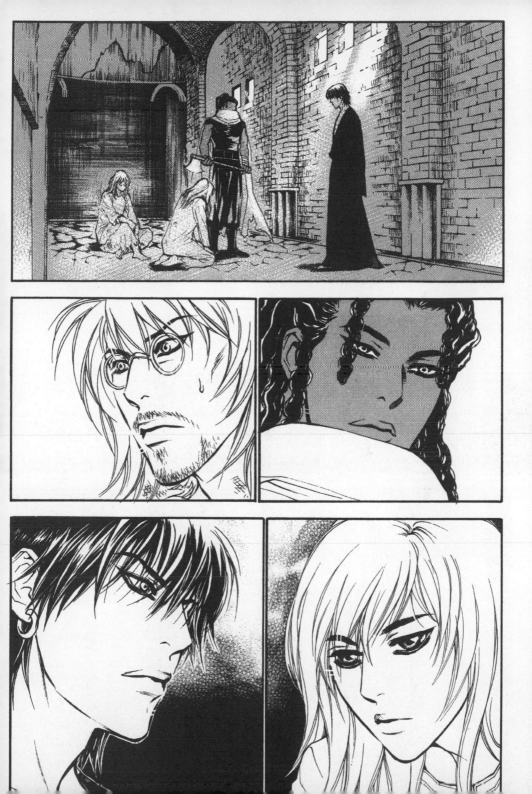

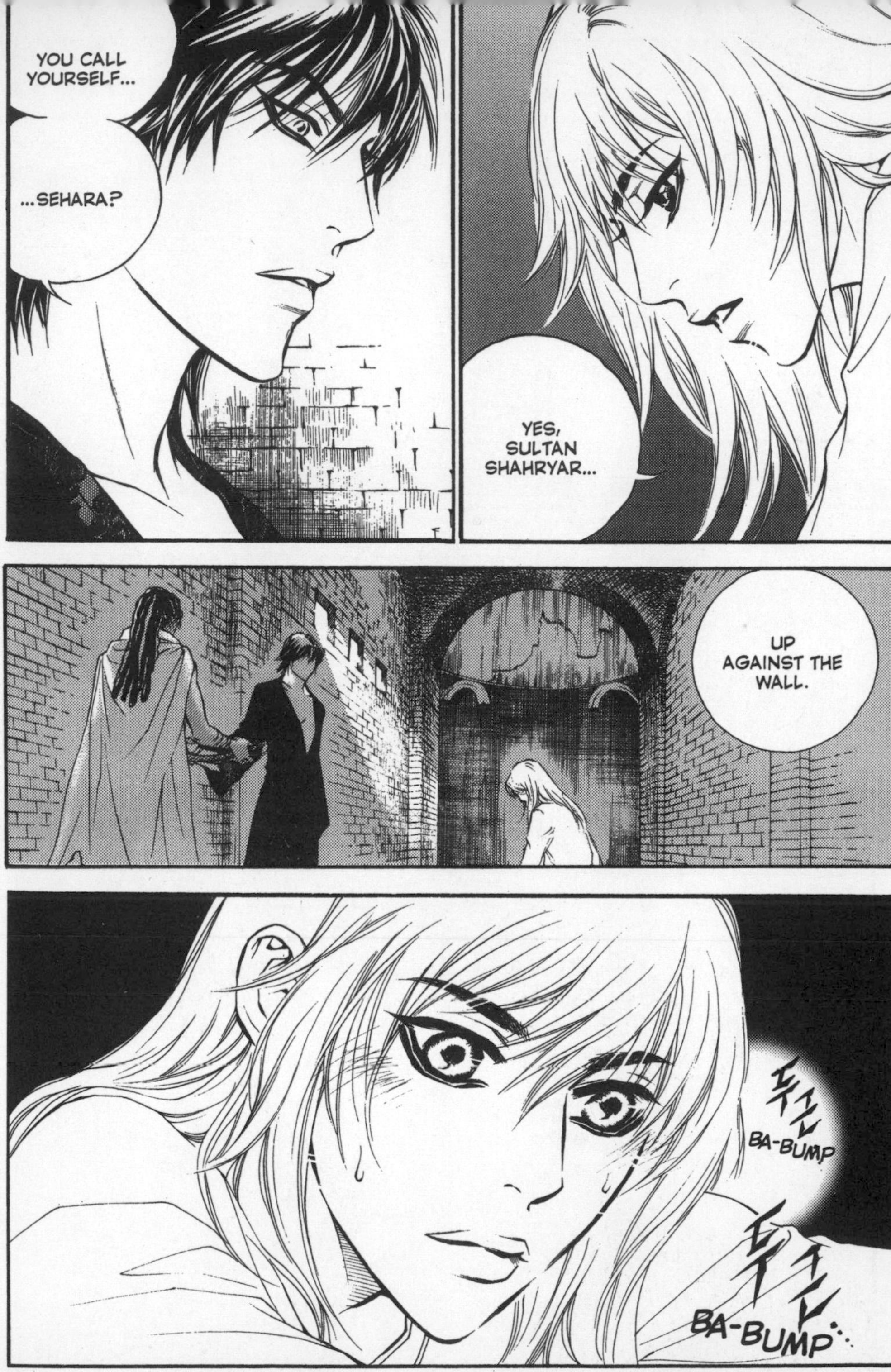
YOU CALL YOURSELF...
...SEHARA?
YES, SULTAN SHAHRYAR...
UP AGAINST THE WALL.
BA-BUMP
BA-BUMP...

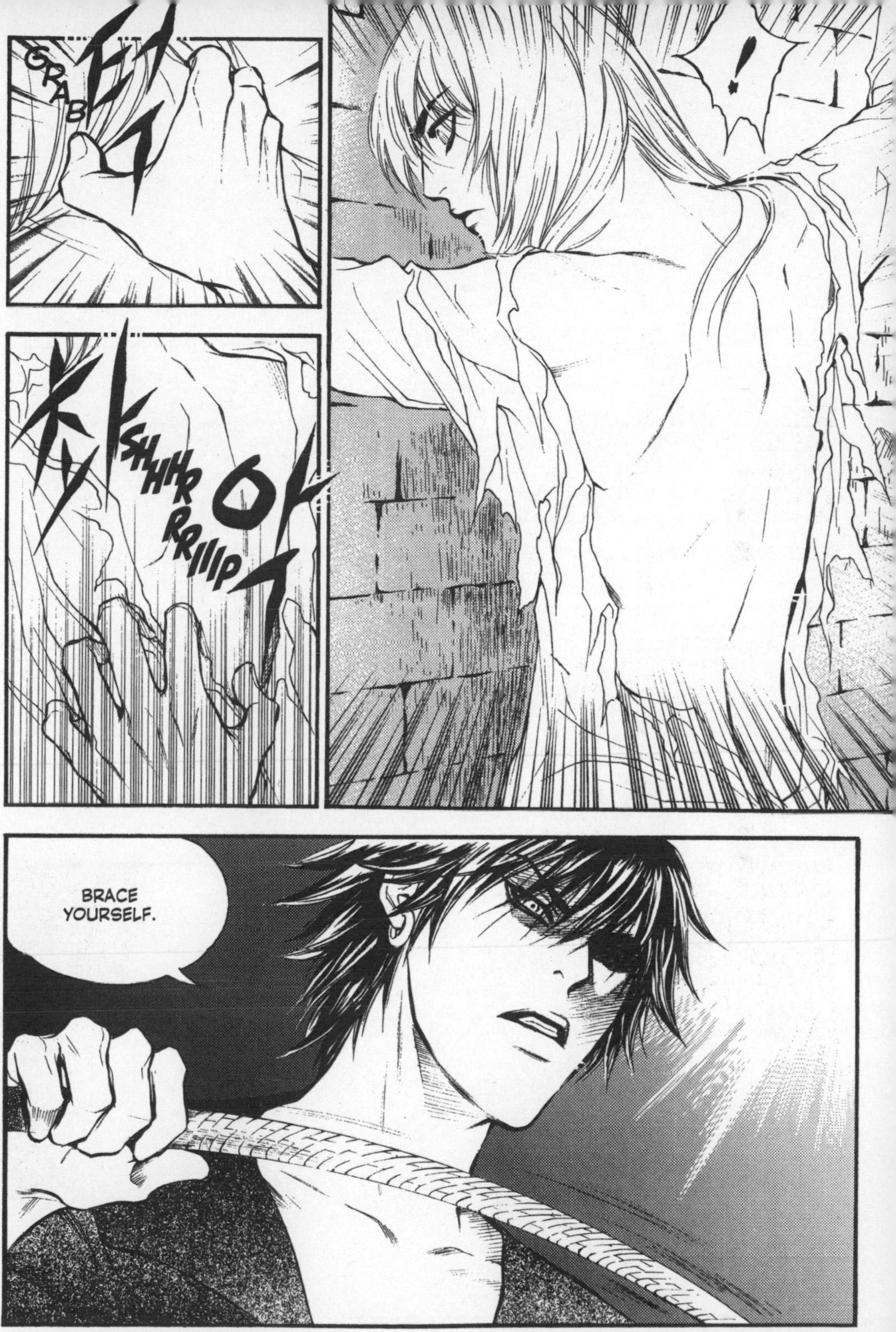
GRAB
SHHHR RRIIIP
!
BRACE YOURSELF.

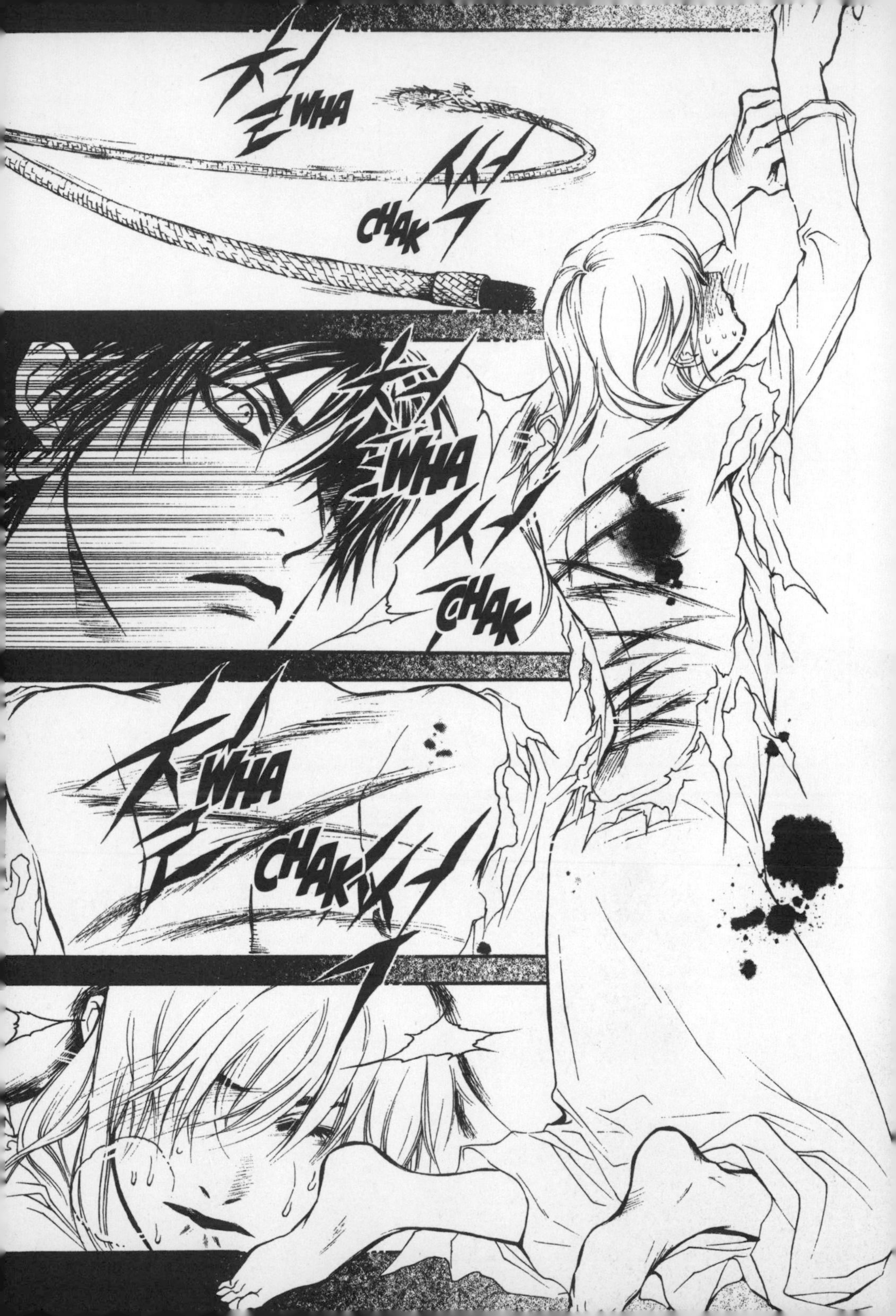
WHA
CHAK
WHA
CHAK
WHA
CHAK

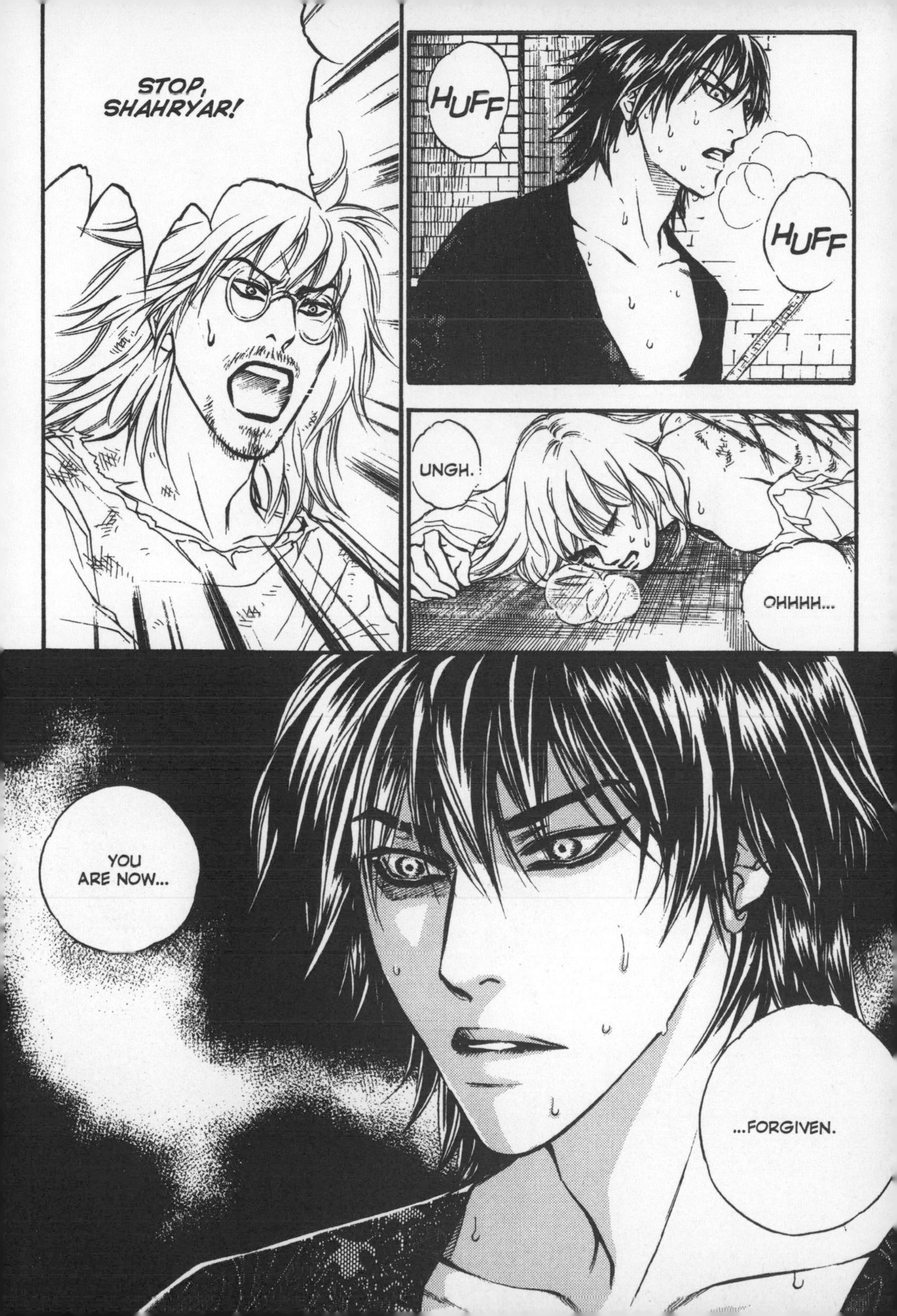
STOP, SHAHRYAR!
HUFF
HUFF
UNGH.
OHHHH...
YOU ARE NOW...
...FORGIVEN.

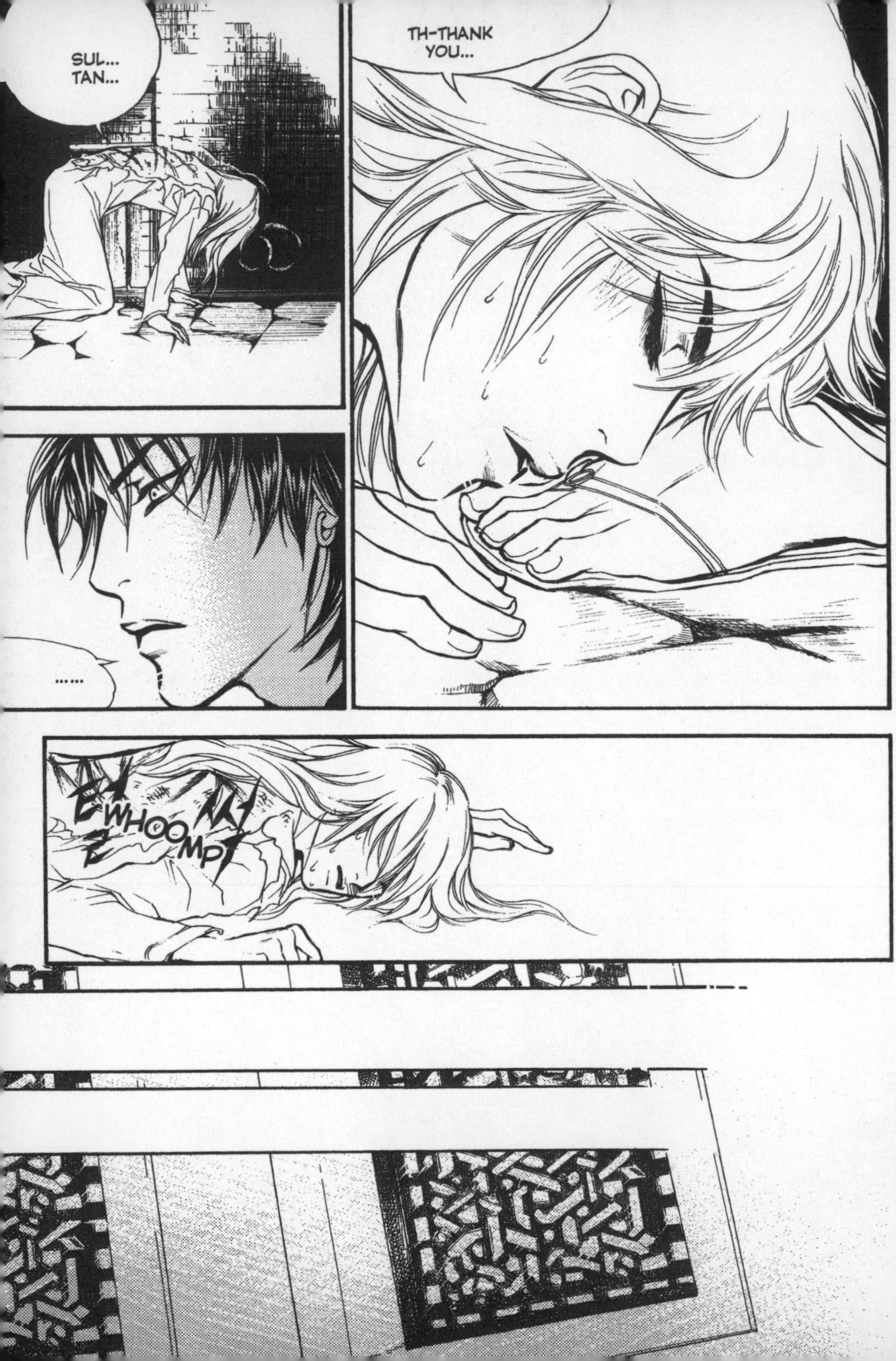
SUL... TAN...
......
TH-THANK YOU...
WHOOMP

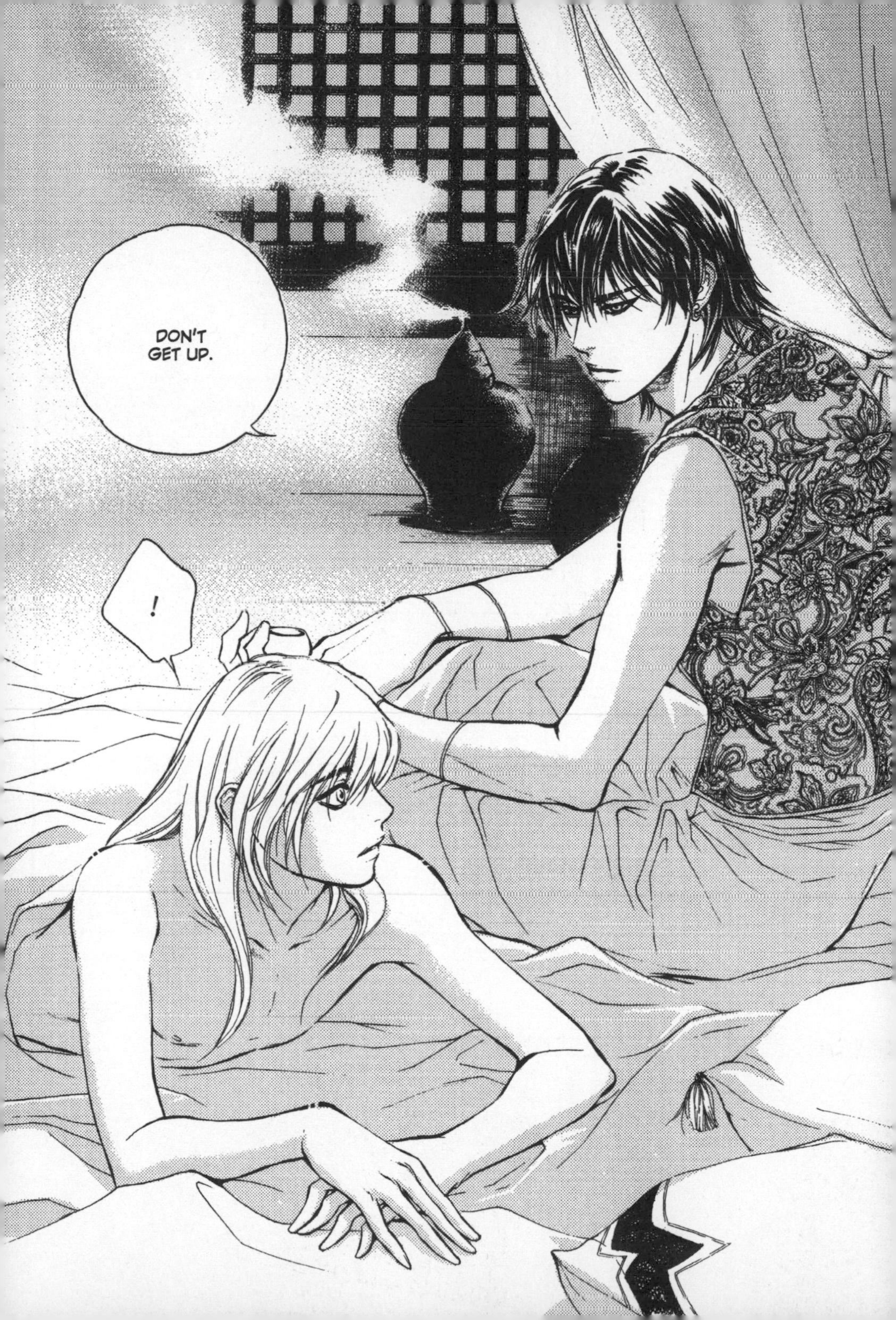
DON'T GET UP.
!

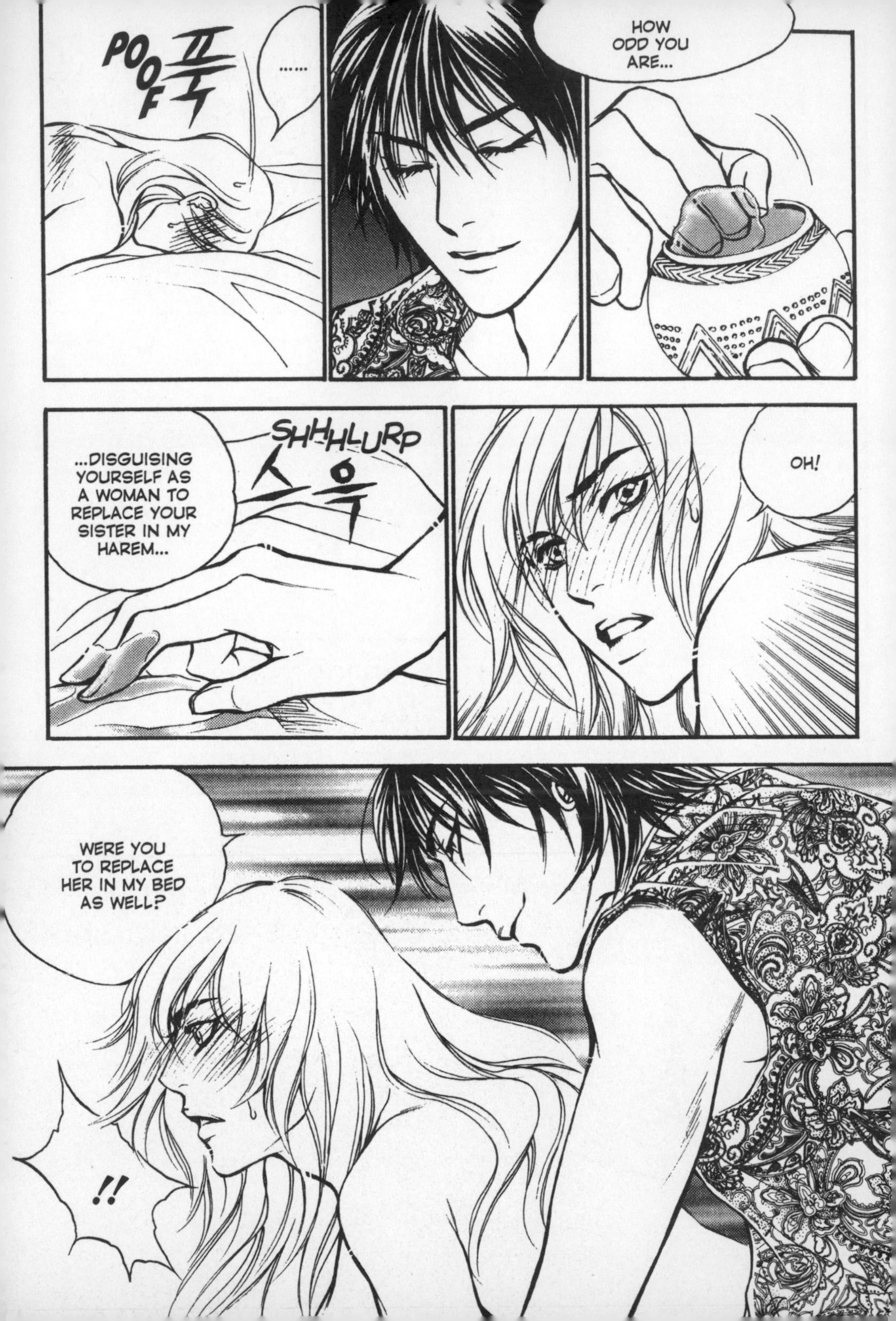
POOF
......
HOW ODD YOU ARE...
...DISGUISING YOURSELF AS A WOMAN TO REPLACE YOUR SISTER IN MY HAREM...
SHHHLURP
OH!
WERE YOU TO REPLACE HER IN MY BED AS WELL?
!!

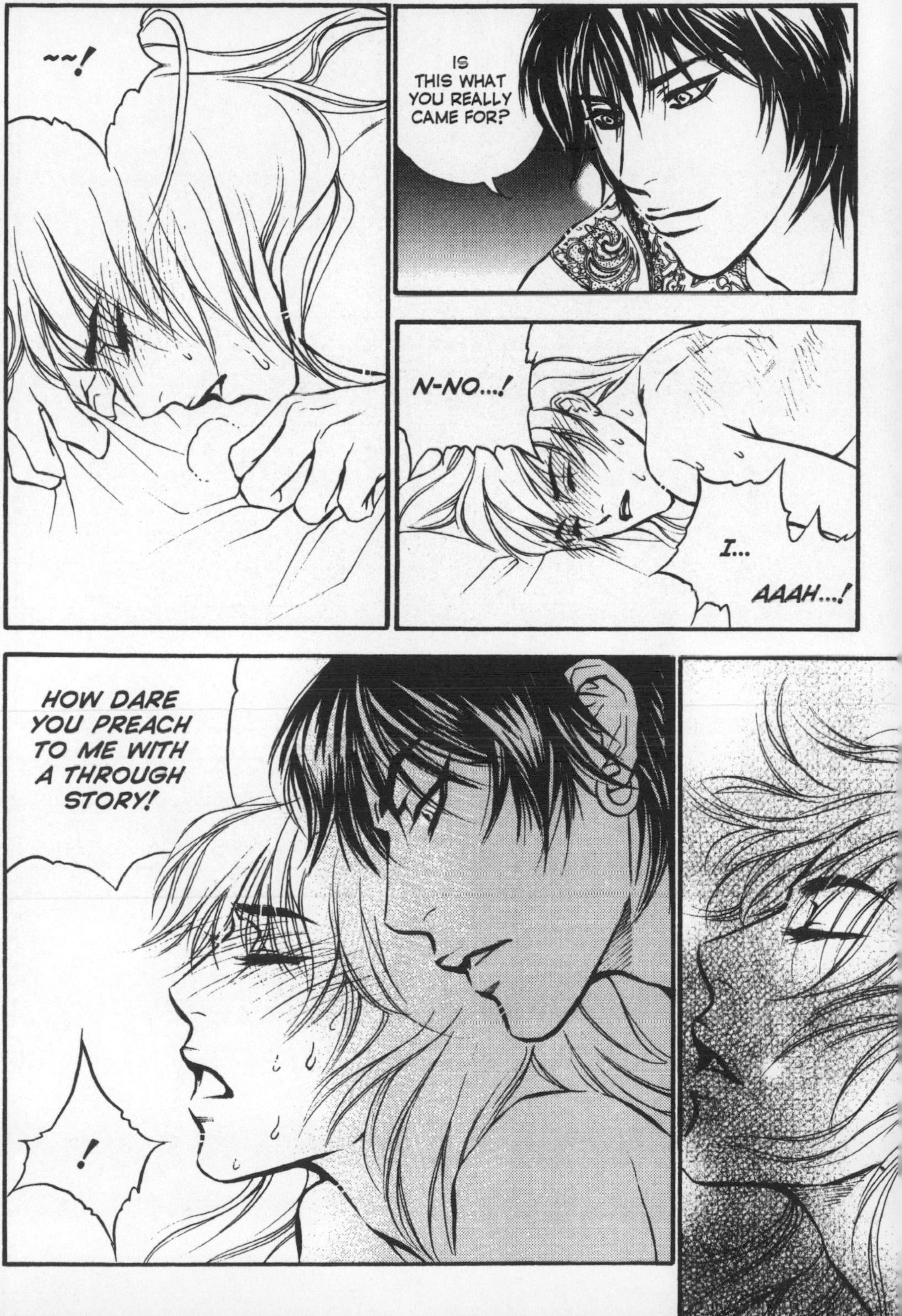
~~!
IS THIS WHAT YOU REALLY CAME FOR?
N-NO...!
I...
AAAH...!
HOW DARE YOU PREACH TO ME WITH A THROUGH STORY!
!

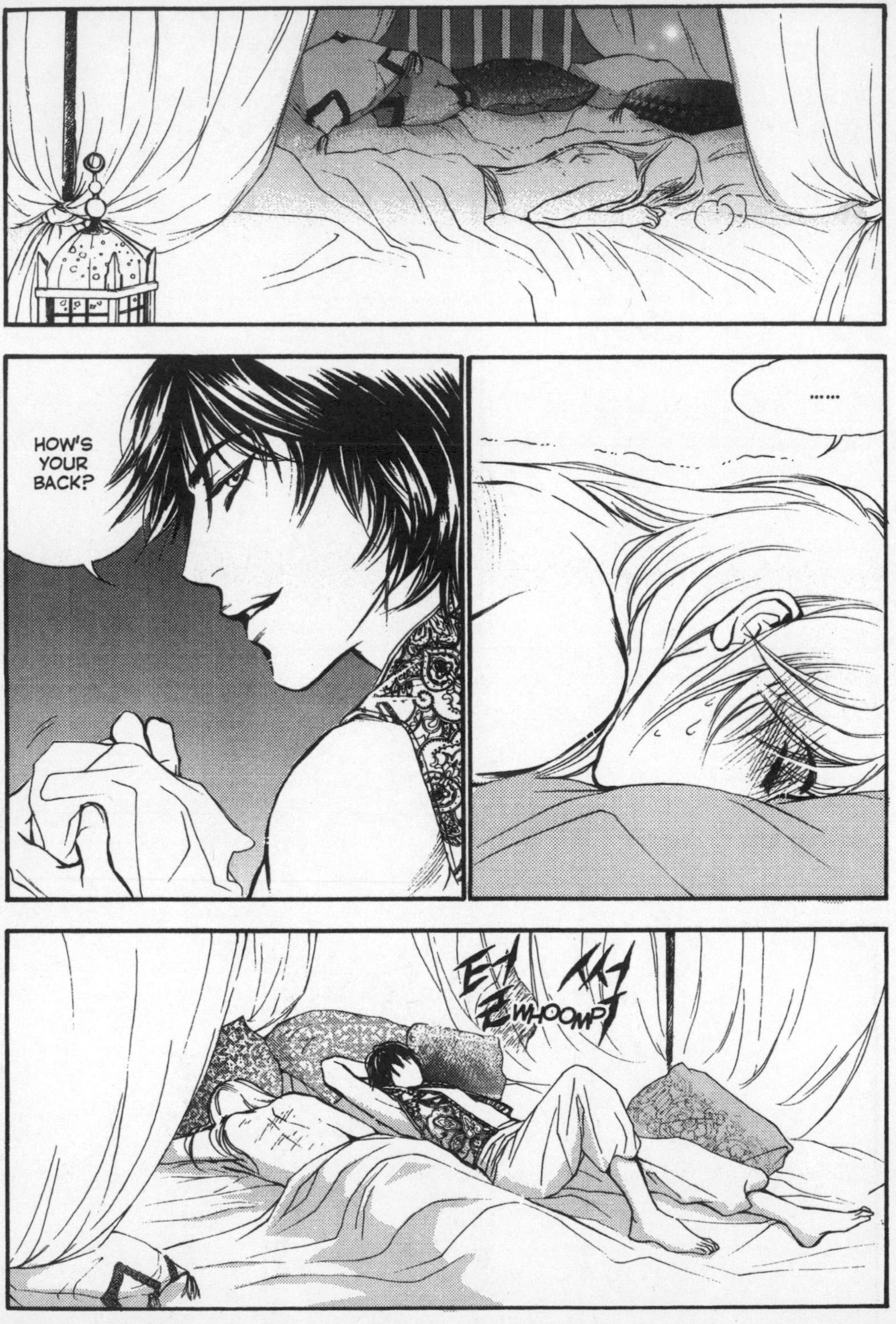
HOW'S YOUR BACK?
......
털썩
WHOOMP

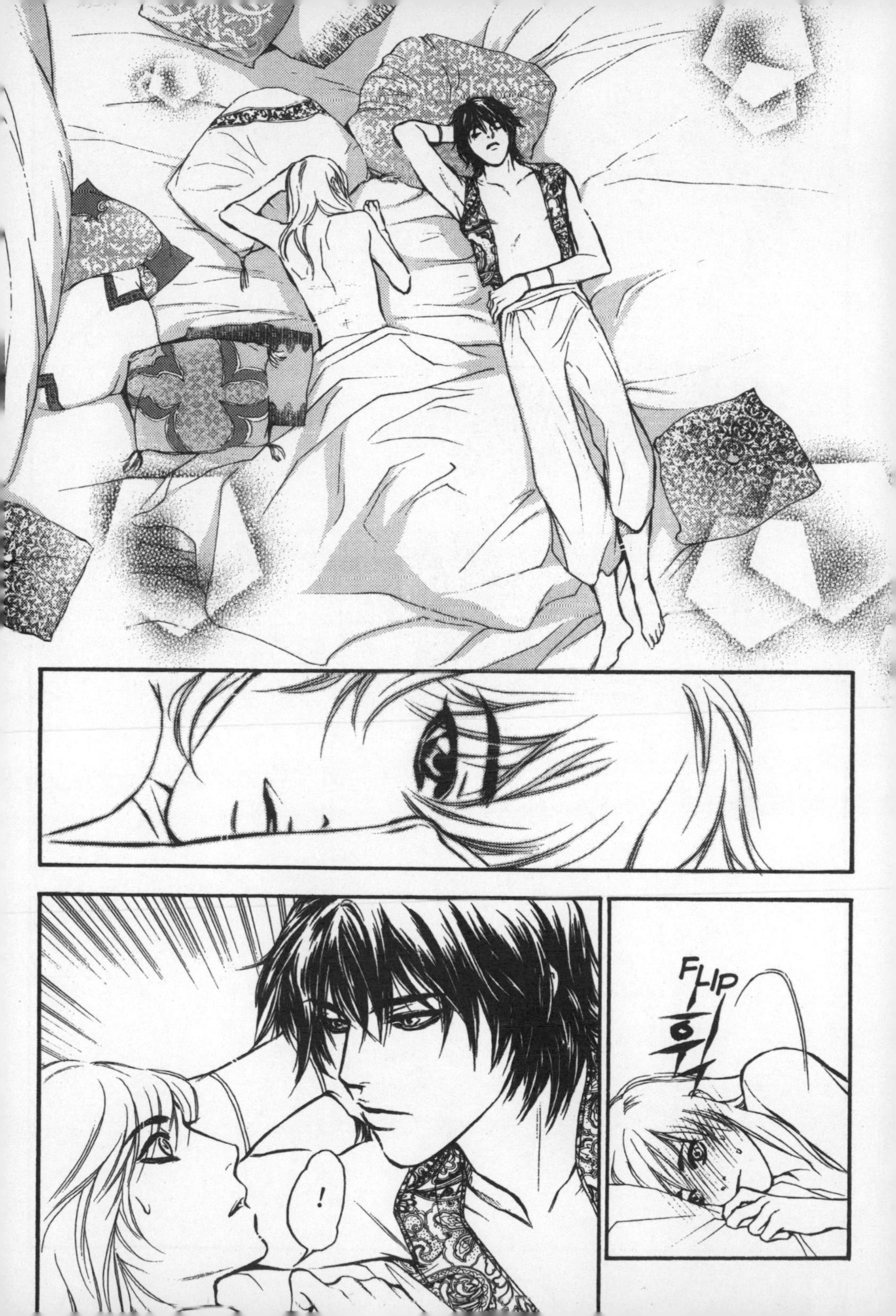
!
FLIP

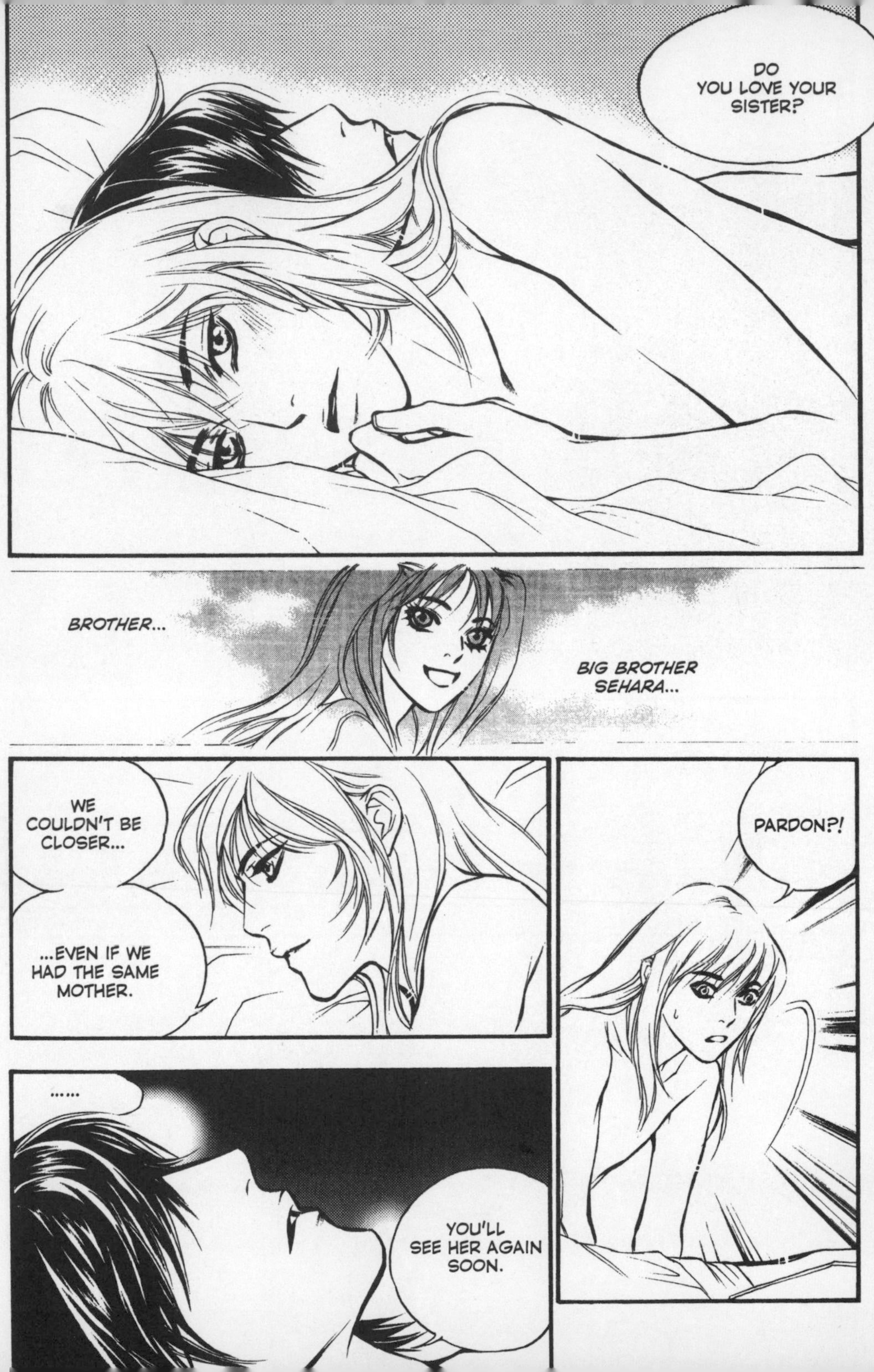
DO YOU LOVE YOUR SISTER?
BROTHER...
BIG BROTHER SEHARA...
WE COULDN'T BE CLOSER...
...EVEN IF WE HAD THE SAME MOTHER.
......
YOU'LL SEE HER AGAIN SOON.
PARDON?!

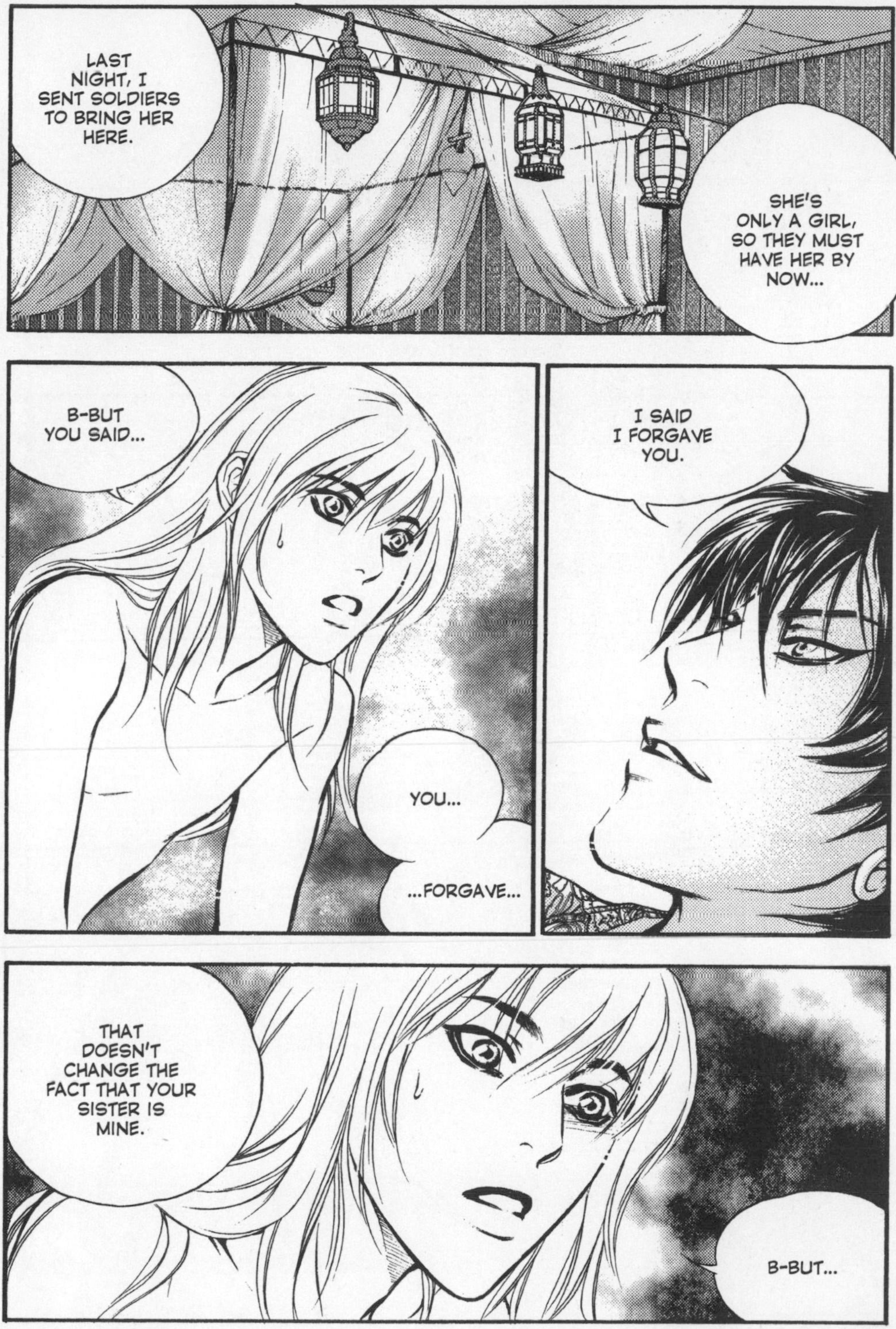
LAST NIGHT, I SENT SOLDIERS TO BRING HER HERE.
SHE'S ONLY A GIRL, SO THEY MUST HAVE HER BY NOW...
B-BUT YOU SAID...
YOU...
...FORGAVE...
I SAID I FORGAVE YOU.
THAT DOESN'T CHANGE THE FACT THAT YOUR SISTER IS MINE.
B-BUT...

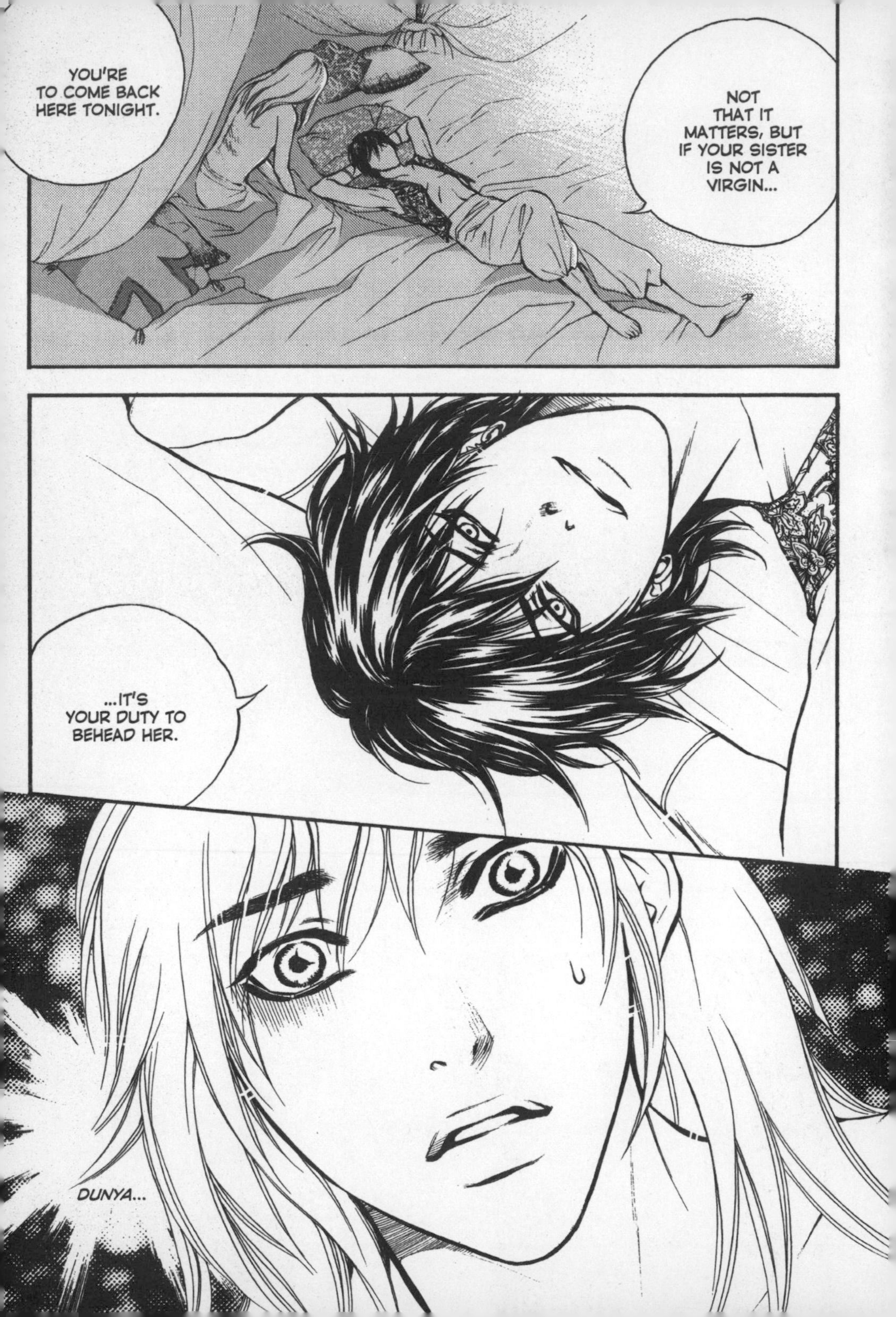
YOU'RE TO COME BACK HERE TONIGHT.
NOT THAT IT MATTERS, BUT IF YOUR SISTER IS NOT A VIRGIN...
...IT'S YOUR DUTY TO BEHEAD HER.
DUNYA...

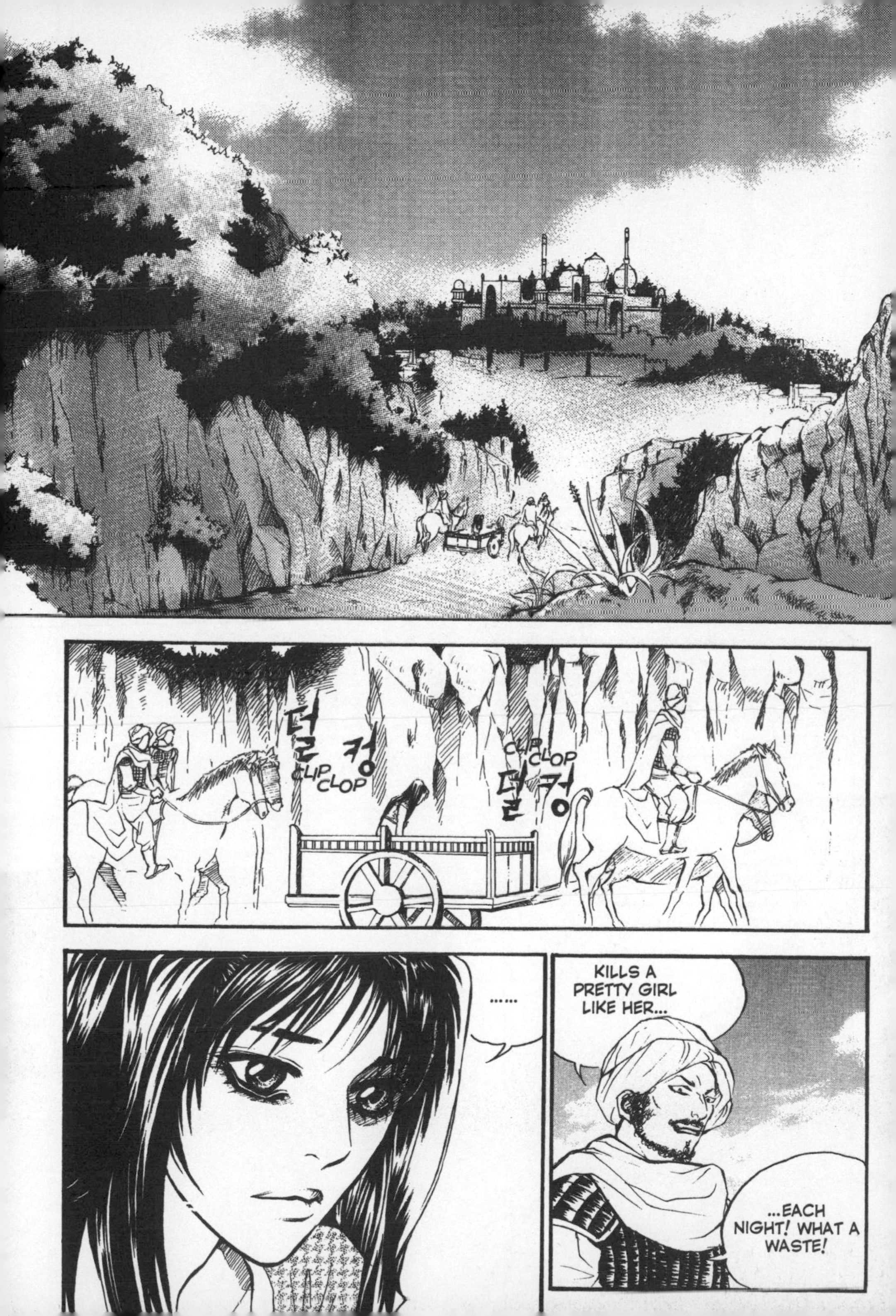
덜컹
CLIP CLOP
CLIP CLOP
덜컹
……
KILLS A PRETTY GIRL LIKE HER...
...EACH NIGHT! WHAT A WASTE!

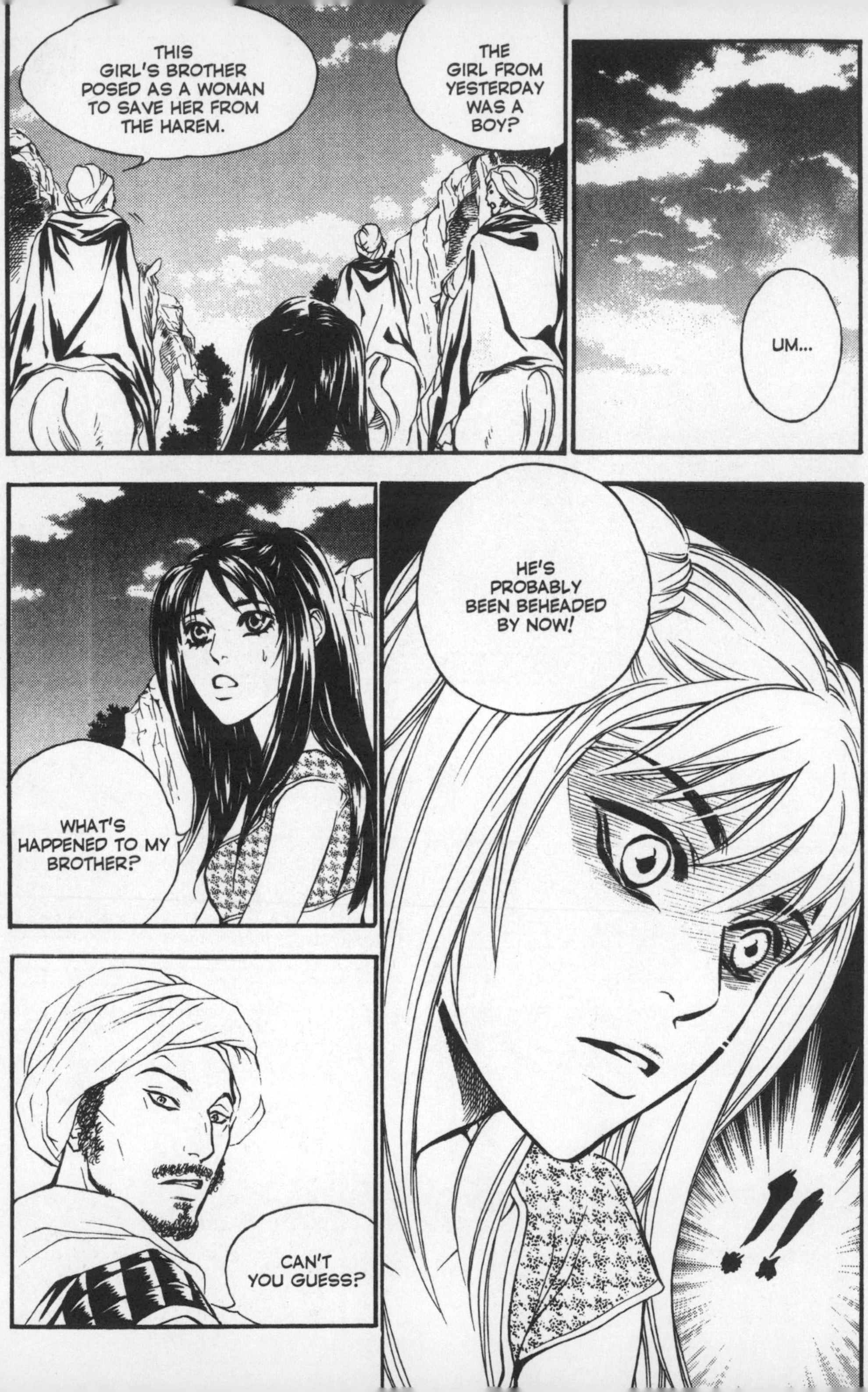
THIS GIRL'S BROTHER POSED AS A WOMAN TO SAVE HER FROM THE HAREM.
THE GIRL FROM YESTERDAY WAS A BOY?
UM...
WHAT'S HAPPENED TO MY BROTHER?
CAN'T YOU GUESS?
HE'S PROBABLY BEEN BEHEADED BY NOW!
!!

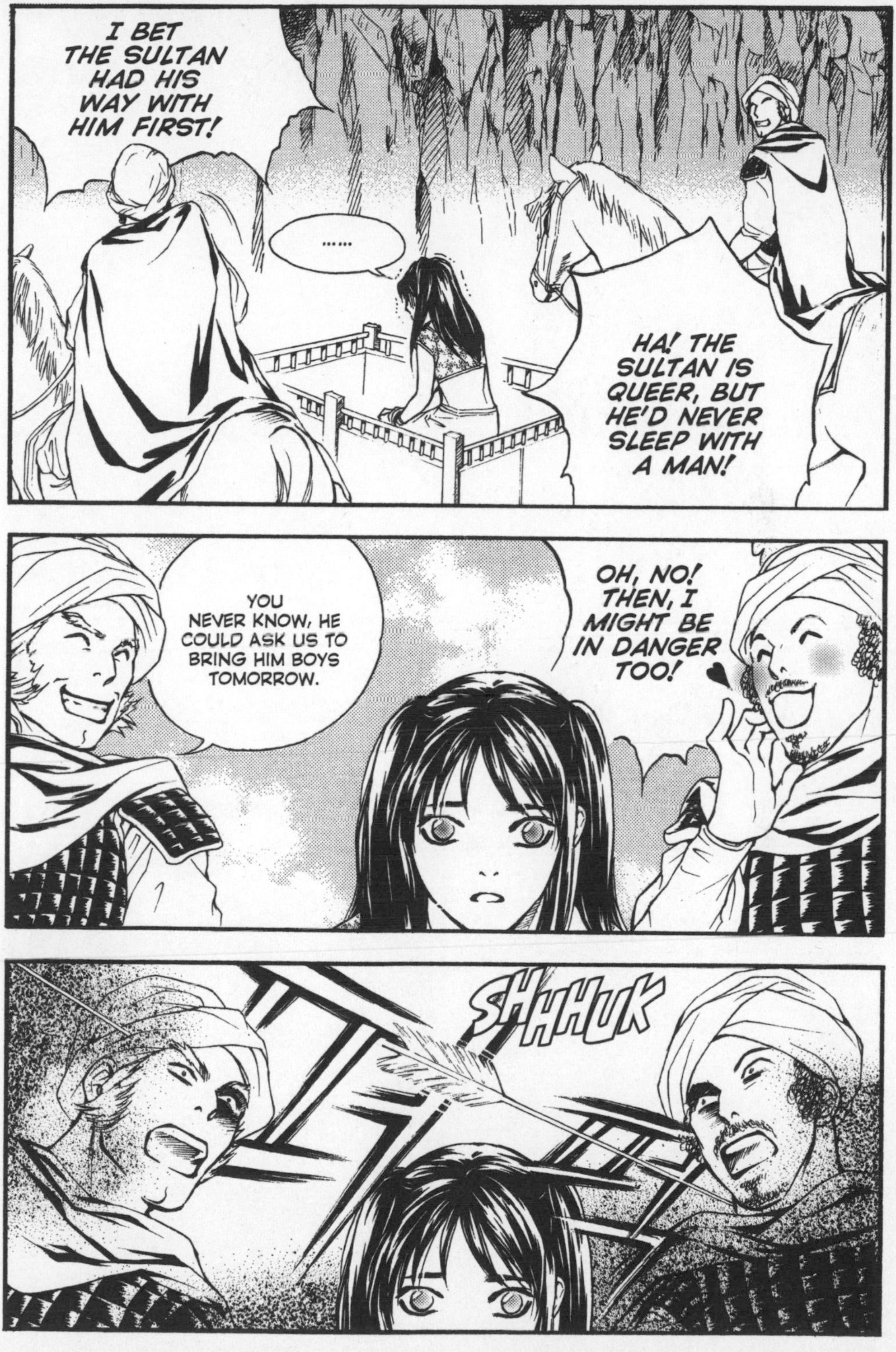
I BET THE SULTAN HAD HIS WAY WITH HIM FIRST!
......
HA! THE SULTAN IS QUEER, BUT HE'D NEVER SLEEP WITH A MAN!
YOU NEVER KNOW, HE COULD ASK US TO BRING HIM BOYS TOMORROW.
OH, NO! THEN, I MIGHT BE IN DANGER TOO!
SHHHUK

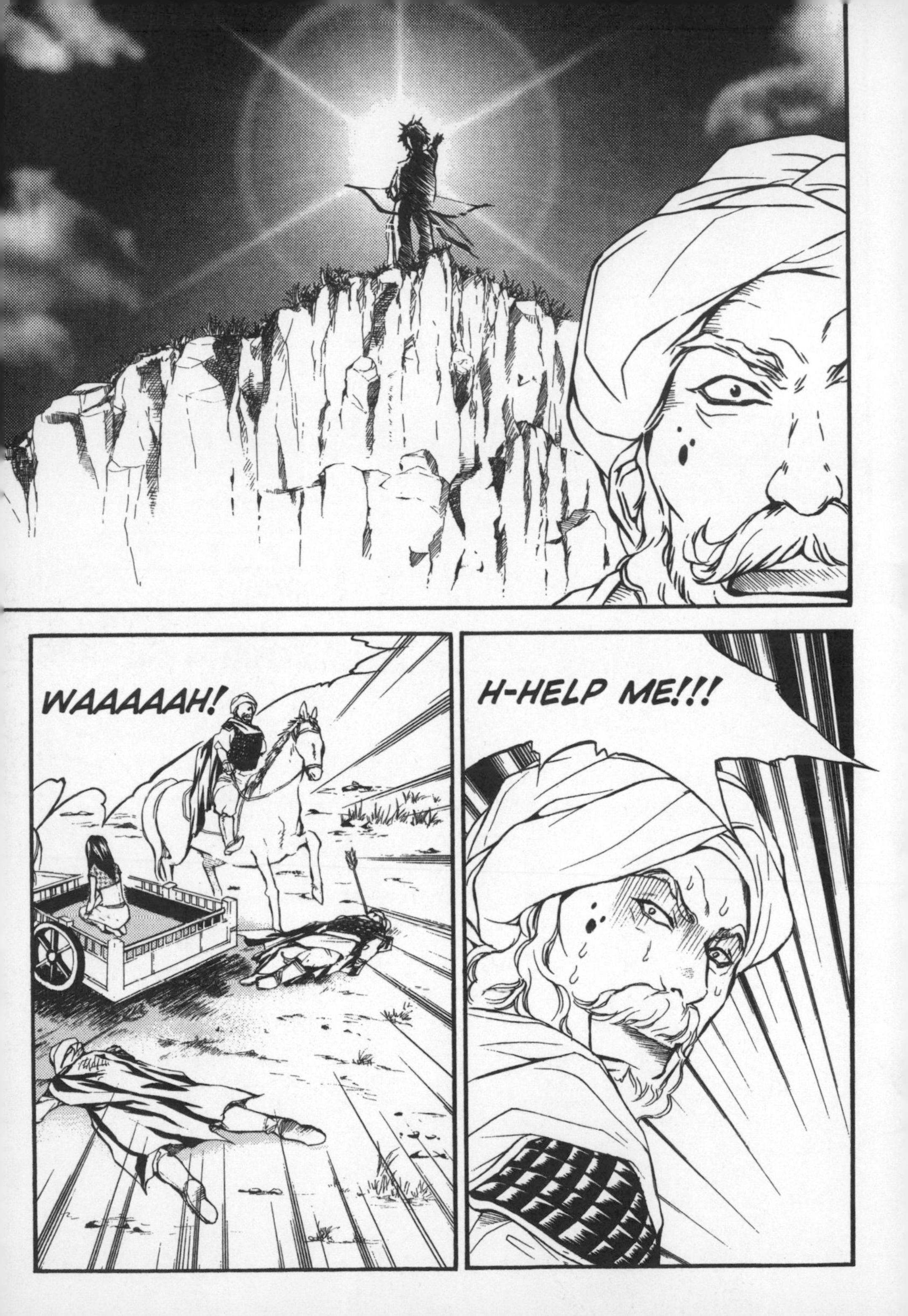
WAAAAAH!
H-HELP ME!!!

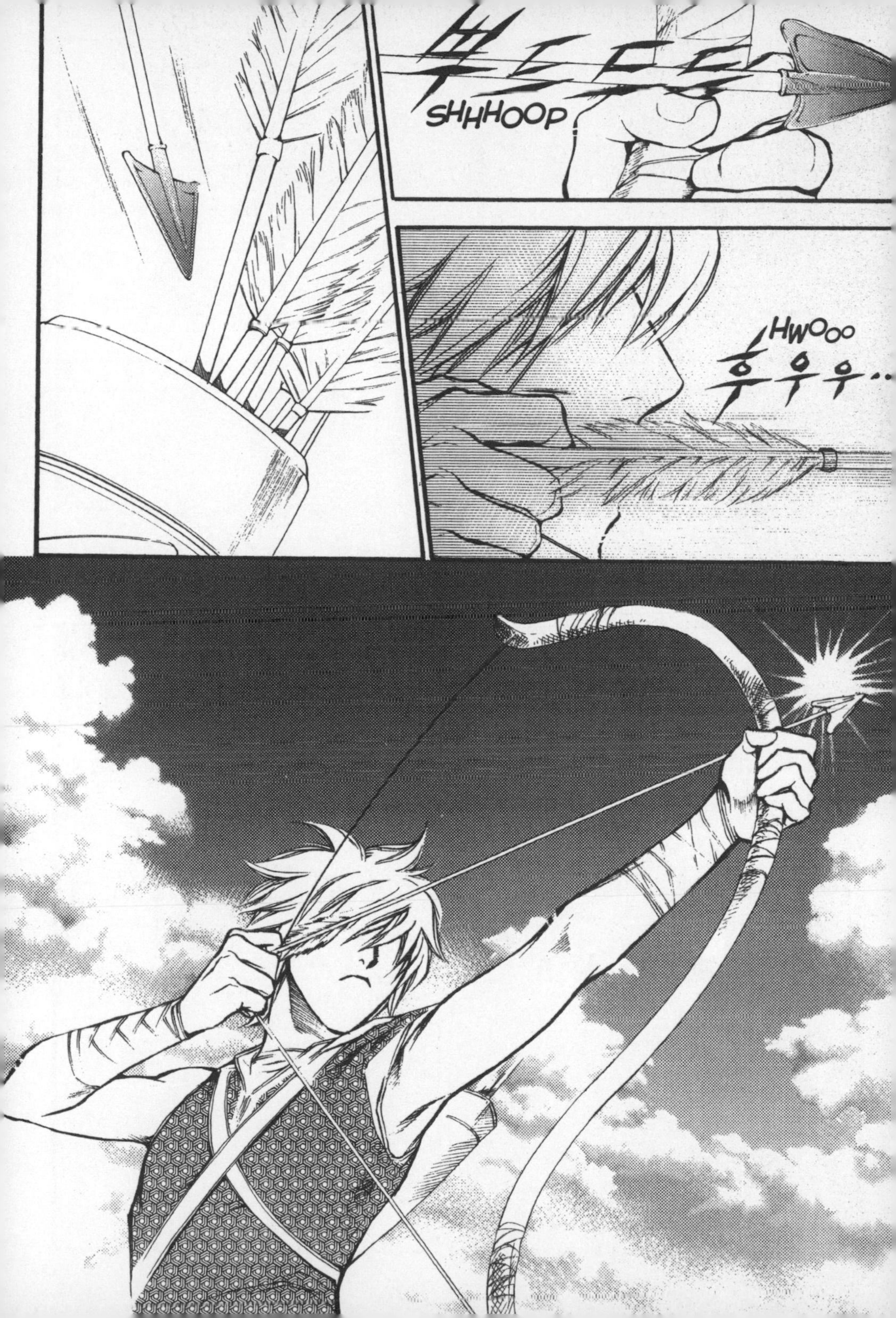
SHHHOOP
HWOOO
후우우…

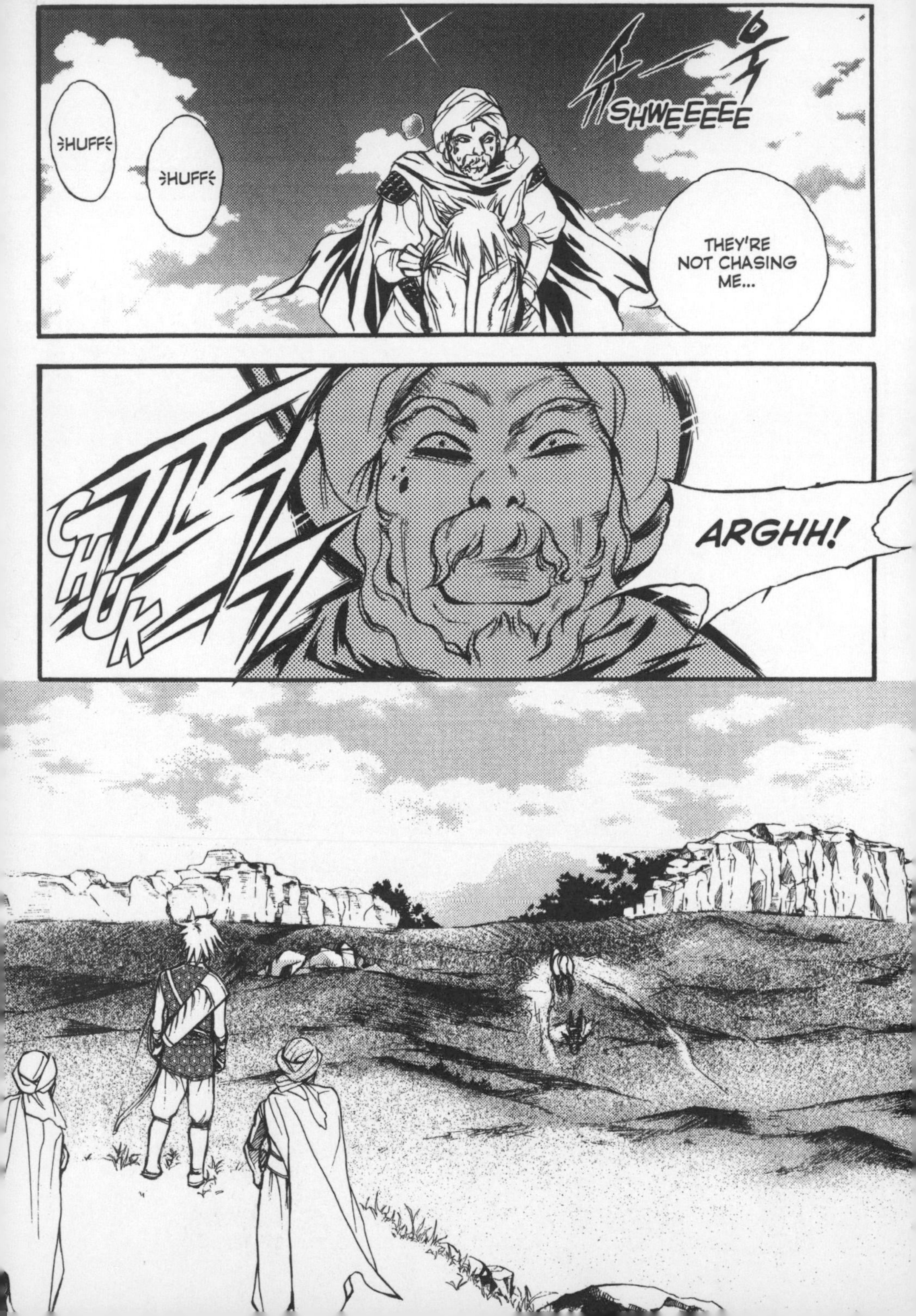

SHWEEEEEE
⁃HUFF⁃
⁃HUFF⁃
THEY'RE NOT CHASING ME...
CHUK
ARGHH!

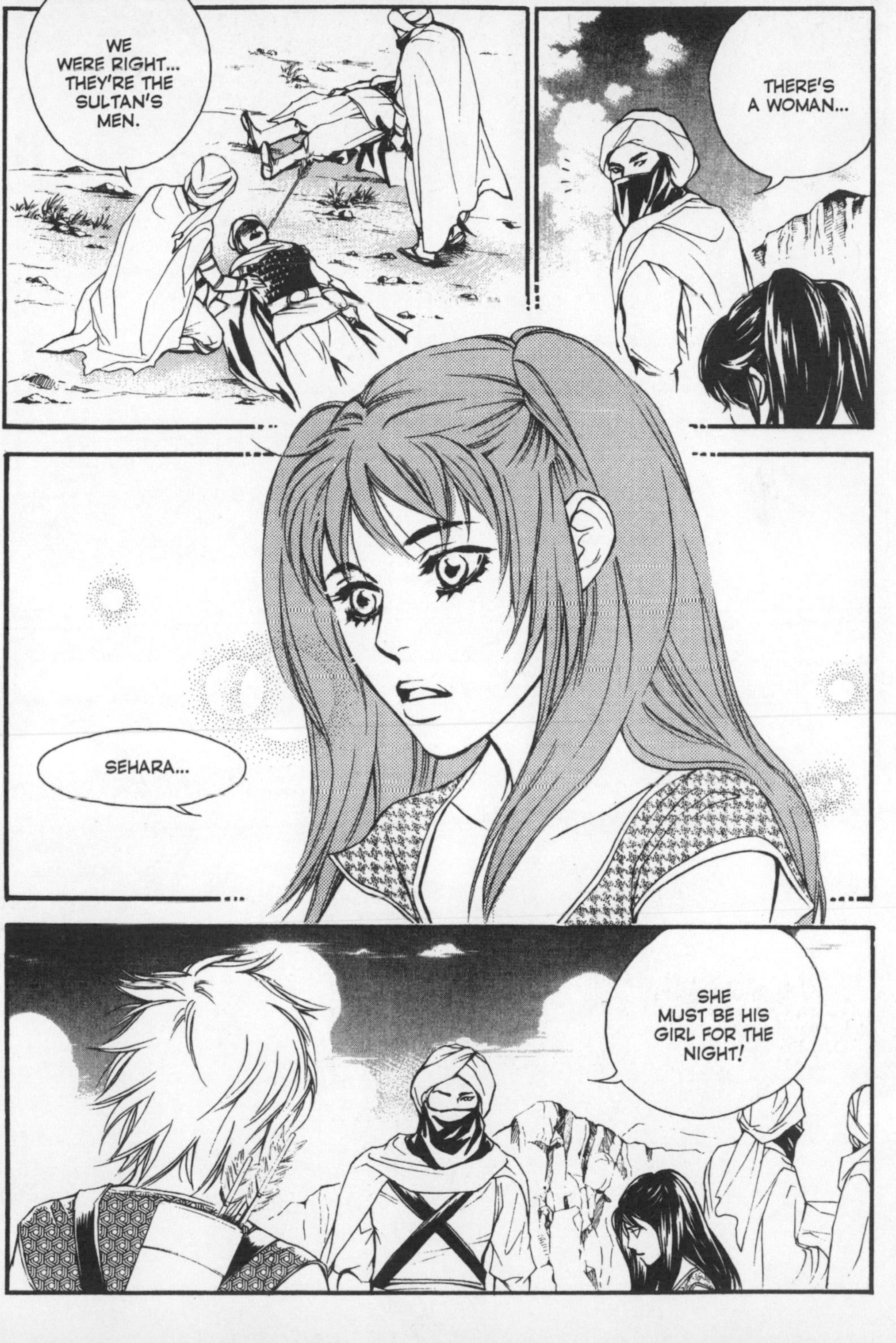
WE WERE RIGHT... THEY'RE THE SULTAN'S MEN.
THERE'S A WOMAN...
SEHARA...
SHE MUST BE HIS GIRL FOR THE NIGHT!

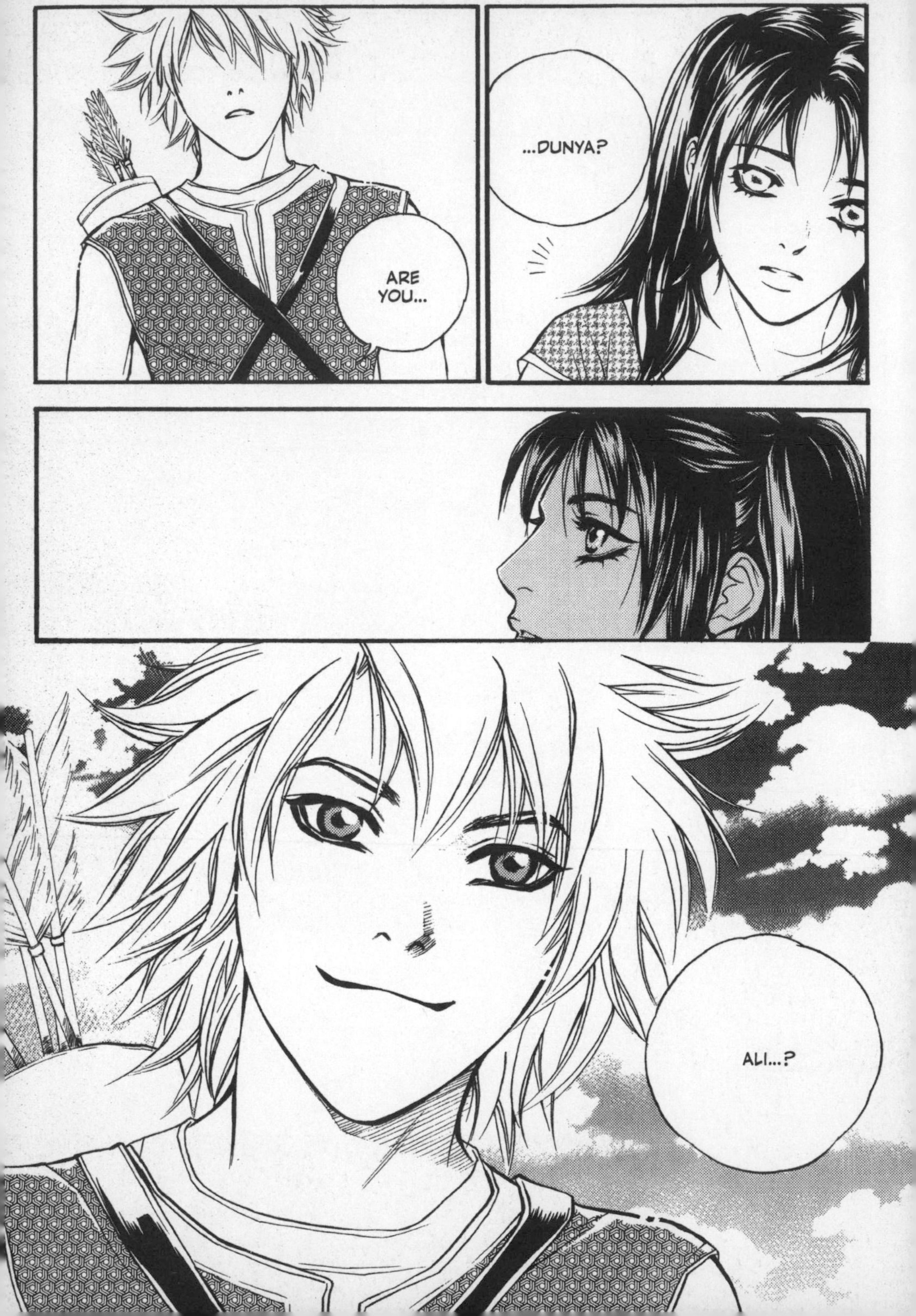
ARE YOU...
...DUNYA?
ALI...?

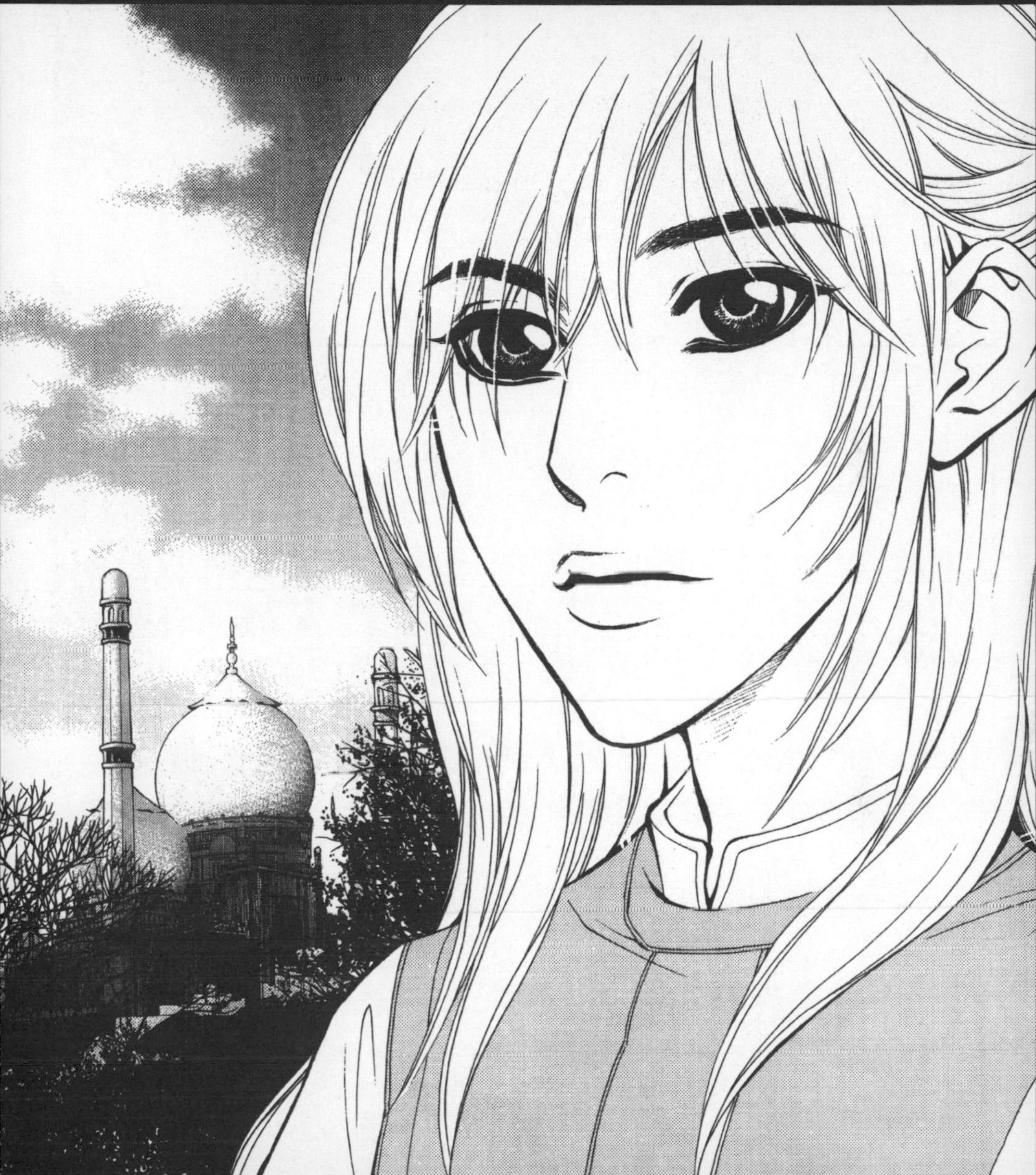

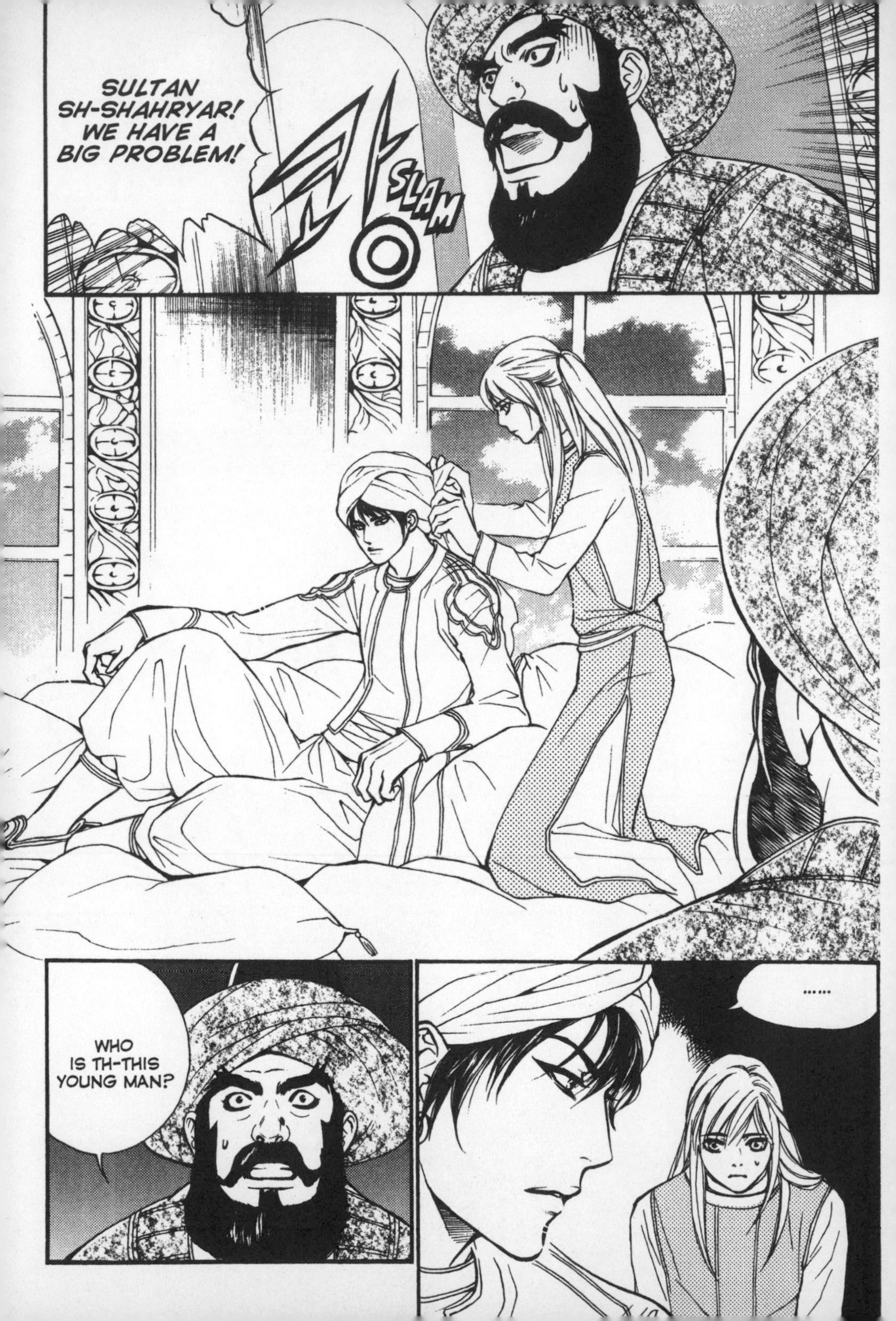
SULTAN SH-SHAHRYAR! WE HAVE A BIG PROBLEM!
SLAM
WHO IS TH-THIS YOUNG MAN?
......

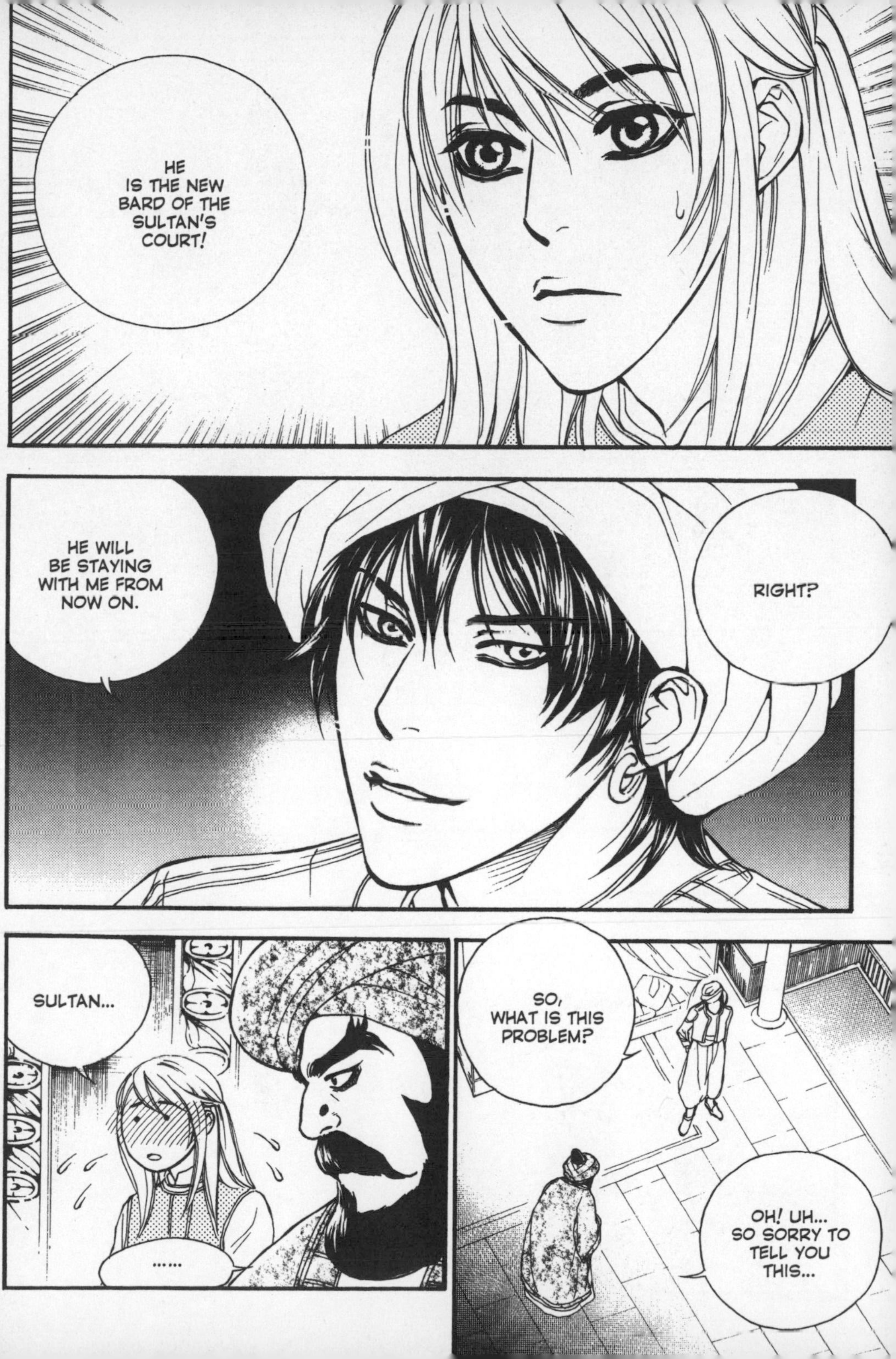
HE IS THE NEW BARD OF THE SULTAN'S COURT!
HE WILL BE STAYING WITH ME FROM NOW ON.
RIGHT?
SULTAN...
......
SO, WHAT IS THIS PROBLEM?
OH! UH... SO SORRY TO TELL YOU THIS...

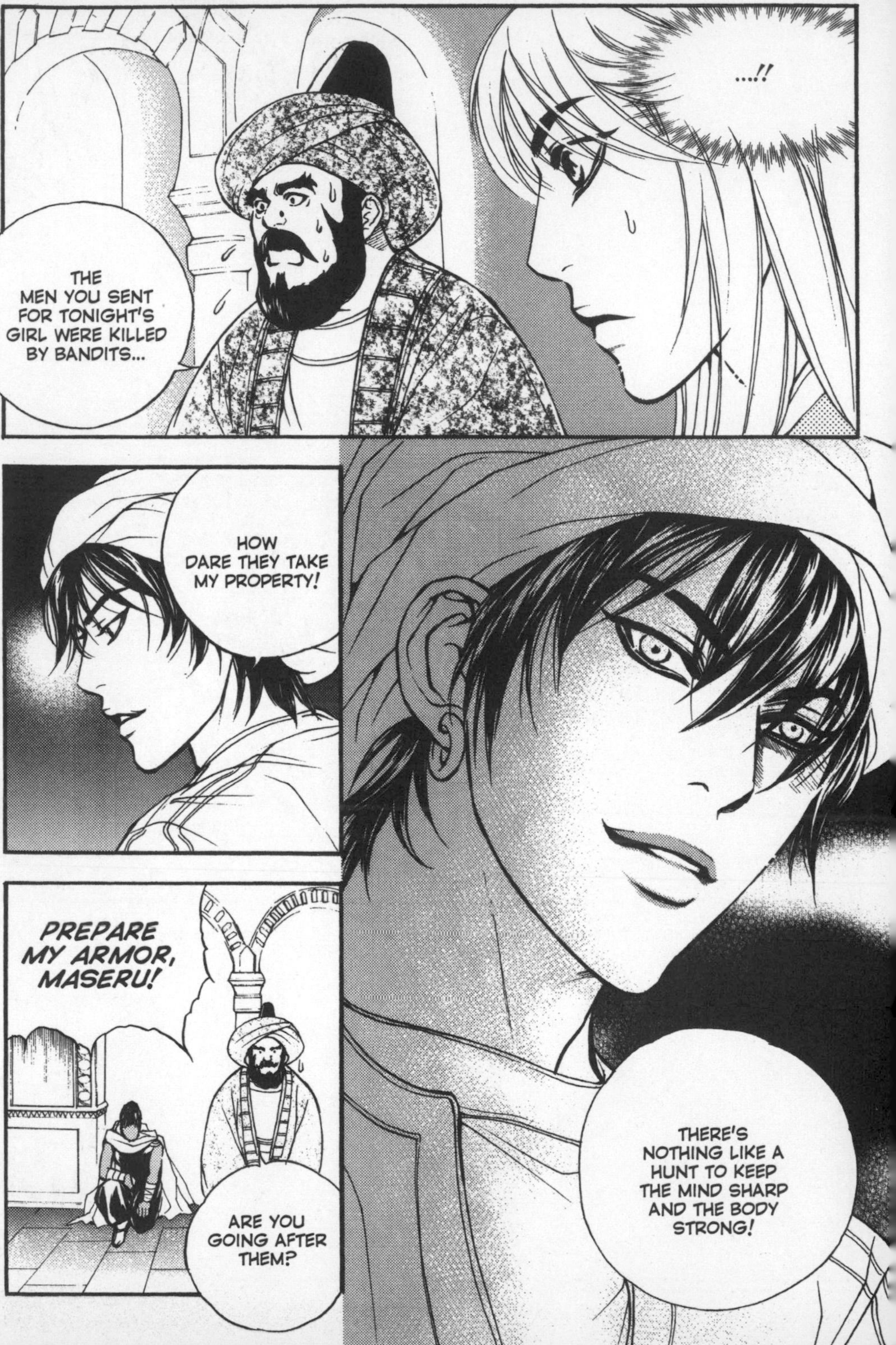
THE MEN YOU SENT FOR TONIGHT'S GIRL WERE KILLED BY BANDITS...
...!!
HOW DARE THEY TAKE MY PROPERTY!
PREPARE MY ARMOR, MASERU!
ARE YOU GOING AFTER THEM?
THERE'S NOTHING LIKE A HUNT TO KEEP THE MIND SHARP AND THE BODY STRONG!

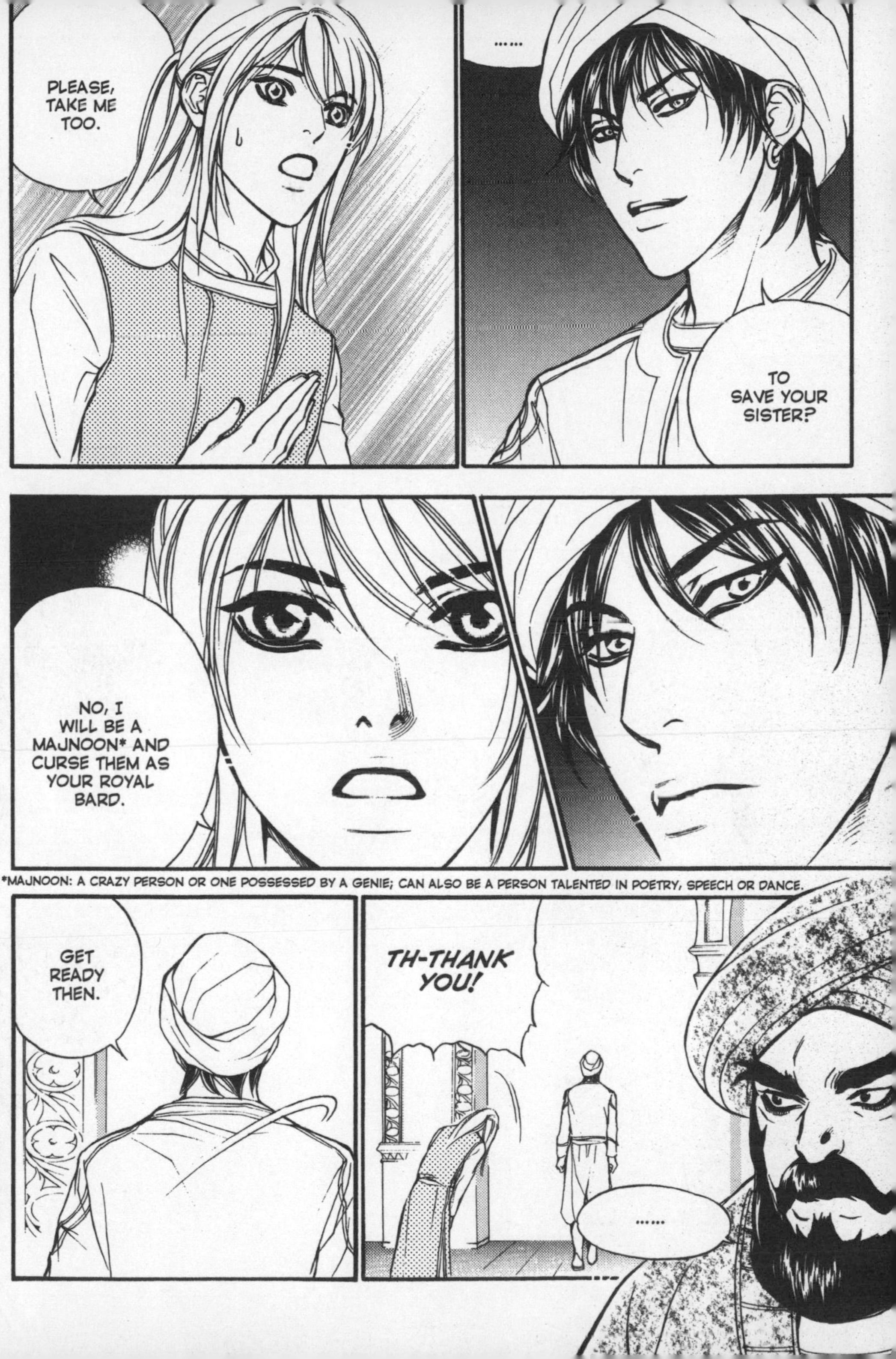
PLEASE, TAKE ME TOO.
......
TO SAVE YOUR SISTER?
NO, I WILL BE A MAJNOON* AND CURSE THEM AS YOUR ROYAL BARD.
GET READY THEN.
TH-THANK YOU!
......

*MAJNOON: A CRAZY PERSON OR ONE POSSESSED BY A GENIE; CAN ALSO BE A PERSON TALENTED IN POETRY, SPEECH OR DANCE.

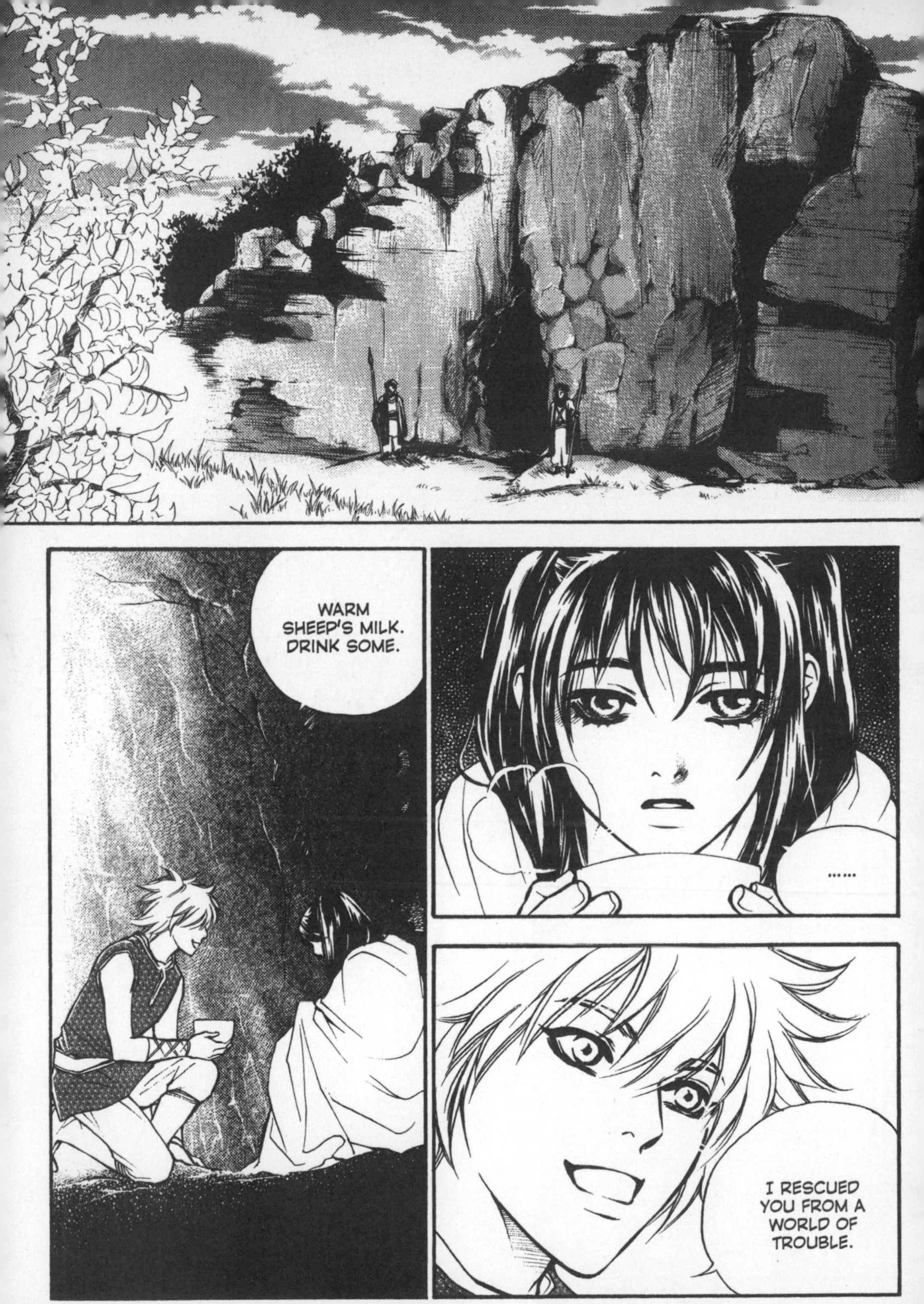
WARM SHEEP'S MILK. DRINK SOME.
......
I RESCUED YOU FROM A WORLD OF TROUBLE.

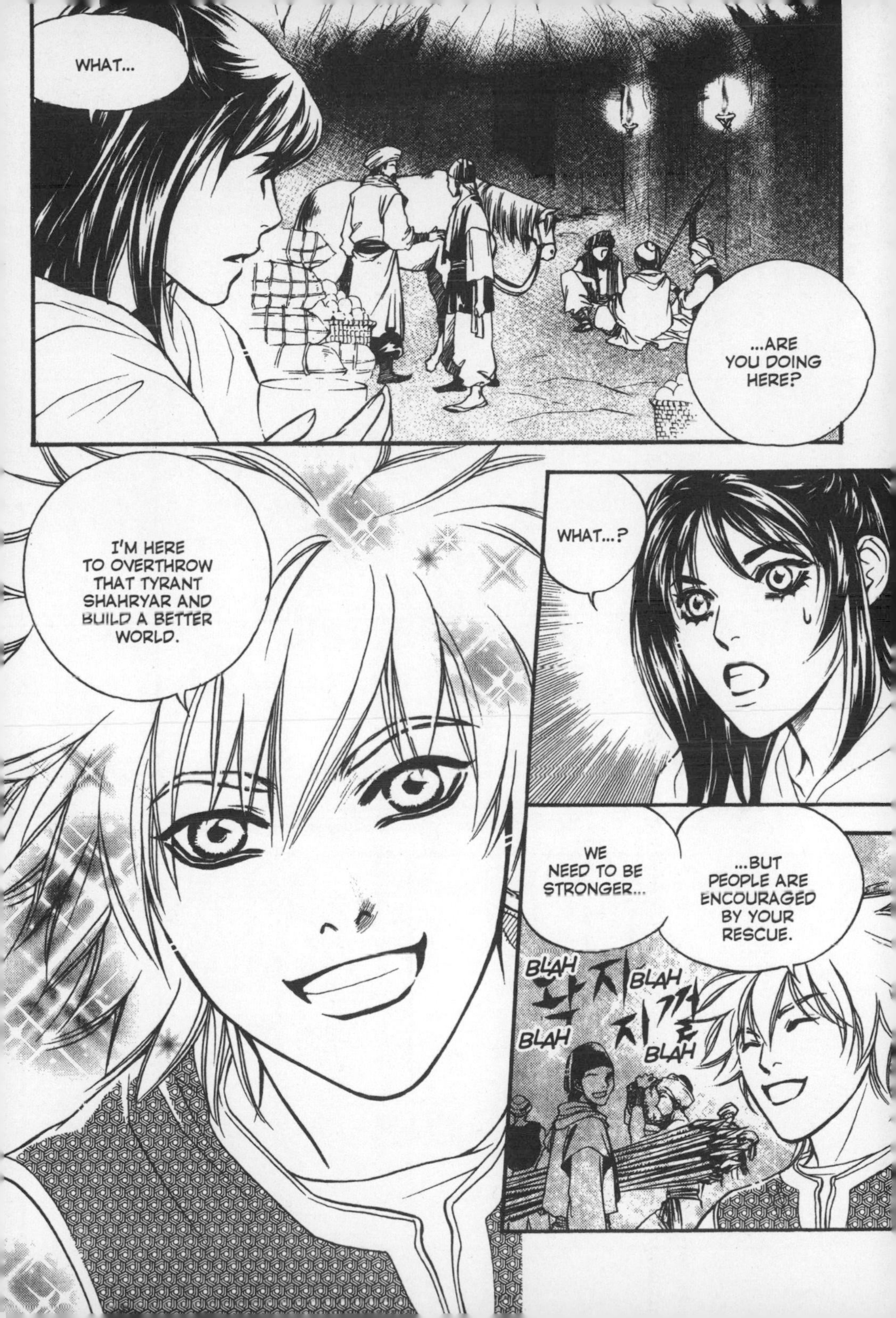
WHAT...
...ARE YOU DOING HERE?
I'M HERE TO OVERTHROW THAT TYRANT SHAHRYAR AND BUILD A BETTER WORLD.
WHAT...?
WE NEED TO BE STRONGER...
...BUT PEOPLE ARE ENCOURAGED BY YOUR RESCUE.
BLAH
BLAH
BLAH
BLAH

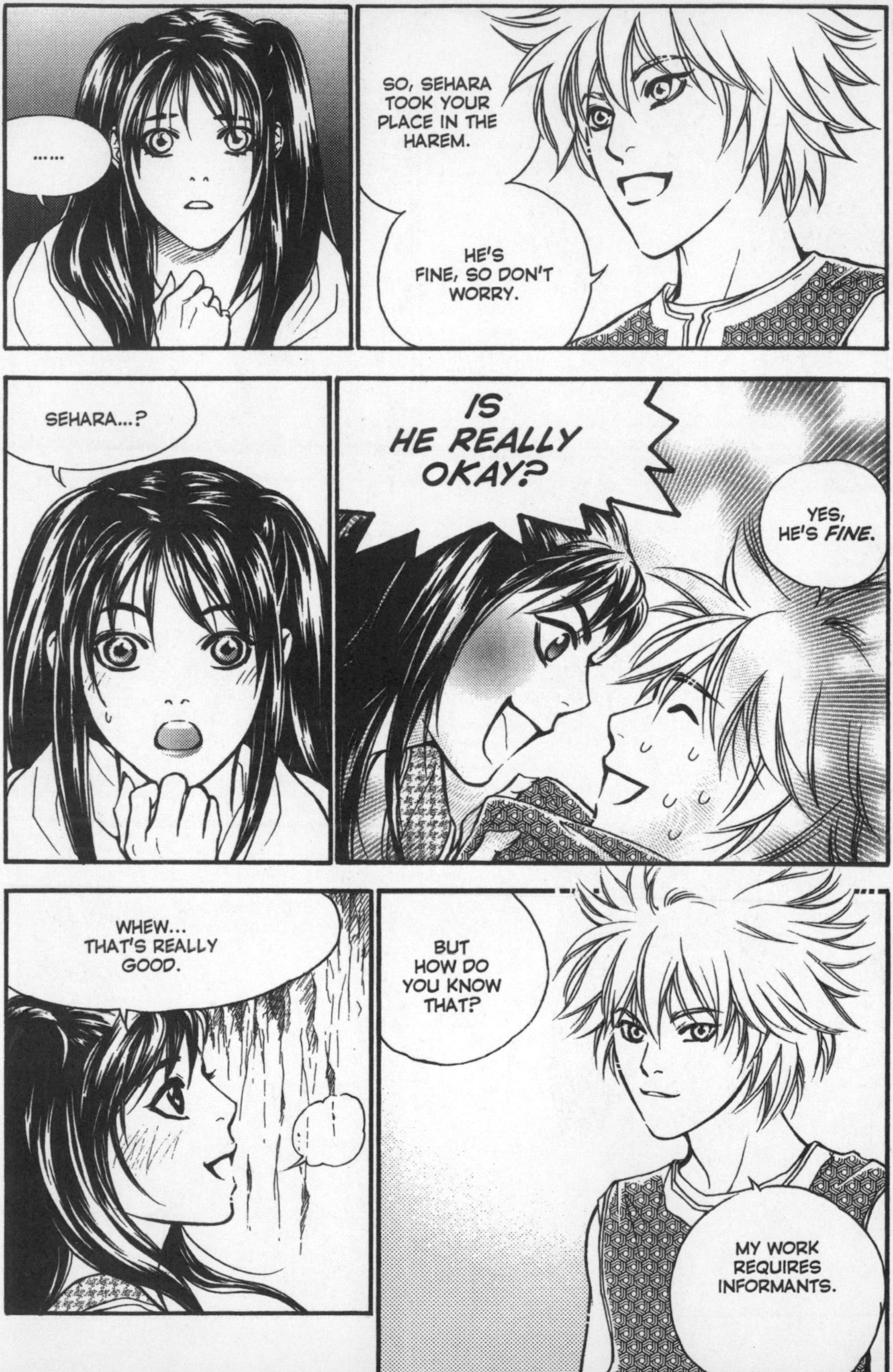
......
SO, SEHARA TOOK YOUR PLACE IN THE HAREM.
HE'S FINE, SO DON'T WORRY.
SEHARA...?
IS HE REALLY OKAY?
YES, HE'S *FINE*.
WHEW... THAT'S REALLY GOOD.
BUT HOW DO YOU KNOW THAT?
MY WORK REQUIRES INFORMANTS.

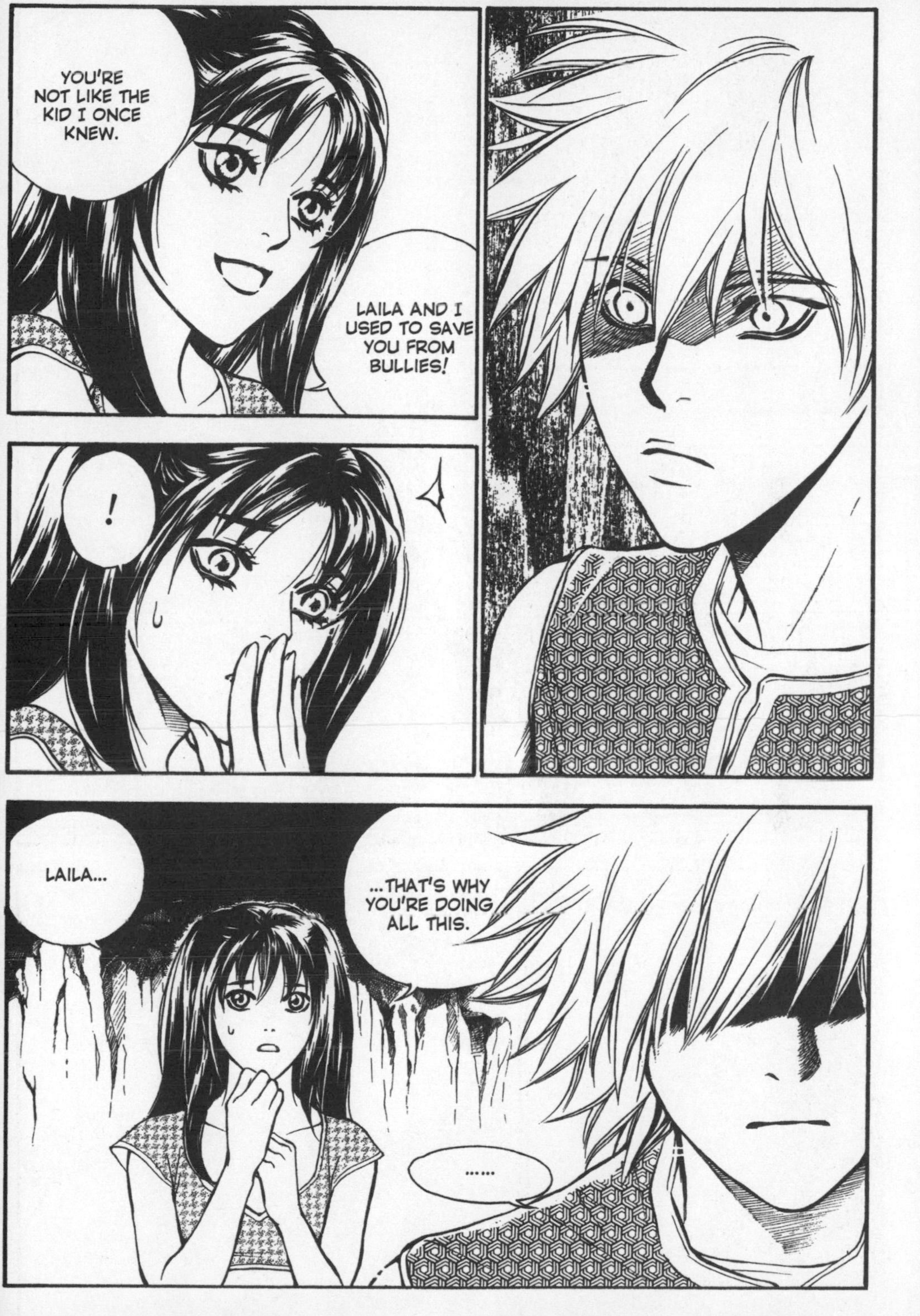
YOU'RE NOT LIKE THE KID I ONCE KNEW.
LAILA AND I USED TO SAVE YOU FROM BULLIES!
!
LAILA...
...THAT'S WHY YOU'RE DOING ALL THIS.
......

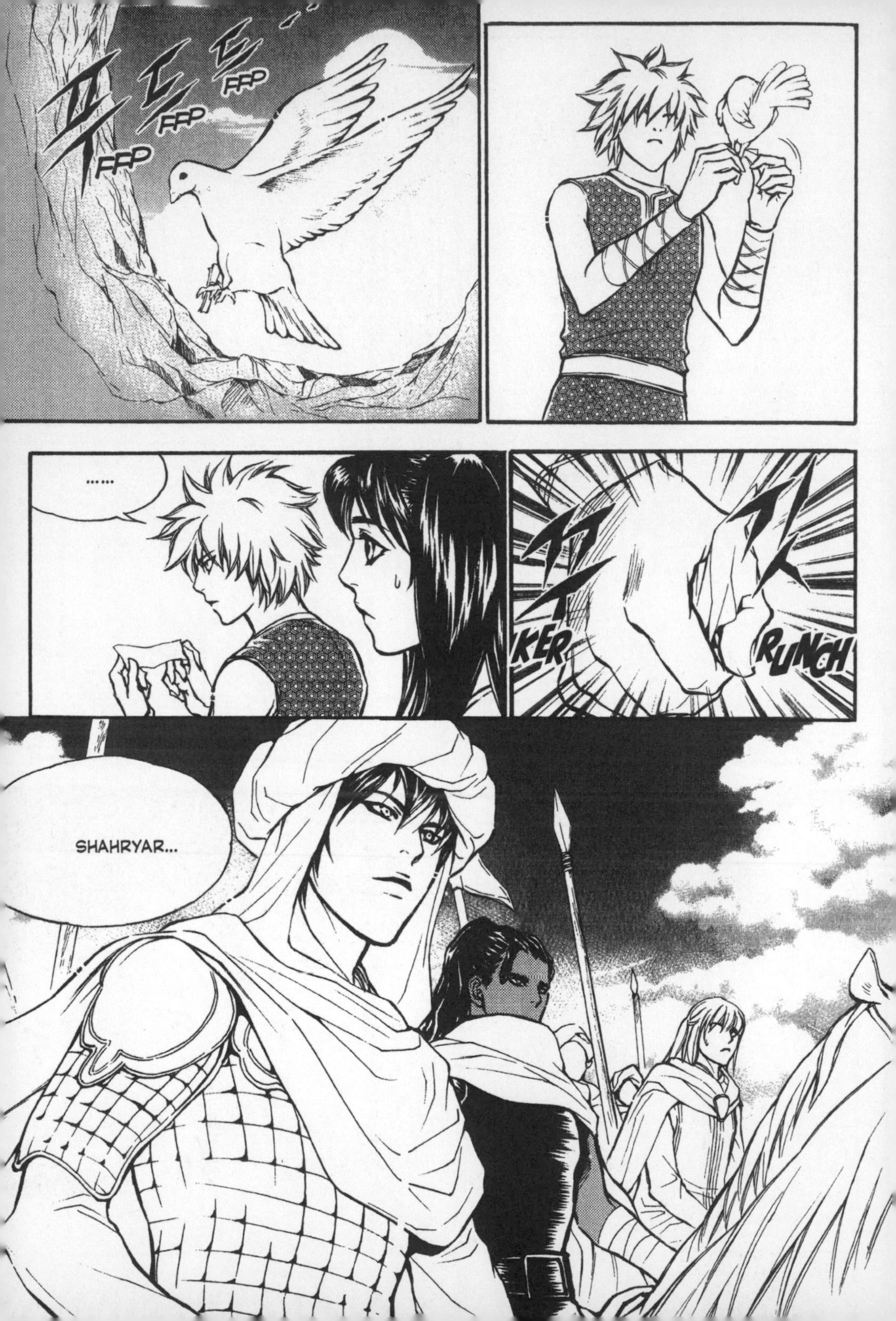
FFP
FFP
FFP
......
KER
RUNCH
SHAHRYAR...

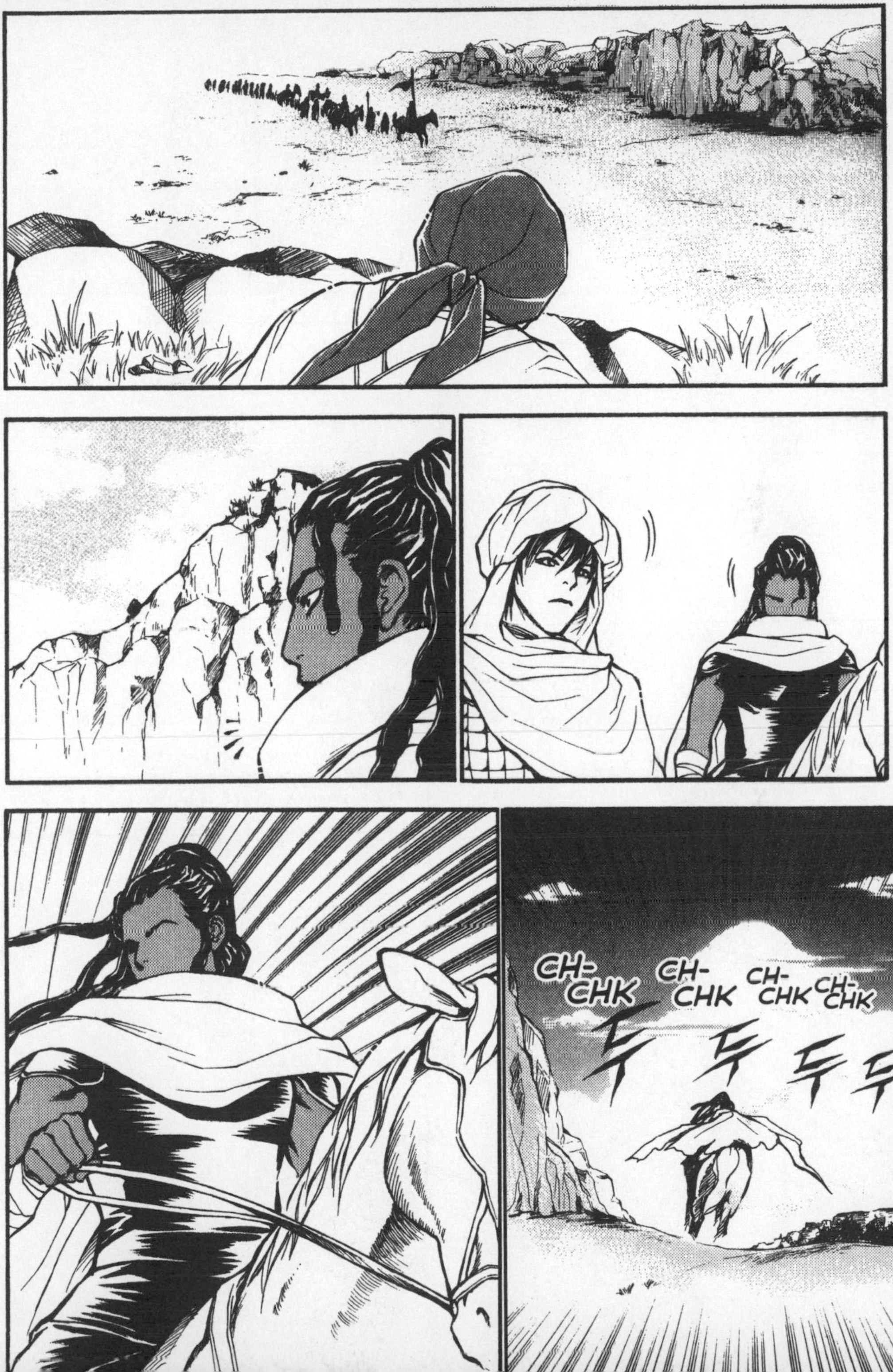
CH-CHK
CH-CHK
CH-CHK
CH-CHK
두 두 두두

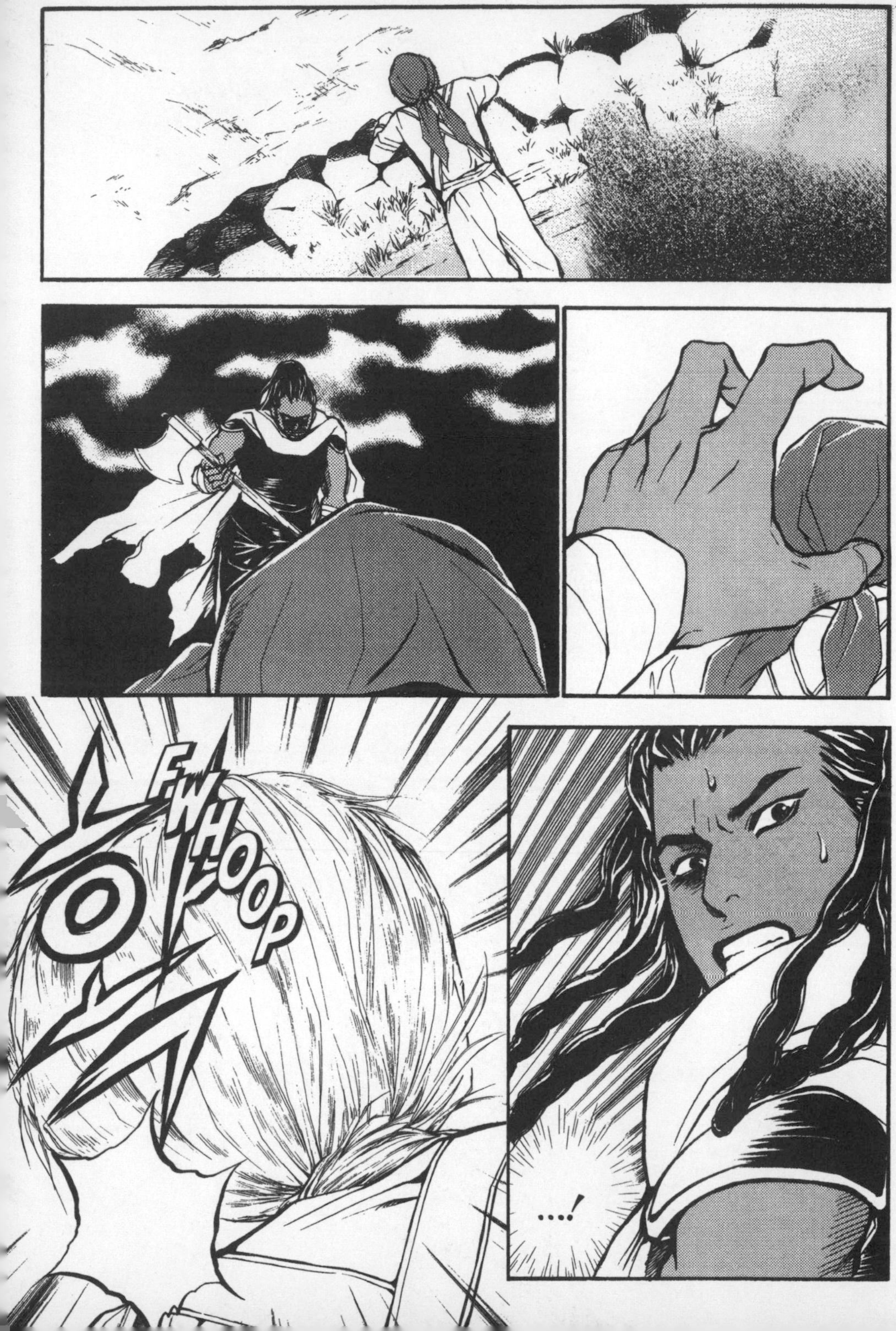
FWHOOP
....!

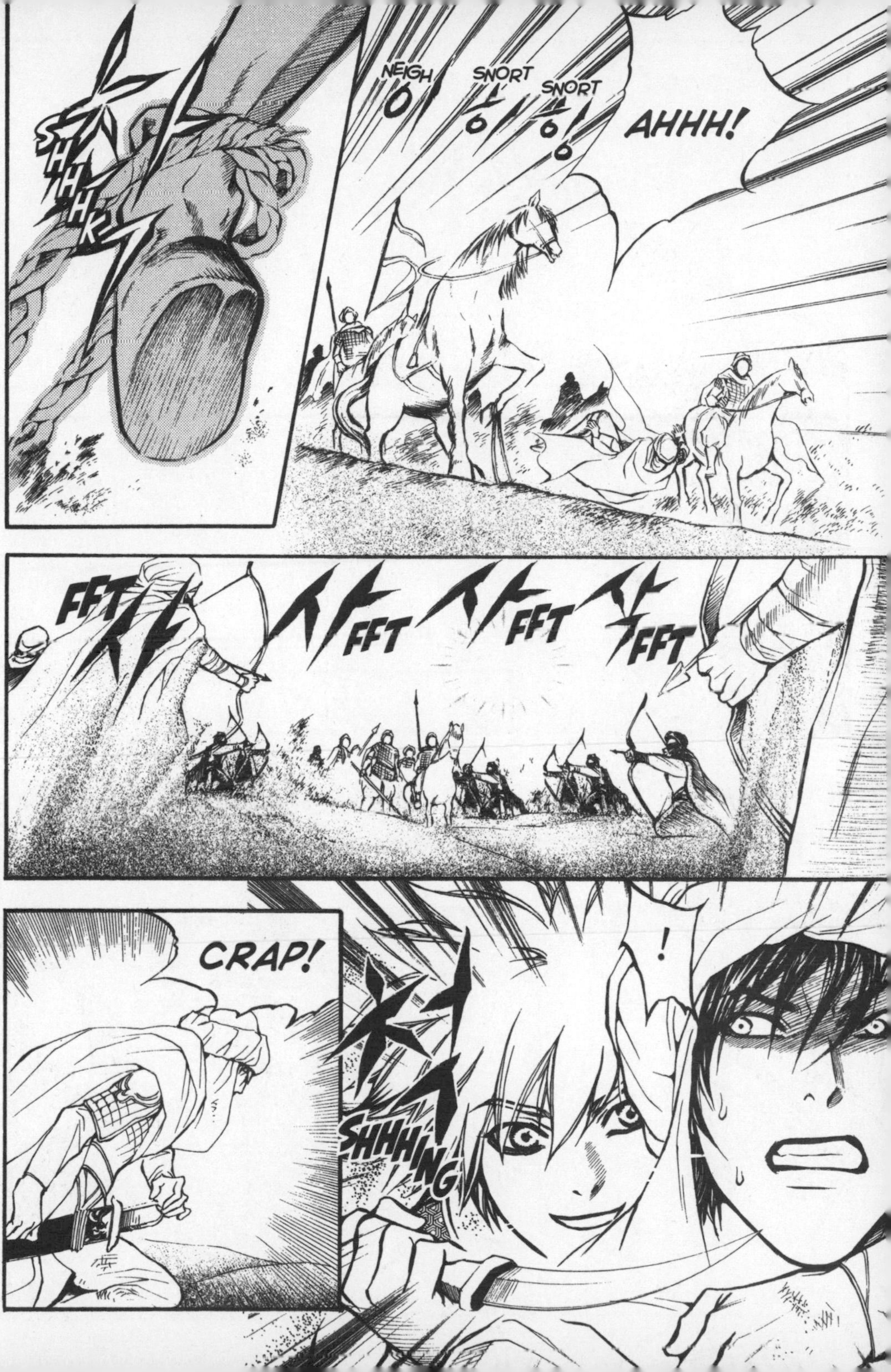
SHHHK
NEIGH
SNORT
SNORT
AHHH!
FFT
FFT
FFT
FFT
CRAP!
!
SHHHING

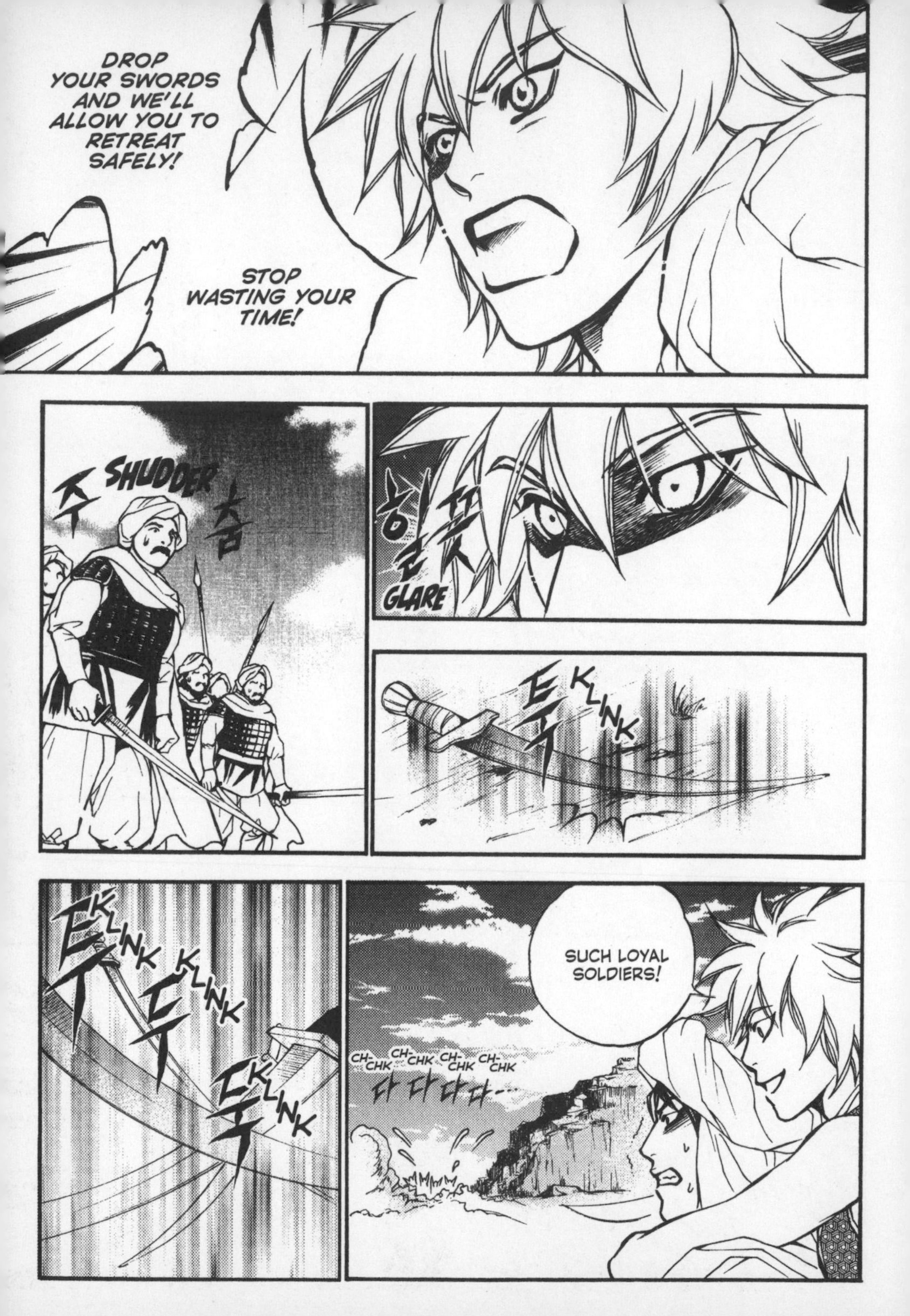
DROP YOUR SWORDS AND WE'LL ALLOW YOU TO RETREAT SAFELY!
STOP WASTING YOUR TIME!
SHUDDER
GLARE
KLINK
KLINK
KLINK
KLINK
SUCH LOYAL SOLDIERS!
CH-CHK CH-CHK CH-CHK CH-CHK
다다다다···

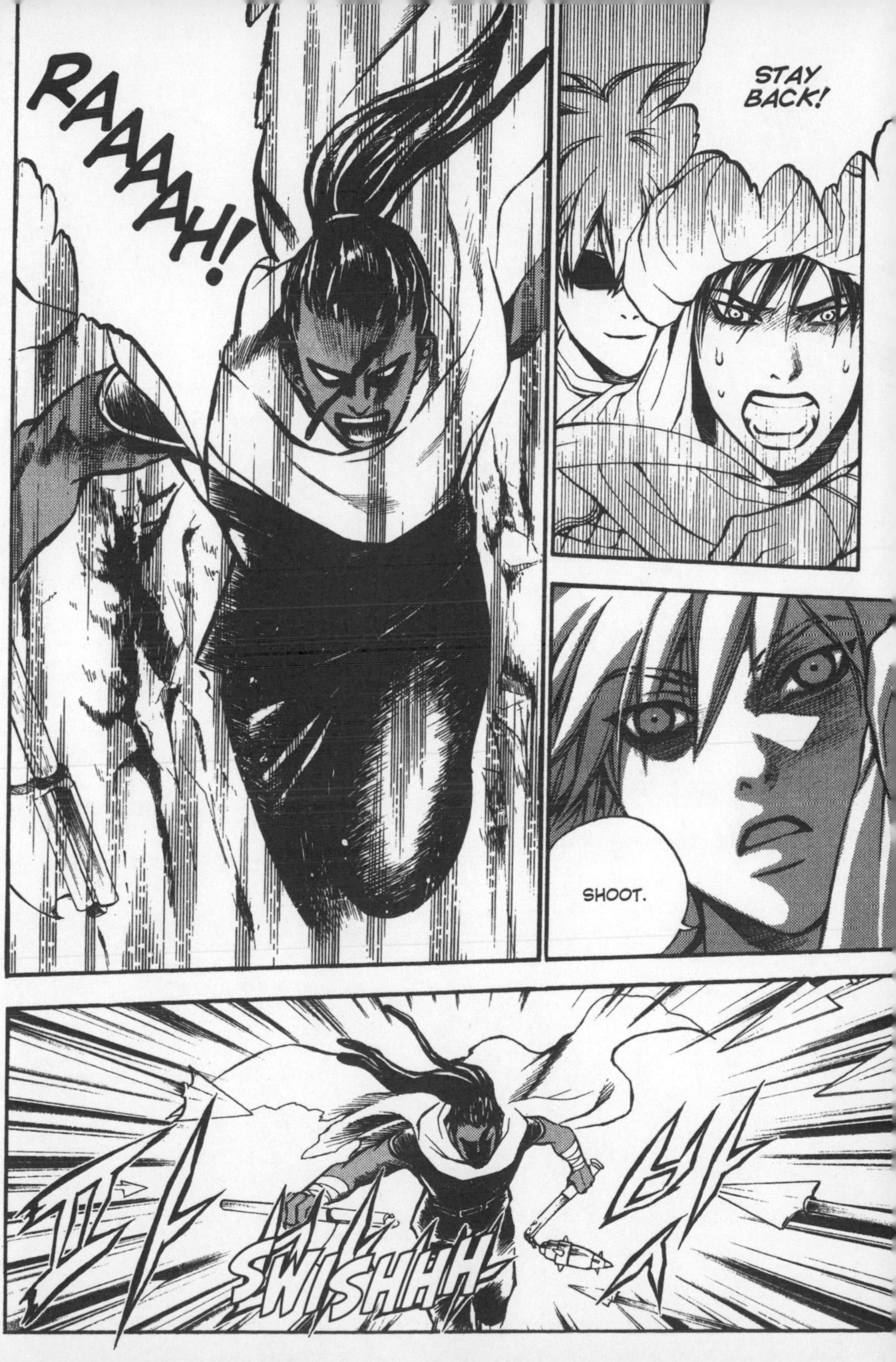
RAAAAAH!
STAY BACK!
SHOOT.
SWISHHH

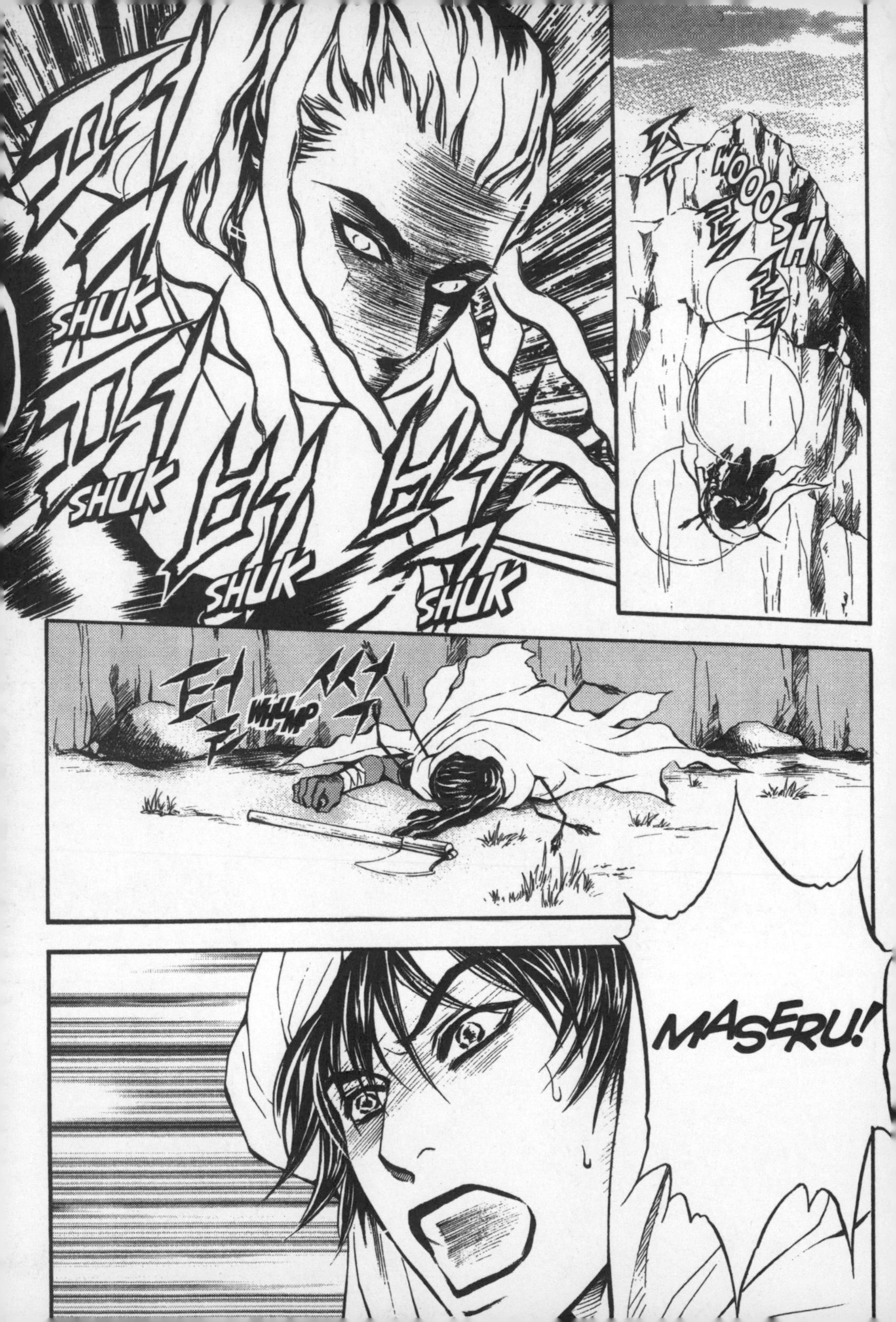
SHUK
SHUK
SHUK
SHUK
WOOOSH
WHUMP
MASERU!

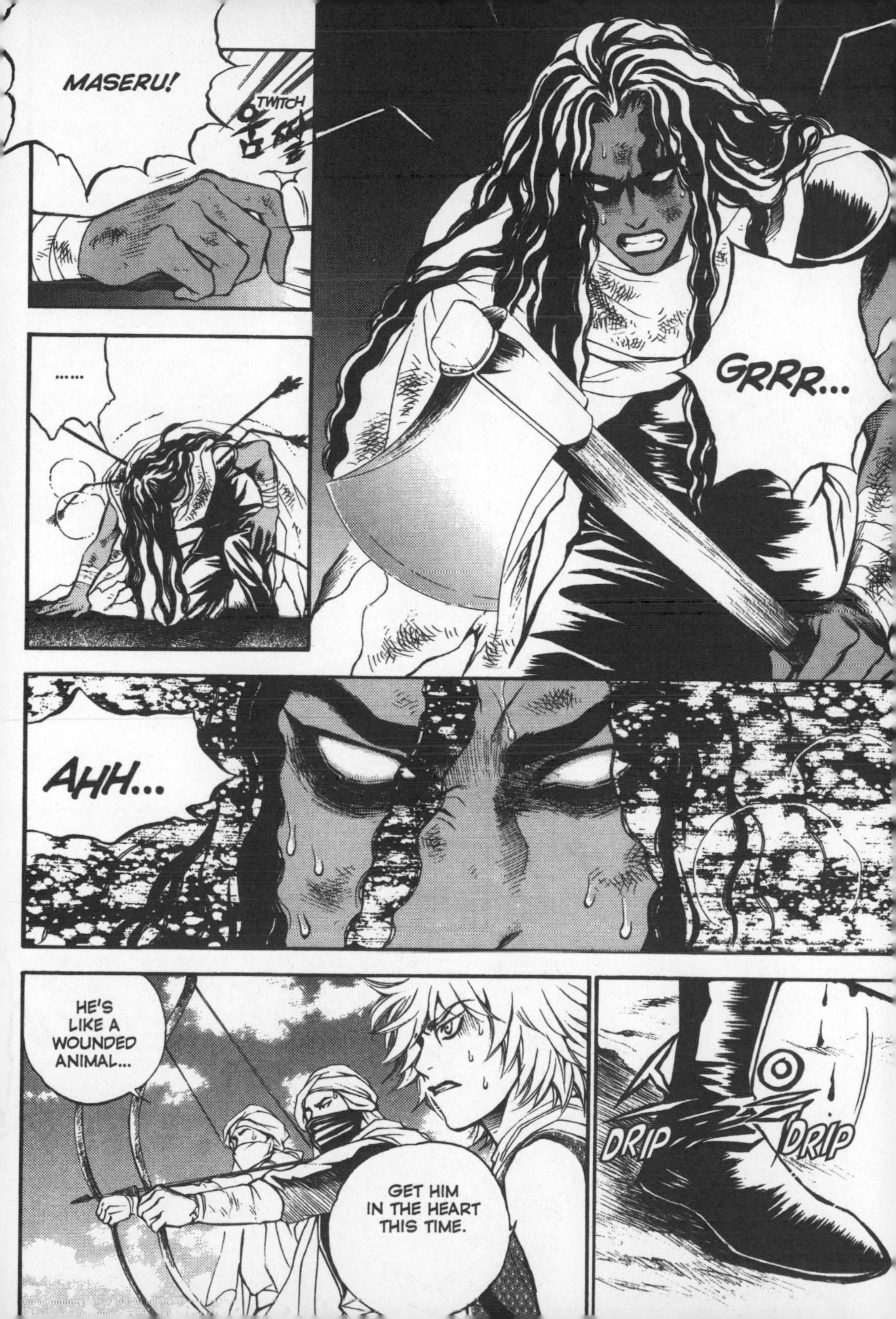
MASERU!
TWITCH
움찔
......
GRRR...
AHH...
HE'S LIKE A WOUNDED ANIMAL...
GET HIM IN THE HEART THIS TIME.
DRIP
DRIP

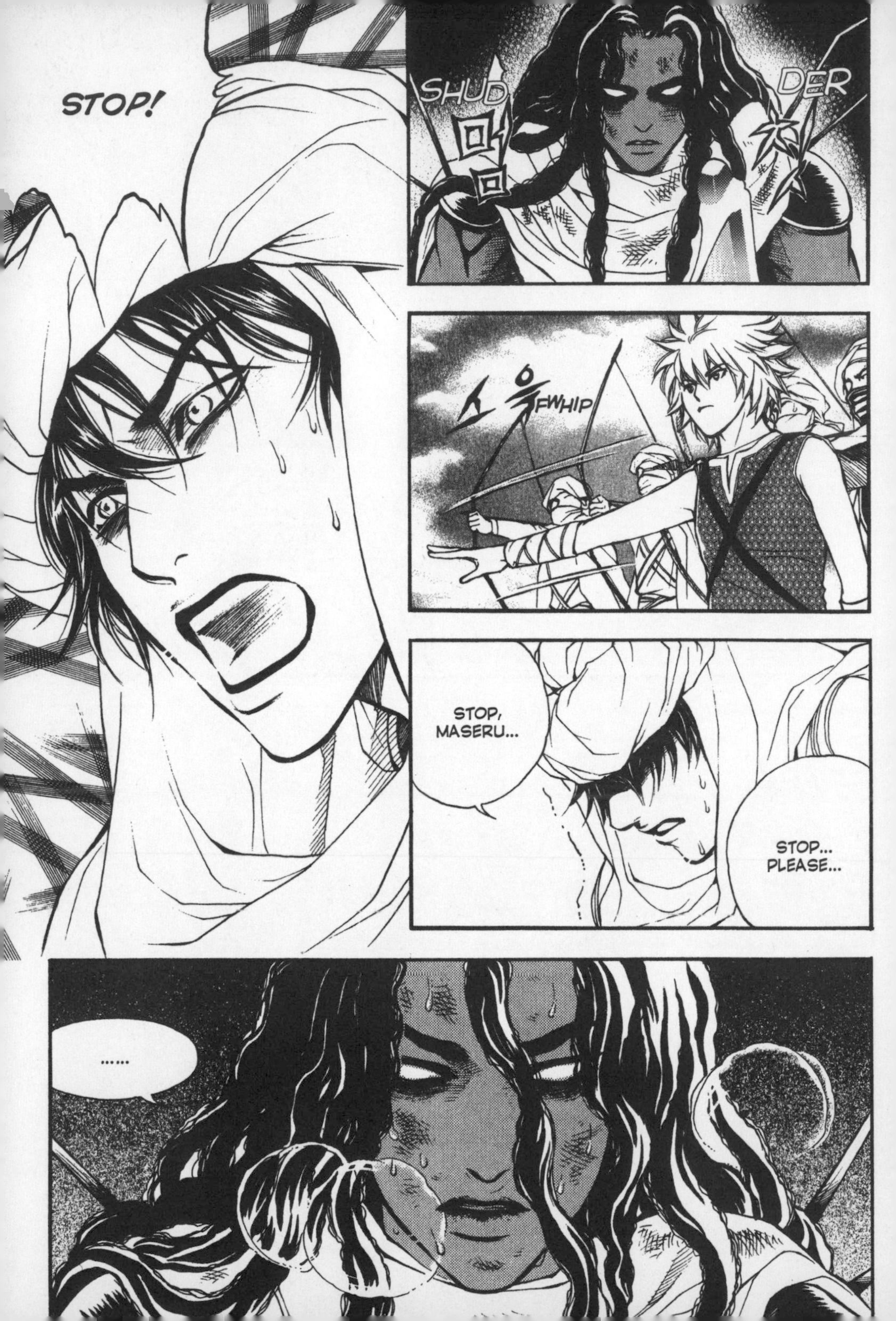
STOP!
SHUD
DER
FWHIP
STOP, MASERU...
STOP... PLEASE...
......

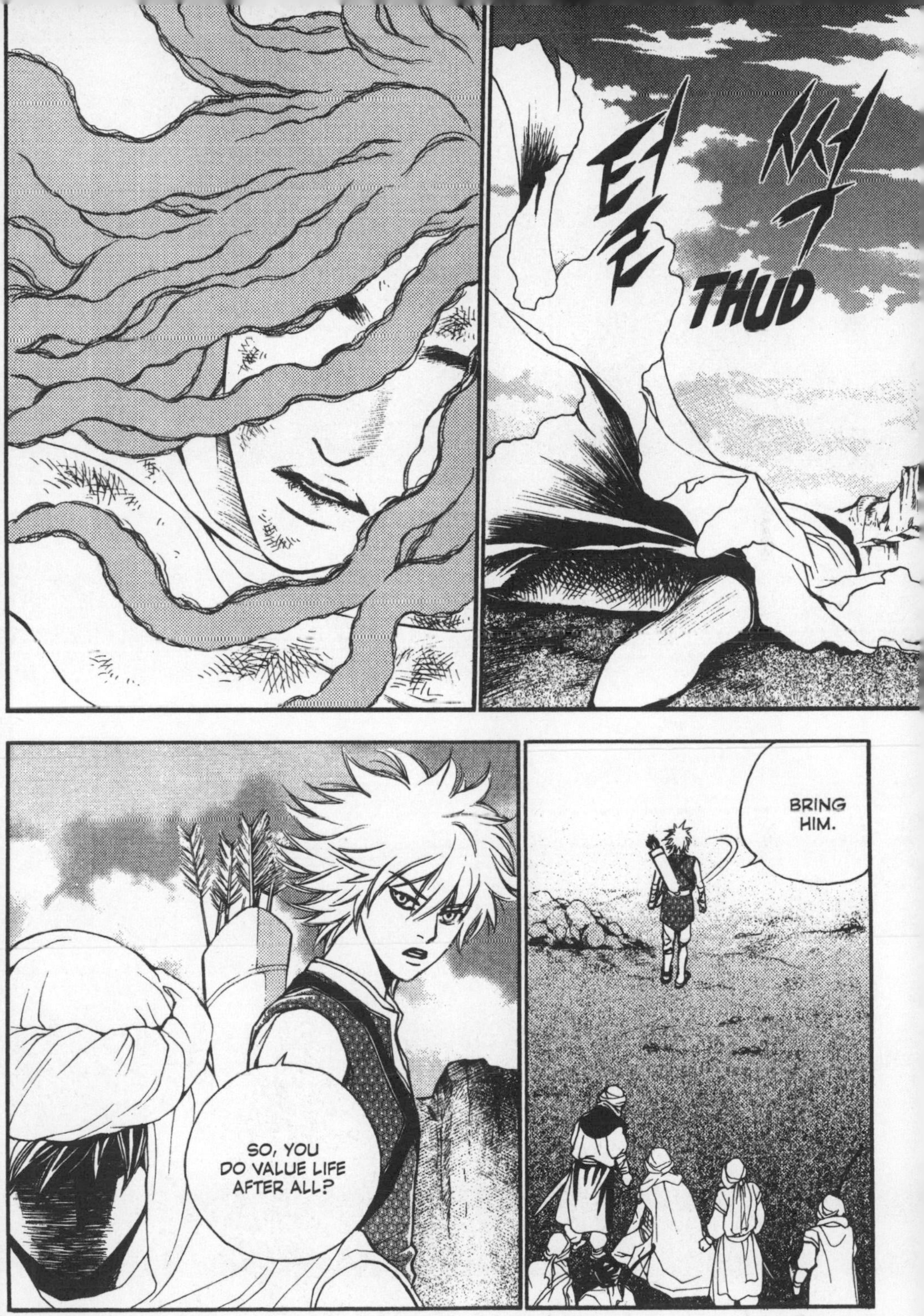
털썩
THUD
SO, YOU DO VALUE LIFE AFTER ALL?
BRING HIM.

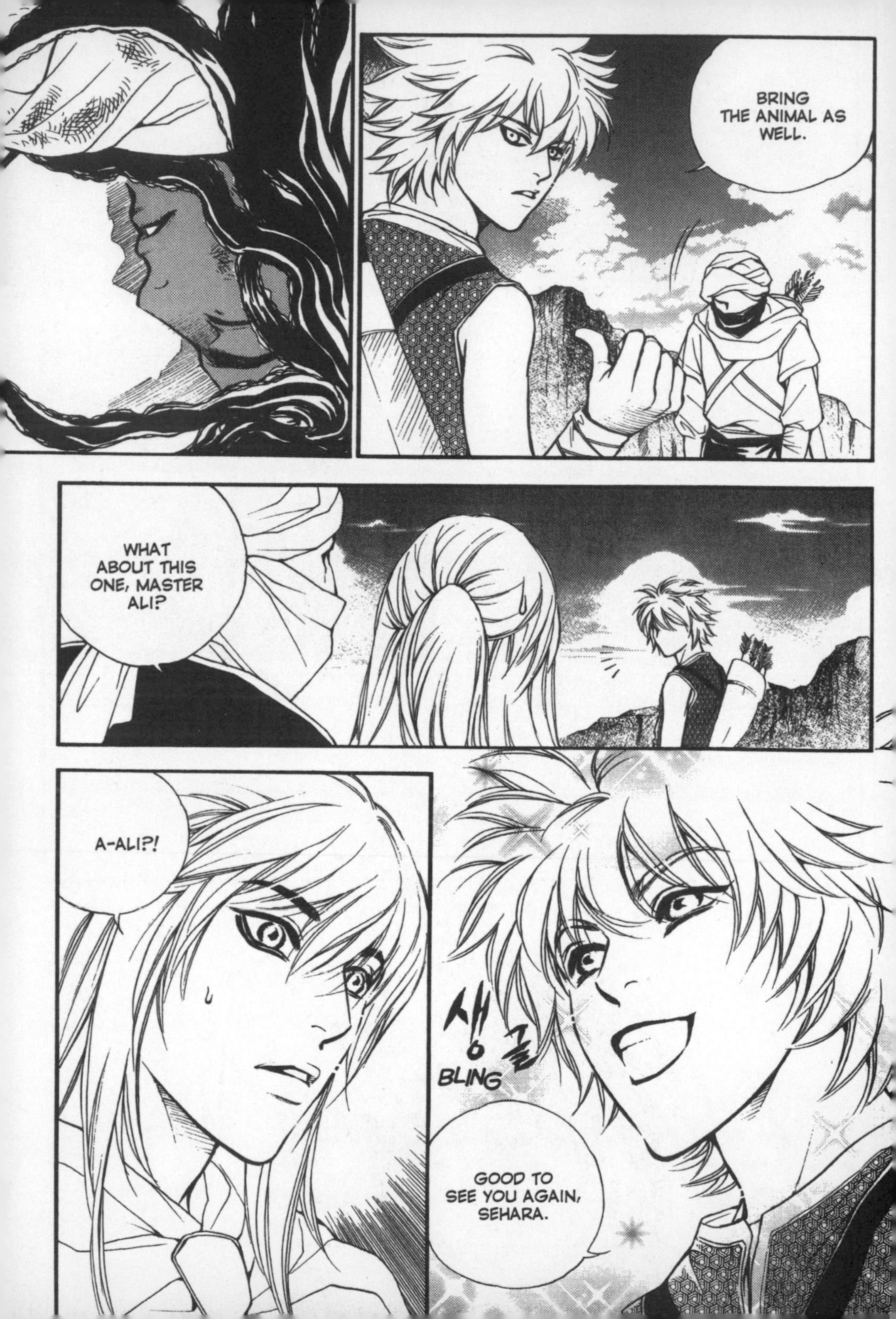
BRING THE ANIMAL AS WELL.
WHAT ABOUT THIS ONE, MASTER ALI?
A-ALI?!
새앵글
BLING
GOOD TO SEE YOU AGAIN, SEHARA.

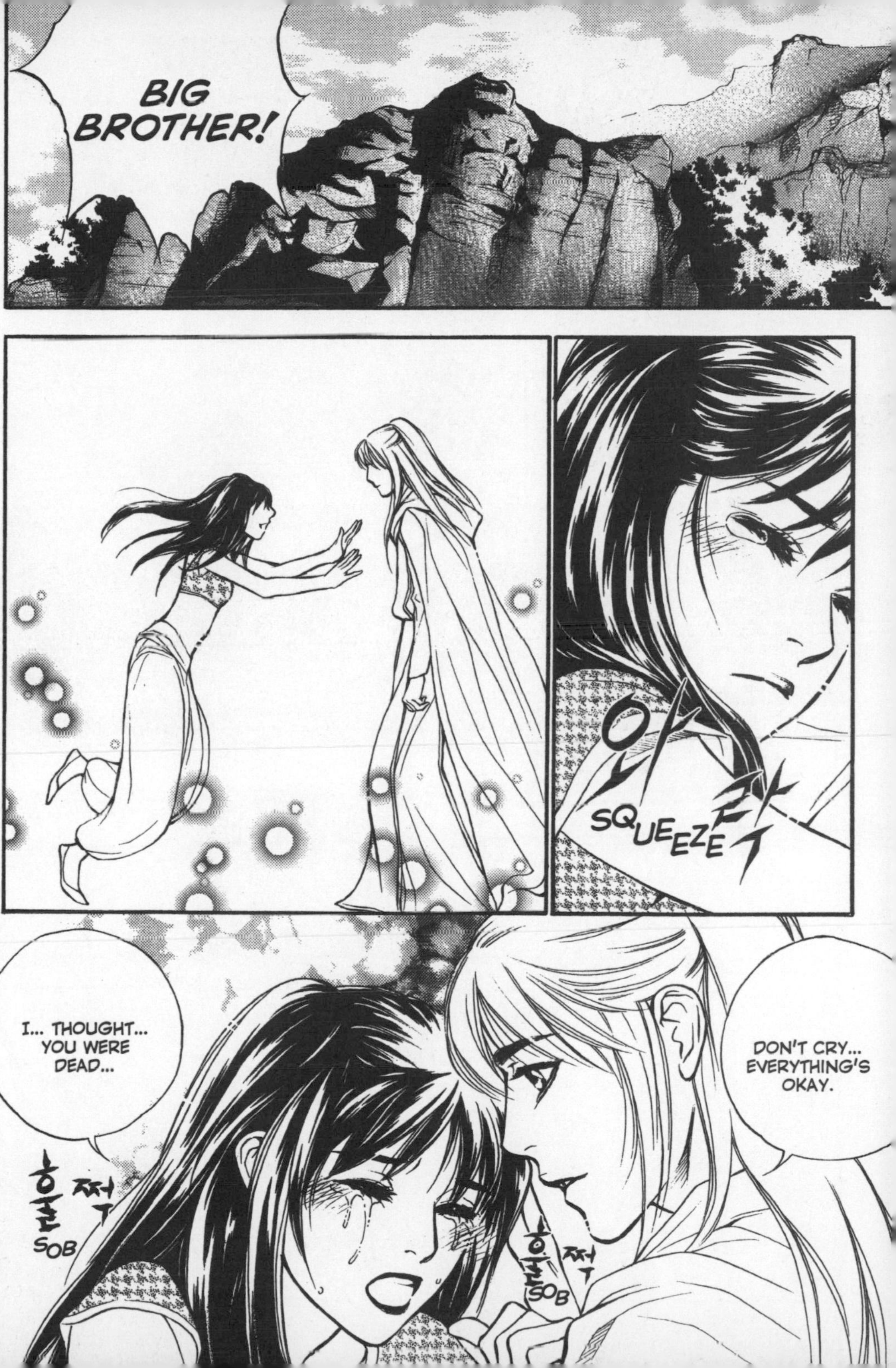
BIG BROTHER!
SQUEEZE
I... THOUGHT... YOU WERE DEAD...
SOB
DON'T CRY... EVERYTHING'S OKAY.
SOB

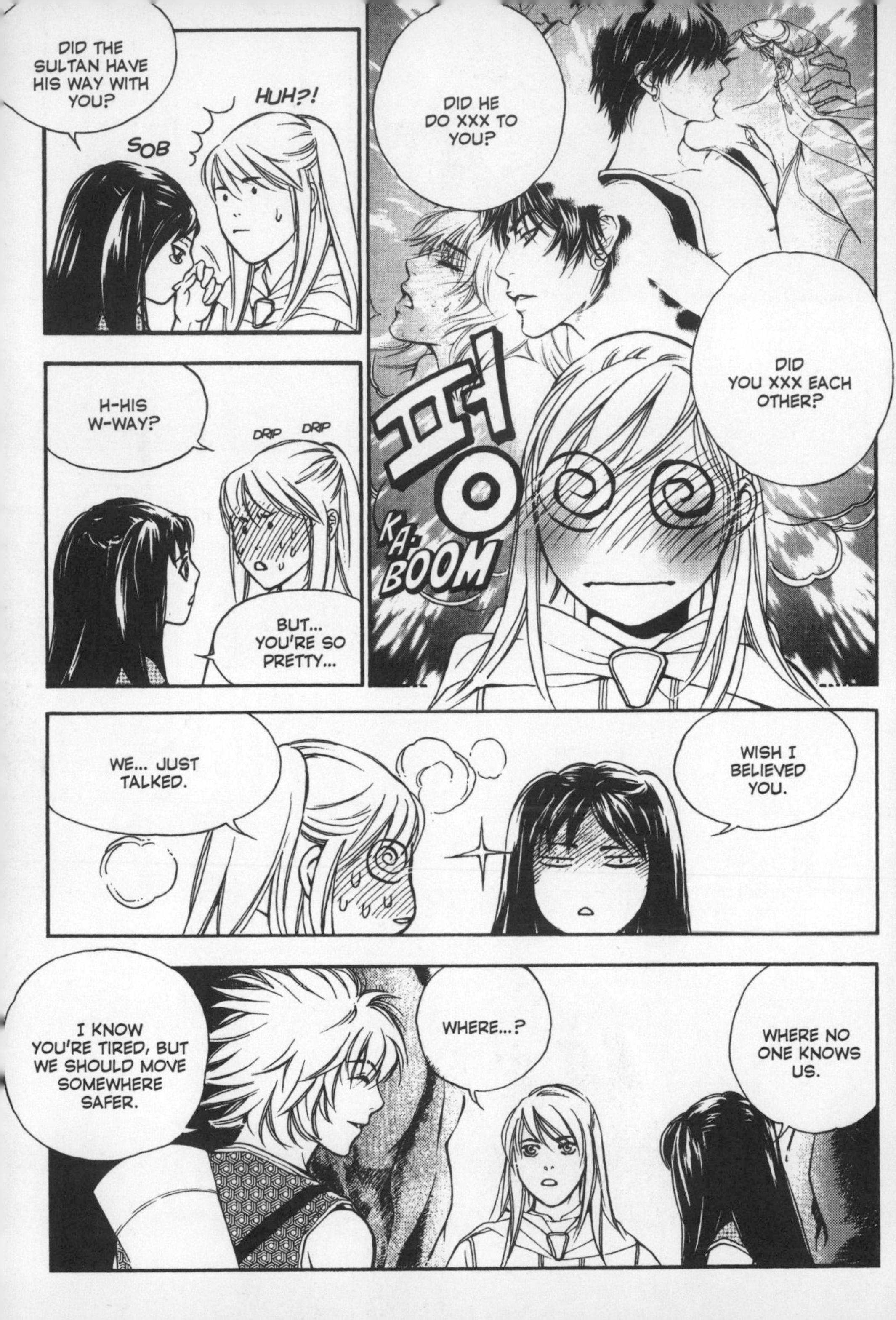
DID THE SULTAN HAVE HIS WAY WITH YOU?
SOB
HUH?!
H-HIS W-WAY?
DRIP DRIP
BUT... YOU'RE SO PRETTY...
DID HE DO XXX TO YOU?
DID YOU XXX EACH OTHER?
KA-BOOM
WE... JUST TALKED.
WISH I BELIEVED YOU.
I KNOW YOU'RE TIRED, BUT WE SHOULD MOVE SOMEWHERE SAFER.
WHERE...?
WHERE NO ONE KNOWS US.

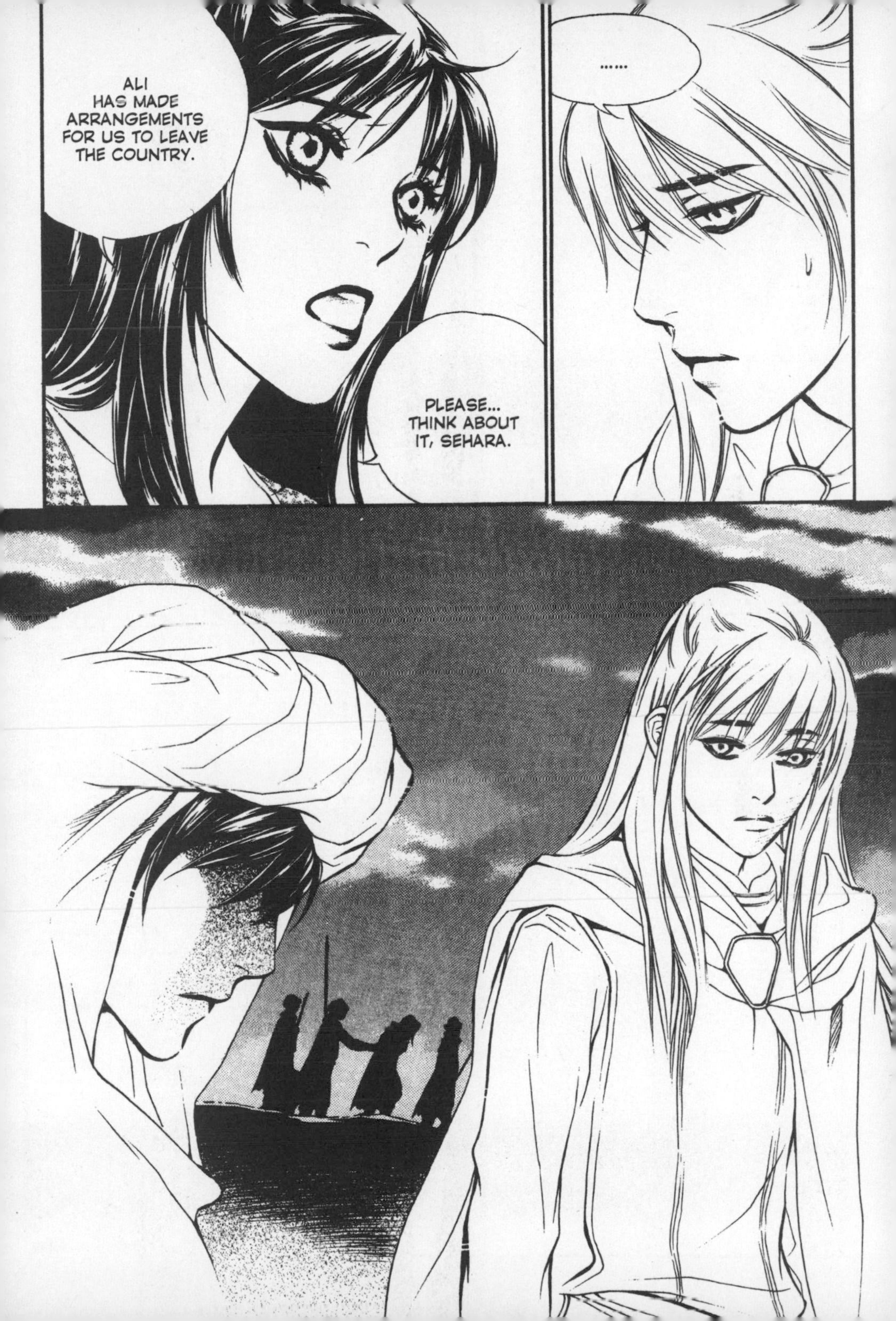
ALI HAS MADE ARRANGEMENTS FOR US TO LEAVE THE COUNTRY.
PLEASE... THINK ABOUT IT, SEHARA.
......

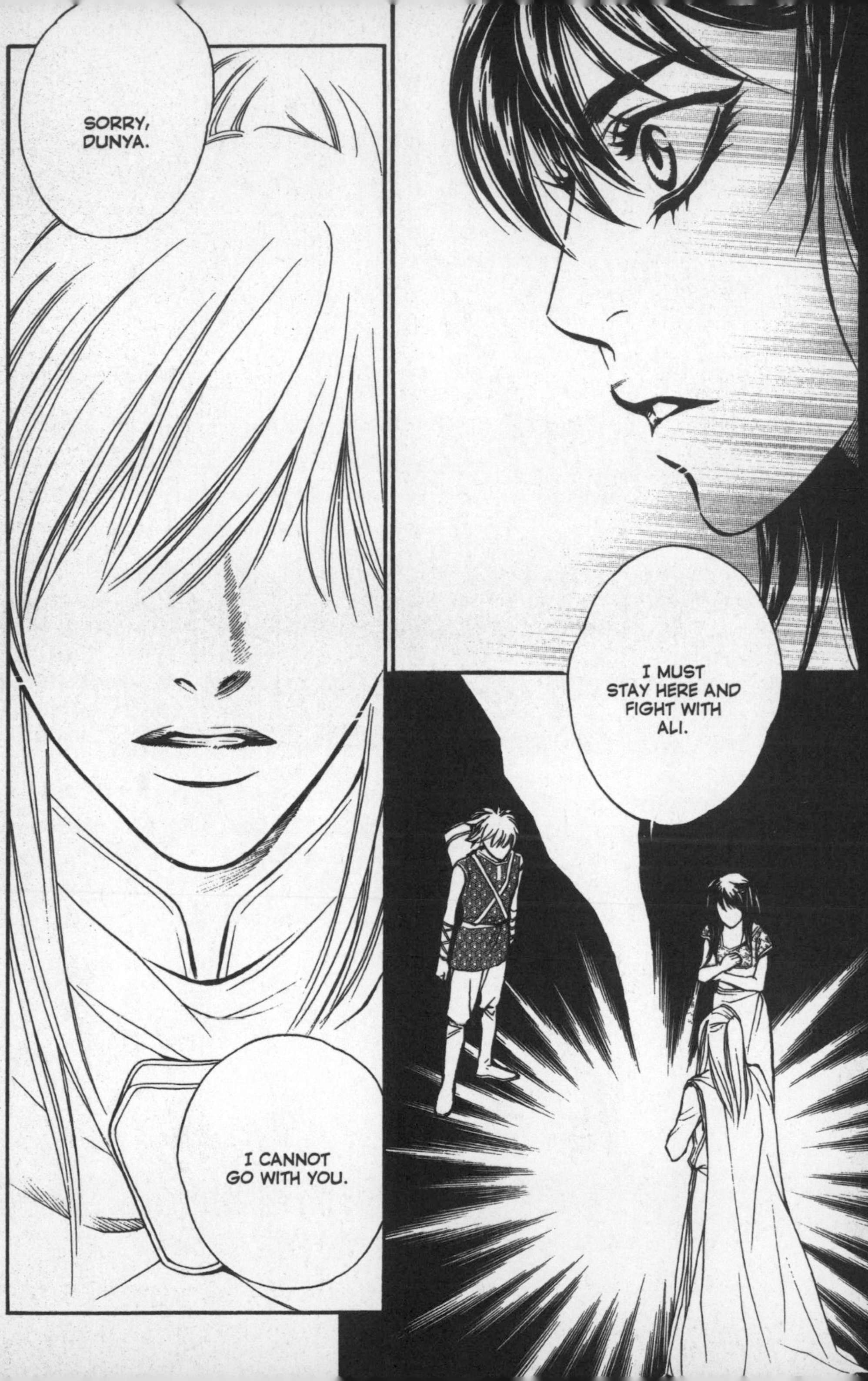
SORRY, DUNYA.
I CANNOT GO WITH YOU.
I MUST STAY HERE AND FIGHT WITH ALI.

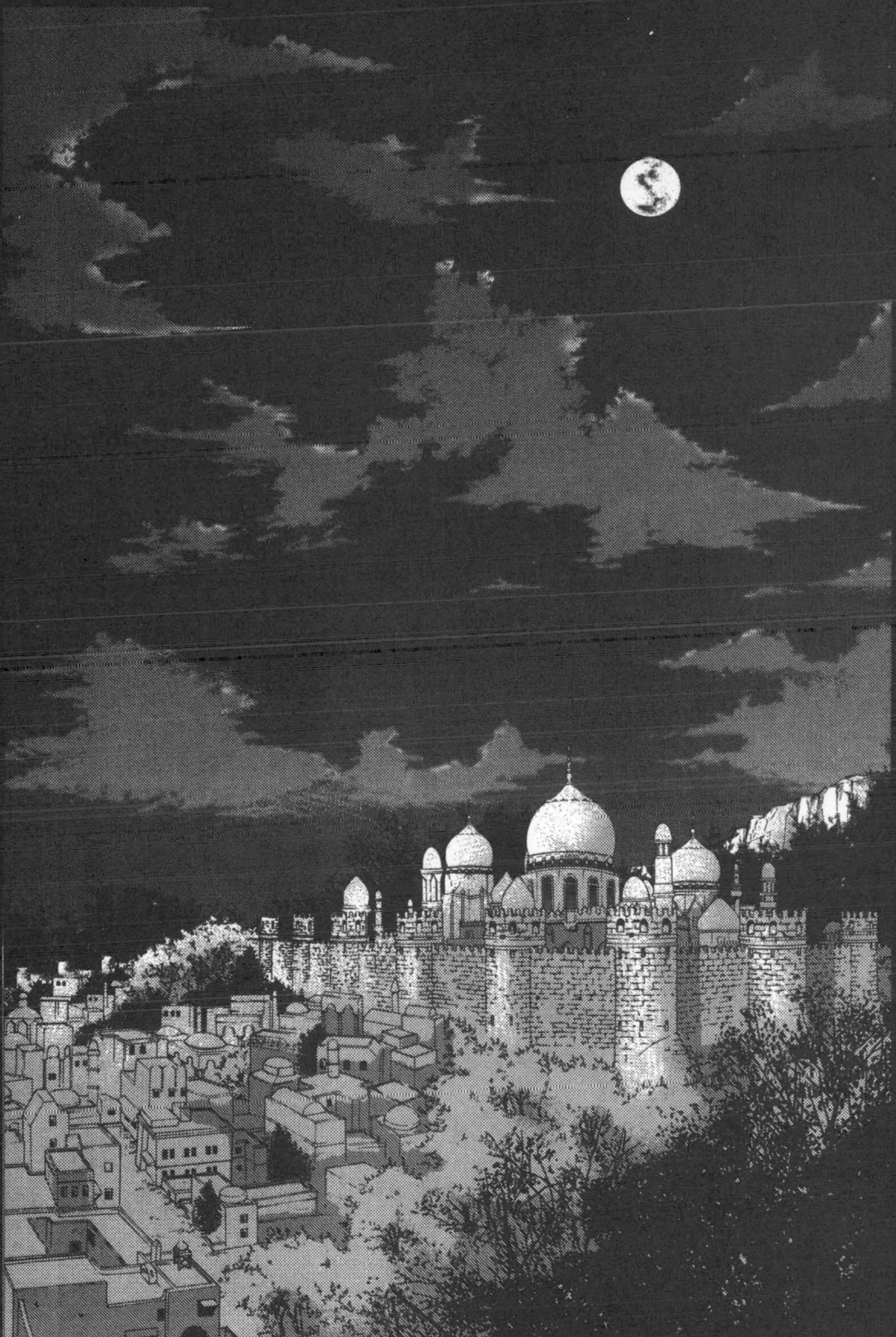

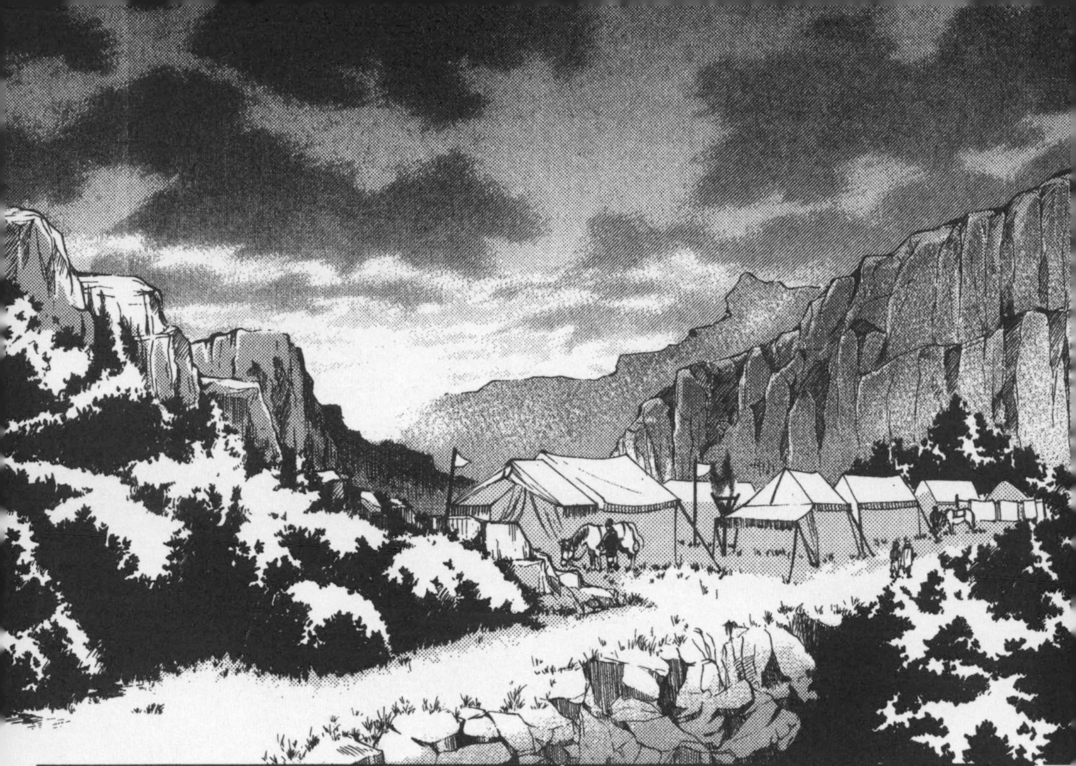

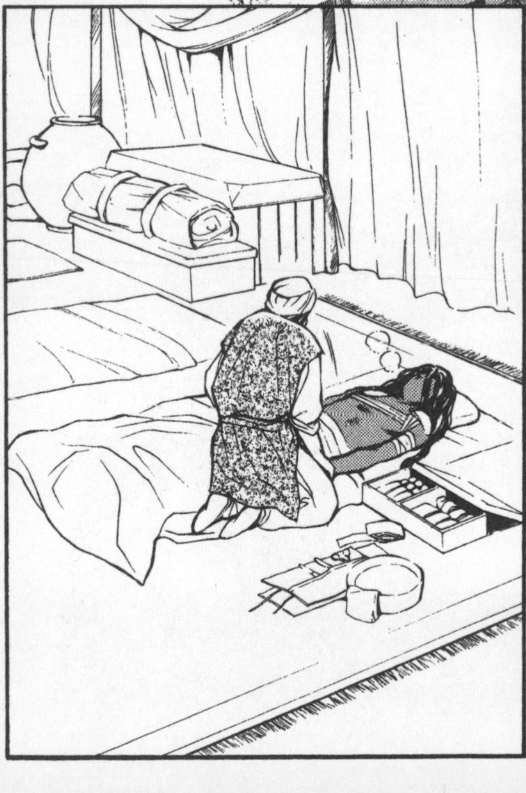

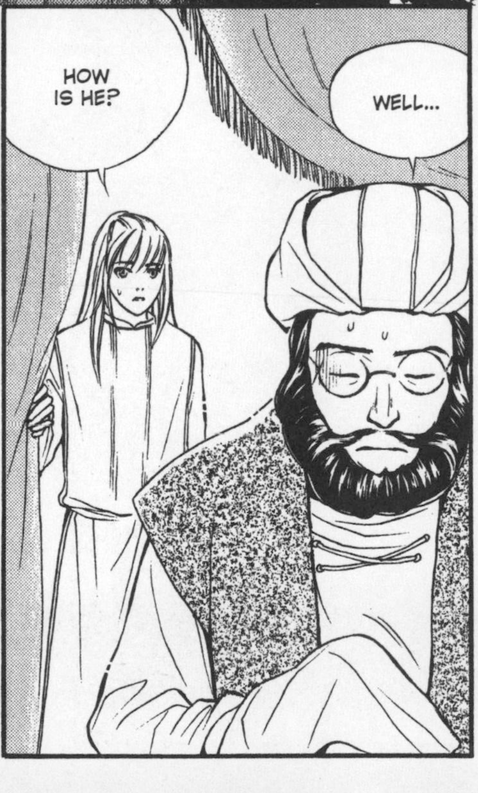
HOW IS HE?
WELL...

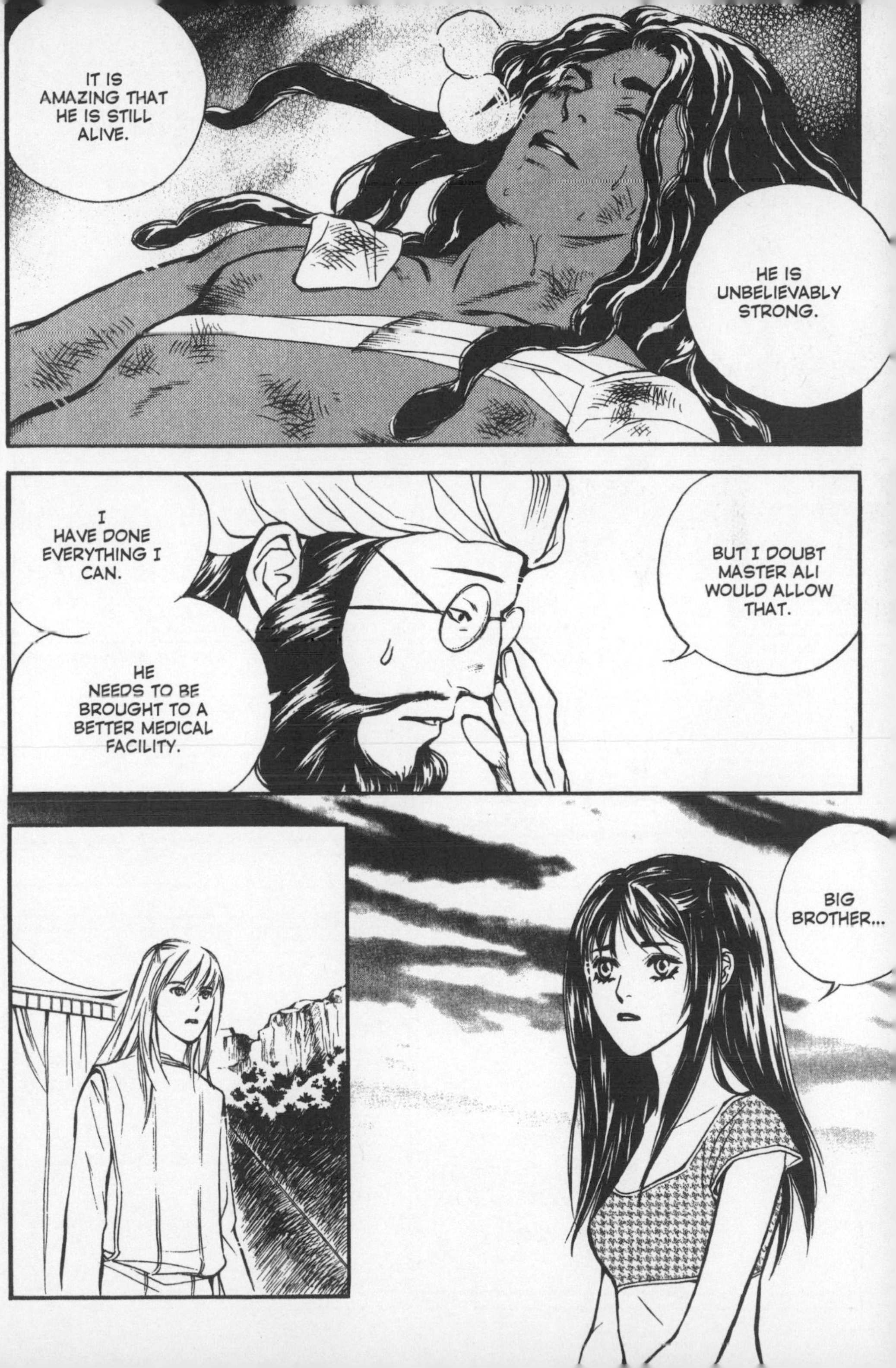
IT IS AMAZING THAT HE IS STILL ALIVE.
HE IS UNBELIEVABLY STRONG.
I HAVE DONE EVERYTHING I CAN.
HE NEEDS TO BE BROUGHT TO A BETTER MEDICAL FACILITY.
BUT I DOUBT MASTER ALI WOULD ALLOW THAT.
BIG BROTHER...

YOU'RE NO SOLDIER...

...YET YOU WANT TO JOIN THIS RESISTANCE!

WHAT'S HAPPENED TO YOU?

YOU'LL BE SAFE WITH ZHAO...

I'LL FOLLOW LATER.

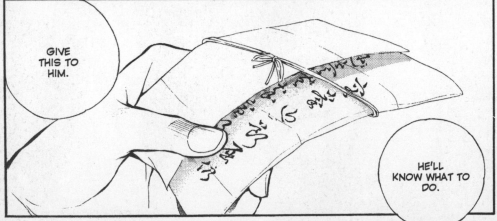

GIVE THIS TO HIM.

HE'LL KNOW WHAT TO DO.

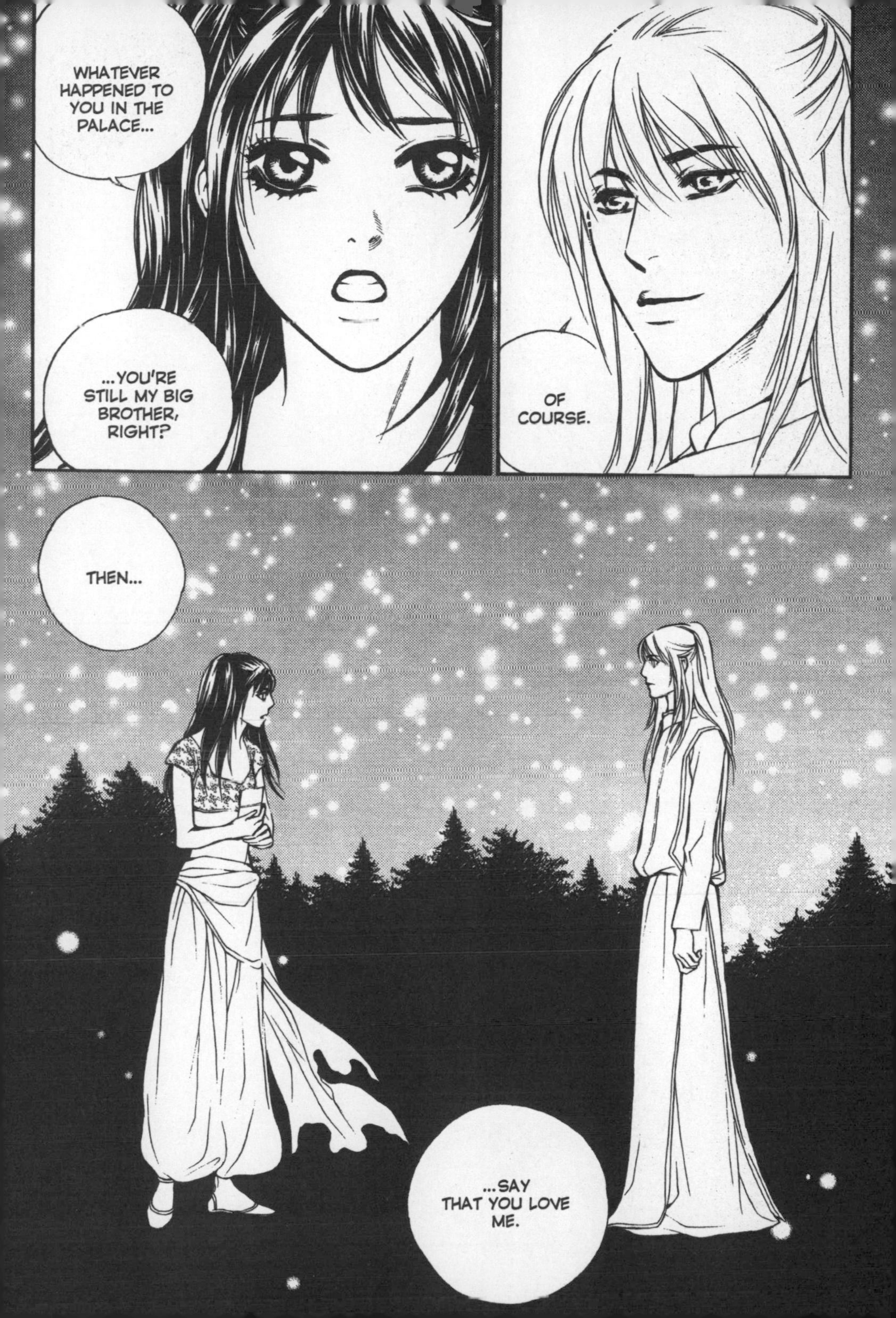
WHATEVER HAPPENED TO YOU IN THE PALACE...
...YOU'RE STILL MY BIG BROTHER, RIGHT?
OF COURSE.
THEN...
...SAY THAT YOU LOVE ME.

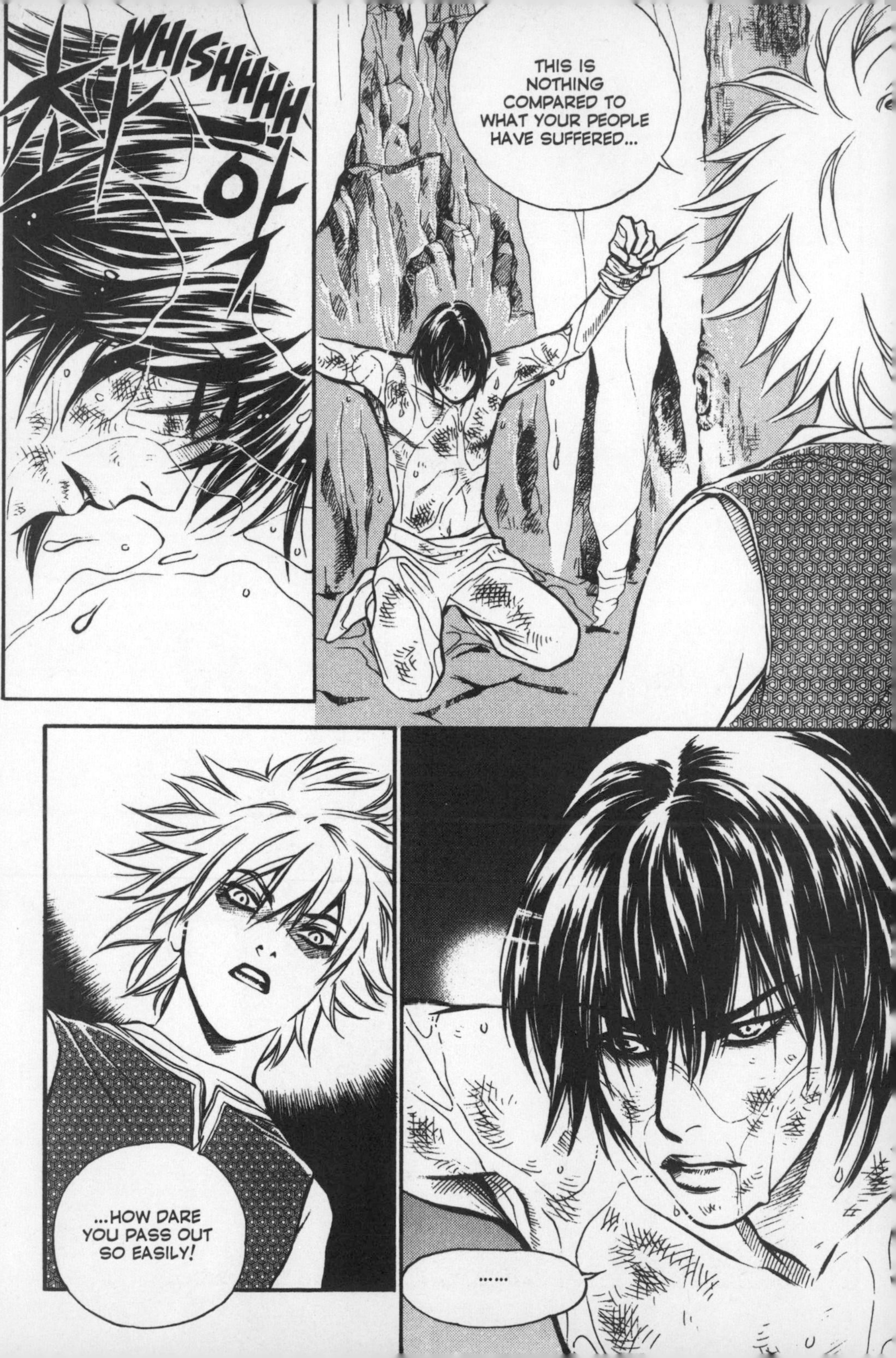
WHISHHHHH
THIS IS NOTHING COMPARED TO WHAT YOUR PEOPLE HAVE SUFFERED...
...HOW DARE YOU PASS OUT SO EASILY!
......

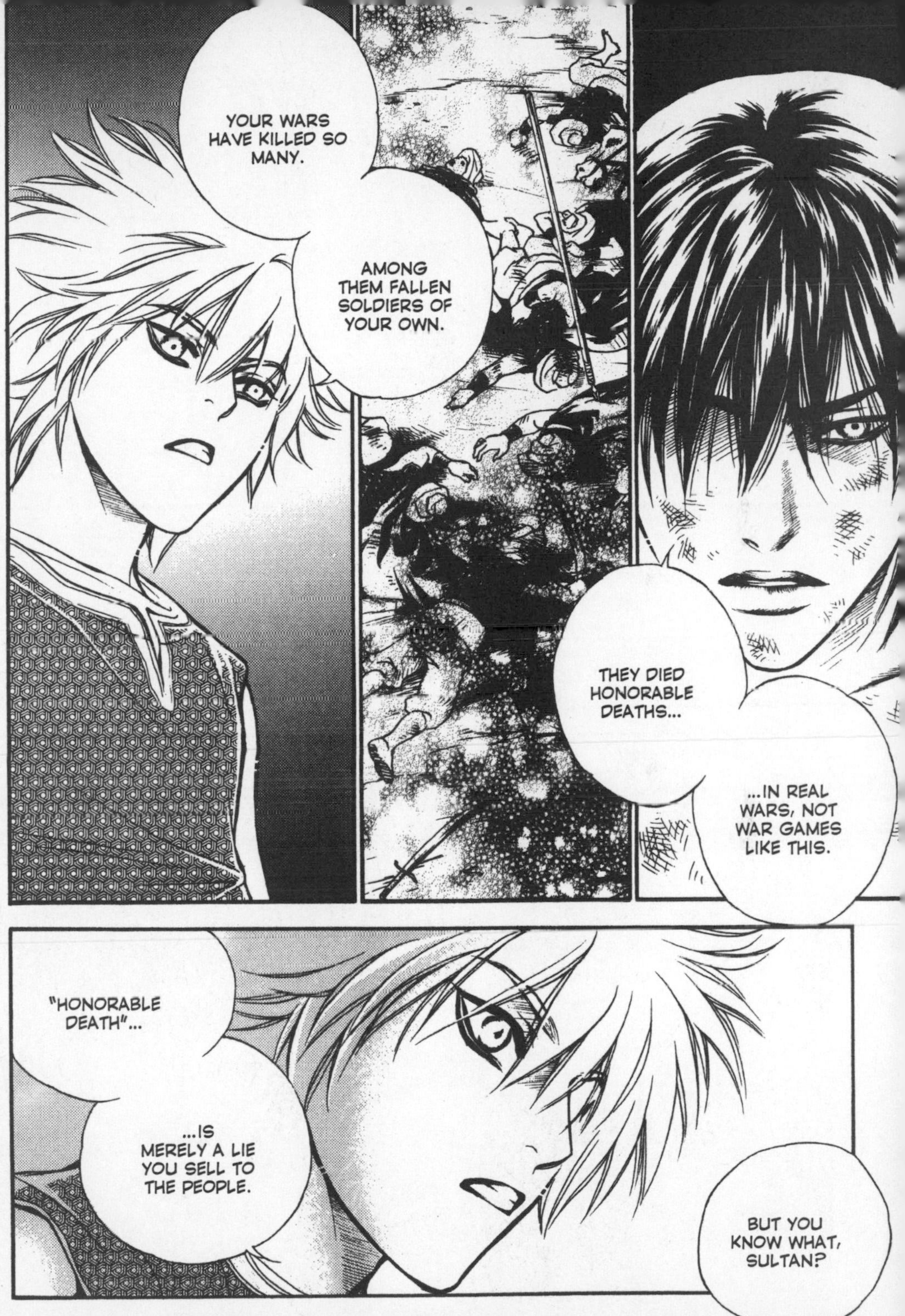
YOUR WARS HAVE KILLED SO MANY.
AMONG THEM FALLEN SOLDIERS OF YOUR OWN.
THEY DIED HONORABLE DEATHS...
...IN REAL WARS, NOT WAR GAMES LIKE THIS.
"HONORABLE DEATH"...
...IS MERELY A LIE YOU SELL TO THE PEOPLE.
BUT YOU KNOW WHAT, SULTAN?

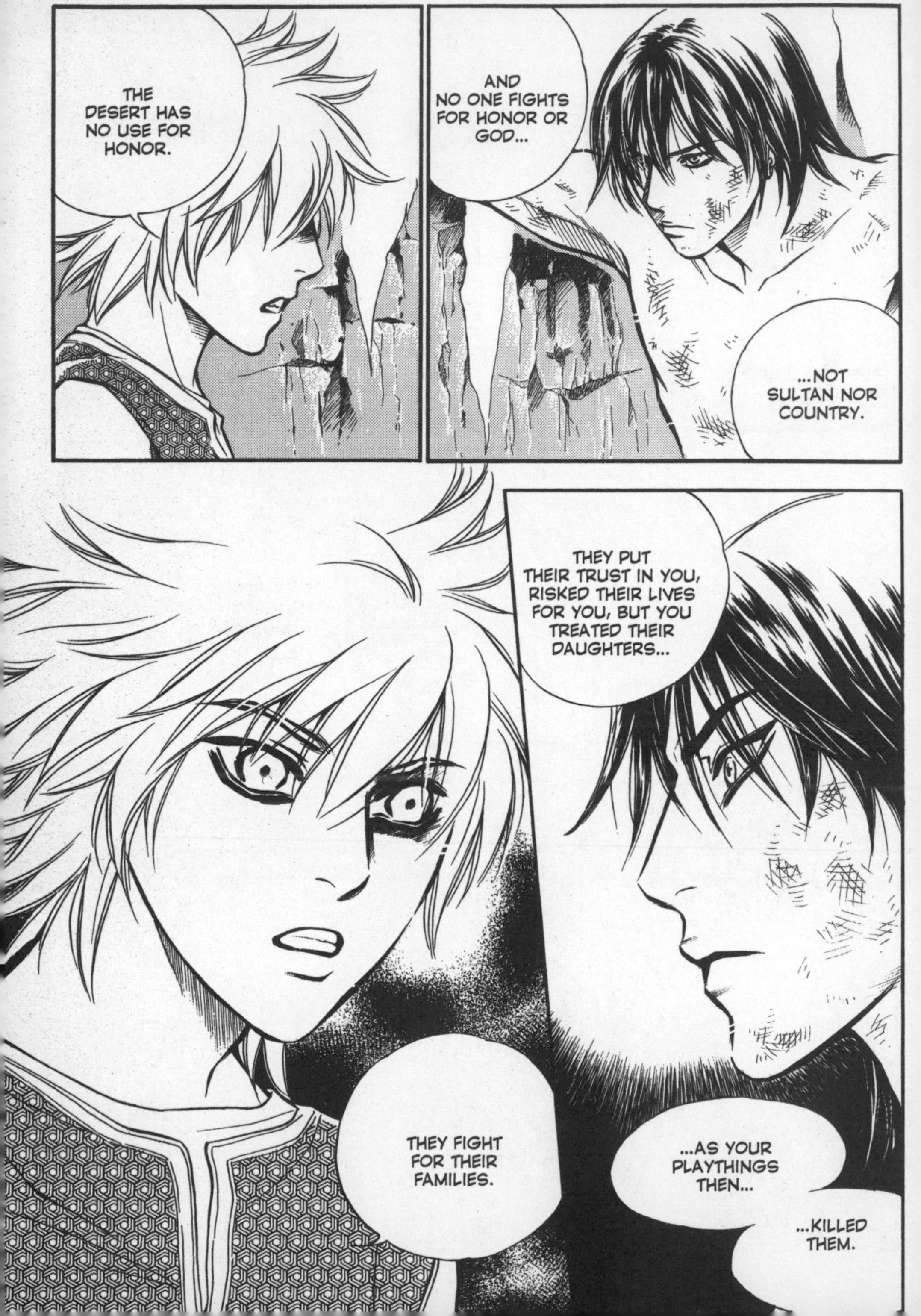
THE DESERT HAS NO USE FOR HONOR.
AND NO ONE FIGHTS FOR HONOR OR GOD...
...NOT SULTAN NOR COUNTRY.
THEY PUT THEIR TRUST IN YOU, RISKED THEIR LIVES FOR YOU, BUT YOU TREATED THEIR DAUGHTERS...
THEY FIGHT FOR THEIR FAMILIES.
...AS YOUR PLAYTHINGS THEN...
...KILLED THEM.

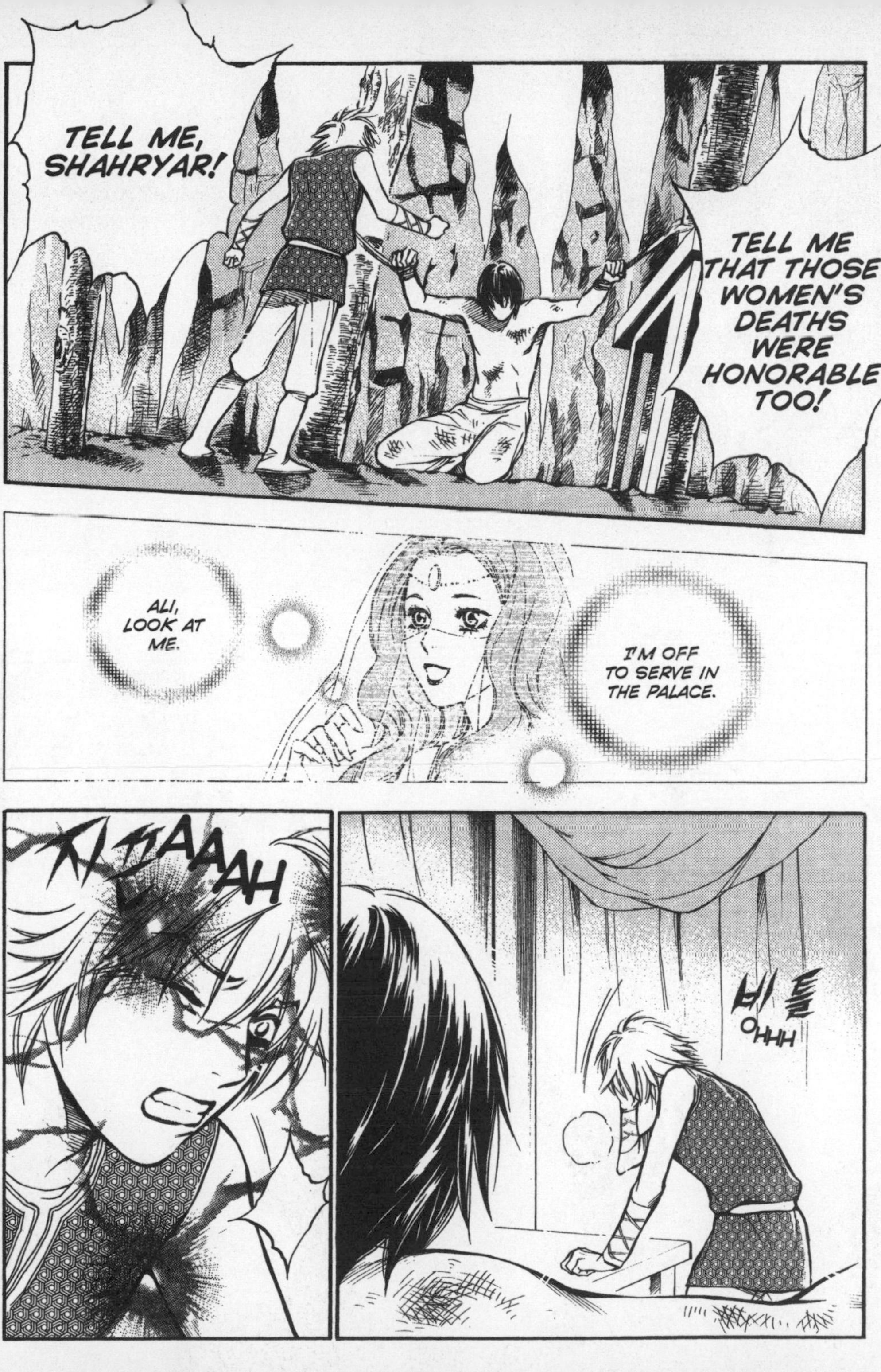
TELL ME, SHAHRYAR!
TELL ME THAT THOSE WOMEN'S DEATHS WERE HONORABLE TOO!
ALI, LOOK AT ME.
I'M OFF TO SERVE IN THE PALACE.
AAAH
비틀
OHHH

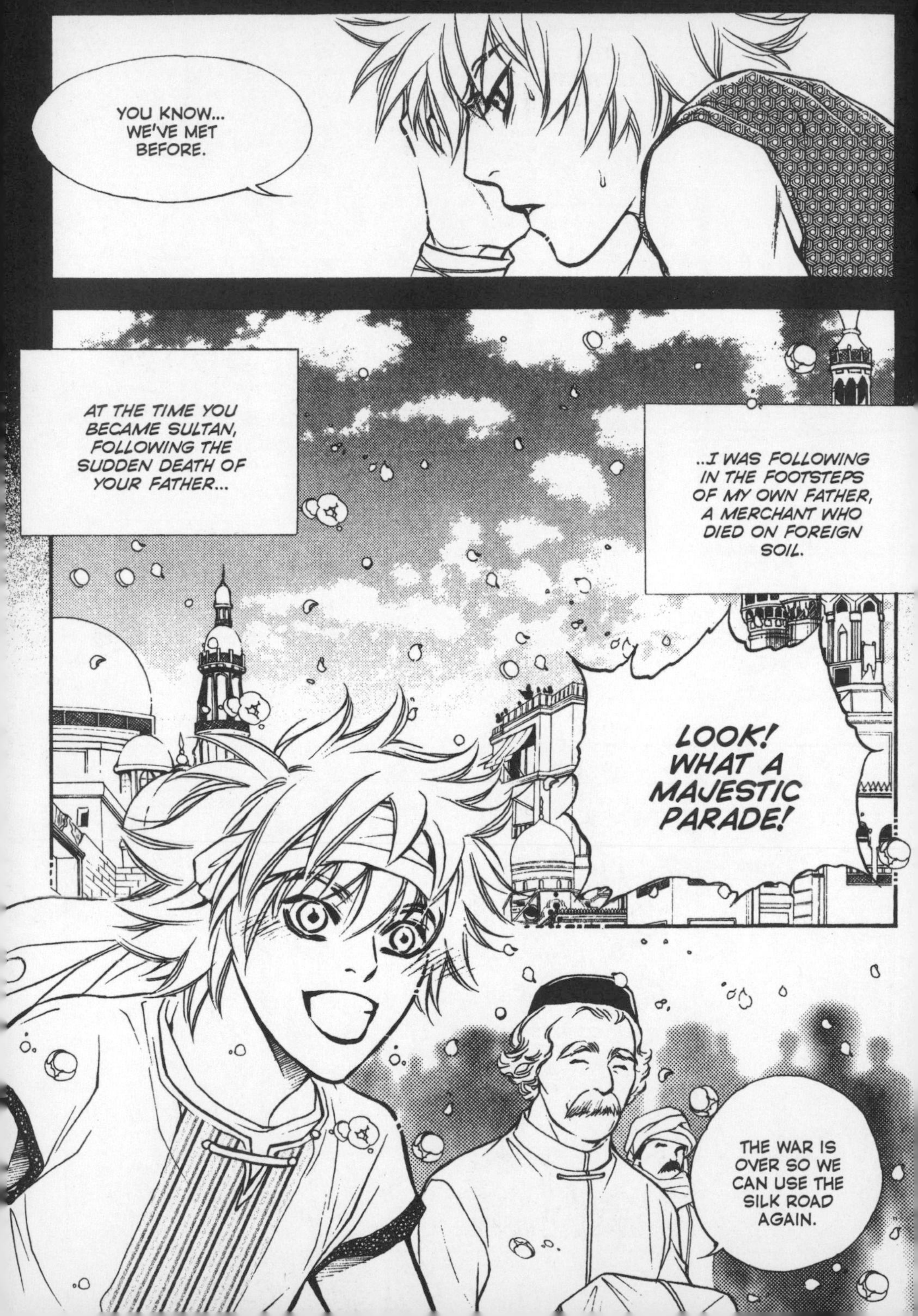
YOU KNOW... WE'VE MET BEFORE.
AT THE TIME YOU BECAME SULTAN, FOLLOWING THE SUDDEN DEATH OF YOUR FATHER...
...I WAS FOLLOWING IN THE FOOTSTEPS OF MY OWN FATHER, A MERCHANT WHO DIED ON FOREIGN SOIL.
LOOK! WHAT A MAJESTIC PARADE!
THE WAR IS OVER SO WE CAN USE THE SILK ROAD AGAIN.

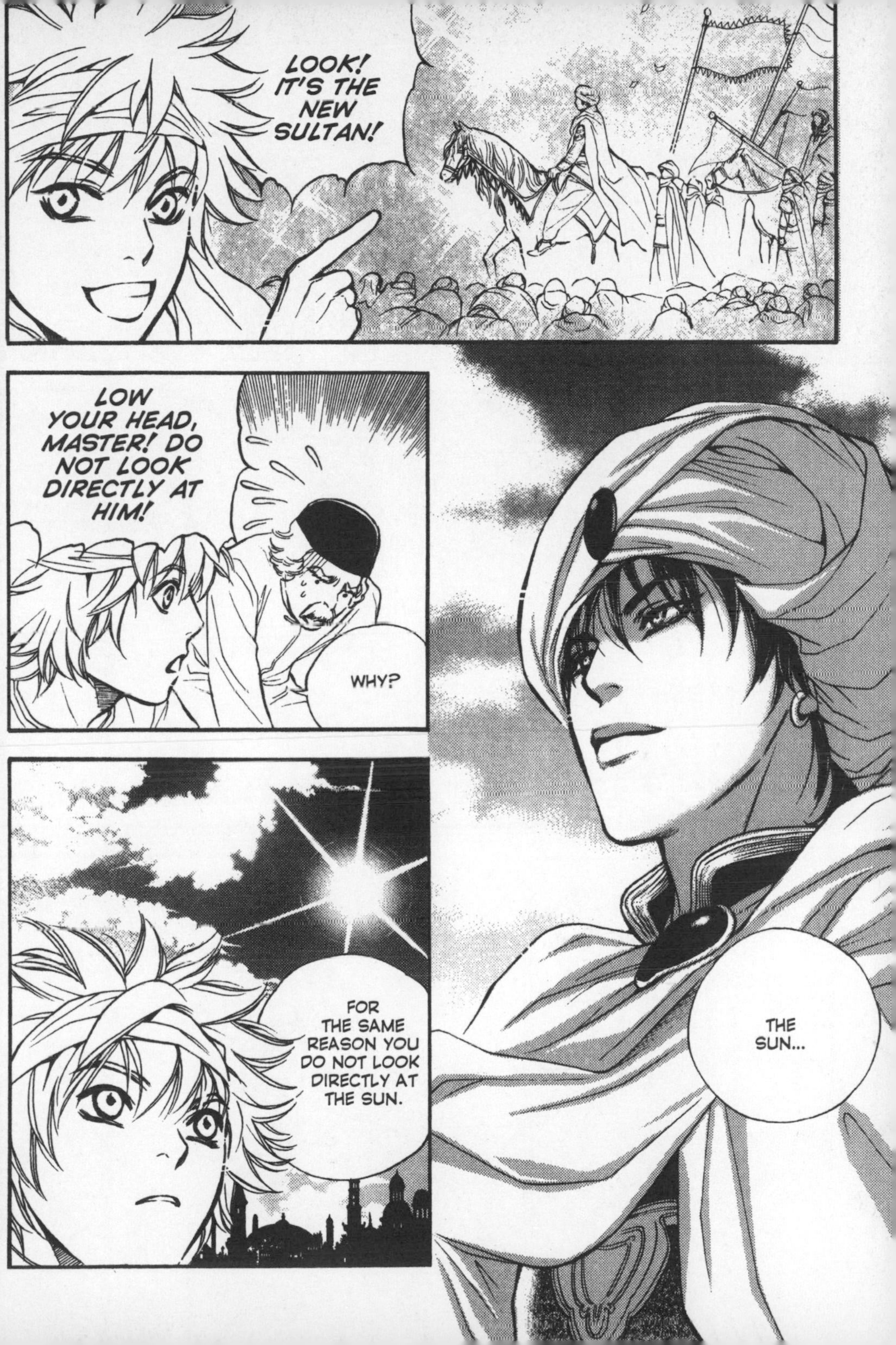
LOOK! IT'S THE NEW SULTAN!
LOW YOUR HEAD, MASTER! DO NOT LOOK DIRECTLY AT HIM!
WHY?
FOR THE SAME REASON YOU DO NOT LOOK DIRECTLY AT THE SUN.
THE SUN...

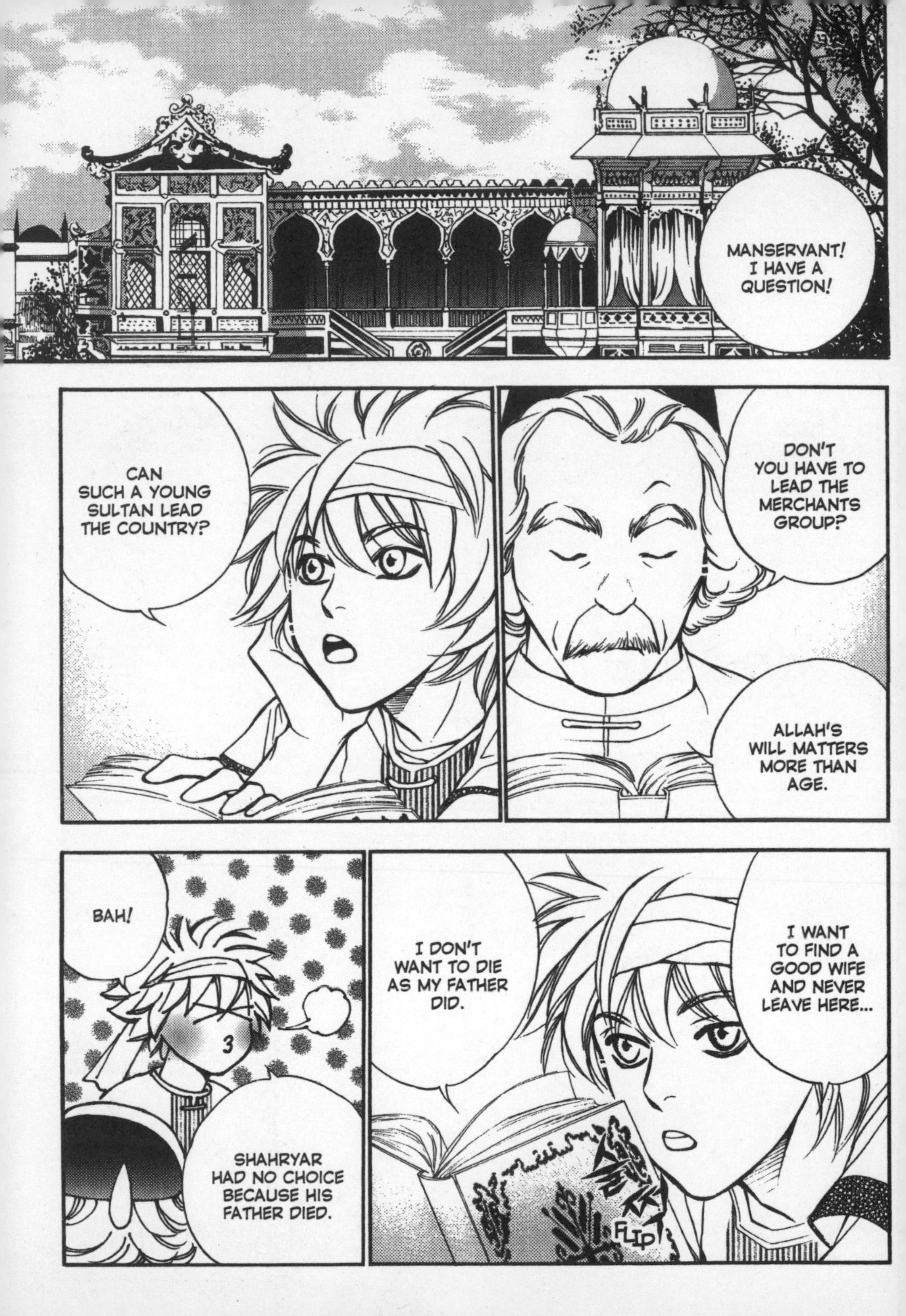
MANSERVANT! I HAVE A QUESTION!
CAN SUCH A YOUNG SULTAN LEAD THE COUNTRY?
DON'T YOU HAVE TO LEAD THE MERCHANTS GROUP?
ALLAH'S WILL MATTERS MORE THAN AGE.
BAH!
SHAHRYAR HAD NO CHOICE BECAUSE HIS FATHER DIED.
I DON'T WANT TO DIE AS MY FATHER DID.
I WANT TO FIND A GOOD WIFE AND NEVER LEAVE HERE...
FLIP

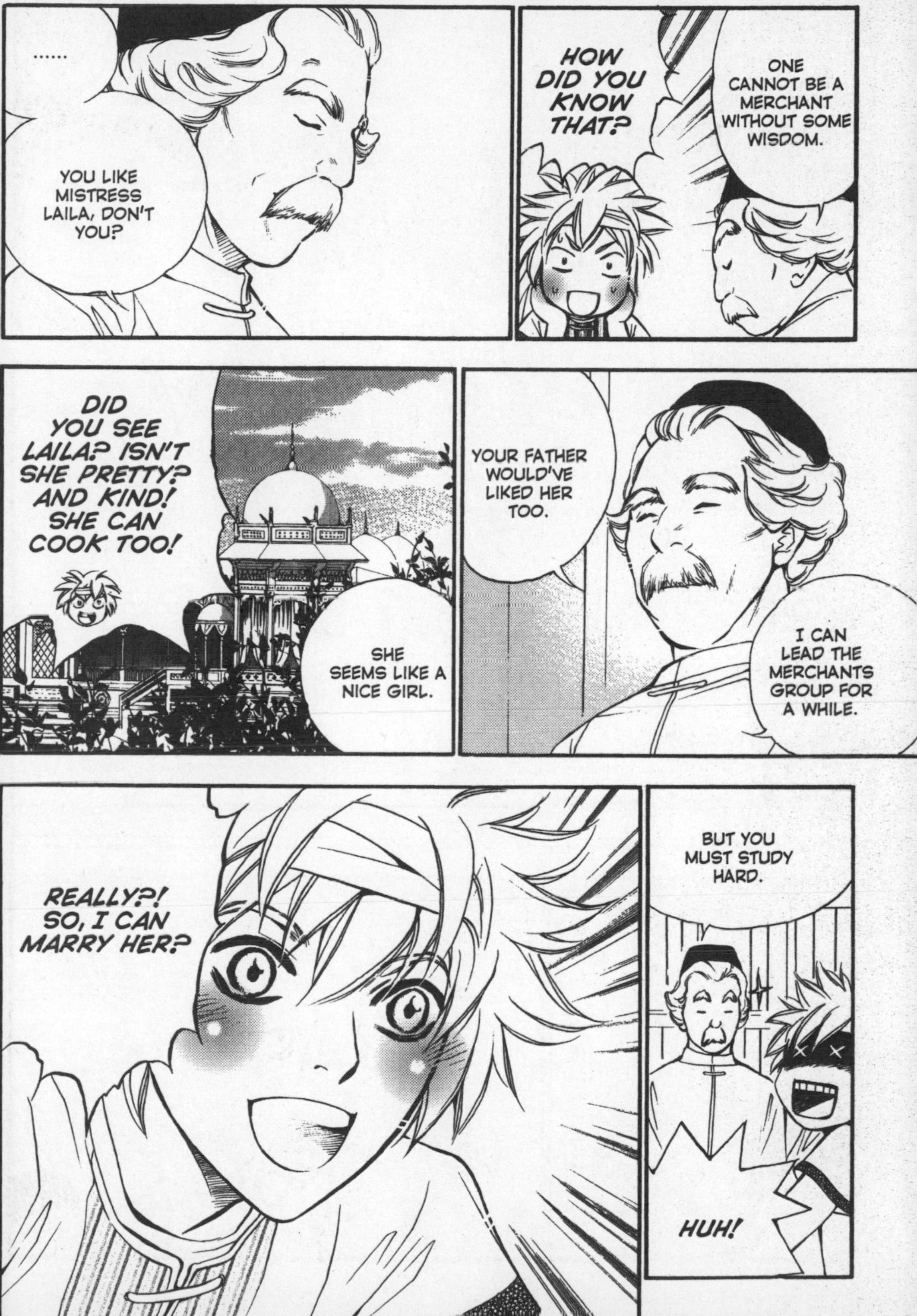
......
YOU LIKE MISTRESS LAILA, DON'T YOU?
HOW DID YOU KNOW THAT?
ONE CANNOT BE A MERCHANT WITHOUT SOME WISDOM.
DID YOU SEE LAILA? ISN'T SHE PRETTY? AND KIND! SHE CAN COOK TOO!
SHE SEEMS LIKE A NICE GIRL.
YOUR FATHER WOULD'VE LIKED HER TOO.
I CAN LEAD THE MERCHANTS GROUP FOR A WHILE.
REALLY?! SO, I CAN MARRY HER?
BUT YOU MUST STUDY HARD.
HUH!

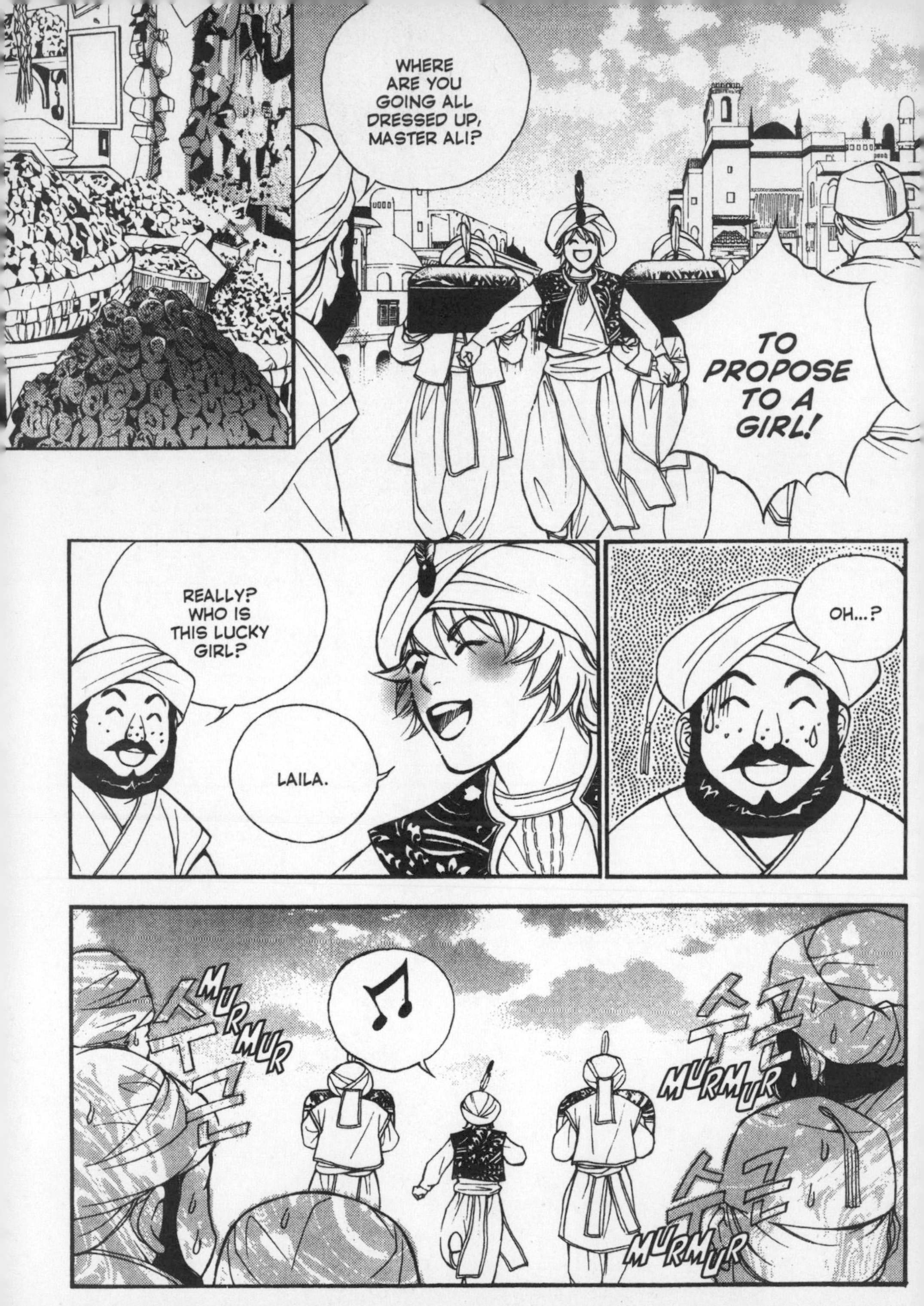
WHERE ARE YOU GOING ALL DRESSED UP, MASTER ALI?
TO PROPOSE TO A GIRL!
REALLY? WHO IS THIS LUCKY GIRL?
LAILA.
OH...?
MURMUR
♫
MURMUR
MURMUR

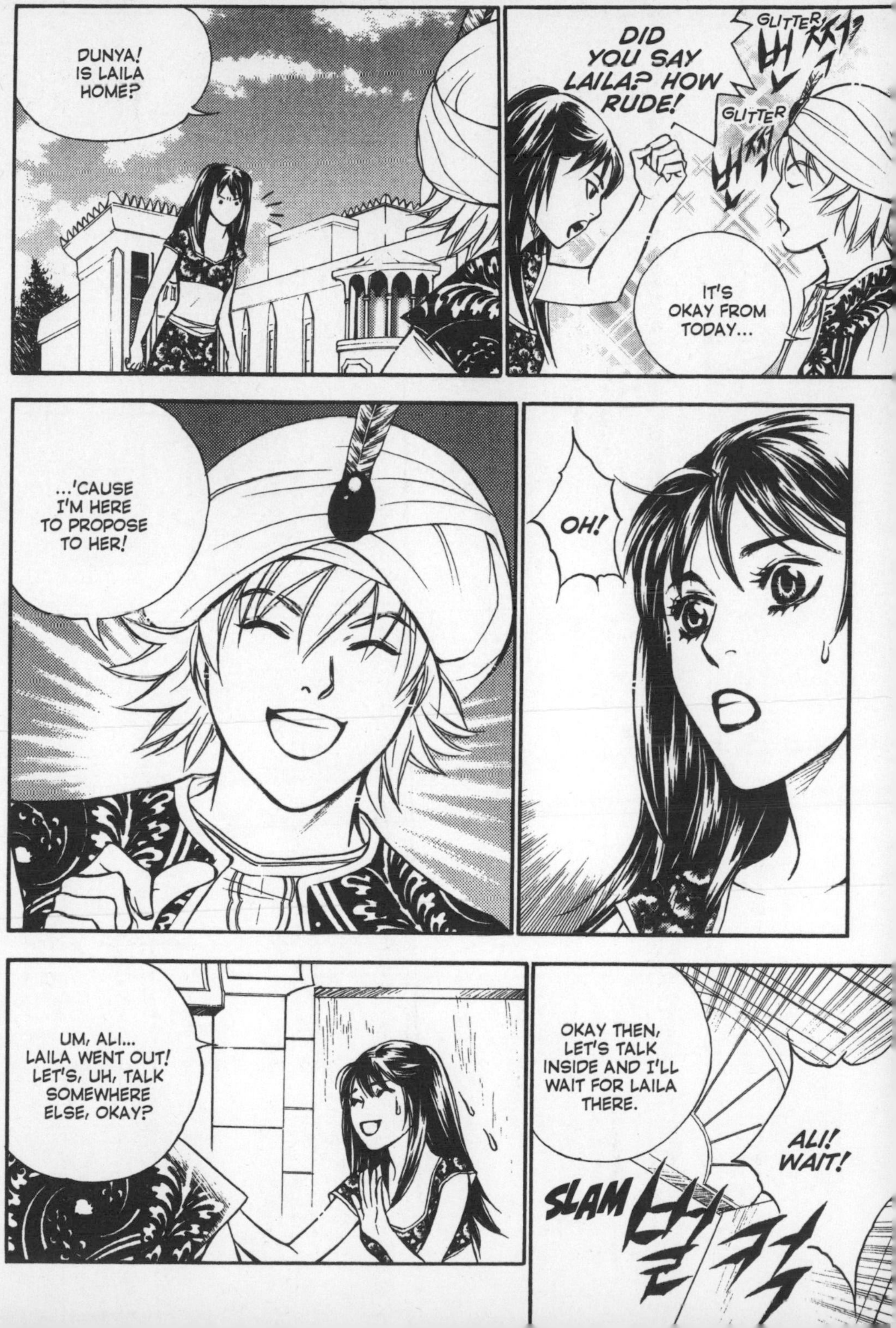
DUNYA! IS LAILA HOME?
DID YOU SAY LAILA? HOW RUDE!
GLITTER
GLITTER
IT'S OKAY FROM TODAY...
...'CAUSE I'M HERE TO PROPOSE TO HER!
OH!
UM, ALI... LAILA WENT OUT! LET'S, UH, TALK SOMEWHERE ELSE, OKAY?
OKAY THEN, LET'S TALK INSIDE AND I'LL WAIT FOR LAILA THERE.
ALI! WAIT!
SLAM
벌컥

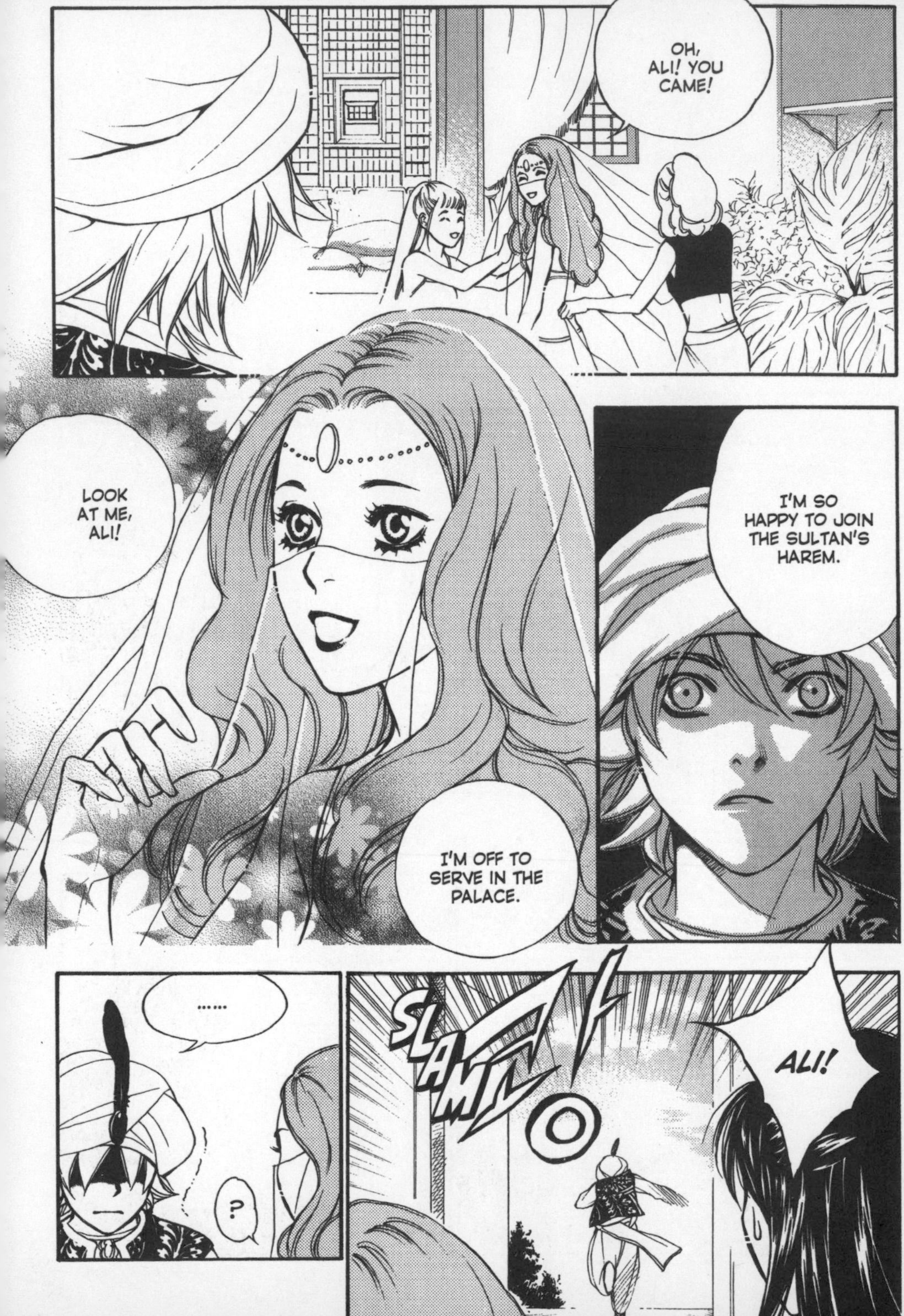
OH, ALI! YOU CAME!
LOOK AT ME, ALI!
I'M OFF TO SERVE IN THE PALACE.
I'M SO HAPPY TO JOIN THE SULTAN'S HAREM.
......
?
SLAM
ALI!

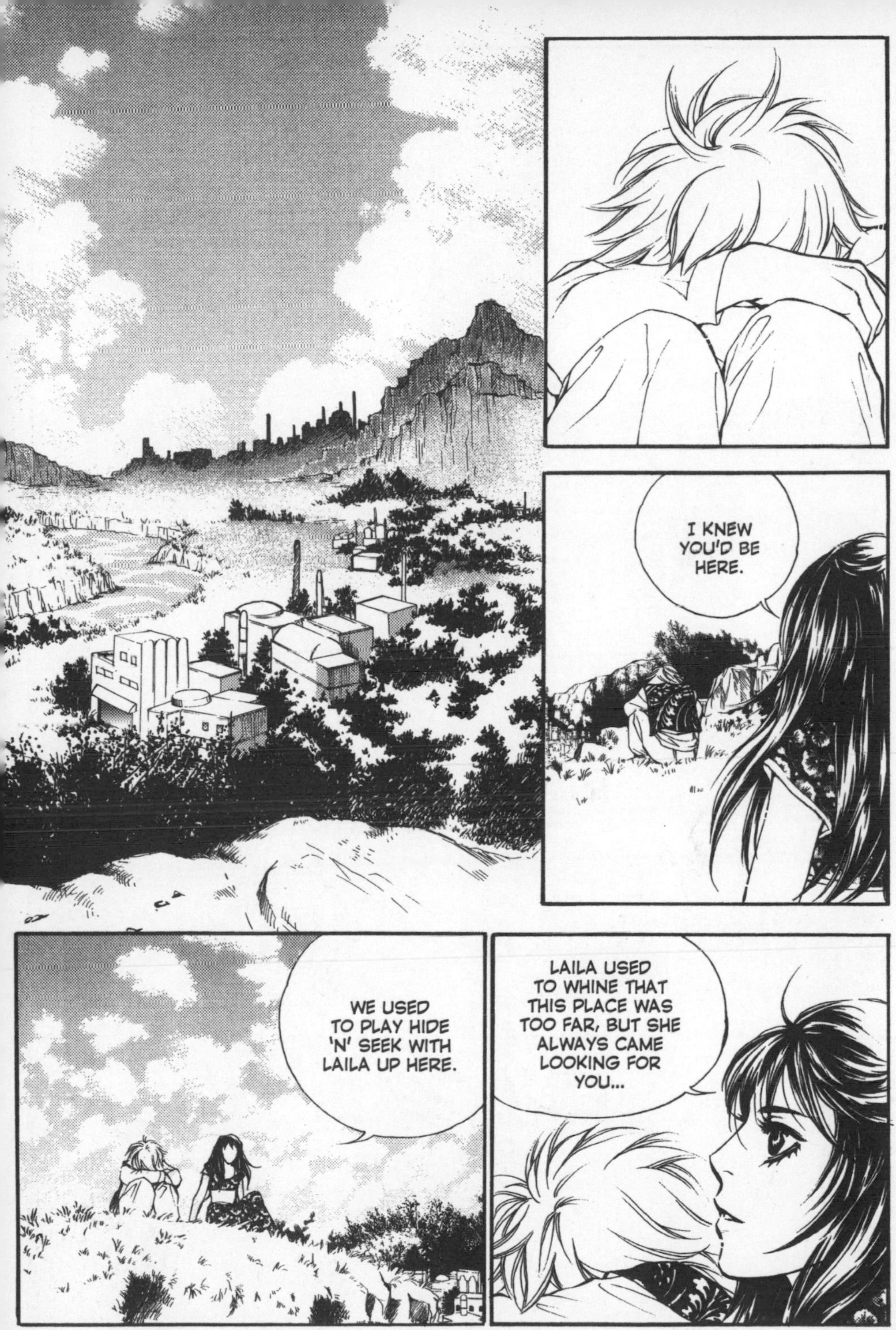
I KNEW YOU'D BE HERE.
WE USED TO PLAY HIDE 'N' SEEK WITH LAILA UP HERE.
LAILA USED TO WHINE THAT THIS PLACE WAS TOO FAR, BUT SHE ALWAYS CAME LOOKING FOR YOU...

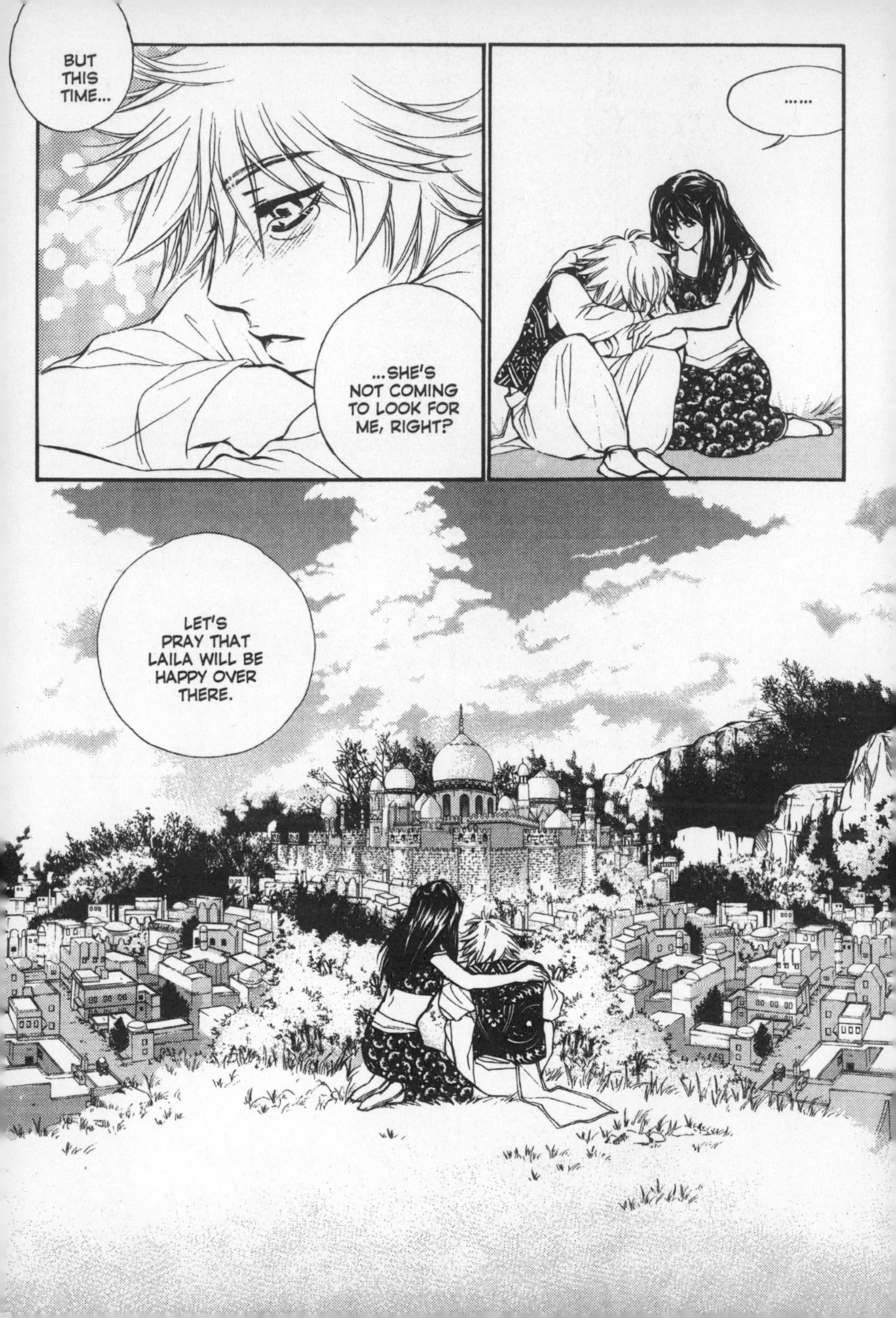
BUT THIS TIME...
...SHE'S NOT COMING TO LOOK FOR ME, RIGHT?
......
LET'S PRAY THAT LAILA WILL BE HAPPY OVER THERE.

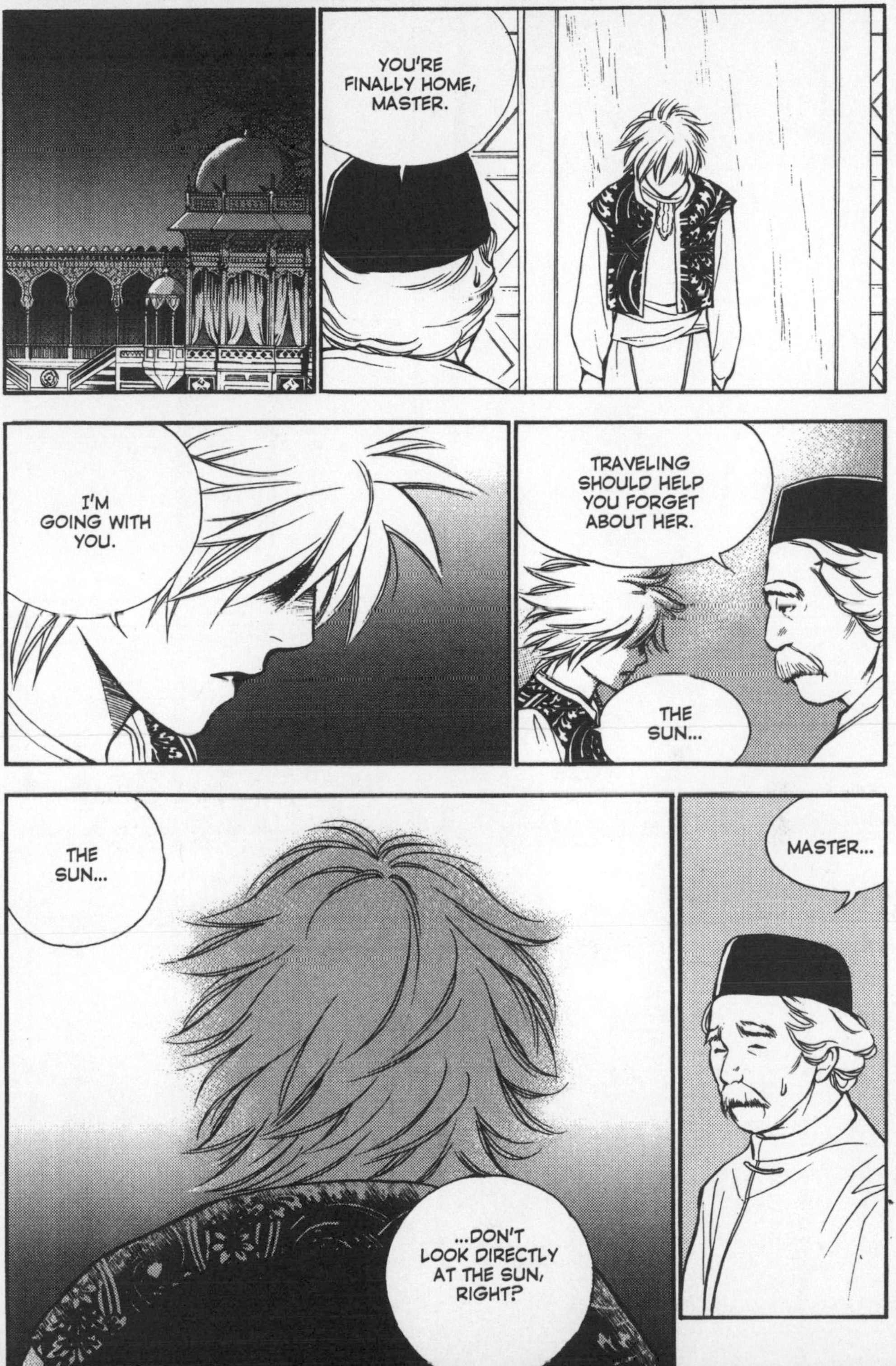
YOU'RE FINALLY HOME, MASTER.
I'M GOING WITH YOU.
TRAVELING SHOULD HELP YOU FORGET ABOUT HER.
THE SUN...
THE SUN...
...DON'T LOOK DIRECTLY AT THE SUN, RIGHT?
MASTER...

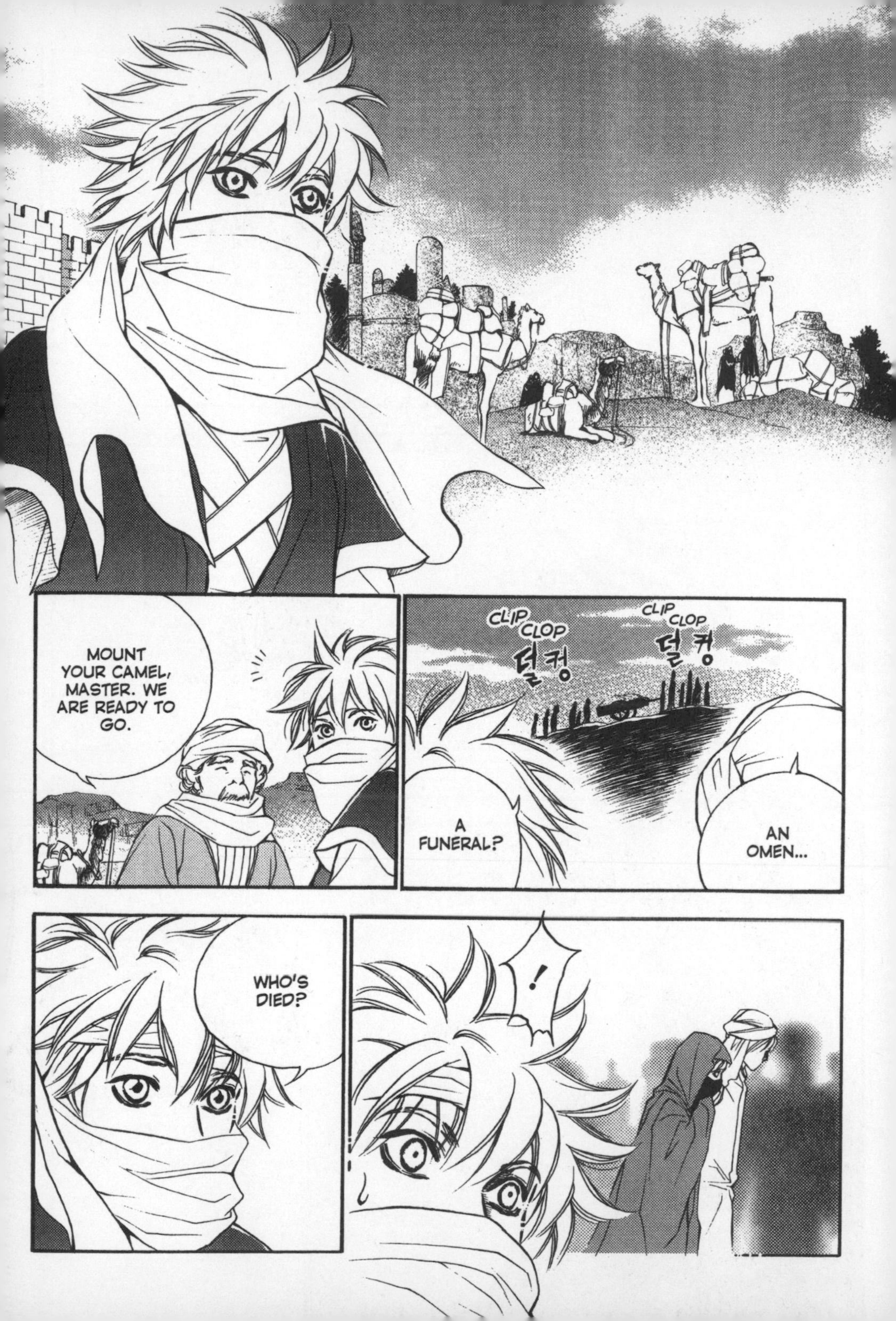
MOUNT YOUR CAMEL, MASTER. WE ARE READY TO GO.
CLIP CLOP
덜컹
CLIP CLOP
덜컹
A FUNERAL?
AN OMEN...
WHO'S DIED?
!

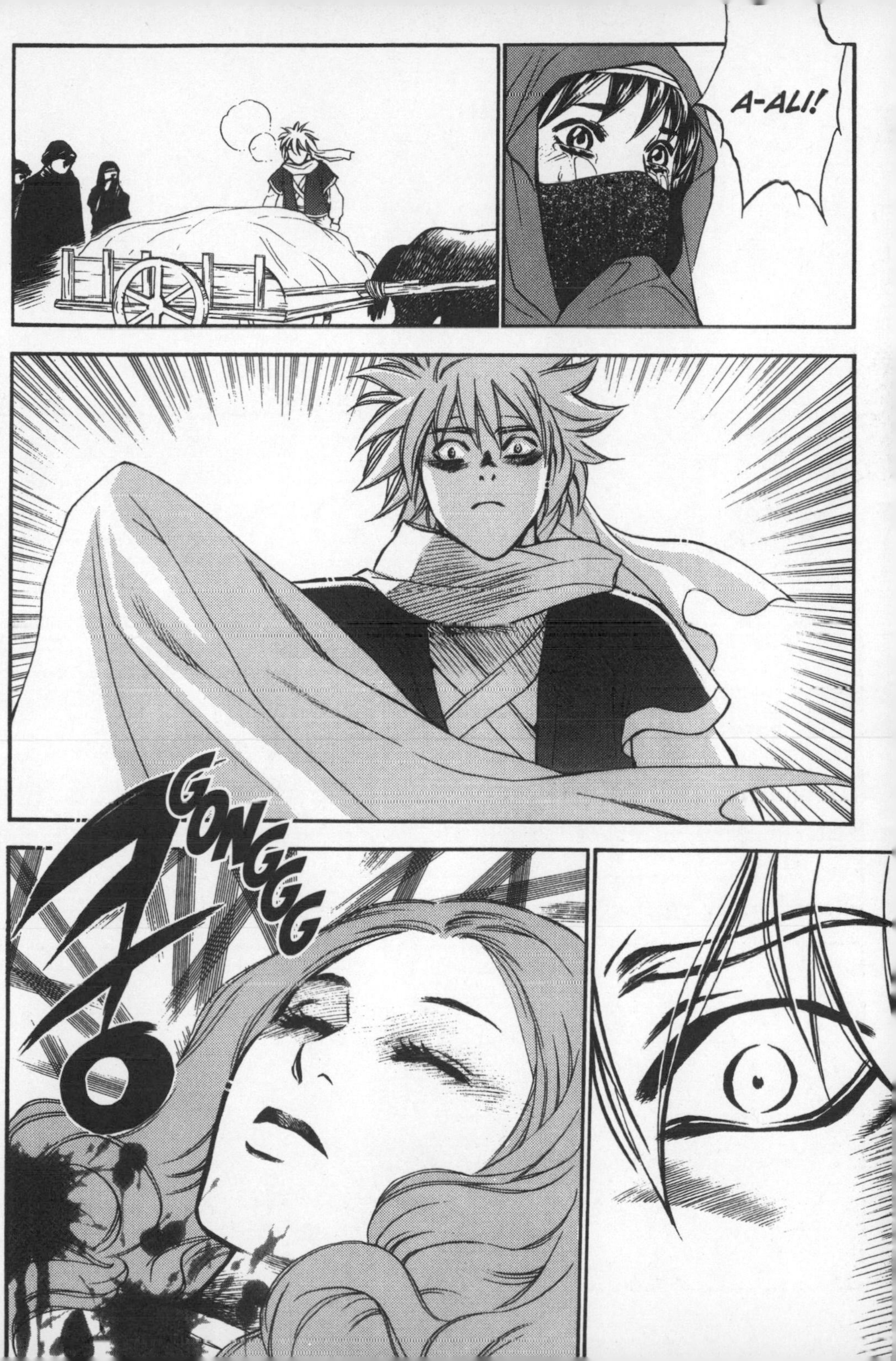
A-ALI!
GONGGG

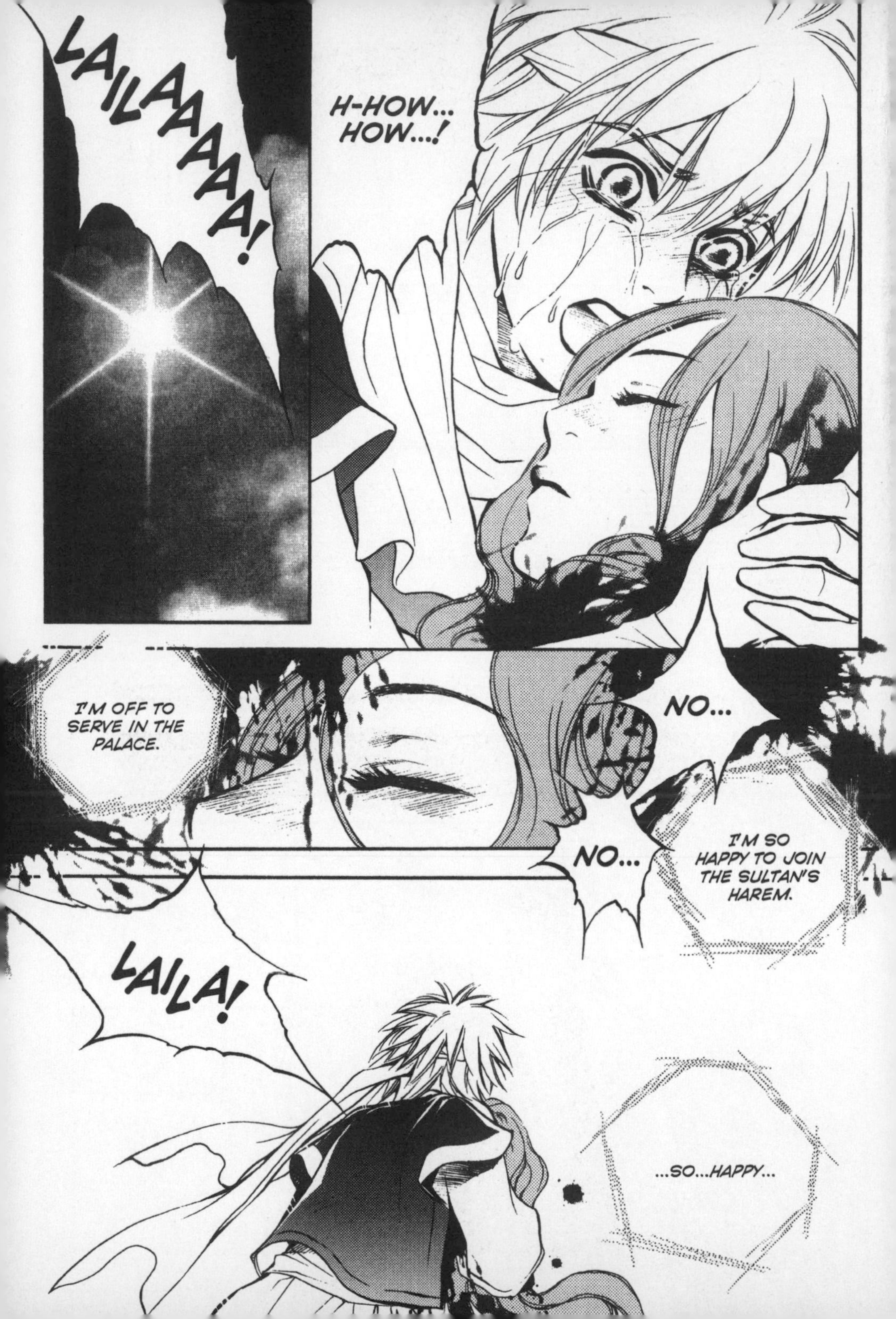
LAILAAAAAA!
H-HOW... HOW...!
I'M OFF TO SERVE IN THE PALACE.
NO...
NO...
I'M SO HAPPY TO JOIN THE SULTAN'S HAREM.
LAILA!
...SO...HAPPY...

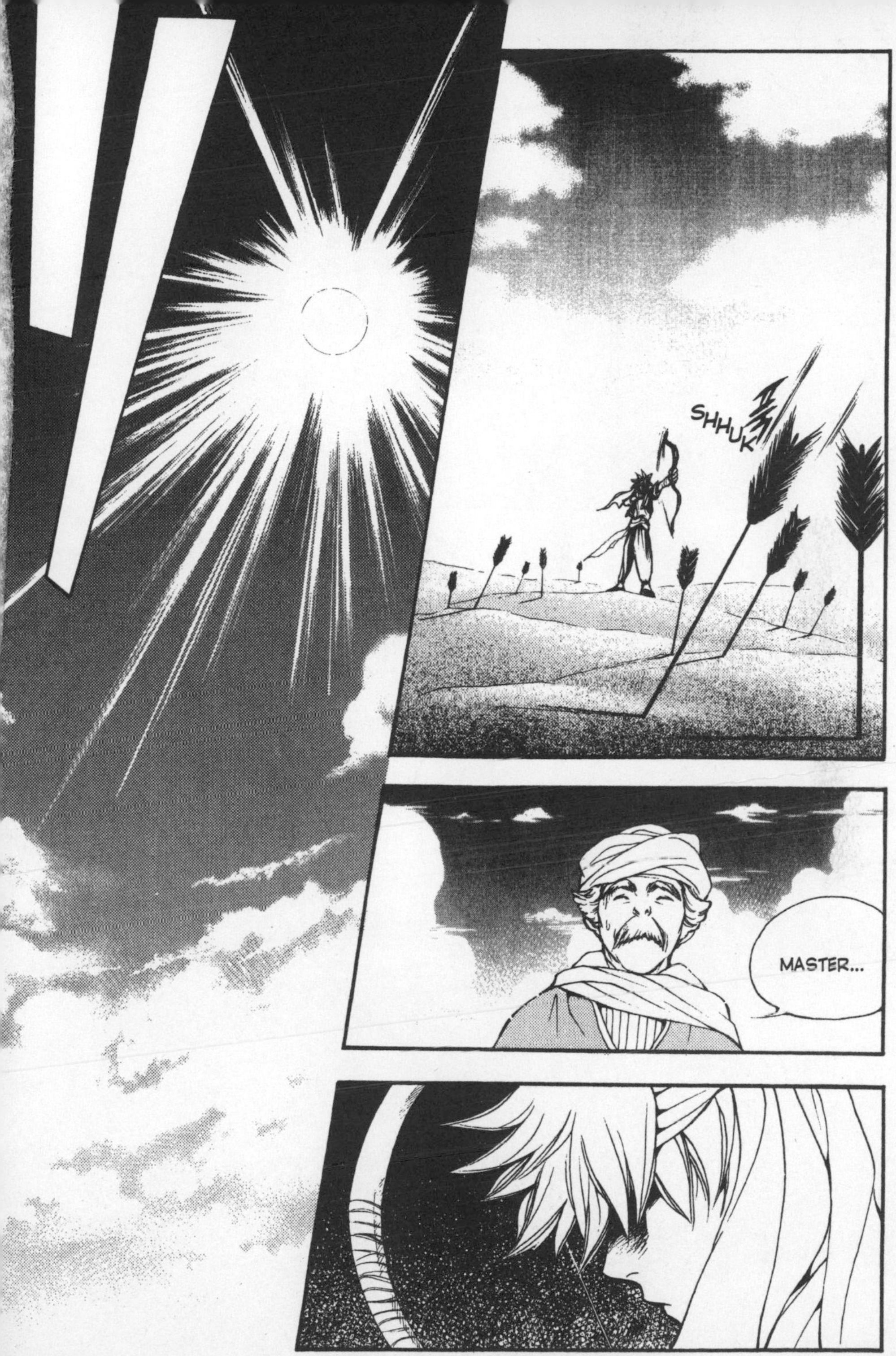
SHHUK
MASTER...

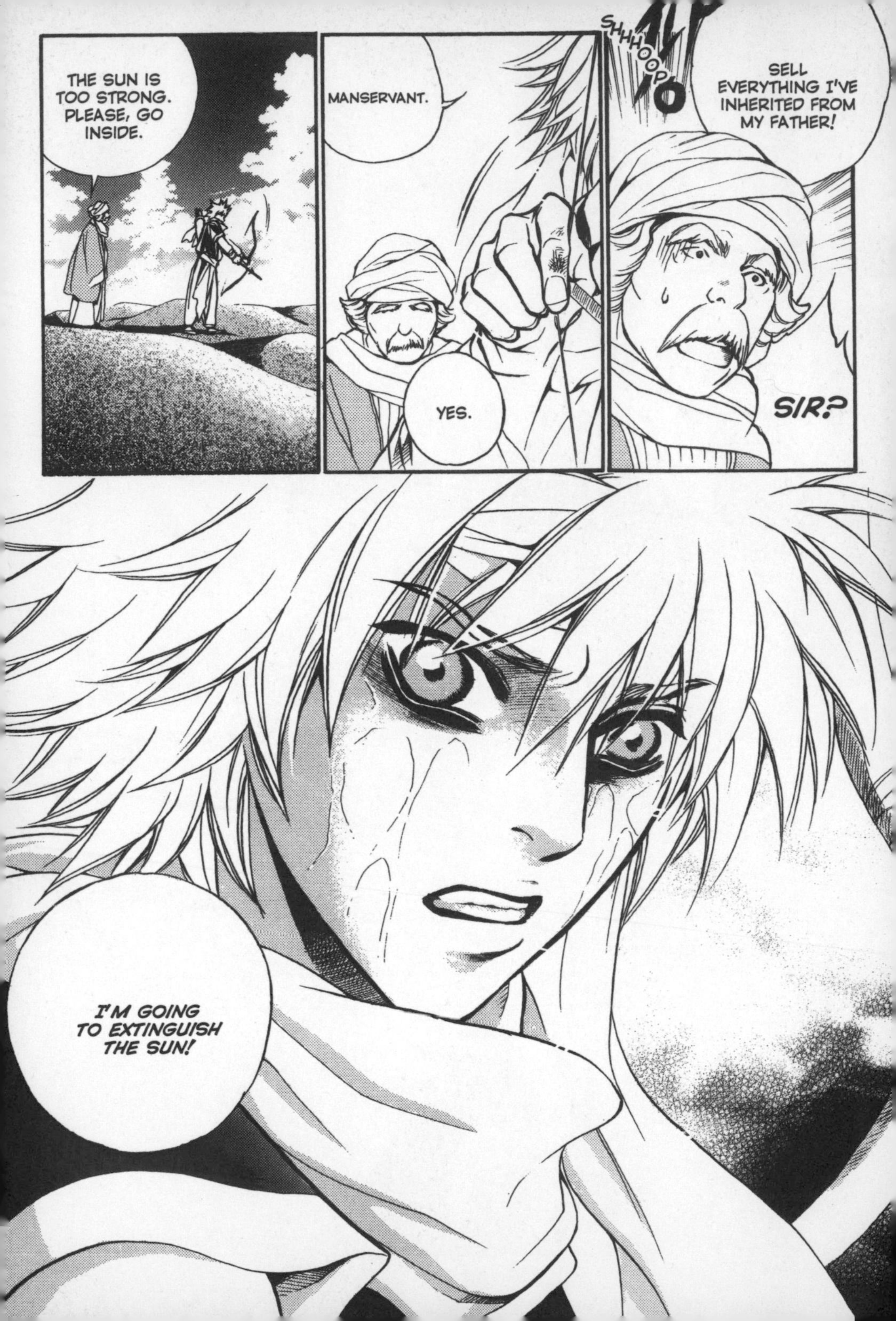
THE SUN IS TOO STRONG. PLEASE, GO INSIDE.
MANSERVANT.
YES.
SHHHOOP
SELL EVERYTHING I'VE INHERITED FROM MY FATHER!
SIR?
I'M GOING TO EXTINGUISH THE SUN!

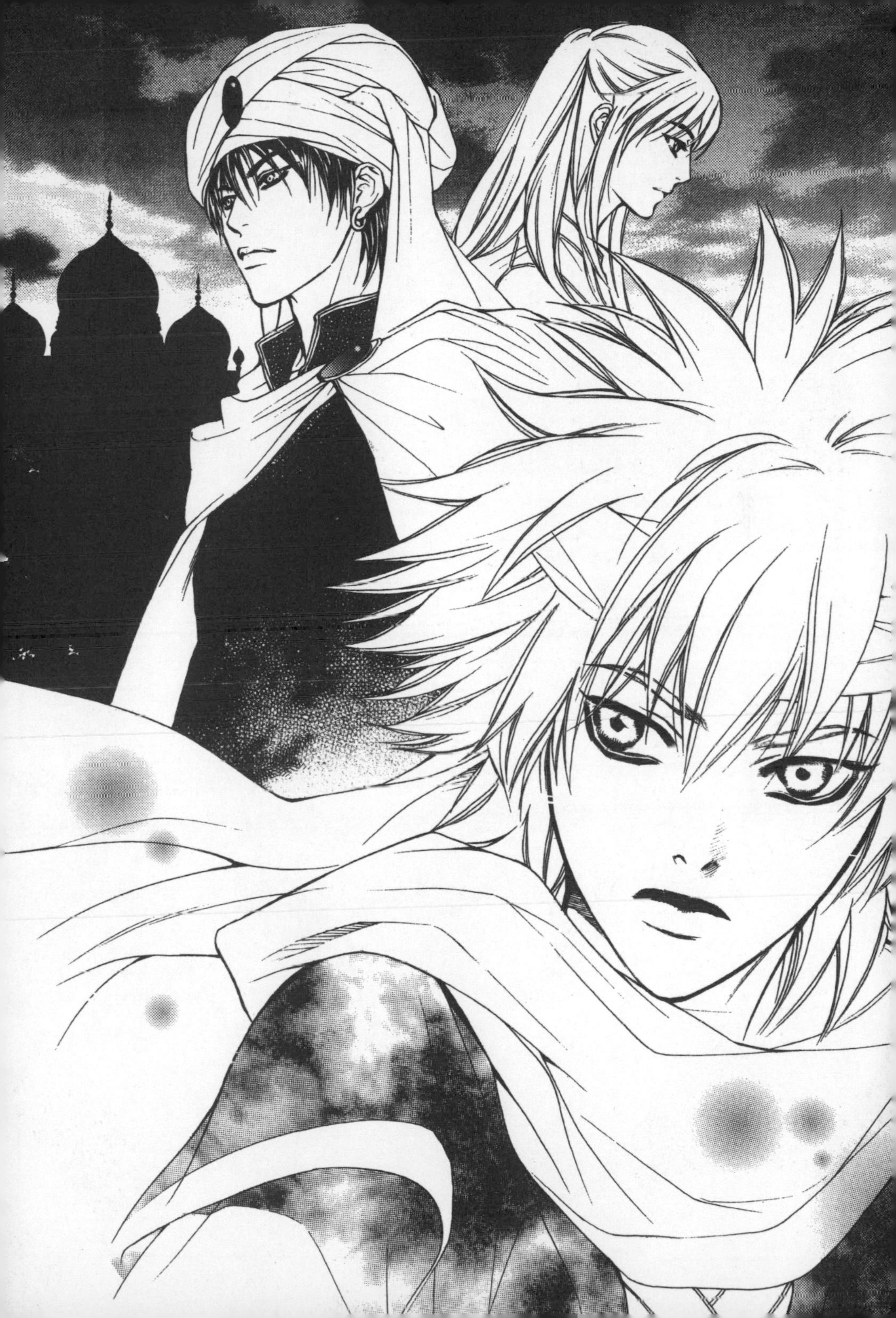

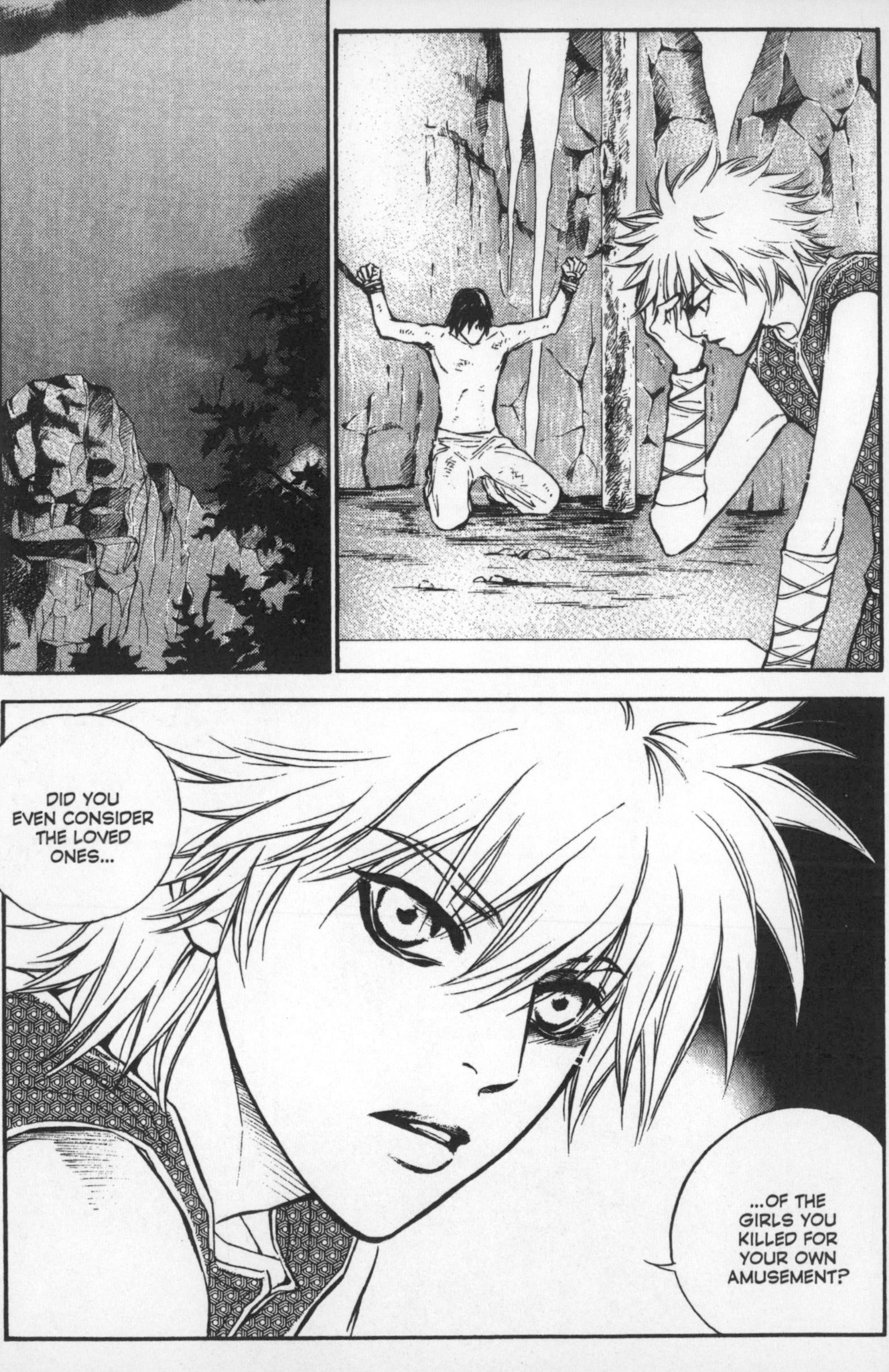
DID YOU EVEN CONSIDER THE LOVED ONES...
...OF THE GIRLS YOU KILLED FOR YOUR OWN AMUSEMENT?

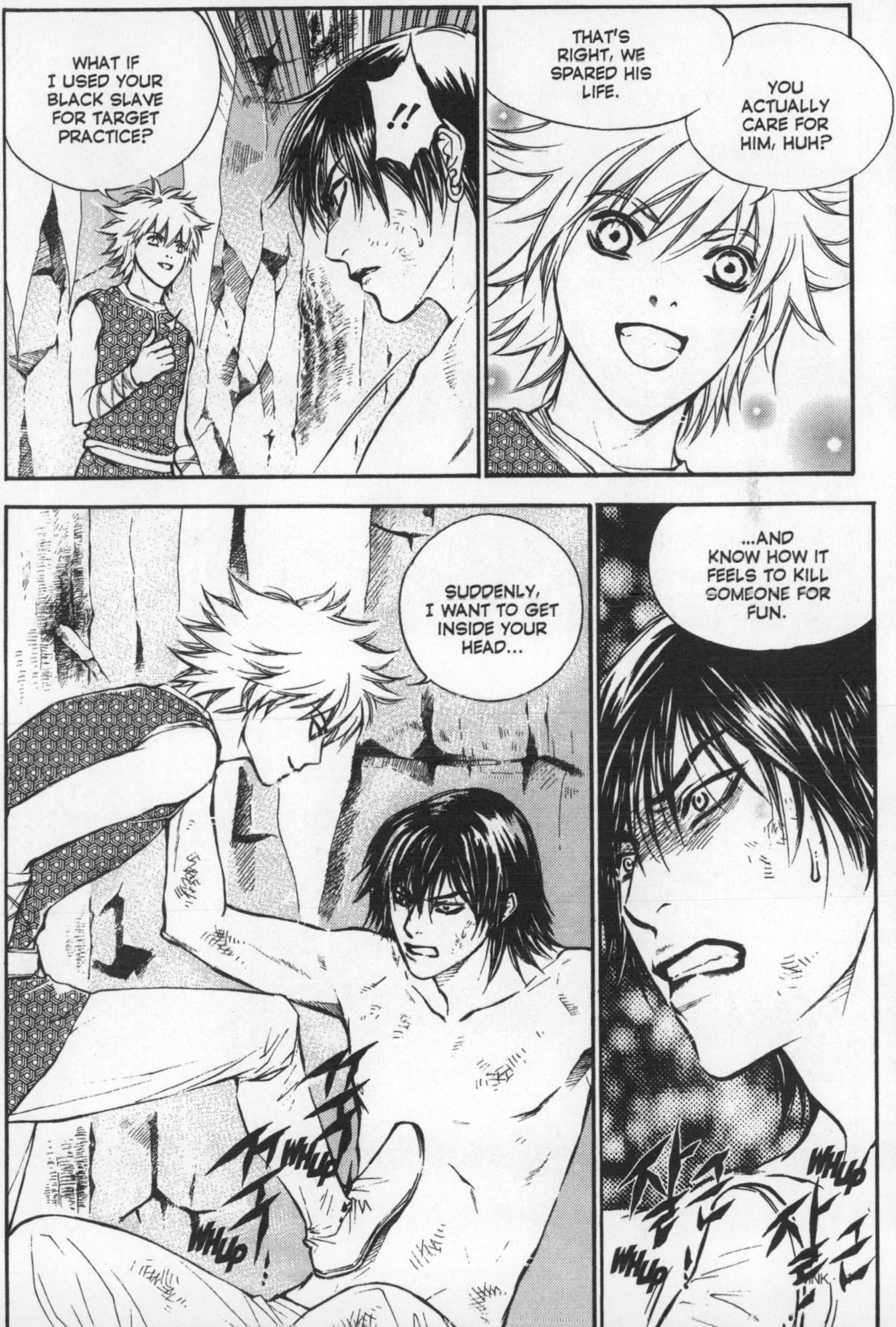
WHAT IF I USED YOUR BLACK SLAVE FOR TARGET PRACTICE?
!!
THAT'S RIGHT, WE SPARED HIS LIFE.
YOU ACTUALLY CARE FOR HIM, HUH?
SUDDENLY, I WANT TO GET INSIDE YOUR HEAD...
WHUP
WHUP
...AND KNOW HOW IT FEELS TO KILL SOMEONE FOR FUN.
WHUP
WHUP

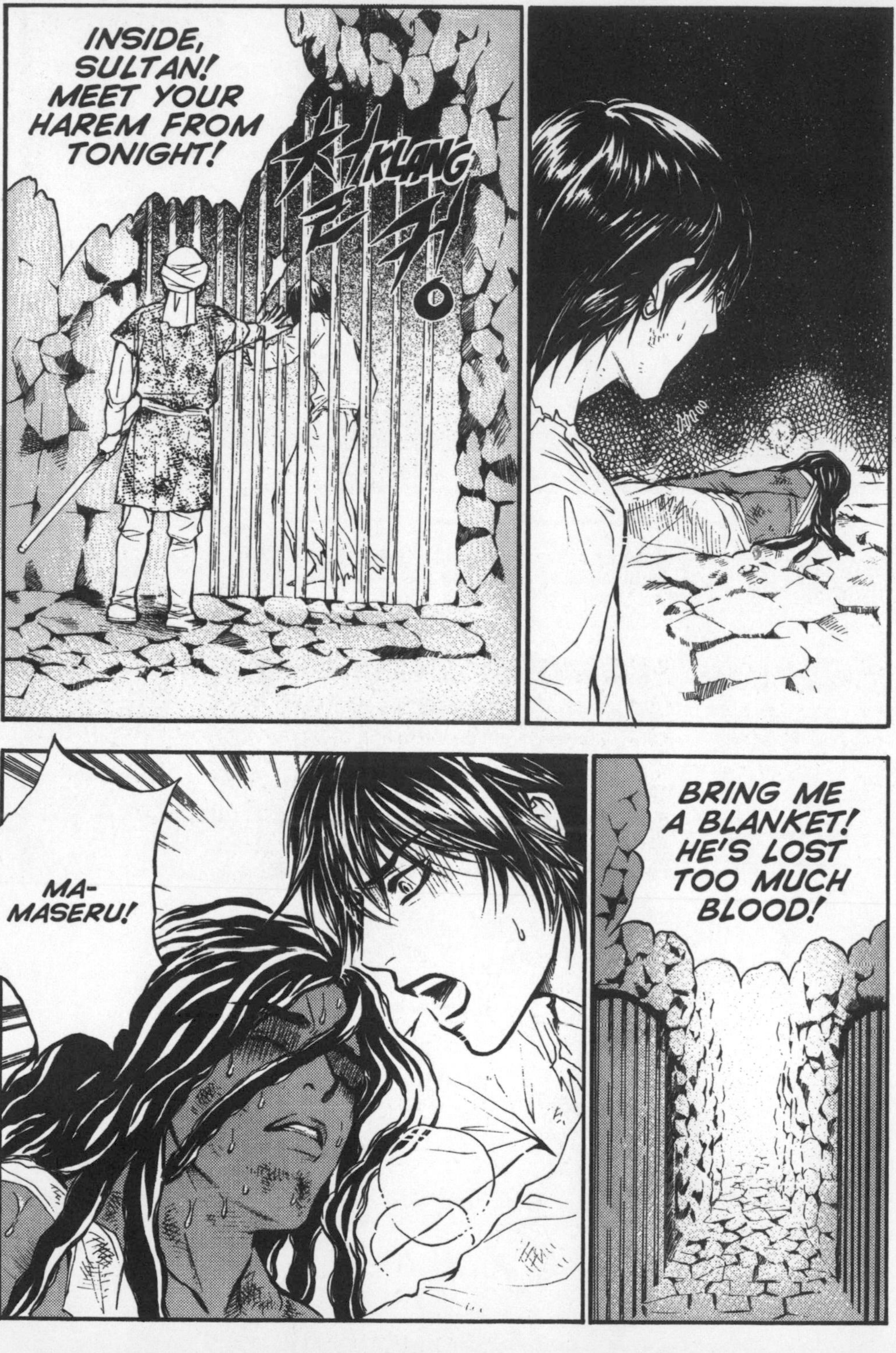
INSIDE, SULTAN! MEET YOUR HAREM FROM TONIGHT!
KLANG
MA-MASERU!
BRING ME A BLANKET! HE'S LOST TOO MUCH BLOOD!

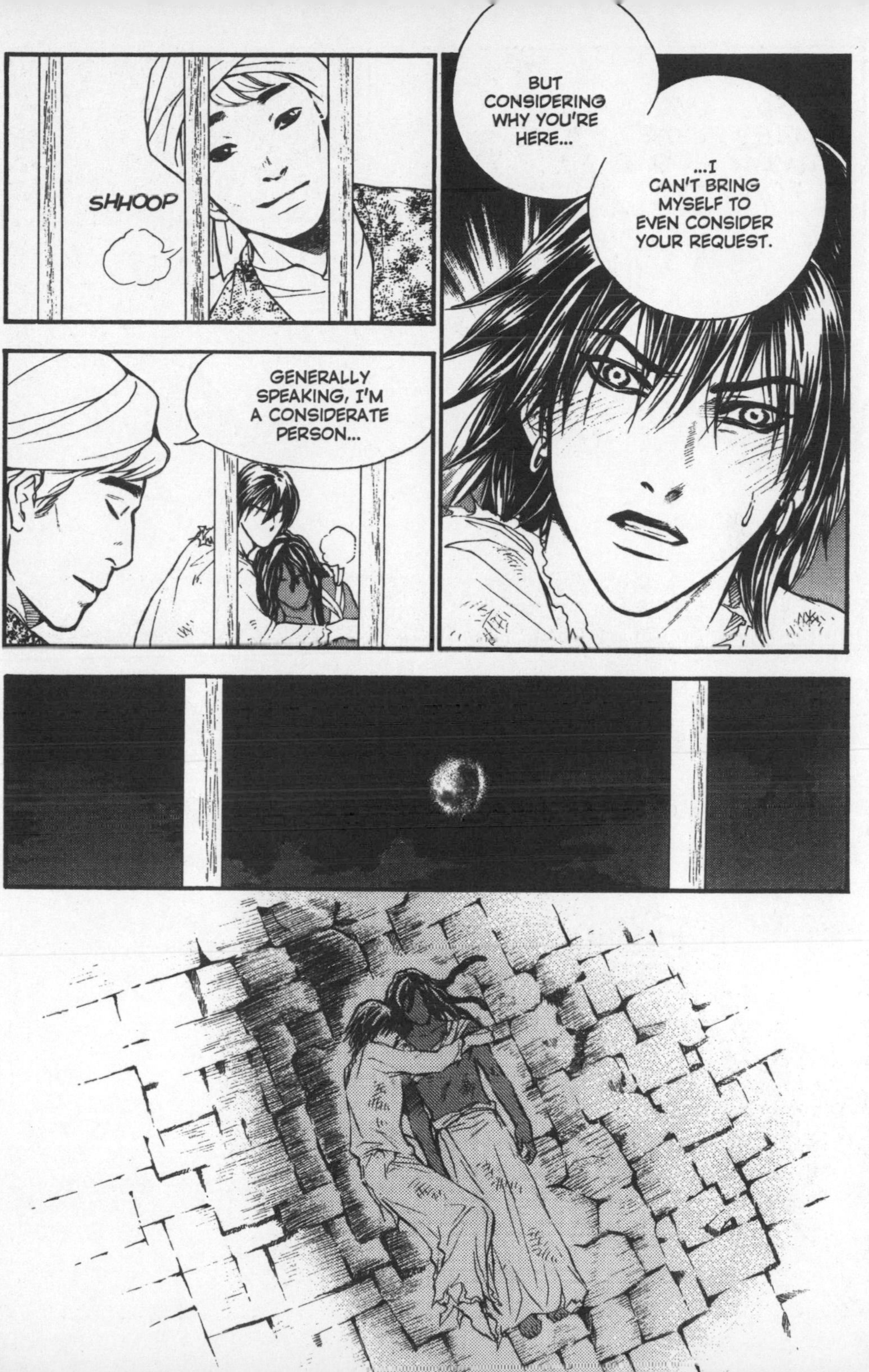
SHHOOP
BUT CONSIDERING WHY YOU'RE HERE...
...I CAN'T BRING MYSELF TO EVEN CONSIDER YOUR REQUEST.
GENERALLY SPEAKING, I'M A CONSIDERATE PERSON...

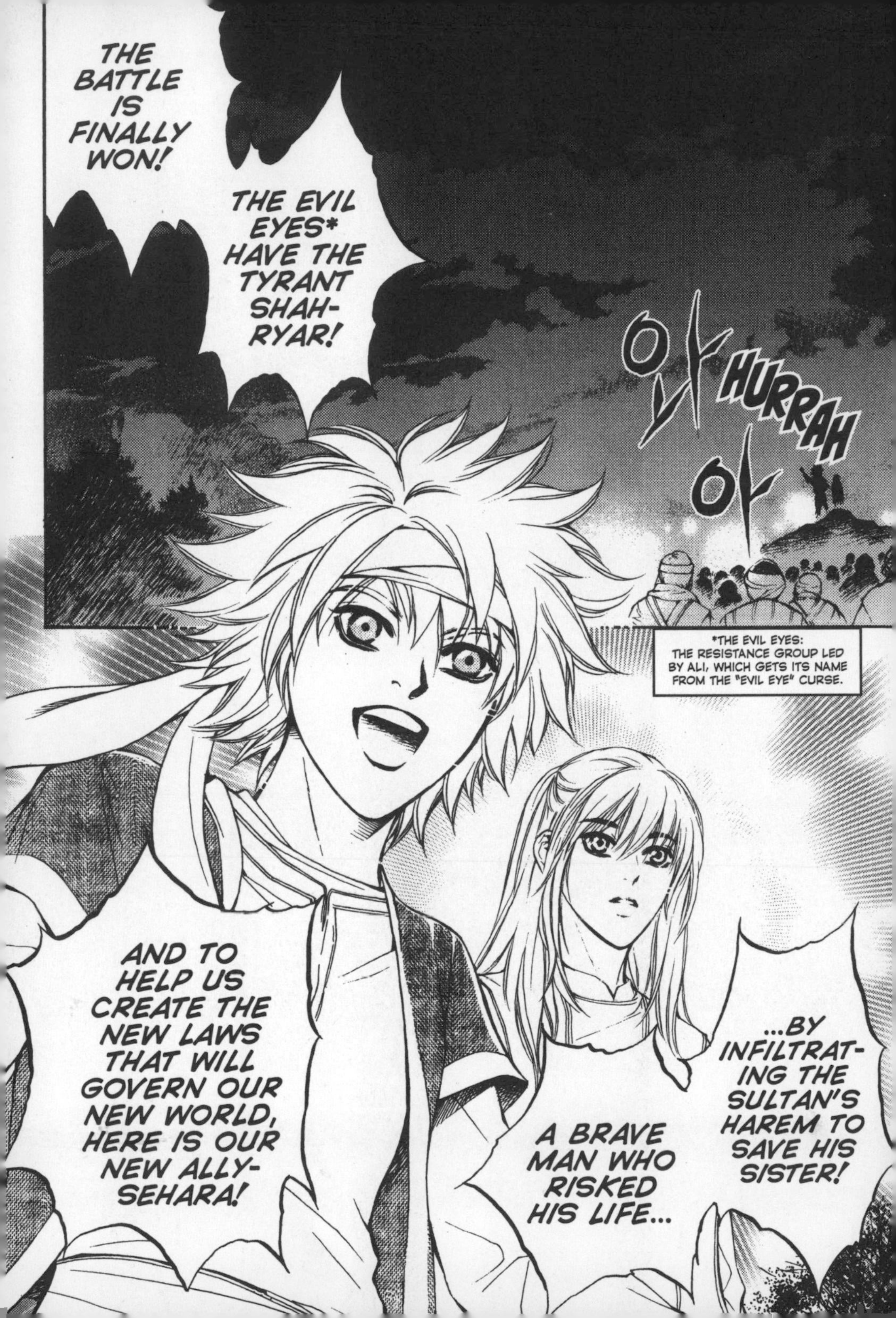
THE BATTLE IS FINALLY WON!
THE EVIL EYES* HAVE THE TYRANT SHAH-RYAR!
와아 HURRAH
*THE EVIL EYES: THE RESISTANCE GROUP LED BY ALI, WHICH GETS ITS NAME FROM THE "EVIL EYE" CURSE.
AND TO HELP US CREATE THE NEW LAWS THAT WILL GOVERN OUR NEW WORLD, HERE IS OUR NEW ALLY-SEHARA!
A BRAVE MAN WHO RISKED HIS LIFE...
...BY INFILTRAT-ING THE SULTAN'S HAREM TO SAVE HIS SISTER!

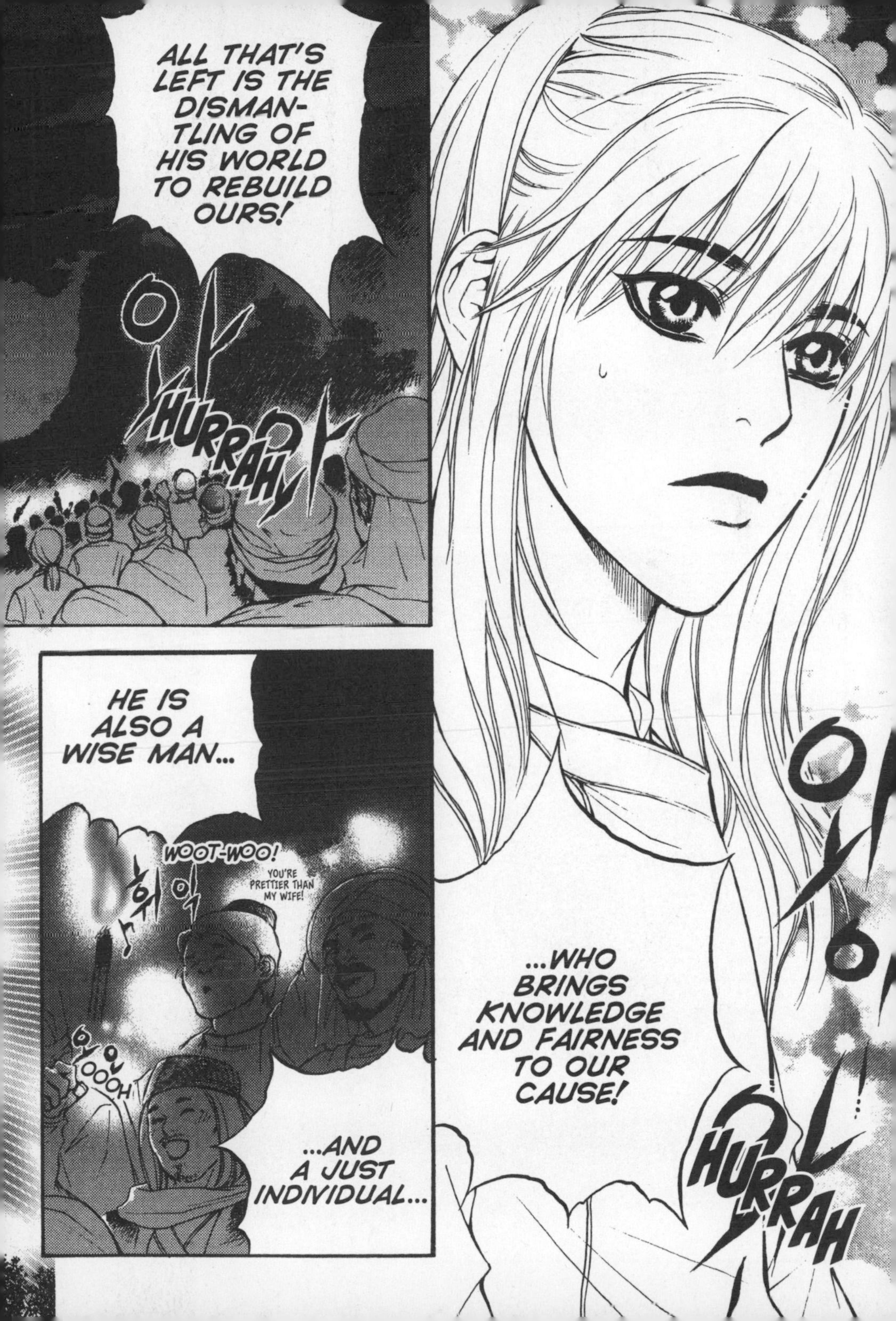
ALL THAT'S LEFT IS THE DISMANTLING OF HIS WORLD TO REBUILD OURS!
HURRAH
HE IS ALSO A WISE MAN...
WOOT-WOO!
YOU'RE PRETTIER THAN MY WIFE!
OOOH
...AND A JUST INDIVIDUAL...
...WHO BRINGS KNOWLEDGE AND FAIRNESS TO OUR CAUSE!
HURRAH

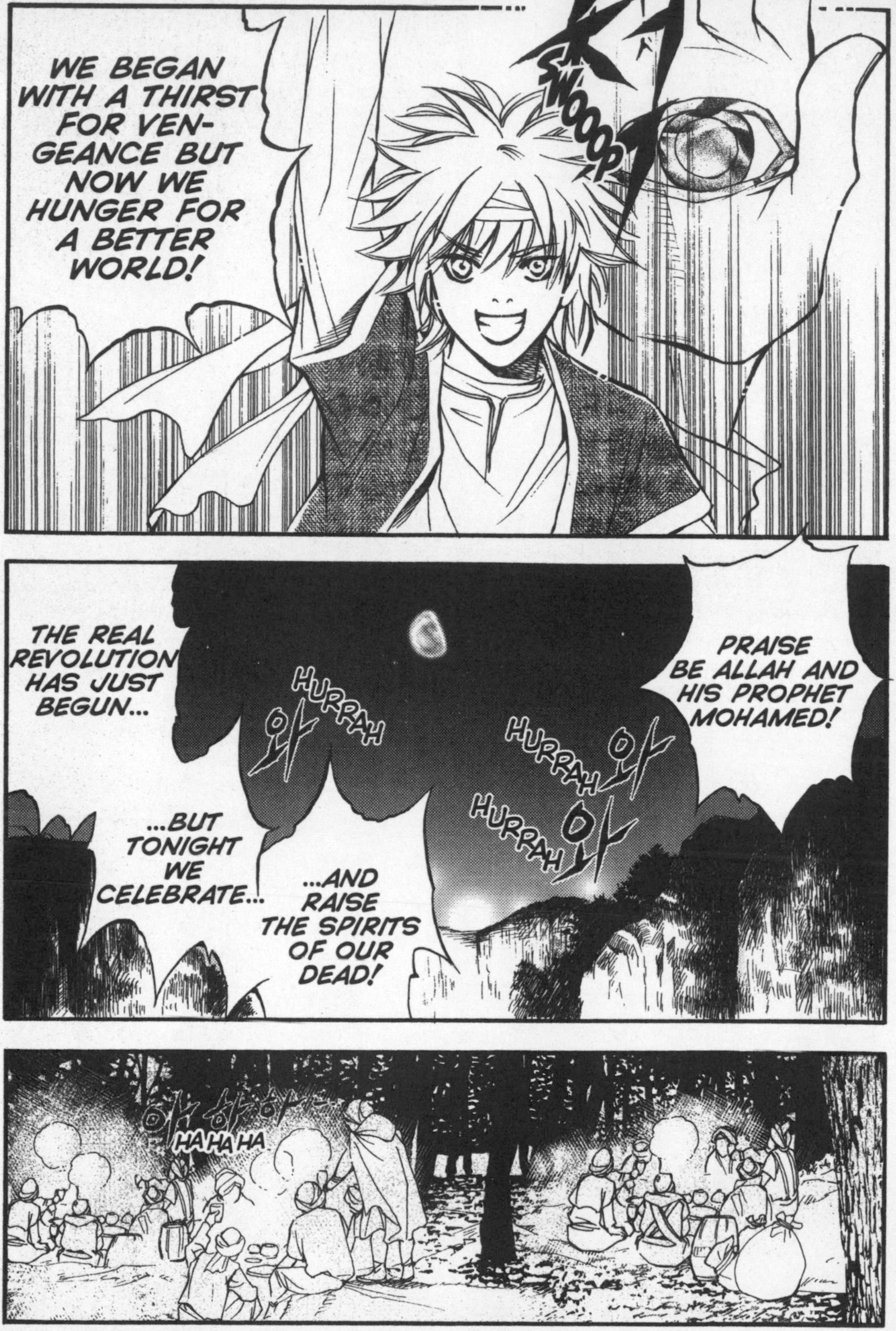

WE BEGAN WITH A THIRST FOR VEN-GEANCE BUT NOW WE HUNGER FOR A BETTER WORLD!
SWOOOP
THE REAL REVOLUTION HAS JUST BEGUN...
와
HURRAH
와
HURRAH
와
HURRAH
PRAISE BE ALLAH AND HIS PROPHET MOHAMED!
...BUT TONIGHT WE CELEBRATE...
...AND RAISE THE SPIRITS OF OUR DEAD!
HA HA HA

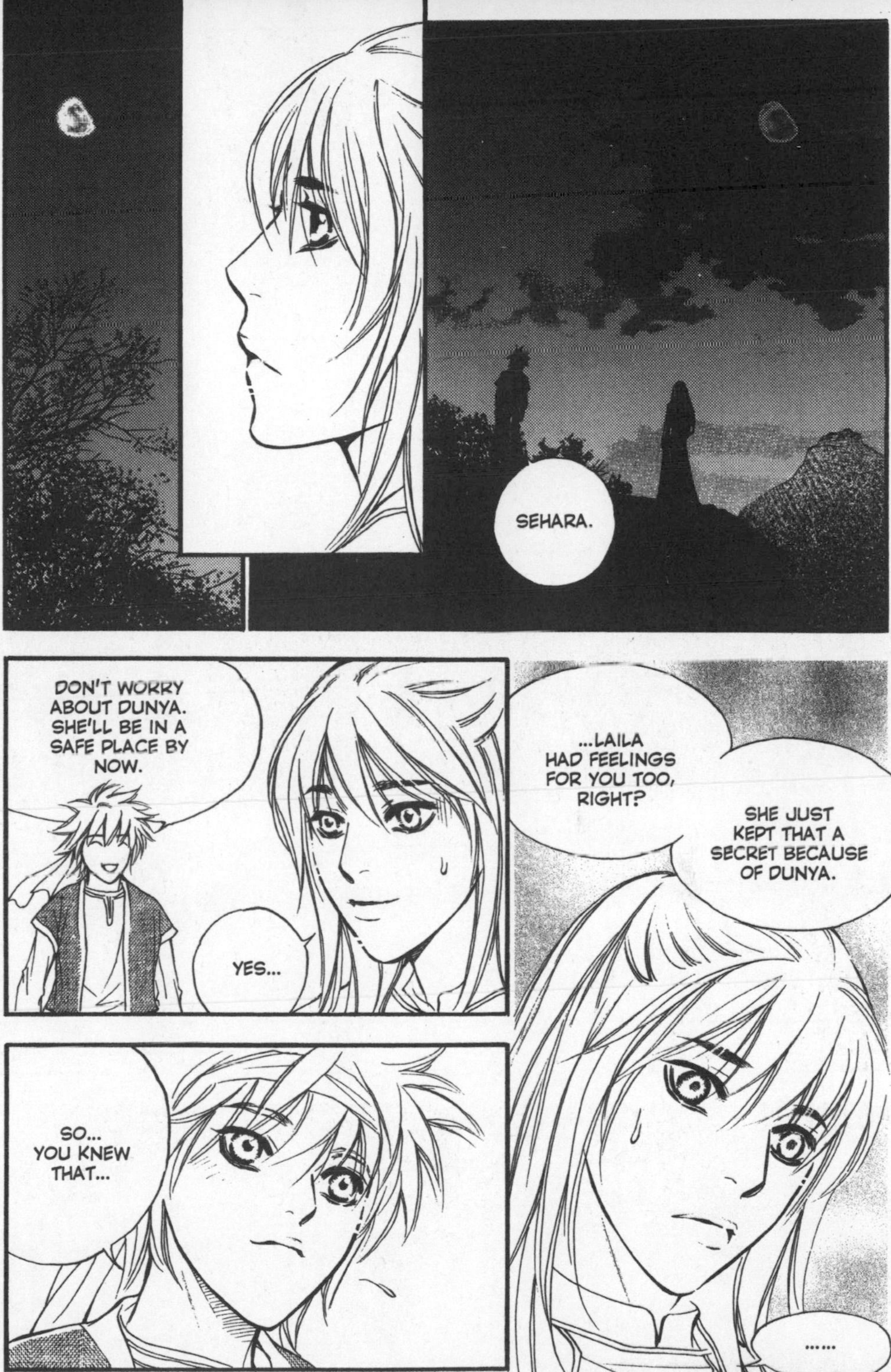
SEHARA.
DON'T WORRY ABOUT DUNYA. SHE'LL BE IN A SAFE PLACE BY NOW.
YES...
SO... YOU KNEW THAT...
...LAILA HAD FEELINGS FOR YOU TOO, RIGHT?
SHE JUST KEPT THAT A SECRET BECAUSE OF DUNYA.
......

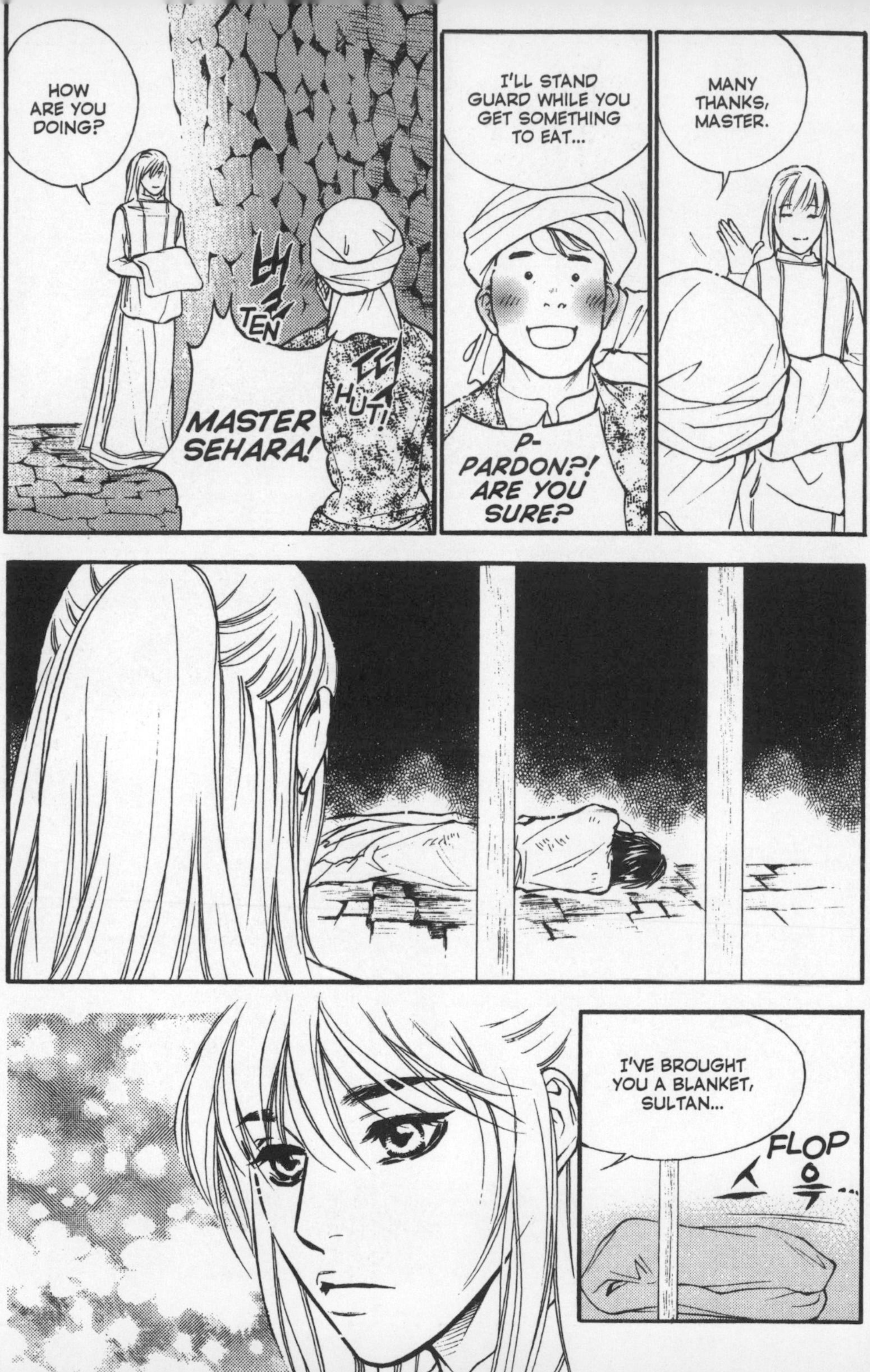
HOW ARE YOU DOING?
TEN-HUT!
MASTER SEHARA!
I'LL STAND GUARD WHILE YOU GET SOMETHING TO EAT...
P-PARDON?! ARE YOU SURE?
MANY THANKS, MASTER.
I'VE BROUGHT YOU A BLANKET, SULTAN...
FLOP

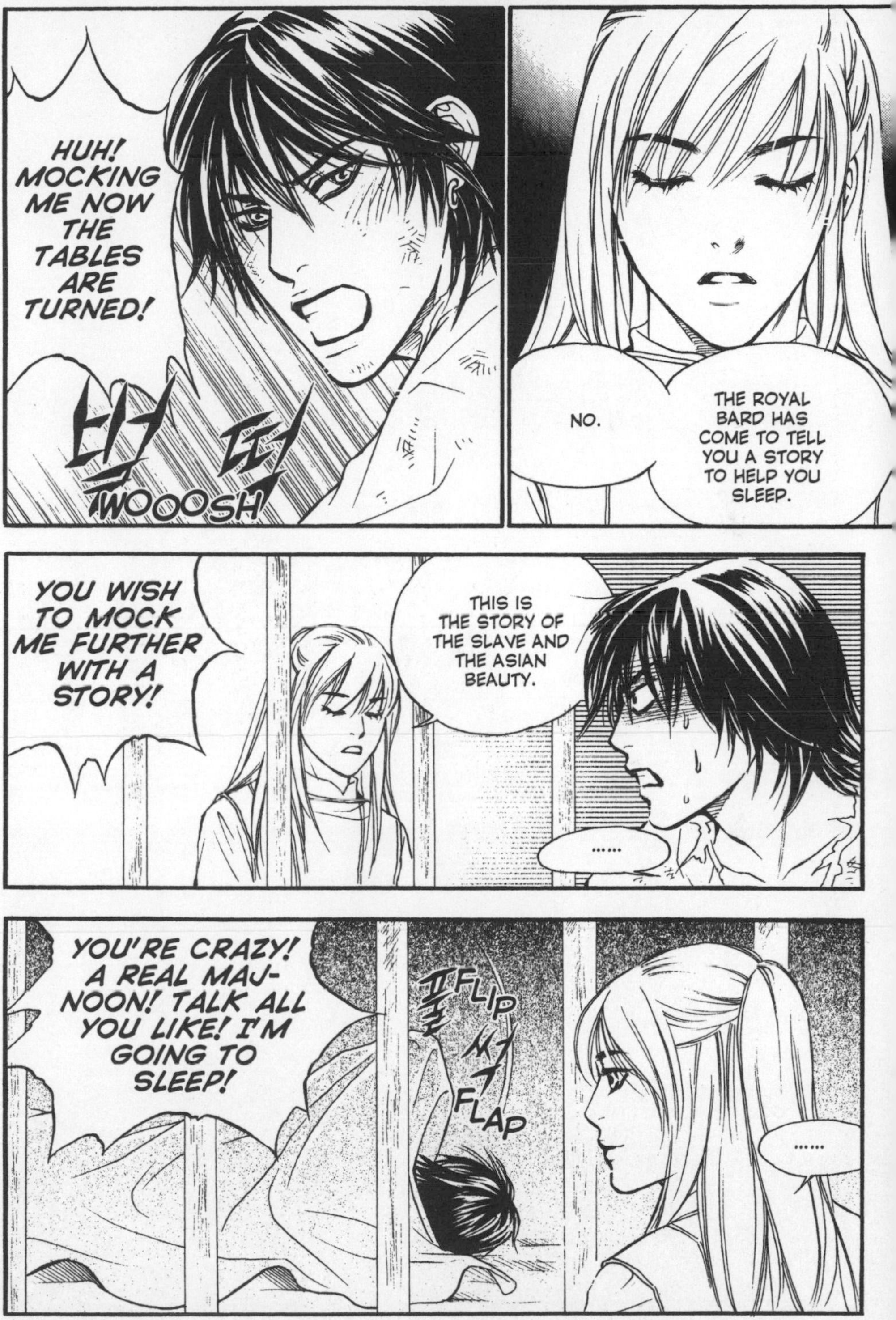
HUH! MOCKING ME NOW THE TABLES ARE TURNED!
WOOOSH
NO.
THE ROYAL BARD HAS COME TO TELL YOU A STORY TO HELP YOU SLEEP.
YOU WISH TO MOCK ME FURTHER WITH A STORY!
THIS IS THE STORY OF THE SLAVE AND THE ASIAN BEAUTY.
......
YOU'RE CRAZY! A REAL MAJ-NOON! TALK ALL YOU LIKE! I'M GOING TO SLEEP!
FLIP
FLAP
......

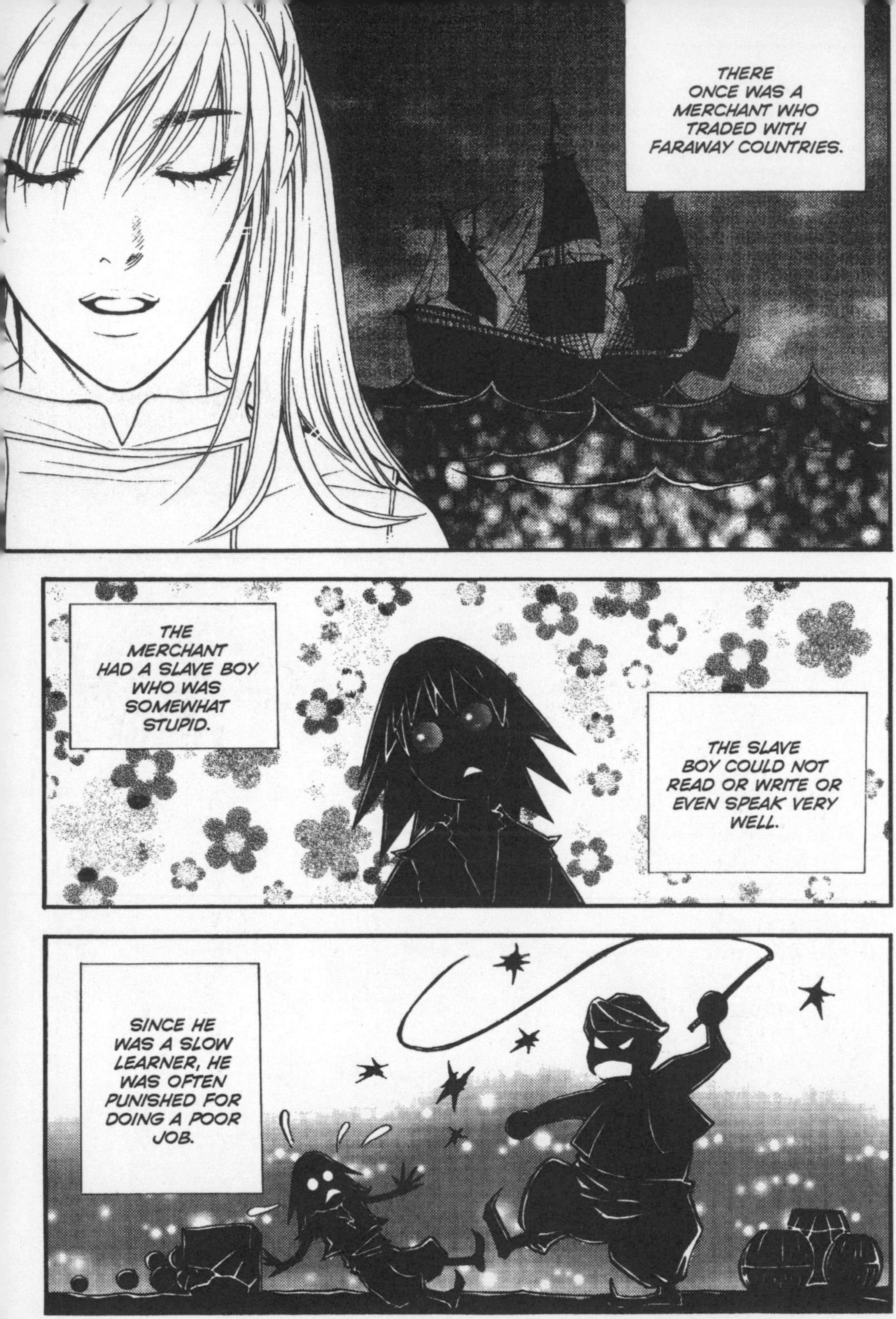
THERE ONCE WAS A MERCHANT WHO TRADED WITH FARAWAY COUNTRIES.
THE MERCHANT HAD A SLAVE BOY WHO WAS SOMEWHAT STUPID.
THE SLAVE BOY COULD NOT READ OR WRITE OR EVEN SPEAK VERY WELL.
SINCE HE WAS A SLOW LEARNER, HE WAS OFTEN PUNISHED FOR DOING A POOR JOB.

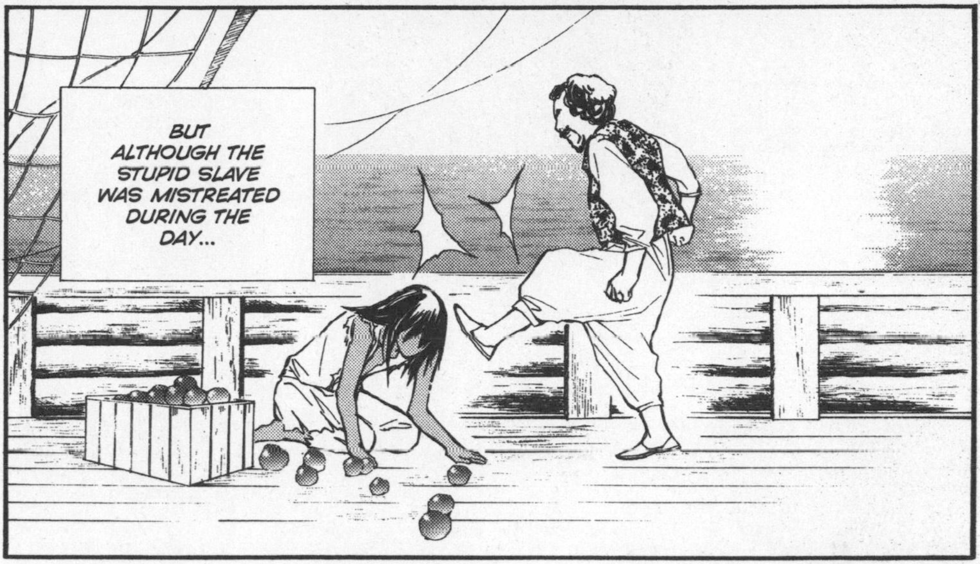
BUT ALTHOUGH THE STUPID SLAVE WAS MISTREATED DURING THE DAY...
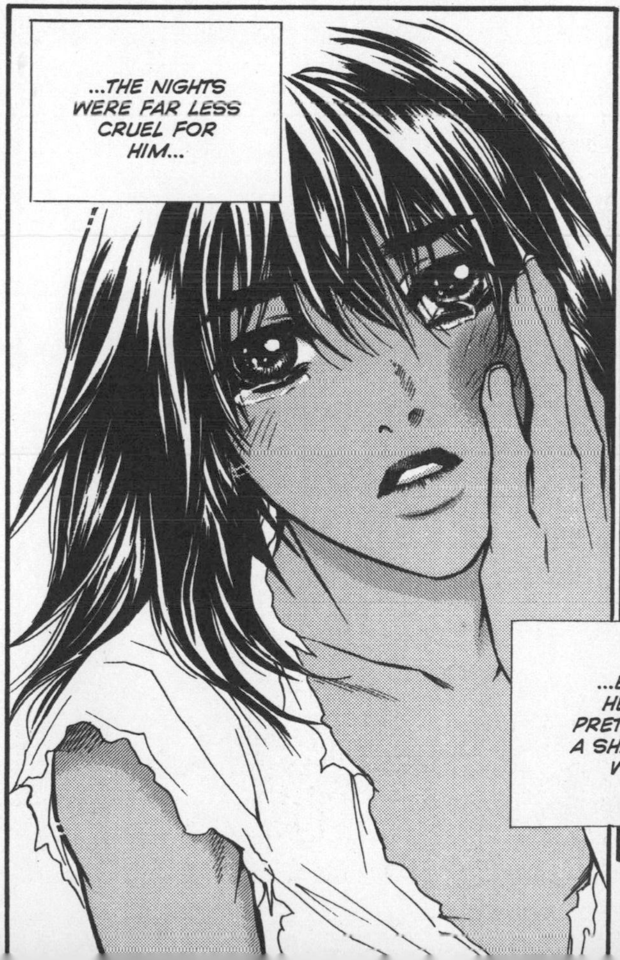
...THE NIGHTS WERE FAR LESS CRUEL FOR HIM...
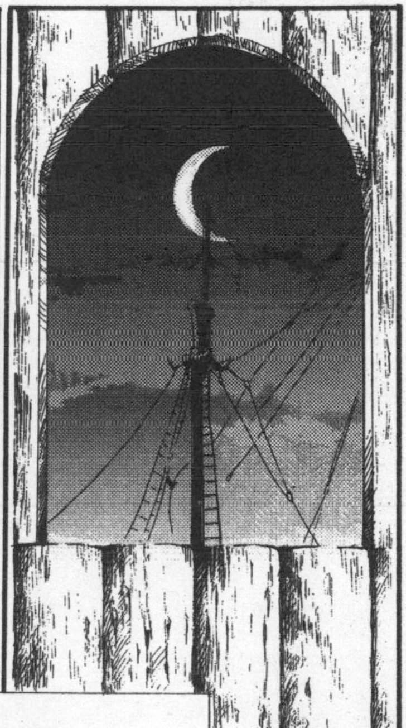
...BECAUSE HE WAS A PRETTY BOY ON A SHIP WITH NO WOMEN.

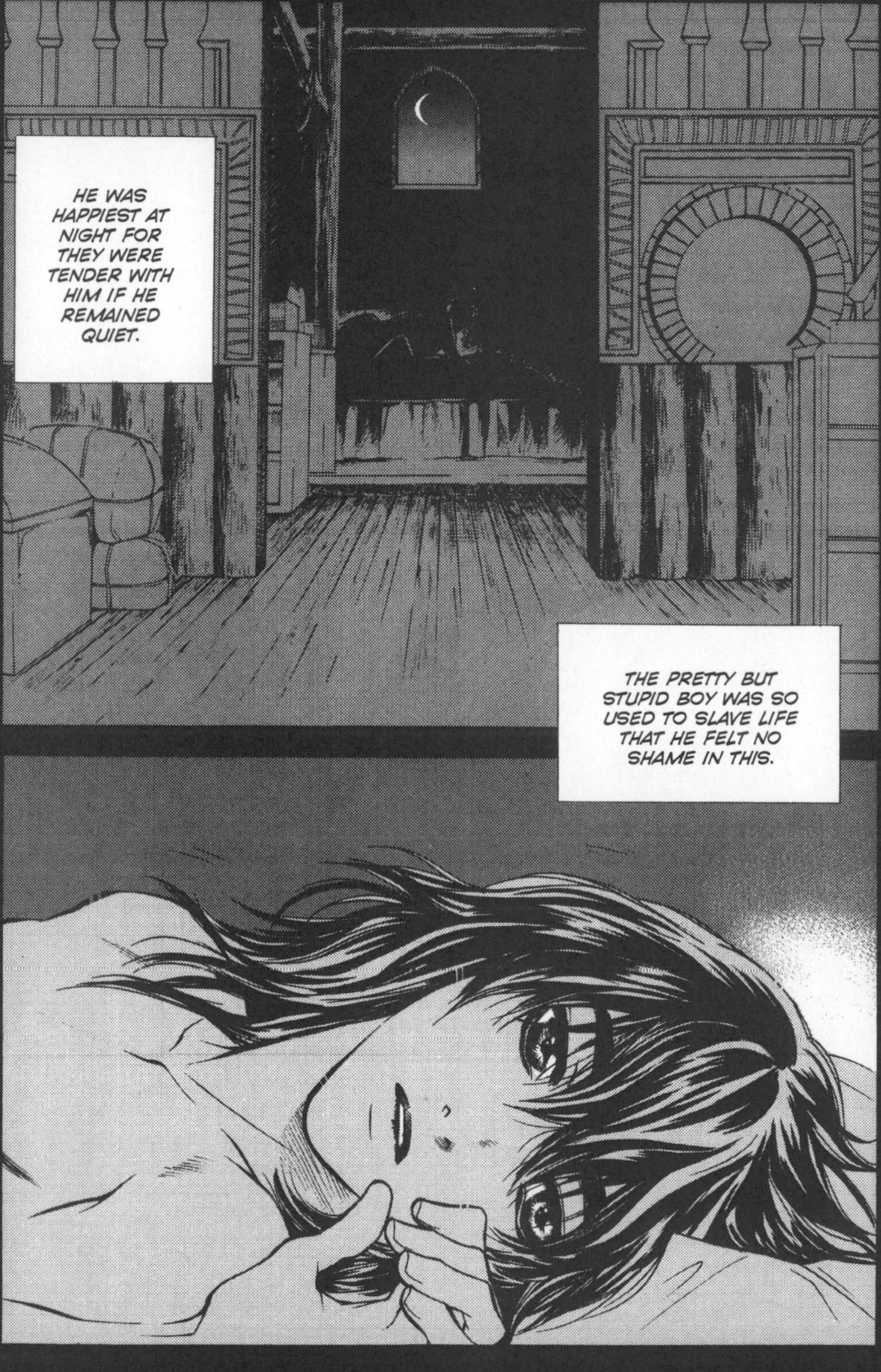
HE WAS HAPPIEST AT NIGHT FOR THEY WERE TENDER WITH HIM IF HE REMAINED QUIET.
THE PRETTY BUT STUPID BOY WAS SO USED TO SLAVE LIFE THAT HE FELT NO SHAME IN THIS.

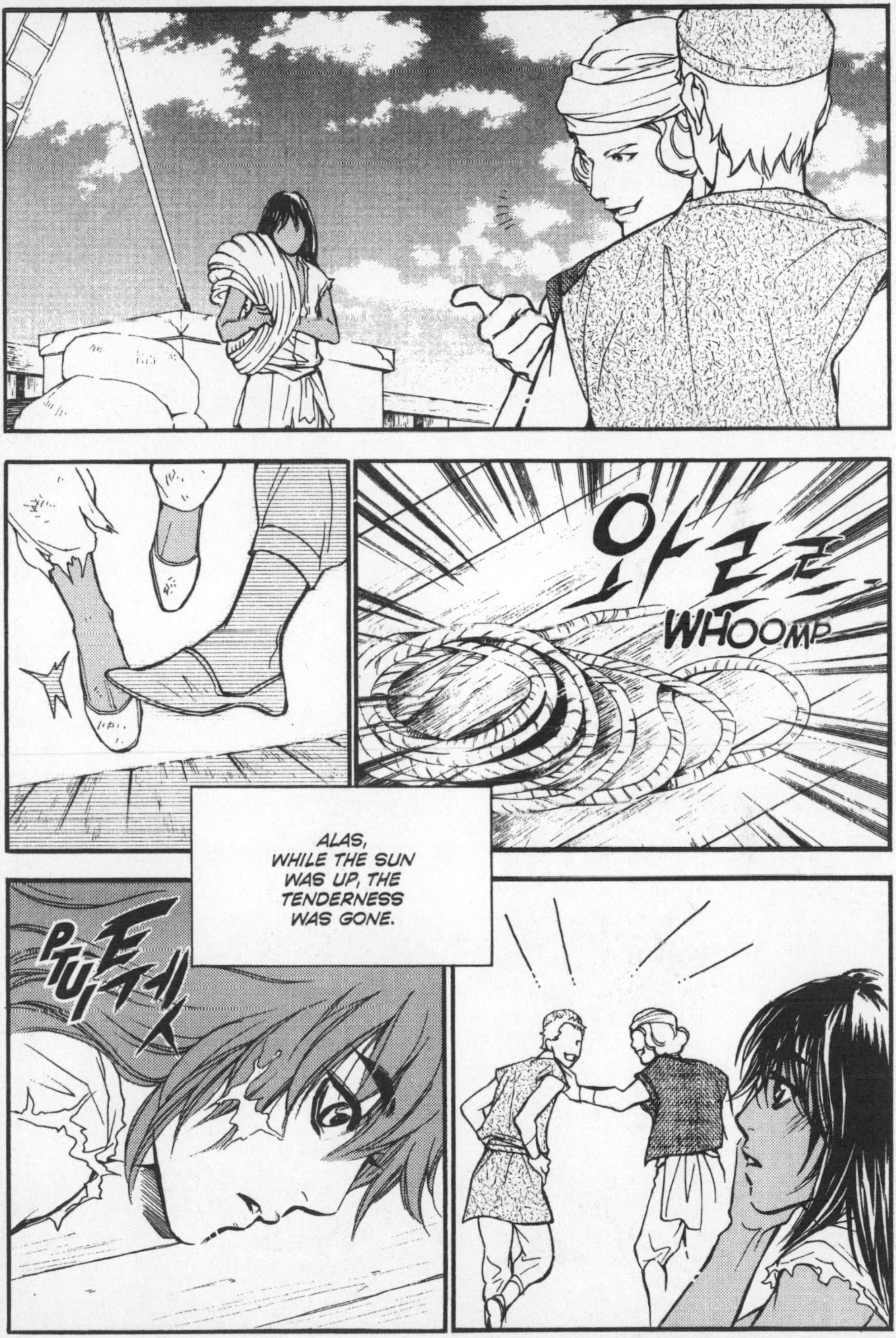
WHOOMP
ALAS, WHILE THE SUN WAS UP, THE TENDERNESS WAS GONE.
PTUI

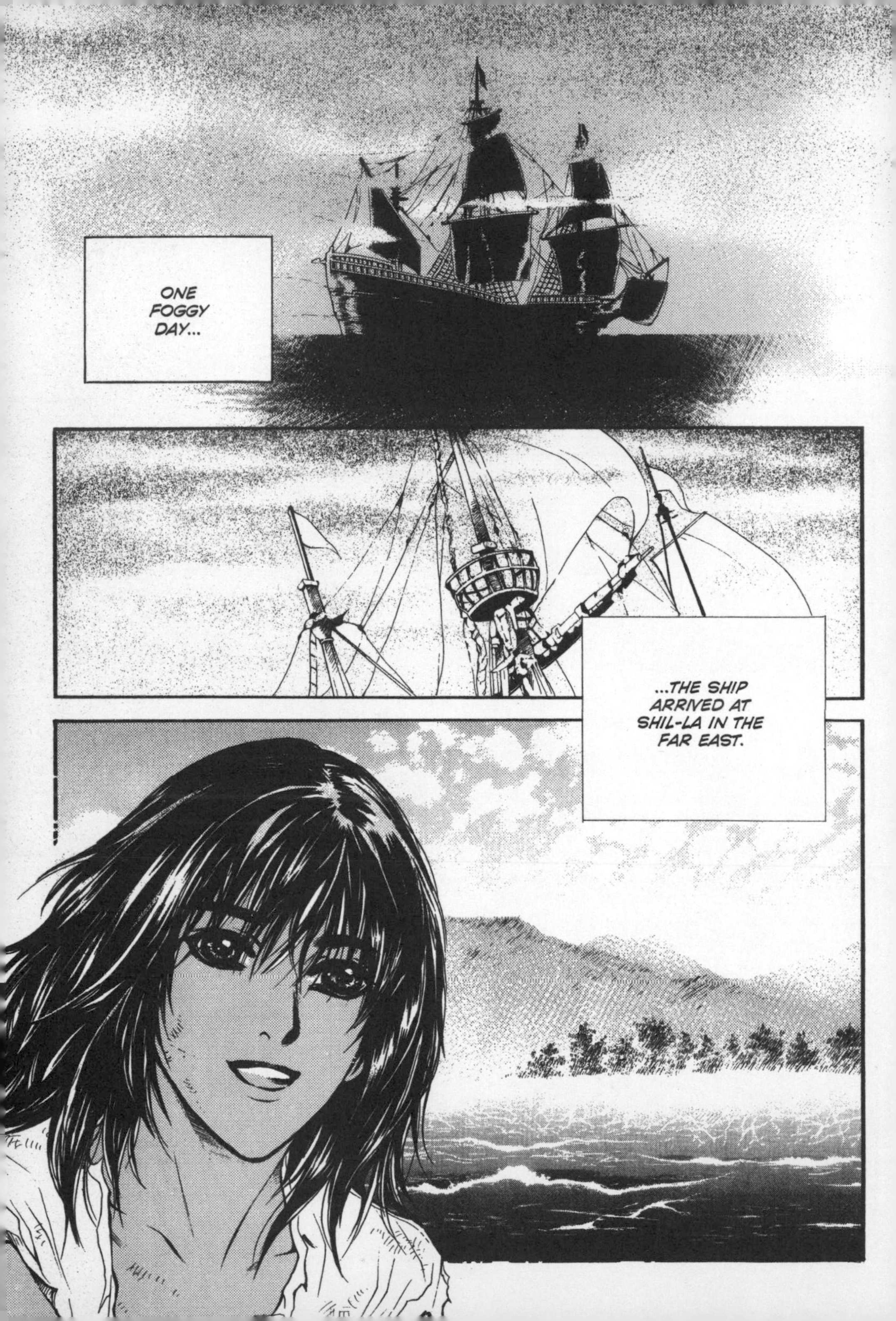
ONE FOGGY DAY...
...THE SHIP ARRIVED AT SHIL-LA IN THE FAR EAST.

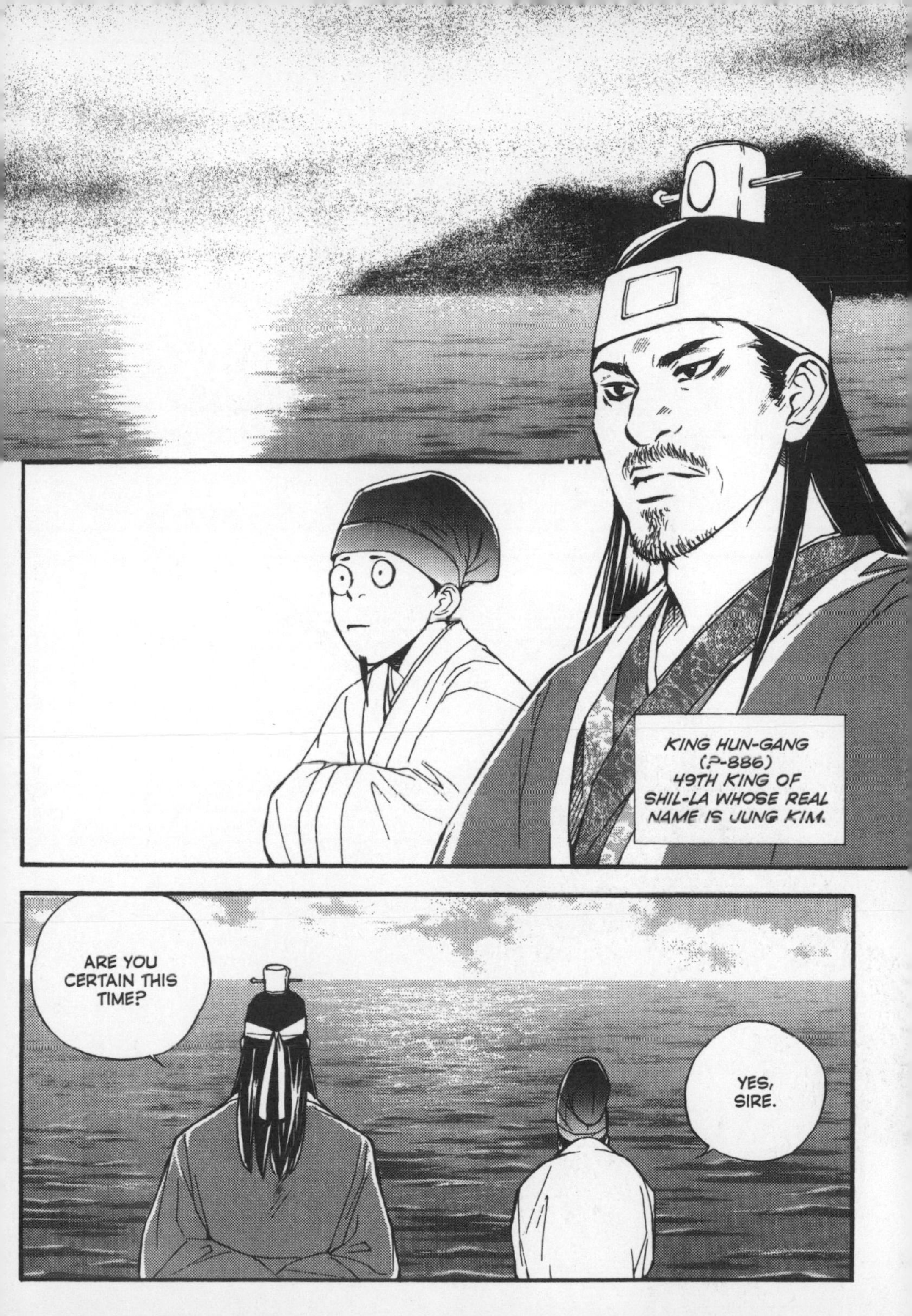
KING HUN-GANG (?-886) 49TH KING OF SHIL-LA WHOSE REAL NAME IS JUNG KIM.
ARE YOU CERTAIN THIS TIME?
YES, SIRE.

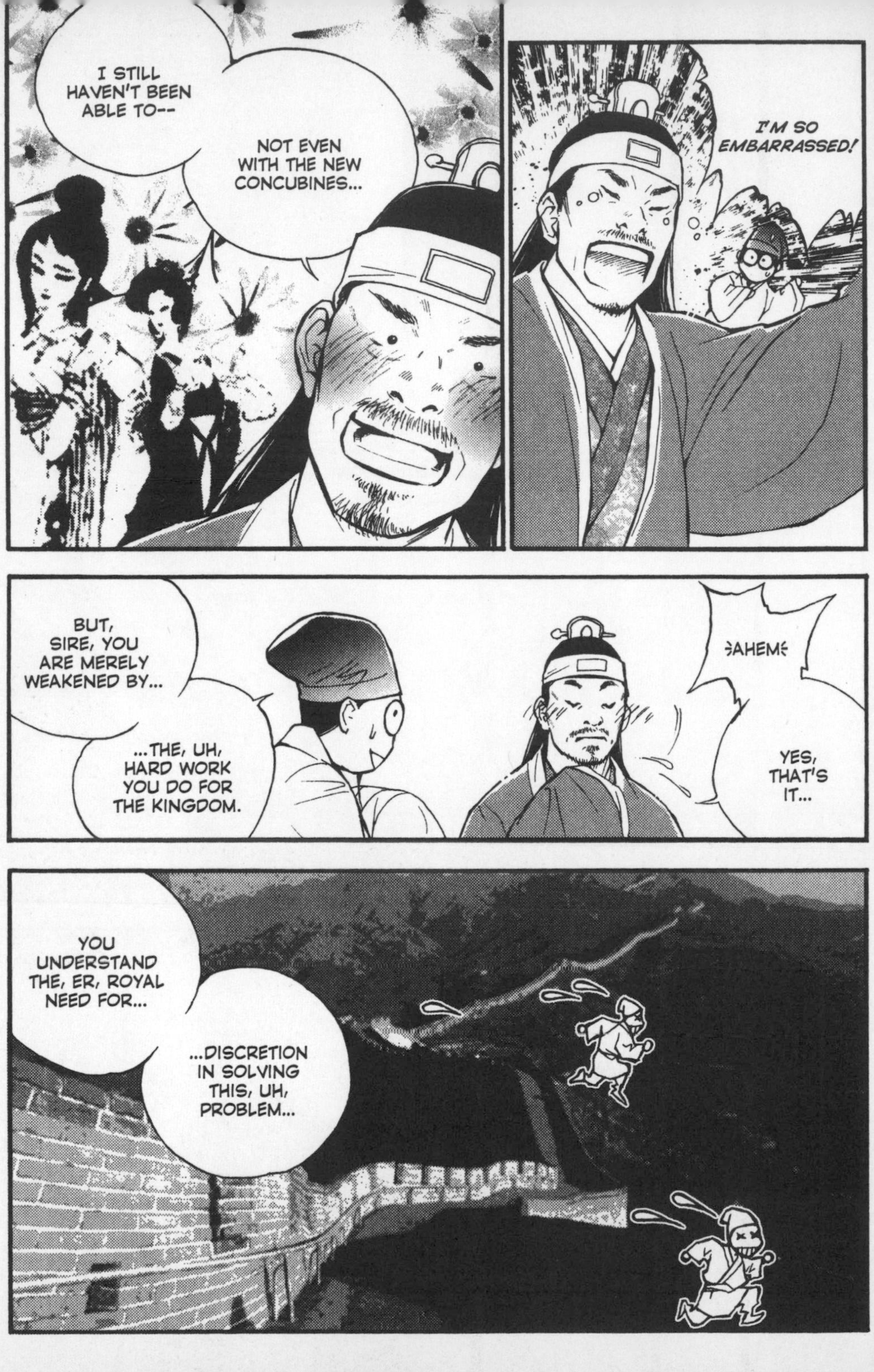
I STILL HAVEN'T BEEN ABLE TO--
NOT EVEN WITH THE NEW CONCUBINES...
I'M SO EMBARRASSED!
BUT, SIRE, YOU ARE MERELY WEAKENED BY...
...THE, UH, HARD WORK YOU DO FOR THE KINGDOM.
AHEM
YES, THAT'S IT...
YOU UNDERSTAND THE, ER, ROYAL NEED FOR...
...DISCRETION IN SOLVING THIS, UH, PROBLEM...

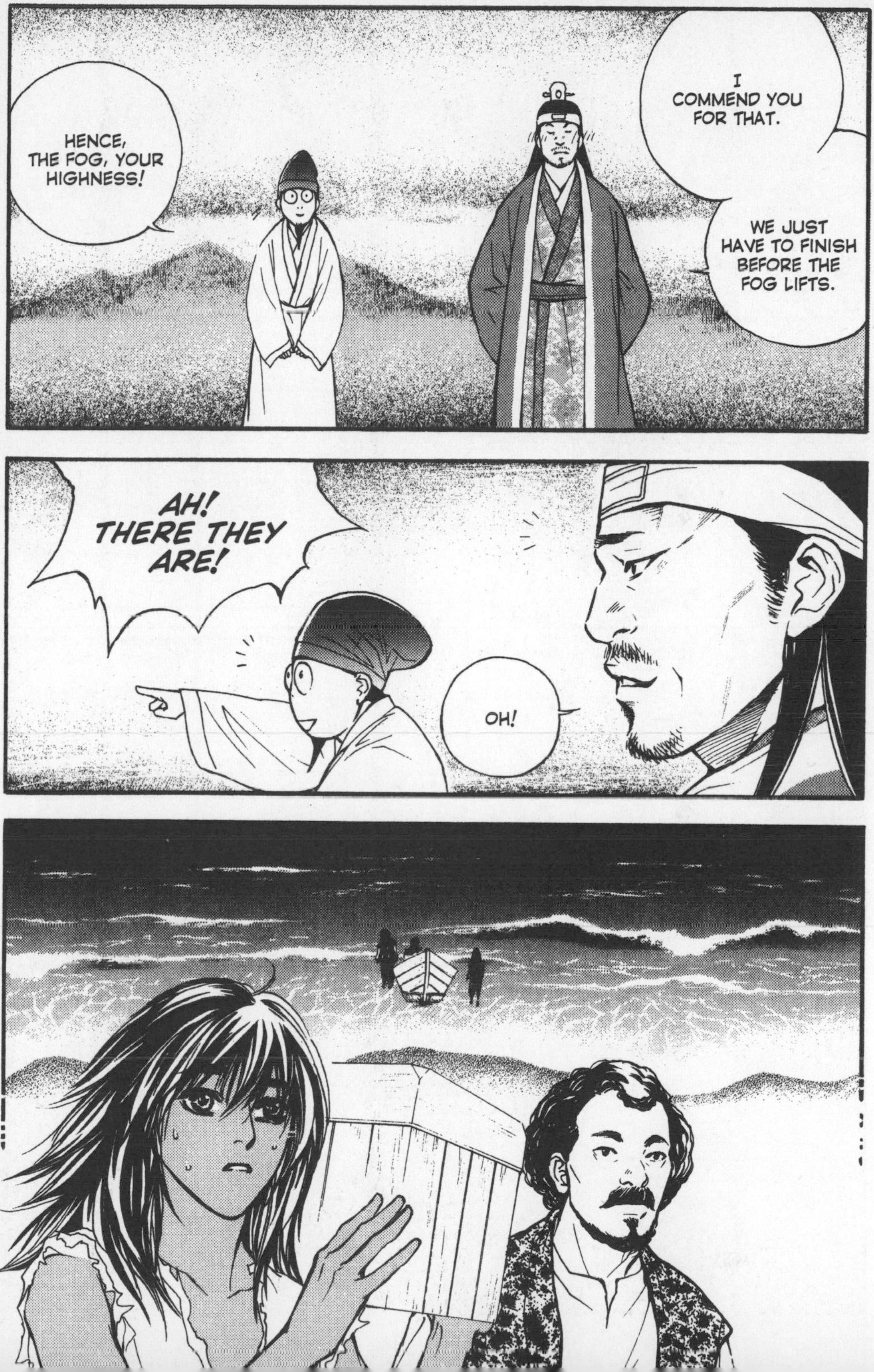
HENCE, THE FOG, YOUR HIGHNESS!
I COMMEND YOU FOR THAT.
WE JUST HAVE TO FINISH BEFORE THE FOG LIFTS.
AH! THERE THEY ARE!
OH!

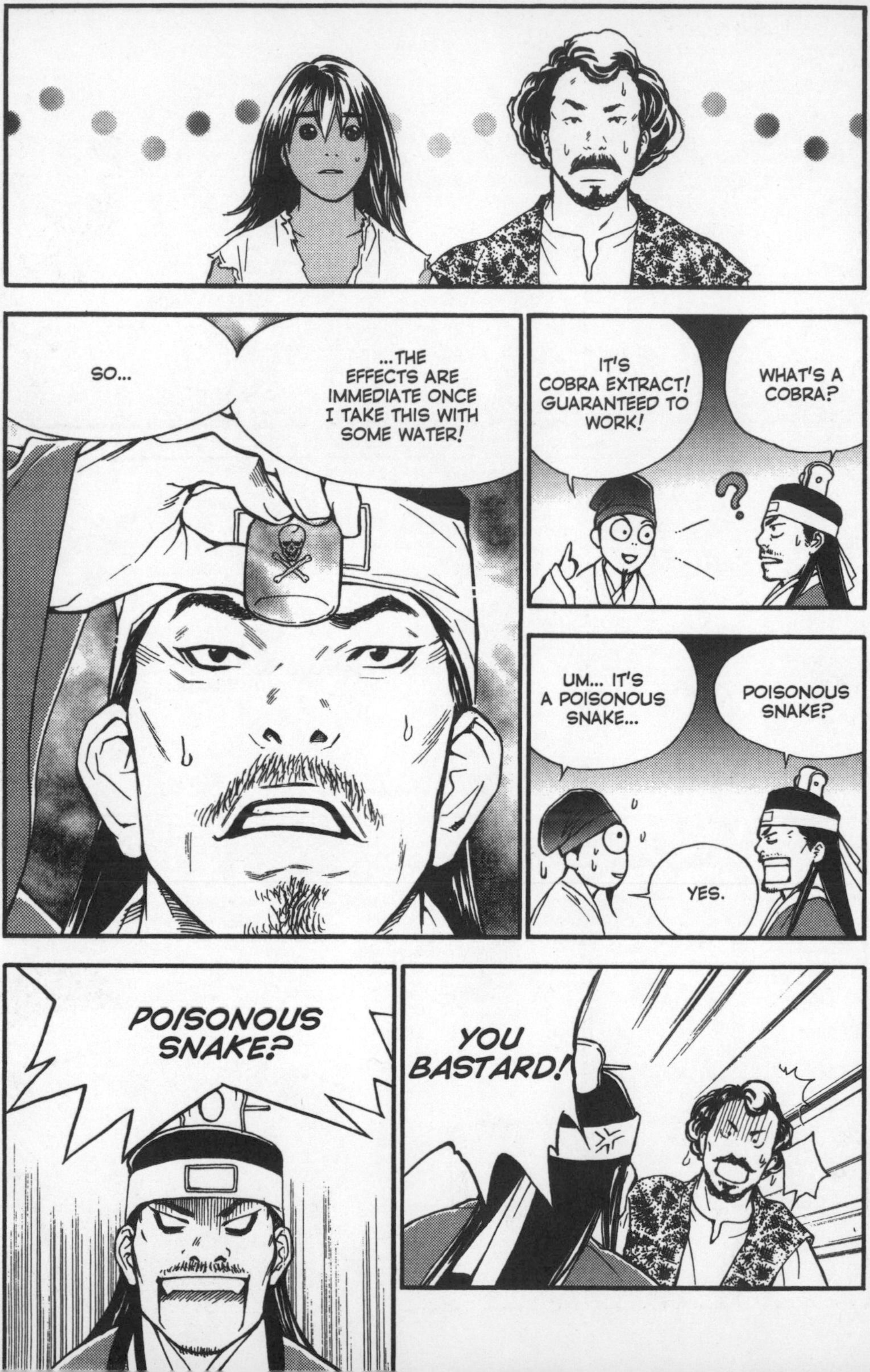
SO...
...THE EFFECTS ARE IMMEDIATE ONCE I TAKE THIS WITH SOME WATER!
IT'S COBRA EXTRACT! GUARANTEED TO WORK!
WHAT'S A COBRA?
UM... IT'S A POISONOUS SNAKE...
POISONOUS SNAKE?
YES.
POISONOUS SNAKE?
YOU BASTARD!

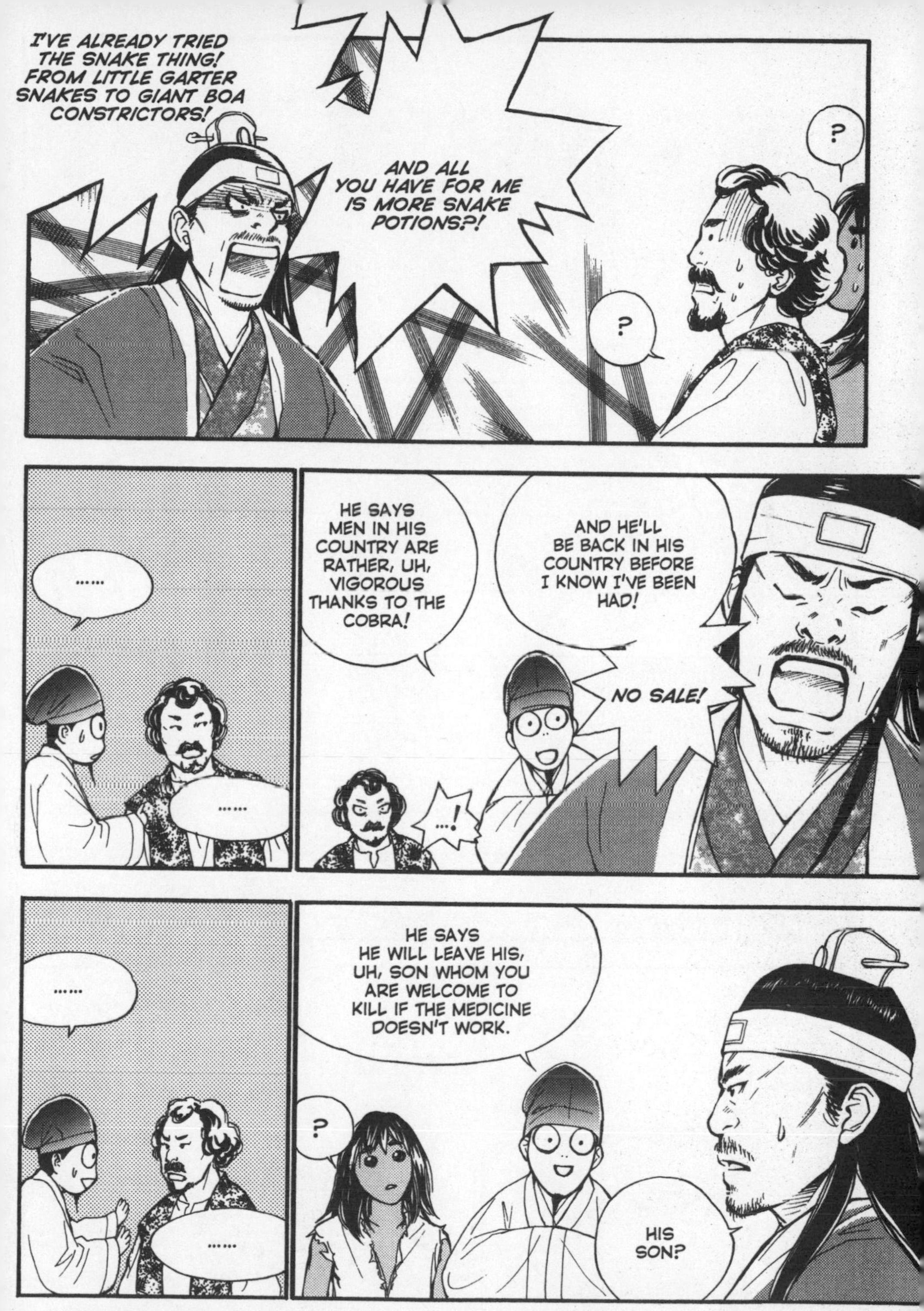
I'VE ALREADY TRIED THE SNAKE THING! FROM LITTLE GARTER SNAKES TO GIANT BOA CONSTRICTORS!
AND ALL YOU HAVE FOR ME IS MORE SNAKE POTIONS?!
?
?
......
......
HE SAYS MEN IN HIS COUNTRY ARE RATHER, UH, VIGOROUS THANKS TO THE COBRA!
AND HE'LL BE BACK IN HIS COUNTRY BEFORE I KNOW I'VE BEEN HAD!
NO SALE!
...!
......
......
HE SAYS HE WILL LEAVE HIS, UH, SON WHOM YOU ARE WELCOME TO KILL IF THE MEDICINE DOESN'T WORK.
?
HIS SON?

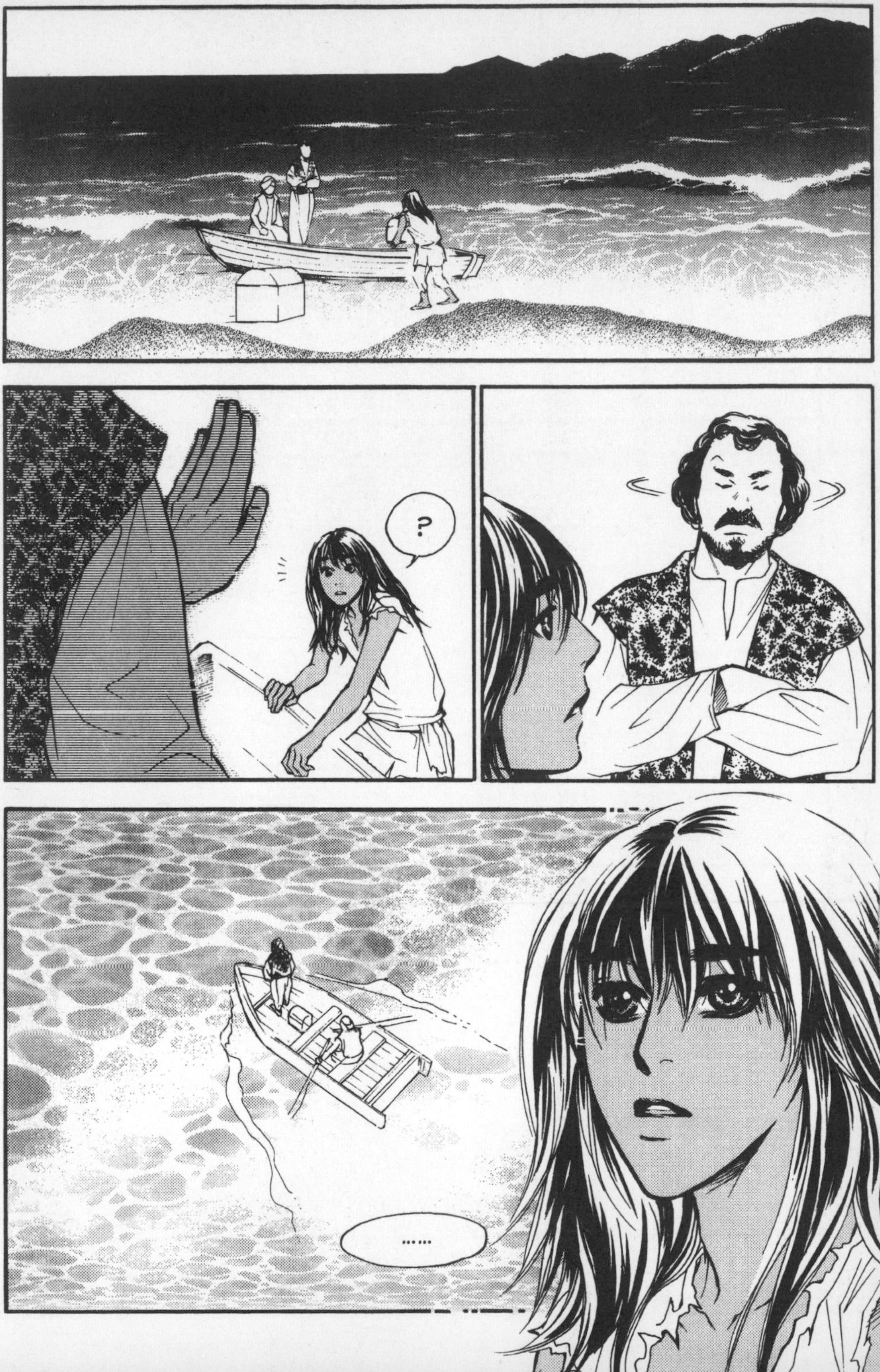
?
……

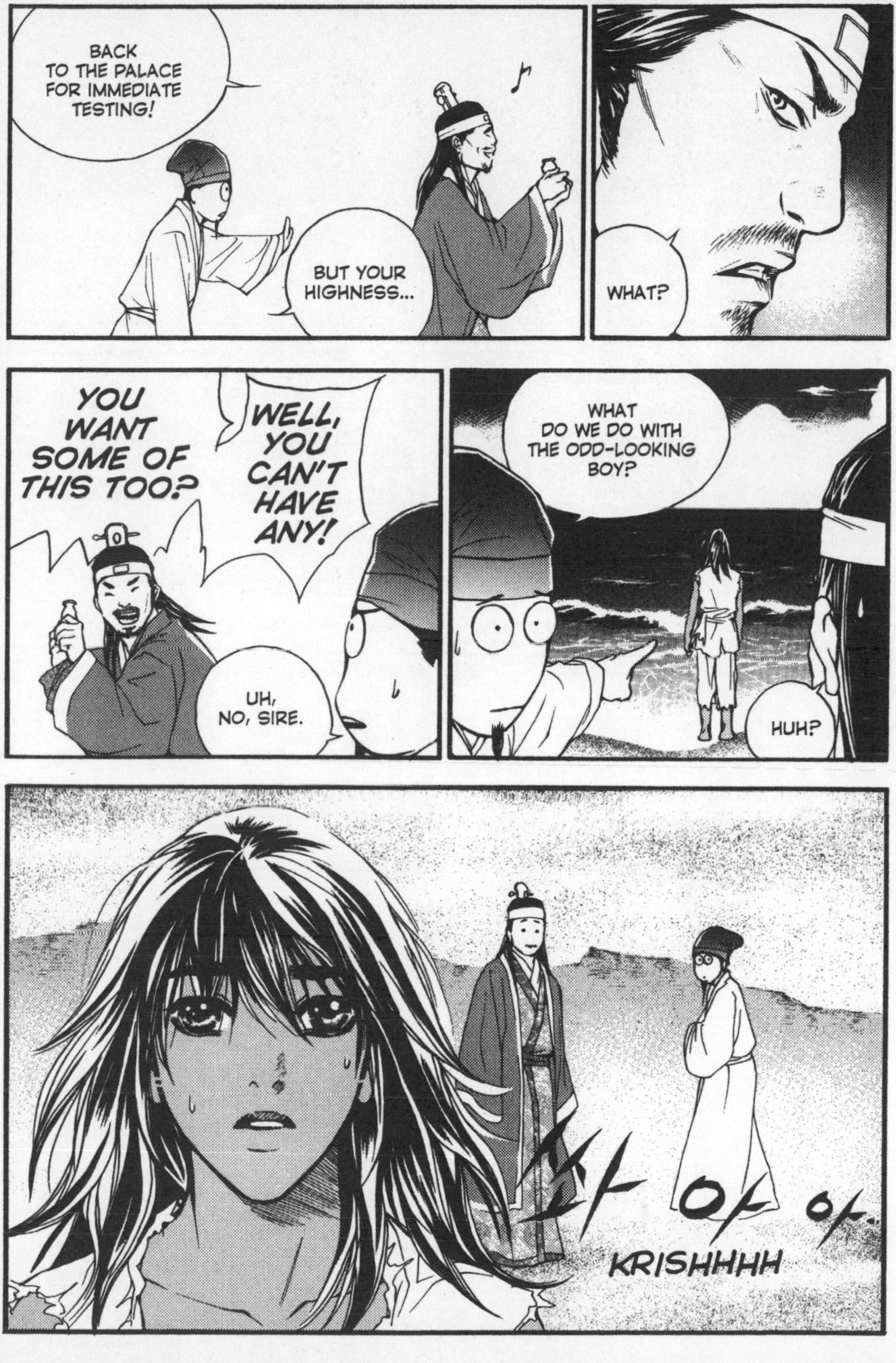
BACK TO THE PALACE FOR IMMEDIATE TESTING!
BUT YOUR HIGHNESS...
WHAT?
YOU WANT SOME OF THIS TOO?
WELL, YOU CAN'T HAVE ANY!
UH, NO, SIRE.
WHAT DO WE DO WITH THE ODD-LOOKING BOY?
HUH?
KRISHHHH

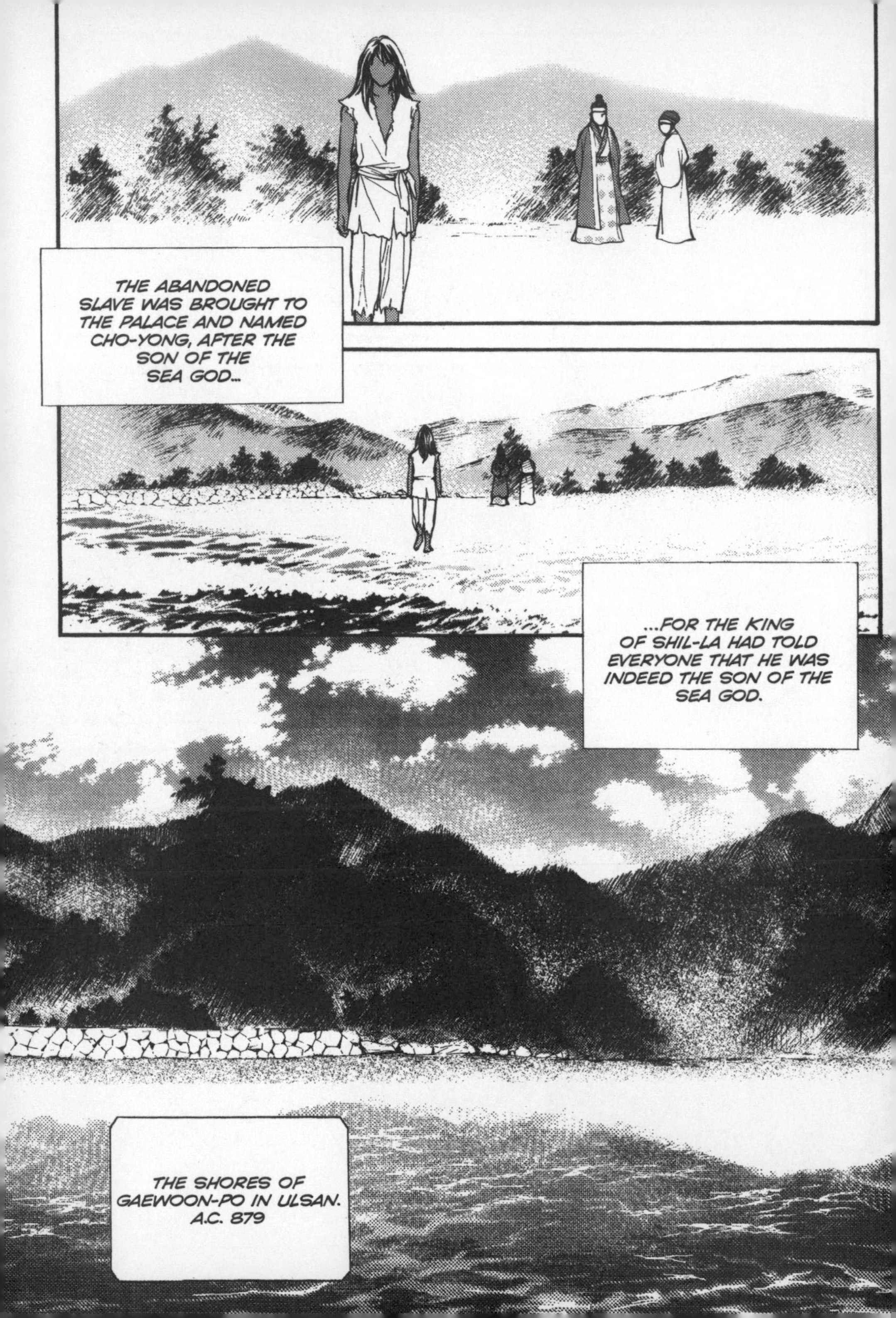
THE ABANDONED SLAVE WAS BROUGHT TO THE PALACE AND NAMED CHO-YONG, AFTER THE SON OF THE SEA GOD...
...FOR THE KING OF SHIL-LA HAD TOLD EVERYONE THAT HE WAS INDEED THE SON OF THE SEA GOD.
THE SHORES OF GAEWOON-PO IN ULSAN. A.C. 879

NIGHT STORY 2

THE TEARS OF CHO-YONG

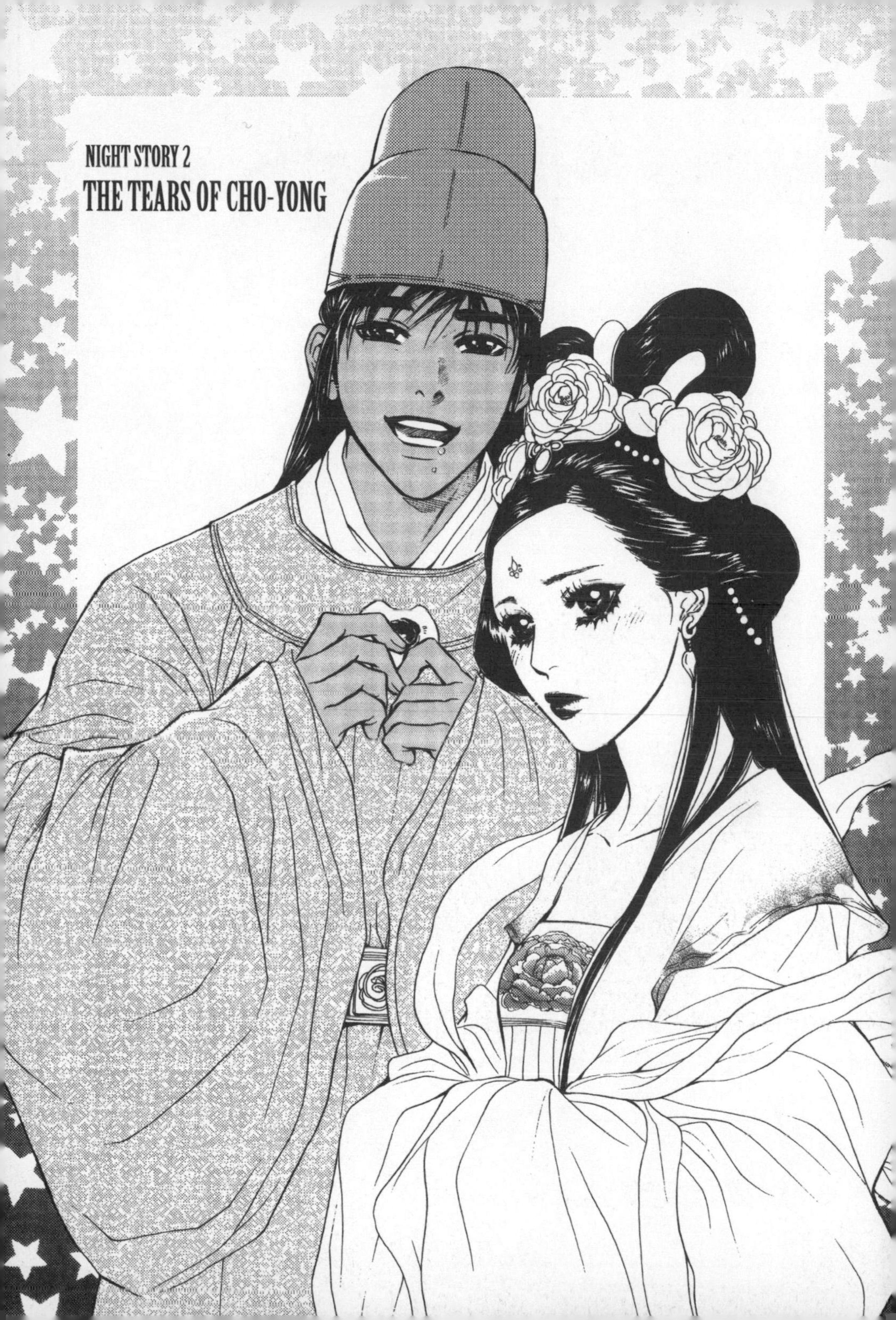

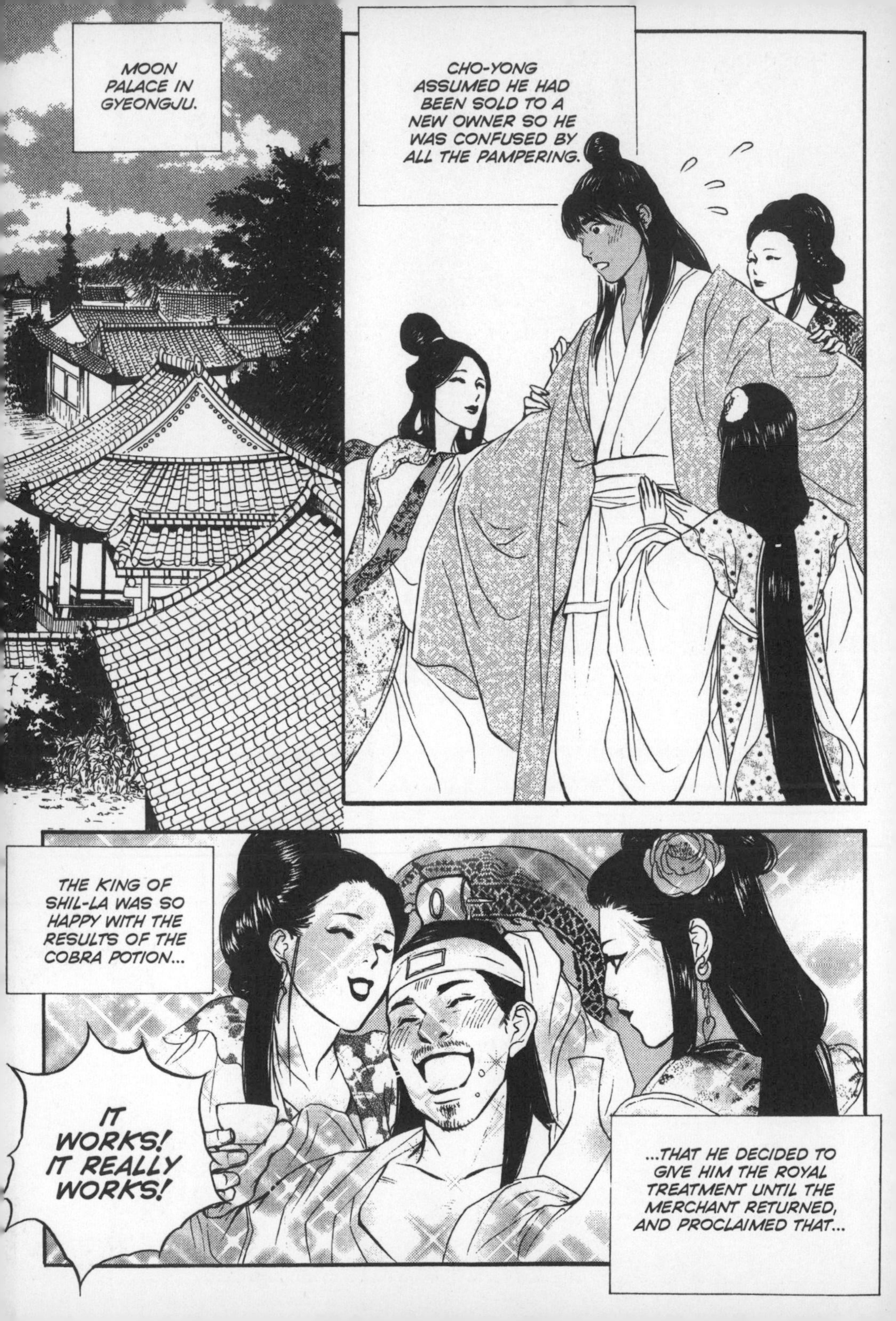
MOON PALACE IN GYEONGJU.
CHO-YONG ASSUMED HE HAD BEEN SOLD TO A NEW OWNER SO HE WAS CONFUSED BY ALL THE PAMPERING.
THE KING OF SHIL-LA WAS SO HAPPY WITH THE RESULTS OF THE COBRA POTION...
IT WORKS! IT REALLY WORKS!
...THAT HE DECIDED TO GIVE HIM THE ROYAL TREATMENT UNTIL THE MERCHANT RETURNED, AND PROCLAIMED THAT...

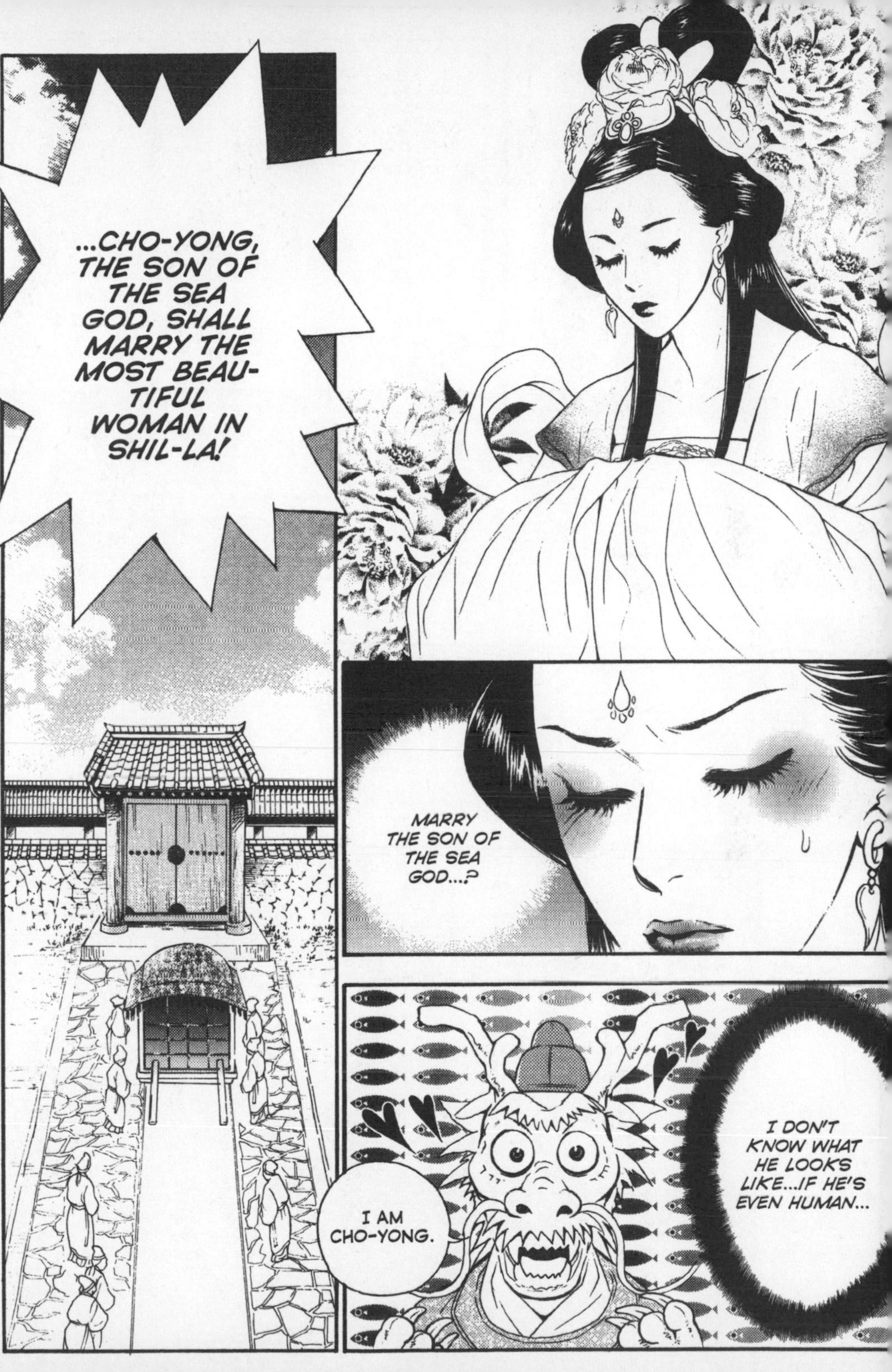
...CHO-YONG, THE SON OF THE SEA GOD, SHALL MARRY THE MOST BEAUTIFUL WOMAN IN SHIL-LA!
MARRY THE SON OF THE SEA GOD...?
I DON'T KNOW WHAT HE LOOKS LIKE...IF HE'S EVEN HUMAN...
I AM CHO-YONG.

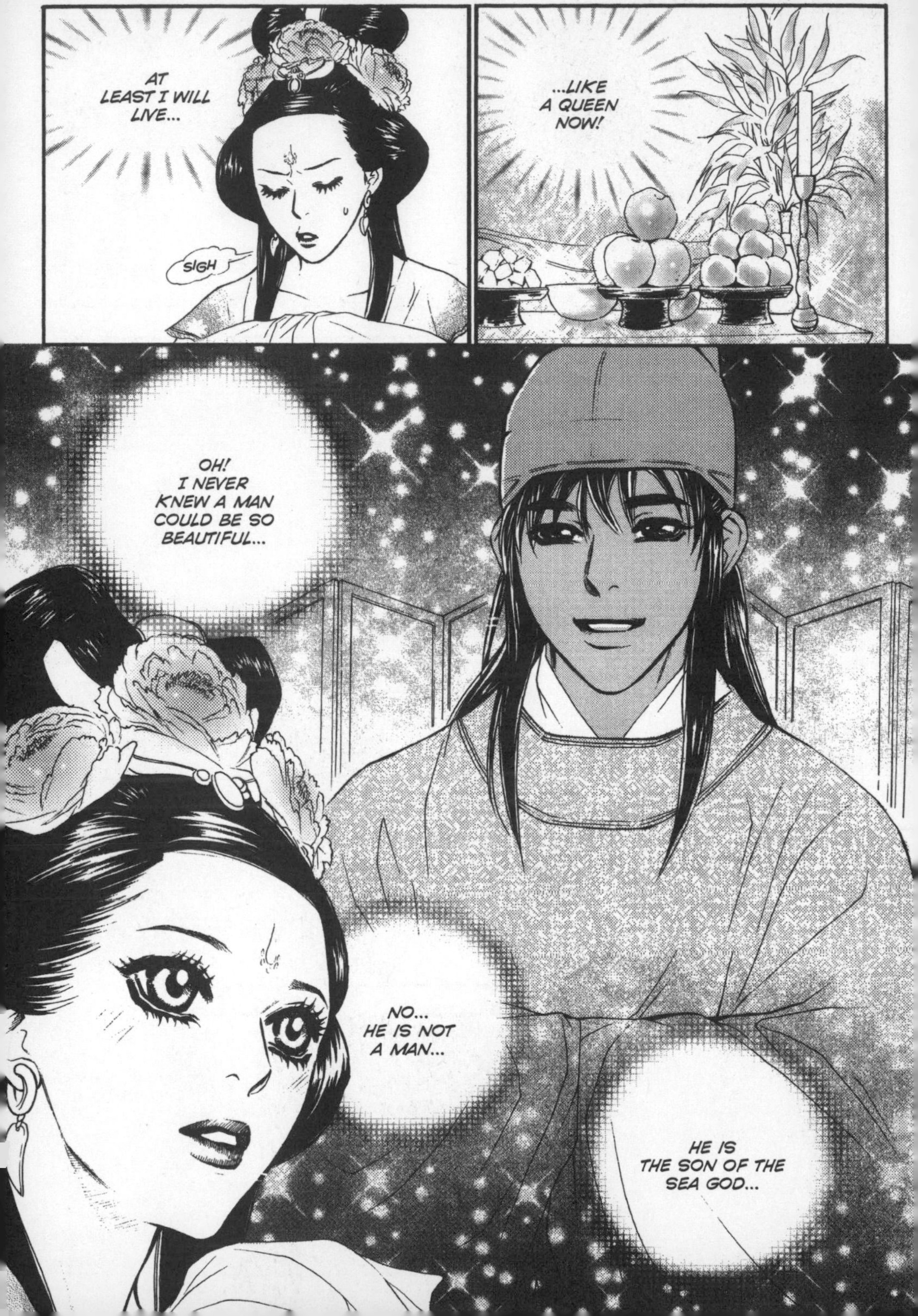
AT LEAST I WILL LIVE...
SIGH
...LIKE A QUEEN NOW!
OH! I NEVER KNEW A MAN COULD BE SO BEAUTIFUL...
NO... HE IS NOT A MAN...
HE IS THE SON OF THE SEA GOD...

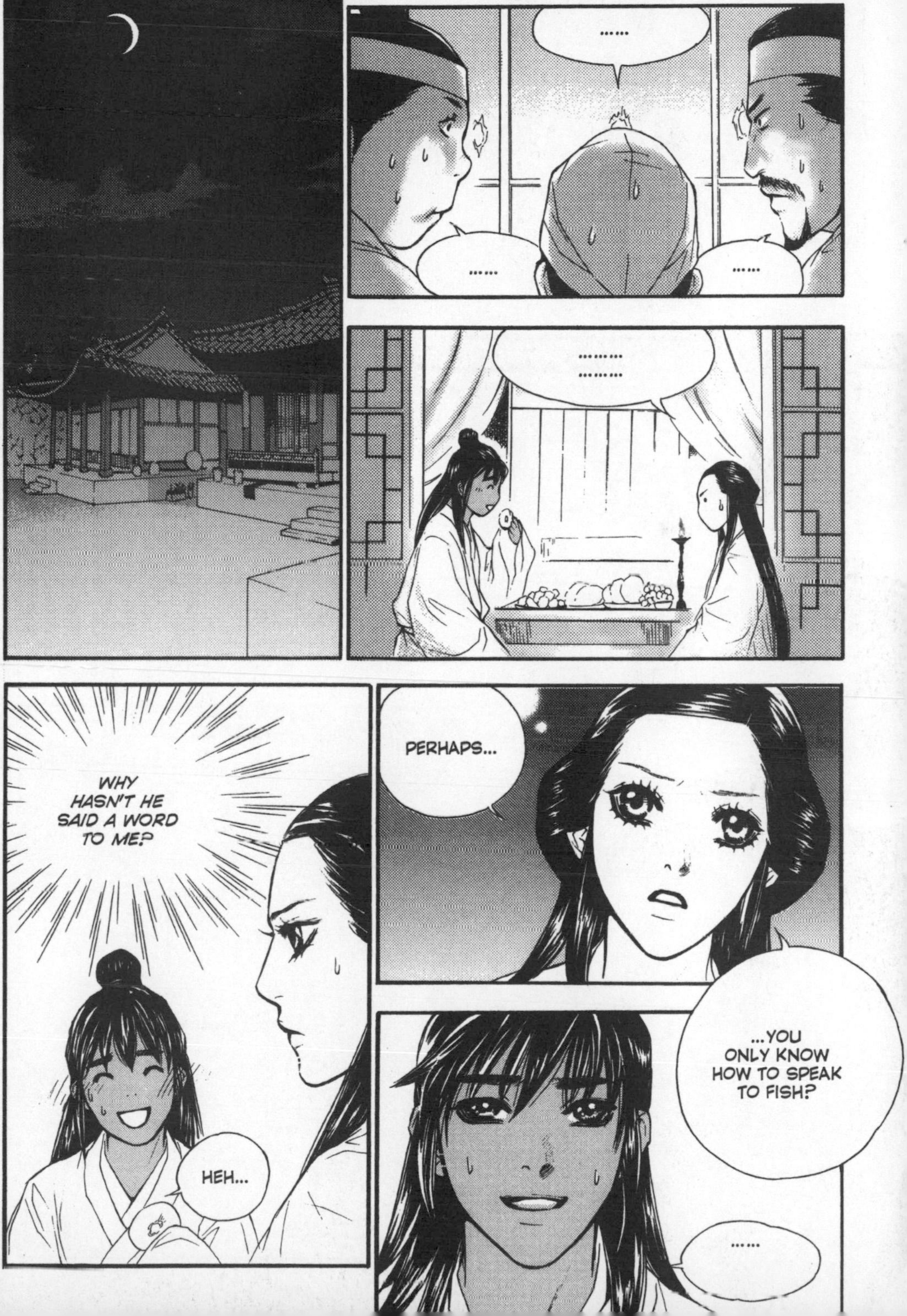
......
......
......
......
......
WHY HASN'T HE SAID A WORD TO ME?
HEH...
PERHAPS...
...YOU ONLY KNOW HOW TO SPEAK TO FISH?
......

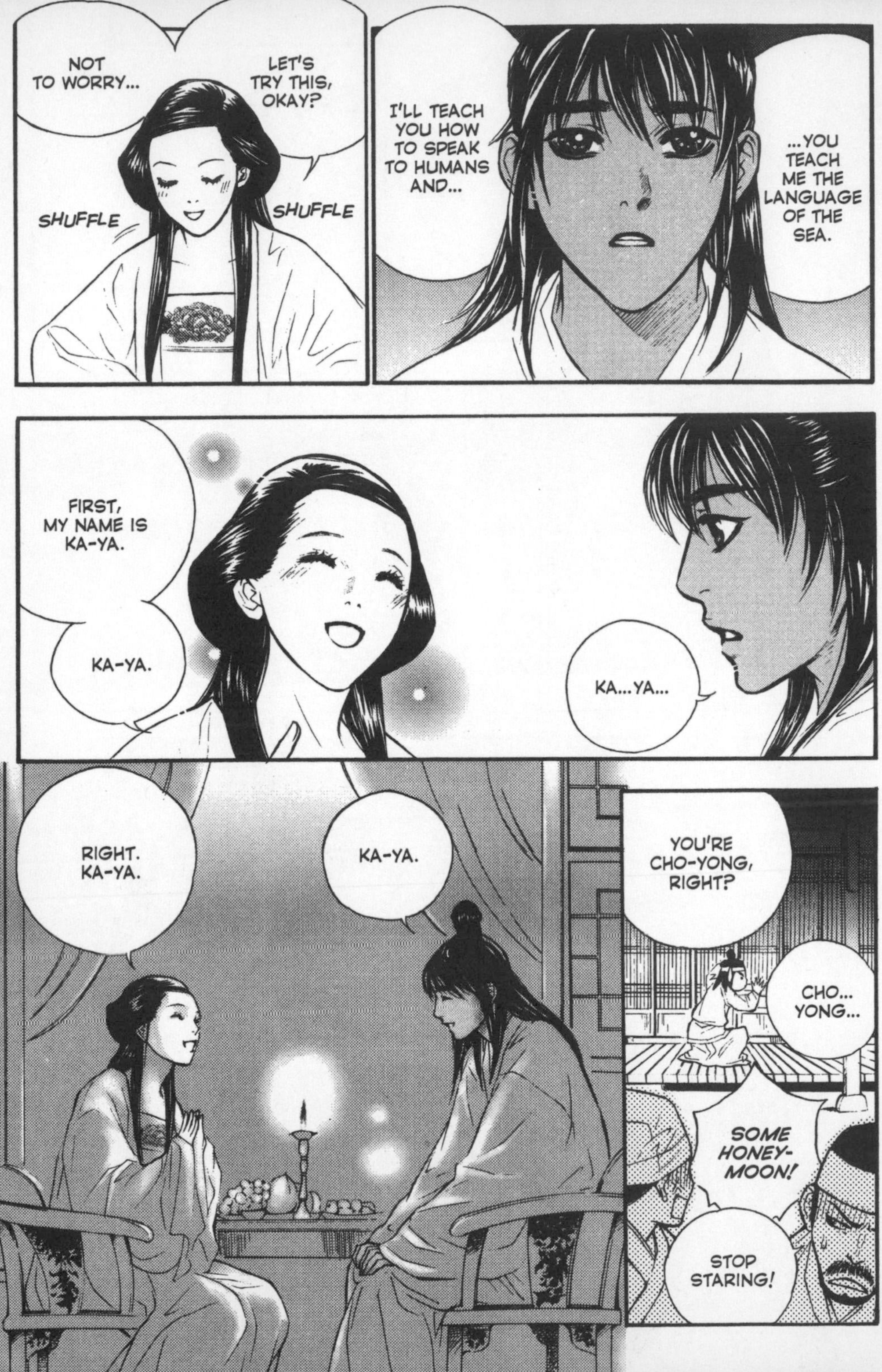
NOT TO WORRY...
LET'S TRY THIS, OKAY?
SHUFFLE
SHUFFLE
I'LL TEACH YOU HOW TO SPEAK TO HUMANS AND...
...YOU TEACH ME THE LANGUAGE OF THE SEA.
FIRST, MY NAME IS KA-YA.
KA-YA.
KA...YA...
RIGHT. KA-YA.
KA-YA.
YOU'RE CHO-YONG, RIGHT?
CHO... YONG...
SOME HONEY-MOON!
STOP STARING!

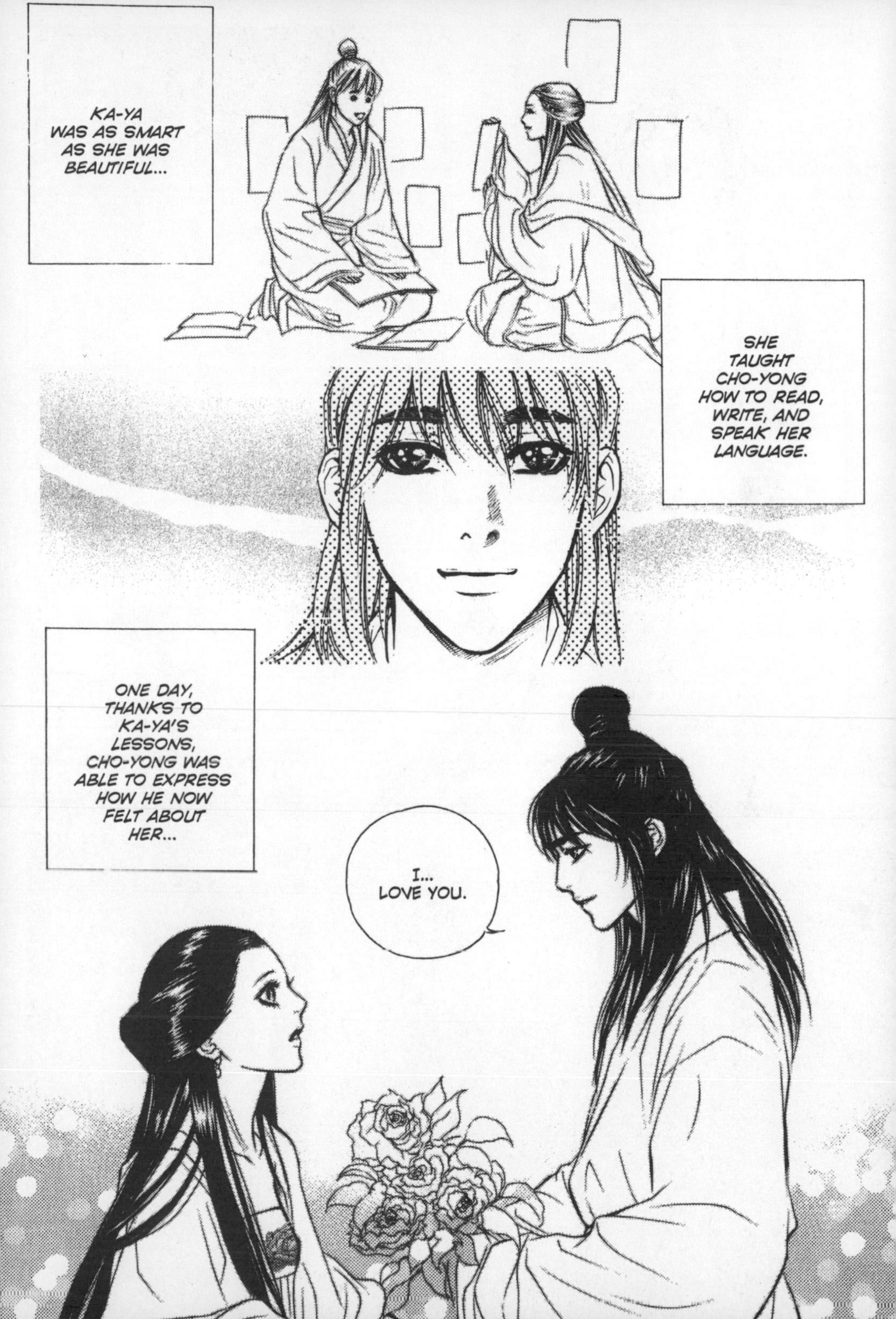
KA-YA WAS AS SMART AS SHE WAS BEAUTIFUL...
SHE TAUGHT CHO-YONG HOW TO READ, WRITE, AND SPEAK HER LANGUAGE.
ONE DAY, THANKS TO KA-YA'S LESSONS, CHO-YONG WAS ABLE TO EXPRESS HOW HE NOW FELT ABOUT HER...
I... LOVE YOU.

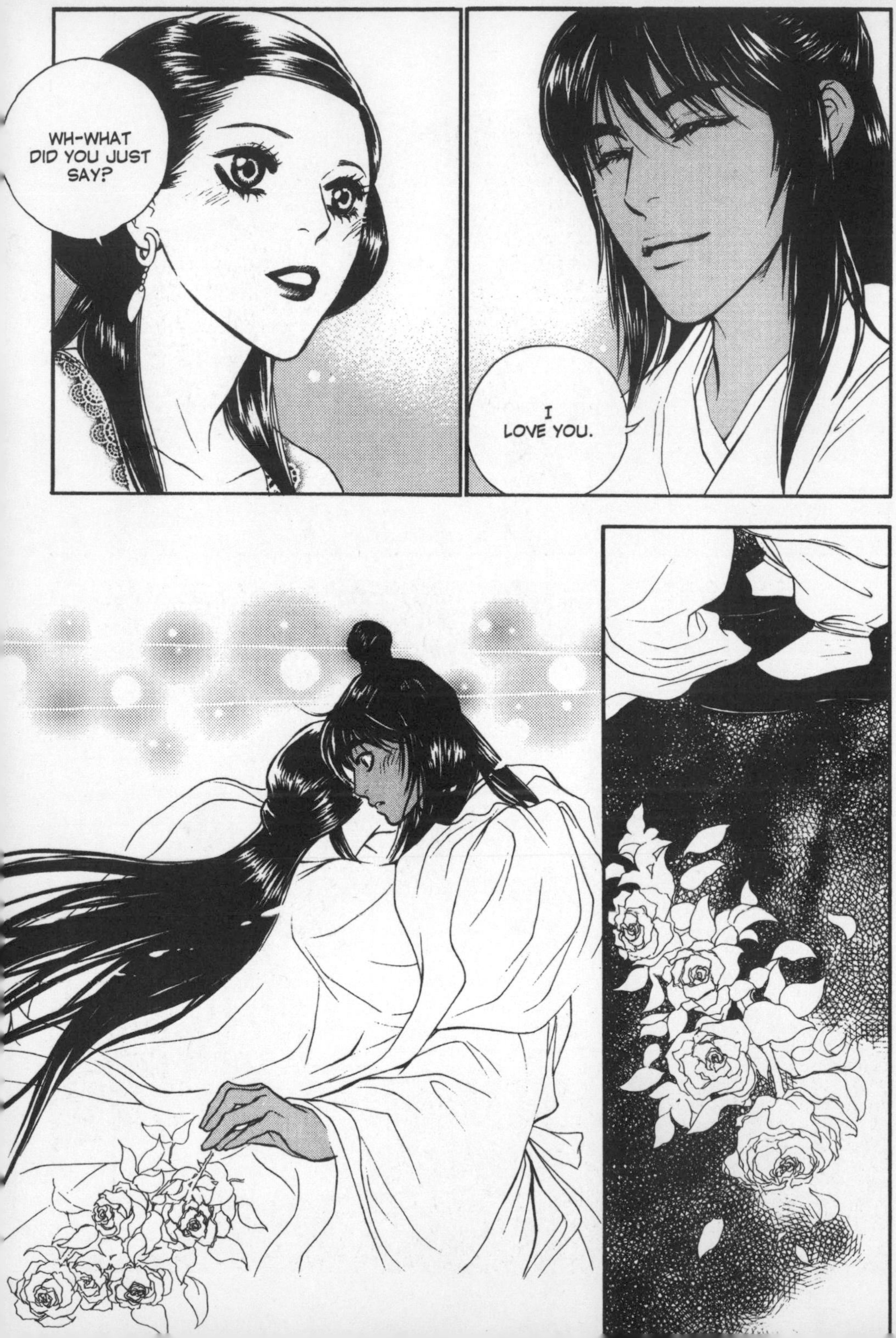
WH-WHAT DID YOU JUST SAY?
I LOVE YOU.

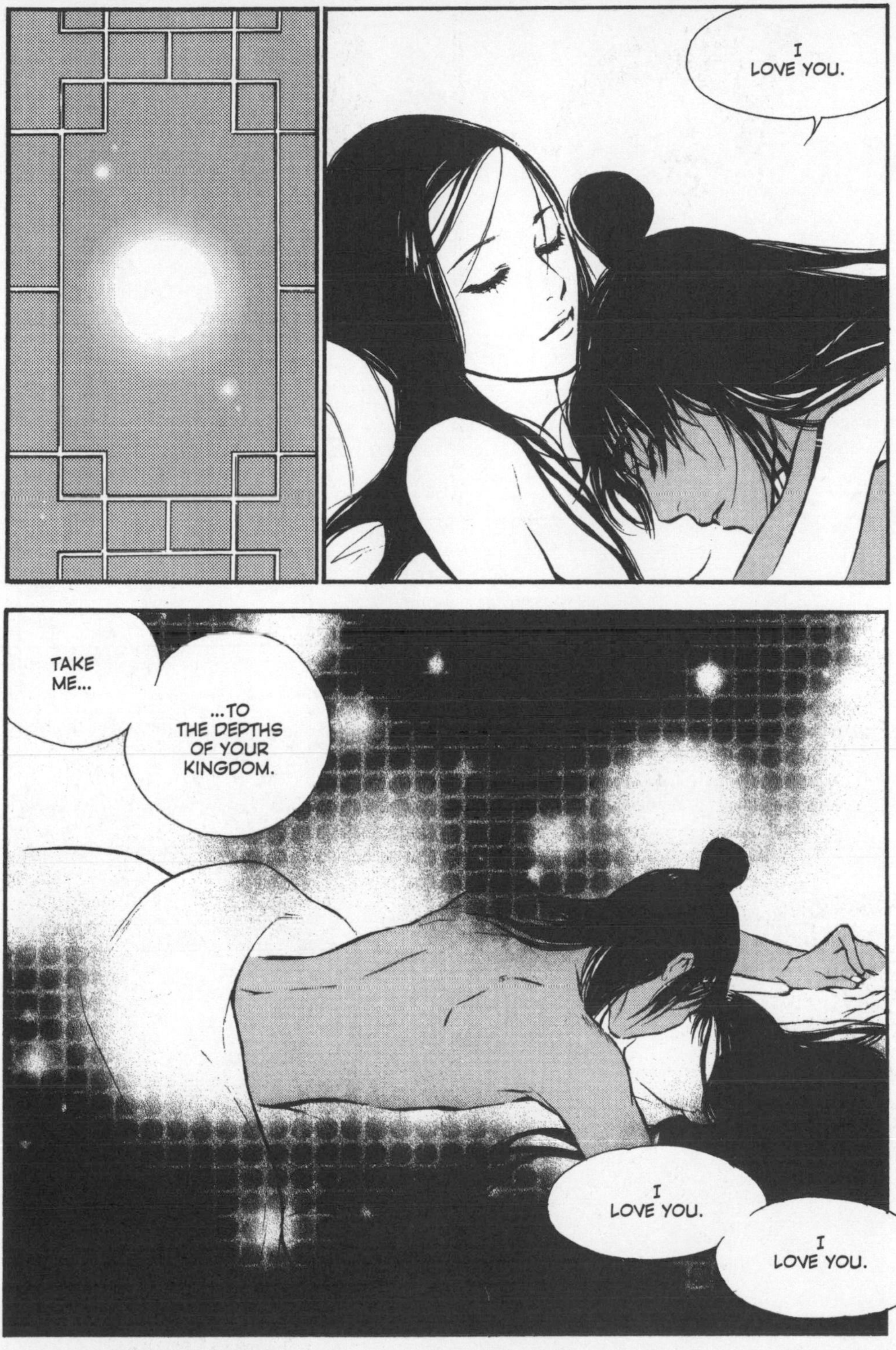
I LOVE YOU.
TAKE ME...
...TO THE DEPTHS OF YOUR KINGDOM.
I LOVE YOU.
I LOVE YOU.

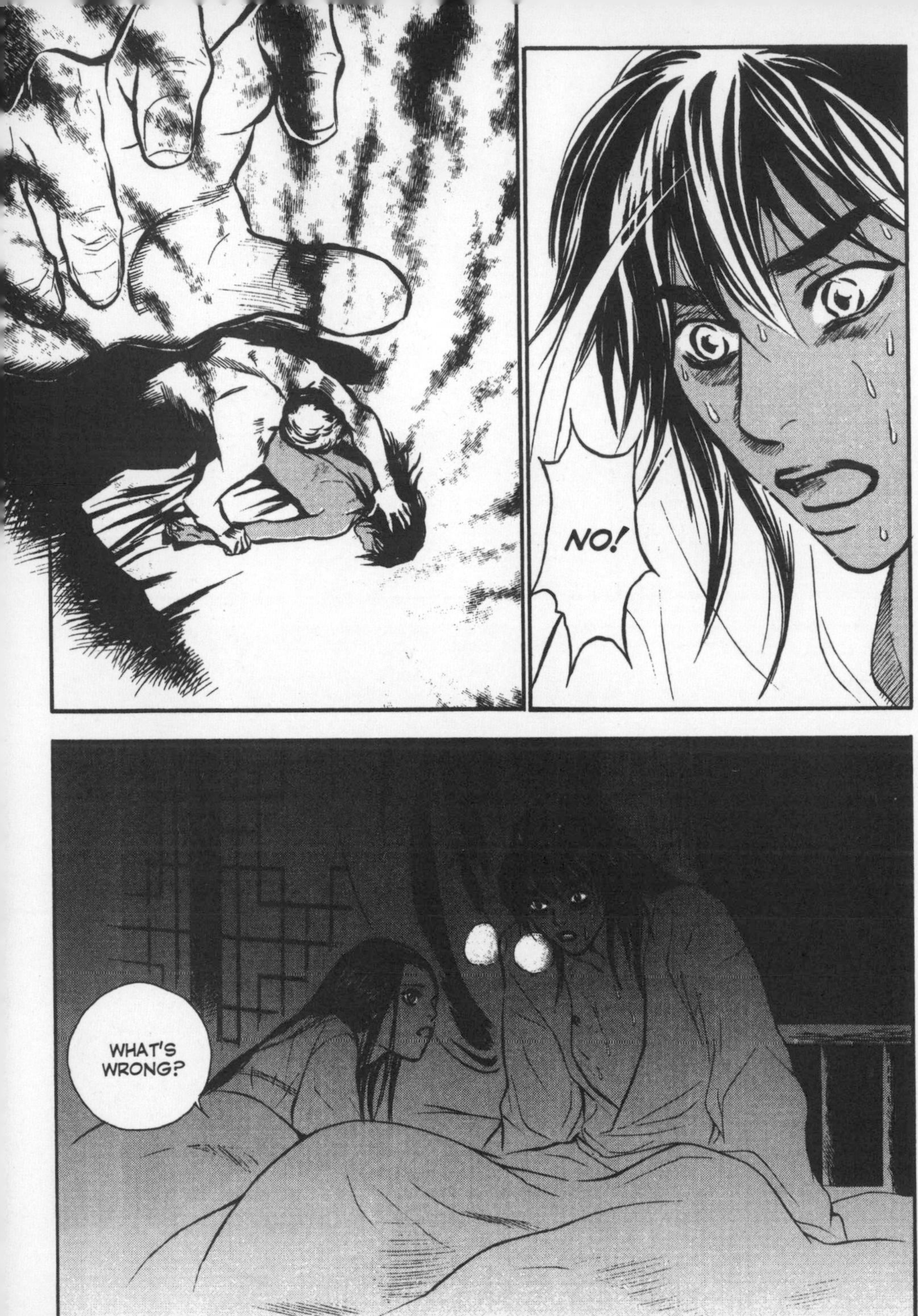
NO!
WHAT'S WRONG?

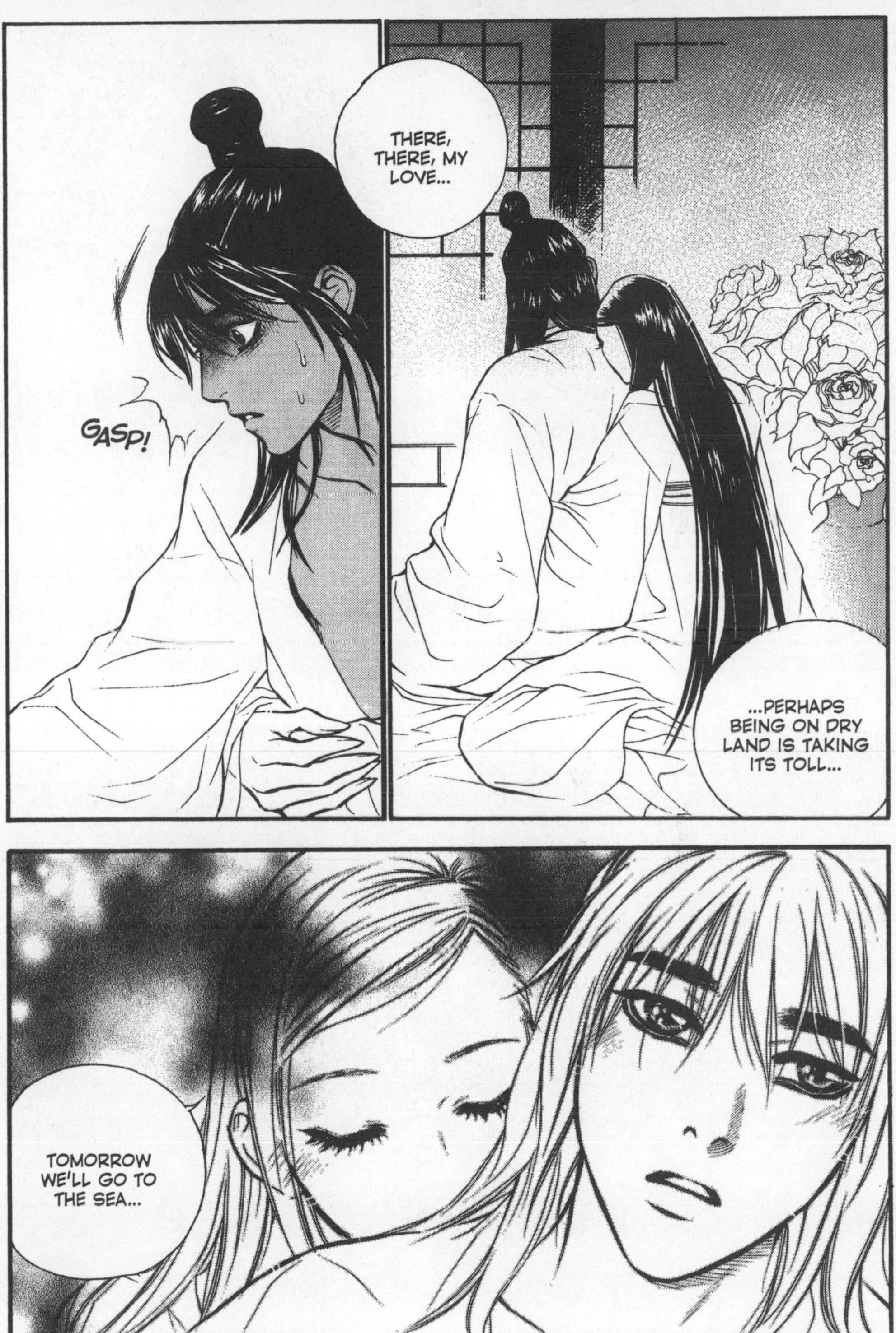
GASP!
THERE, THERE, MY LOVE...
...PERHAPS BEING ON DRY LAND IS TAKING ITS TOLL...
TOMORROW WE'LL GO TO THE SEA...

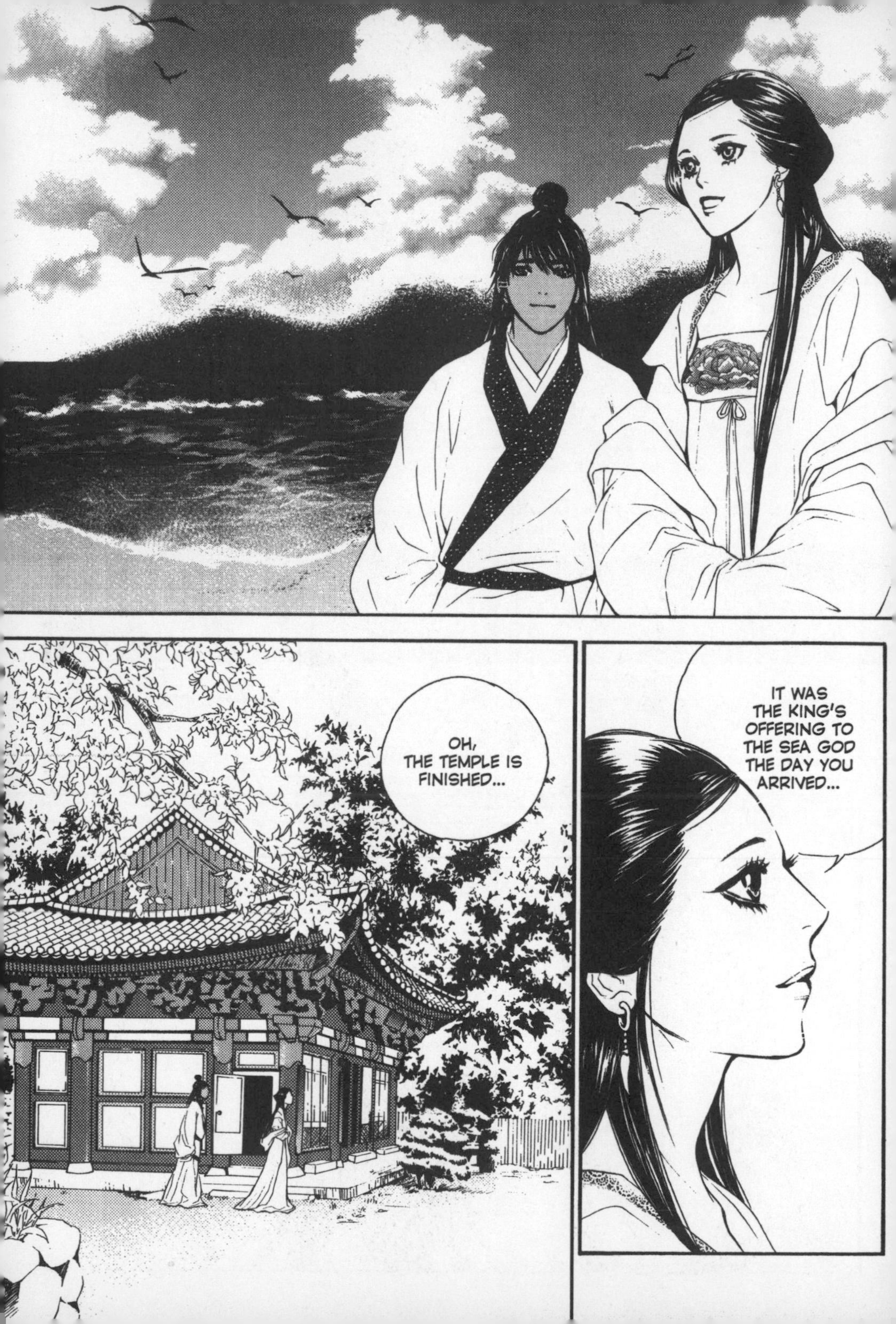
OH, THE TEMPLE IS FINISHED...
IT WAS THE KING'S OFFERING TO THE SEA GOD THE DAY YOU ARRIVED...

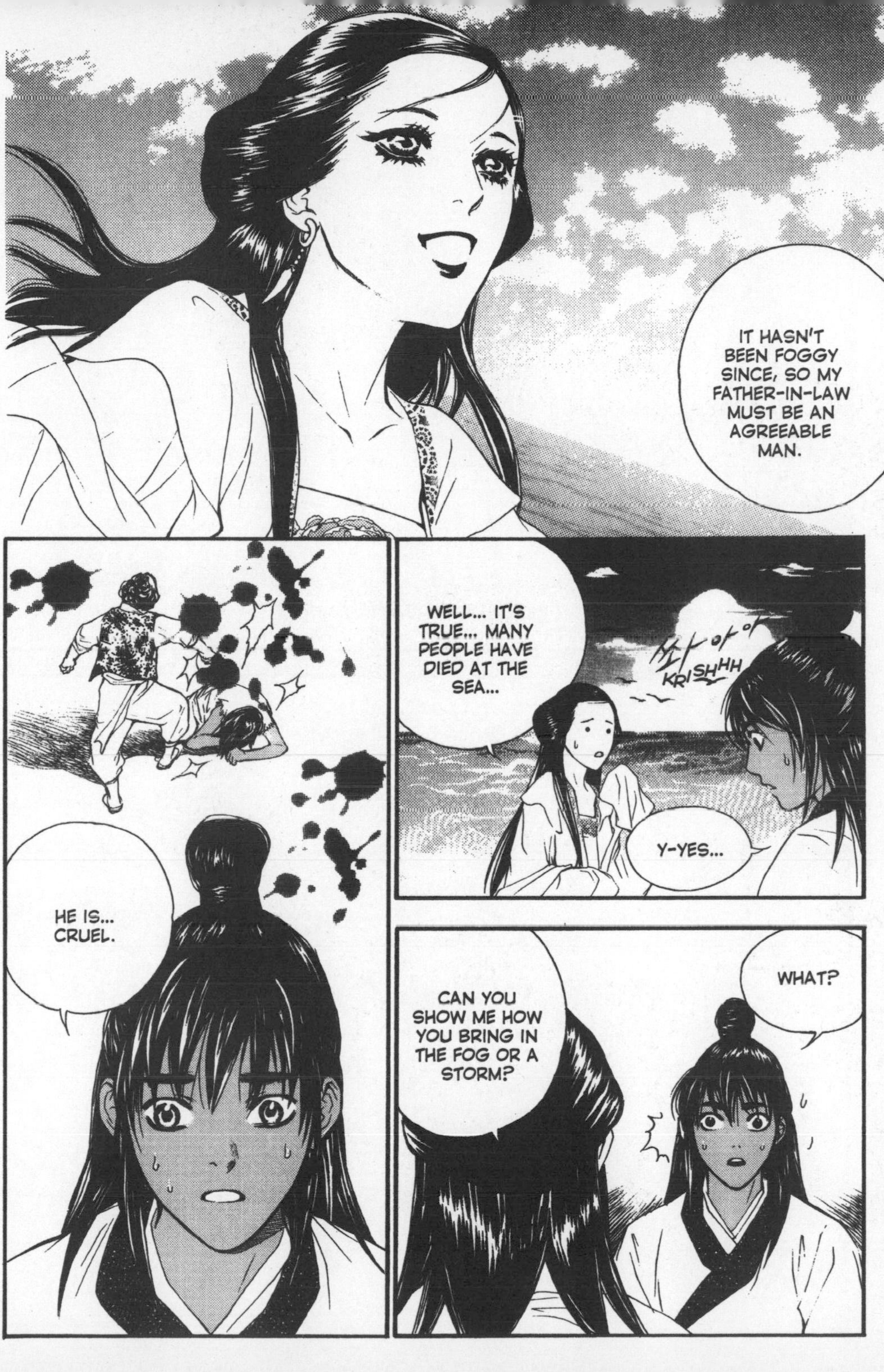
IT HASN'T BEEN FOGGY SINCE, SO MY FATHER-IN-LAW MUST BE AN AGREEABLE MAN.
HE IS... CRUEL.
WELL... IT'S TRUE... MANY PEOPLE HAVE DIED AT THE SEA...
쏴아아
KRISHHH
Y-YES...
CAN YOU SHOW ME HOW YOU BRING IN THE FOG OR A STORM?
WHAT?

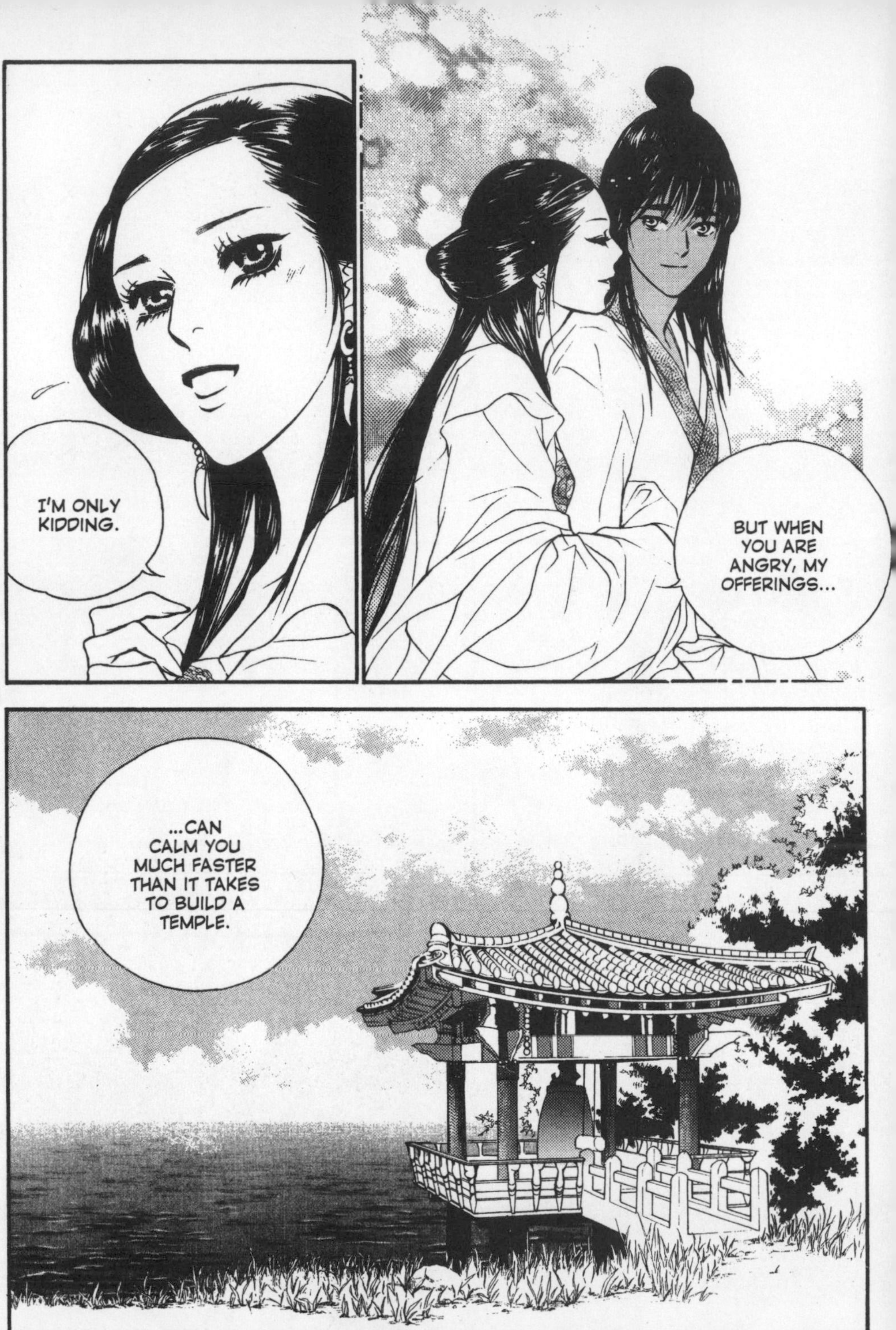
I'M ONLY KIDDING.
BUT WHEN YOU ARE ANGRY, MY OFFERINGS...
...CAN CALM YOU MUCH FASTER THAN IT TAKES TO BUILD A TEMPLE.

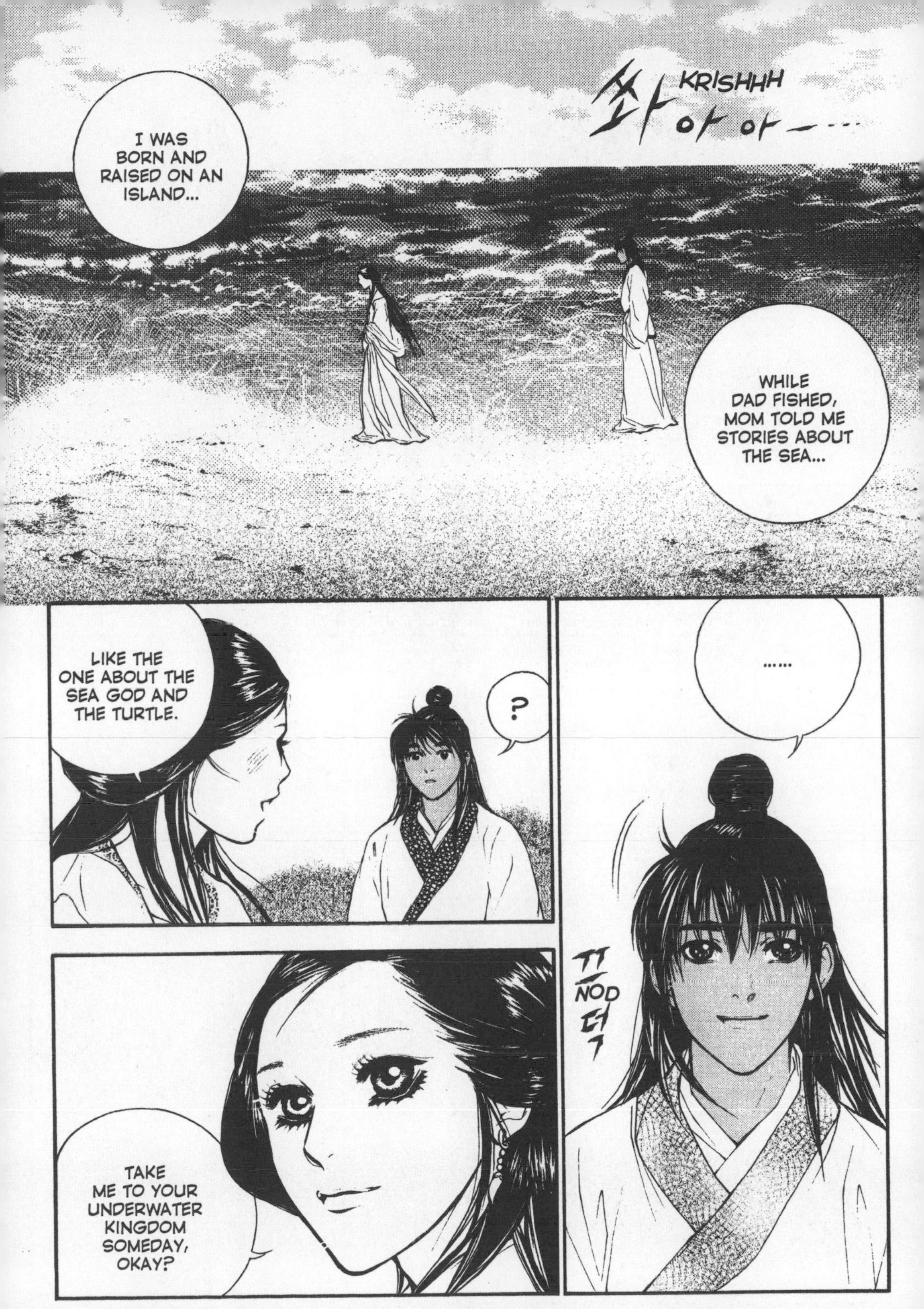

쏴아아
KRISHHH
I WAS BORN AND RAISED ON AN ISLAND...
WHILE DAD FISHED, MOM TOLD ME STORIES ABOUT THE SEA...
LIKE THE ONE ABOUT THE SEA GOD AND THE TURTLE.
?
......
끄덕
NOD
TAKE ME TO YOUR UNDERWATER KINGDOM SOMEDAY, OKAY?

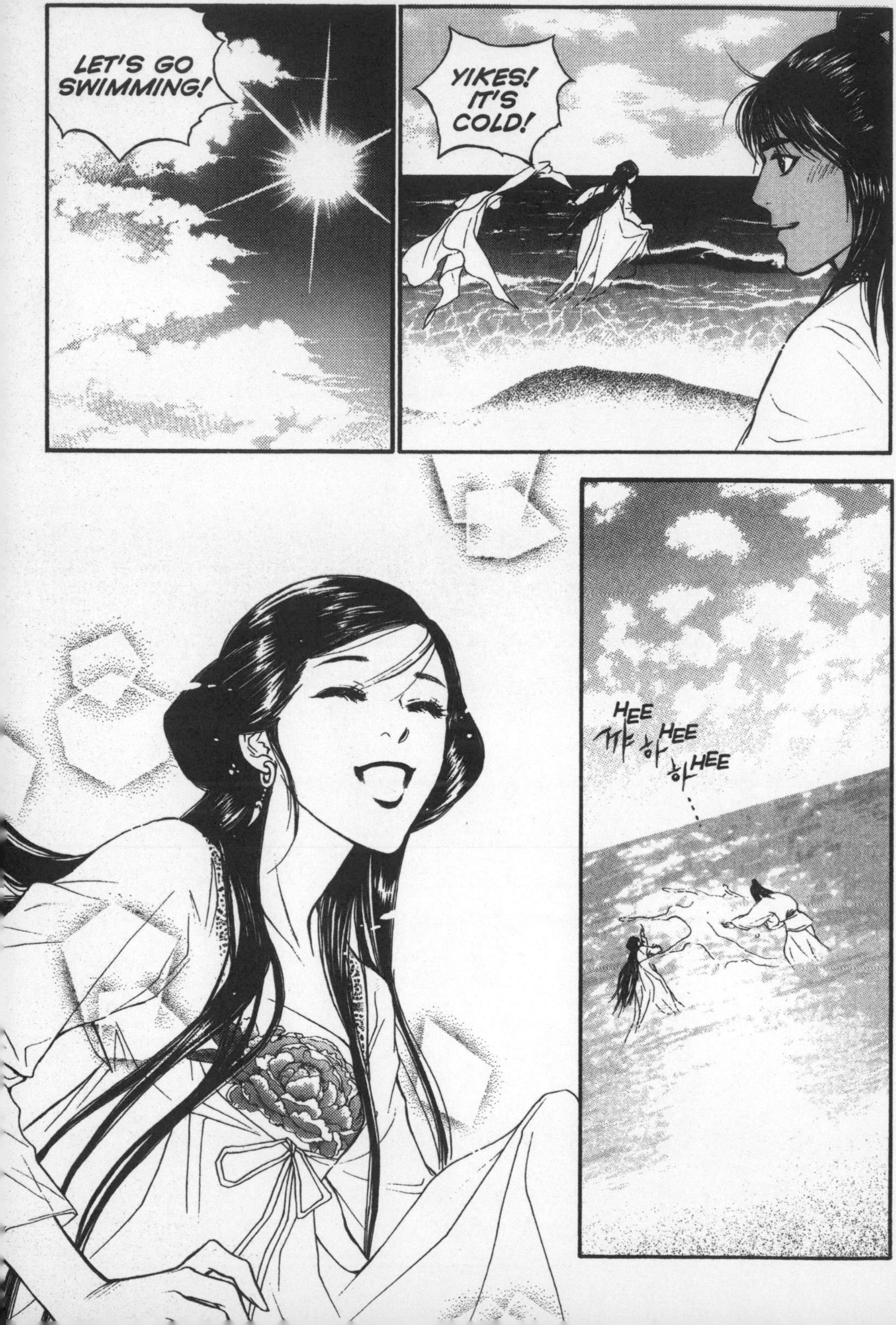
LET'S GO SWIMMING!
YIKES! IT'S COLD!
꺄 하 하
HEE HEE HEE

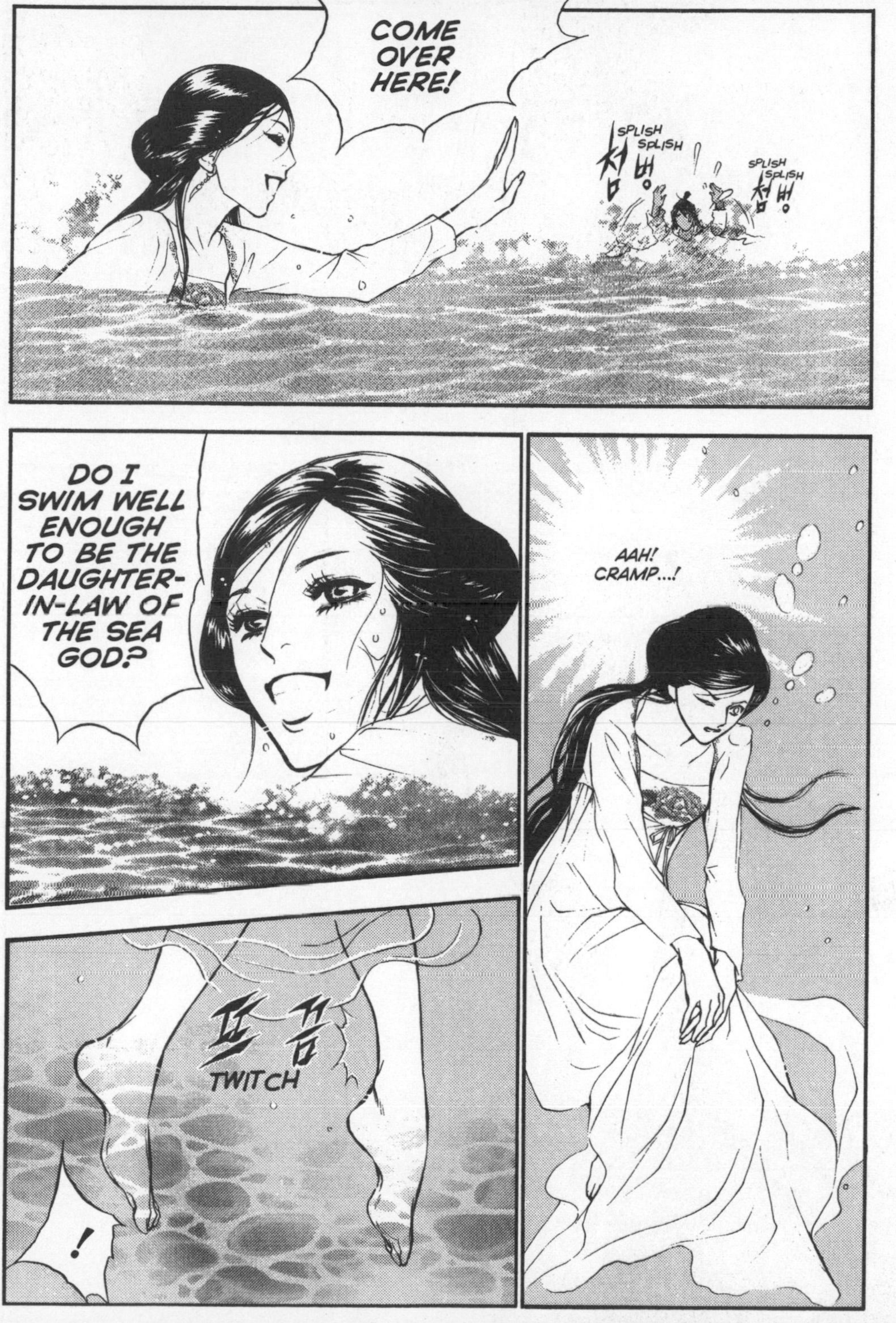

COME OVER HERE!
첨벙 SPLISH SPLISH
!
첨벙 SPLISH SPLISH
DO I SWIM WELL ENOUGH TO BE THE DAUGHTER-IN-LAW OF THE SEA GOD?
TWITCH
!
AAH! CRAMP...!

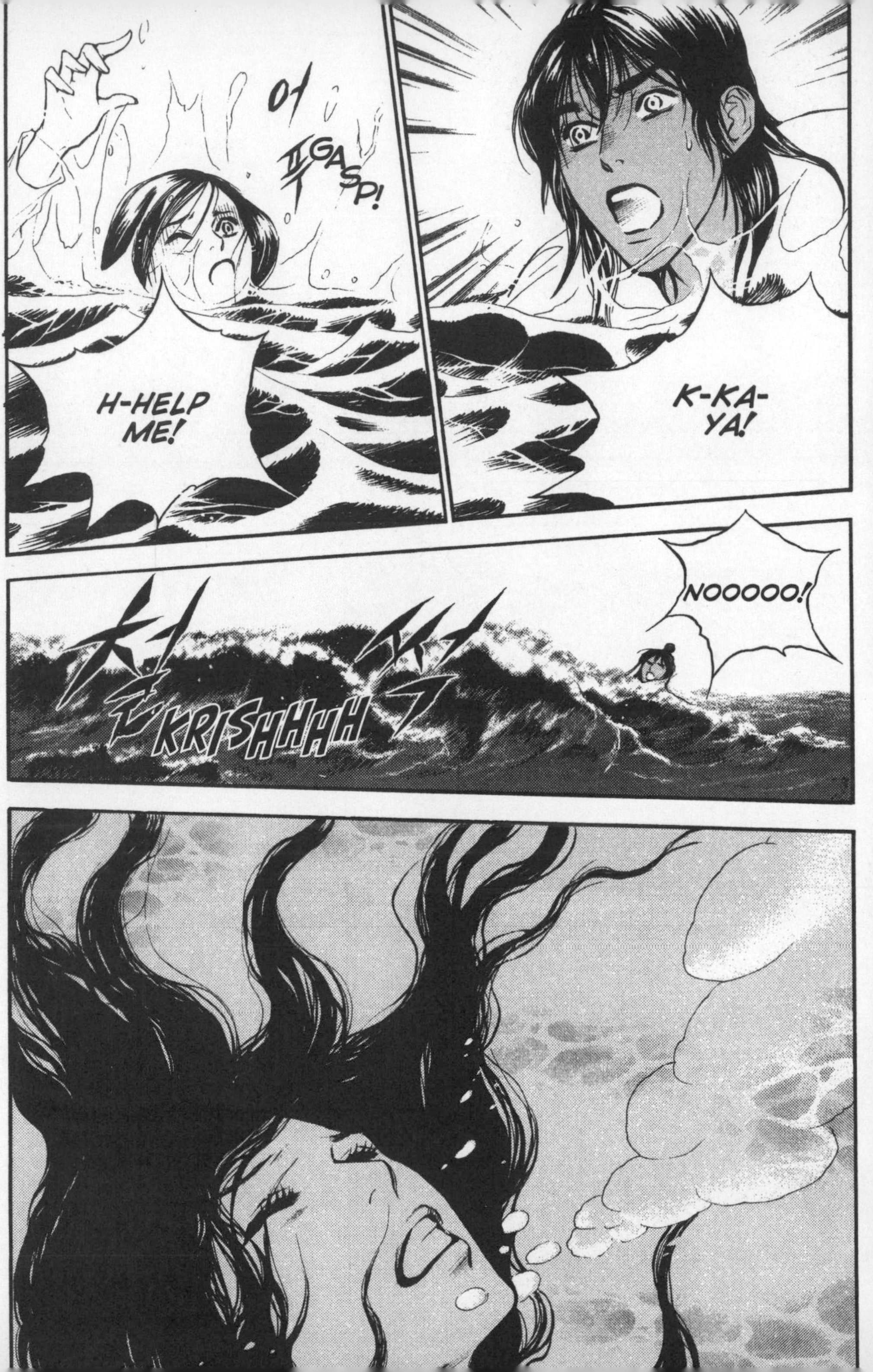
GASP!
H-HELP ME!
K-KA-YA!
NOOOOO!
KRISHHHH

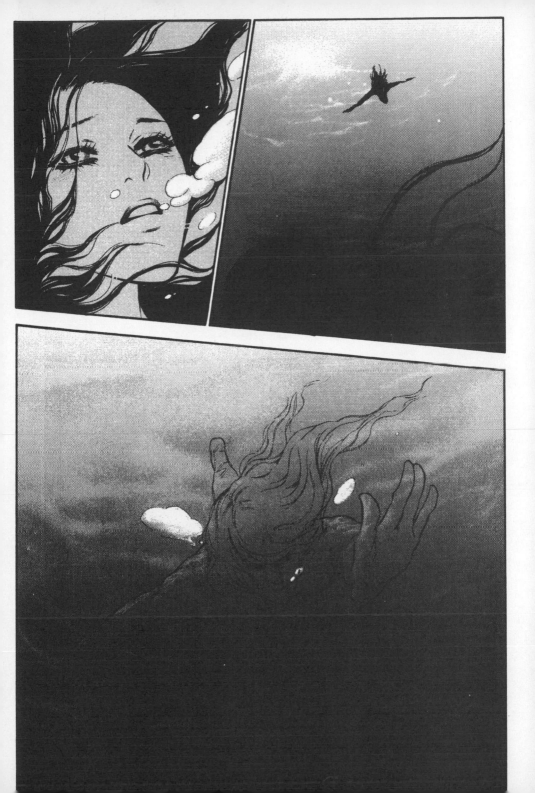

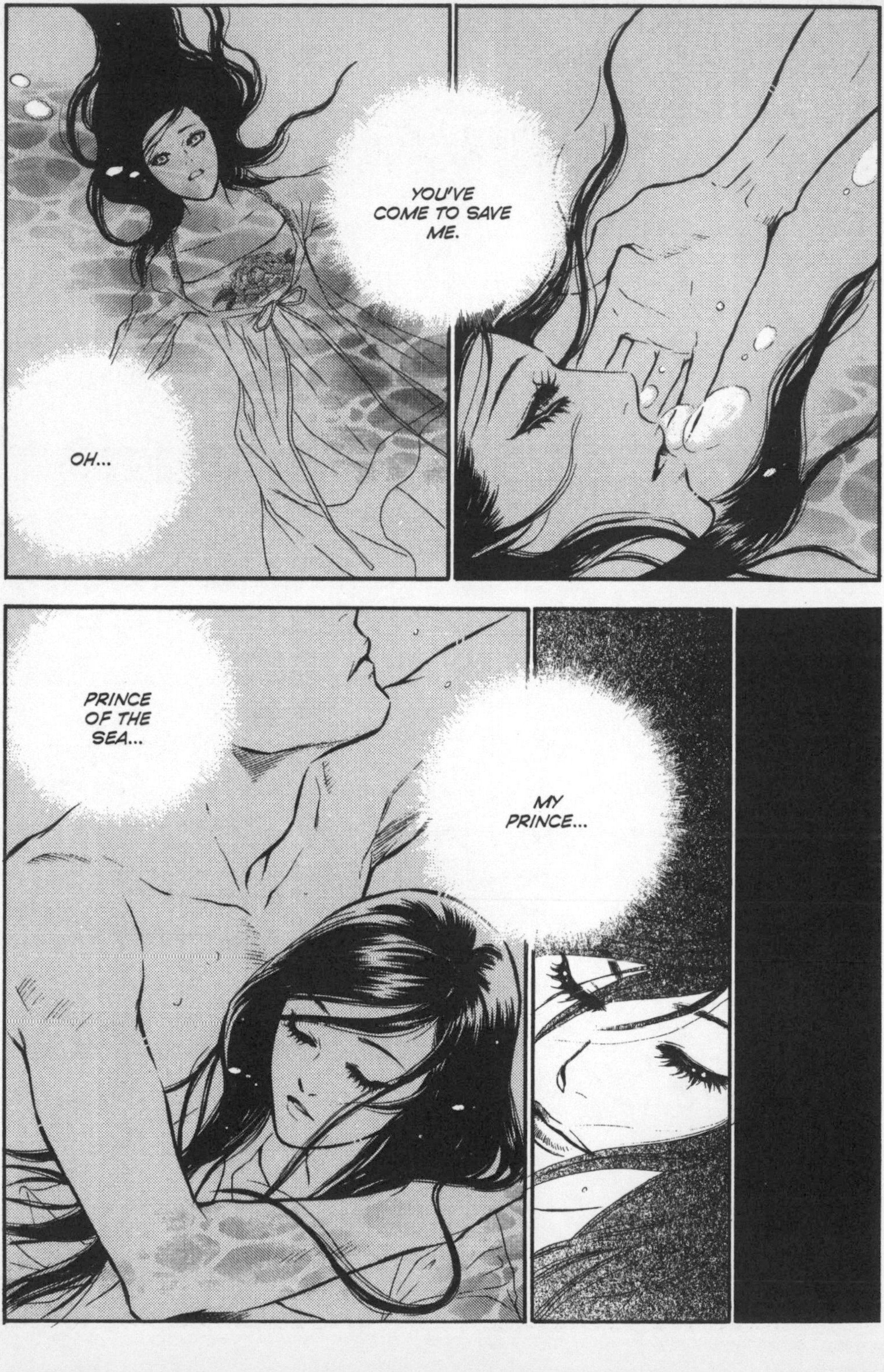
OH...
YOU'VE COME TO SAVE ME.
PRINCE OF THE SEA...
MY PRINCE...

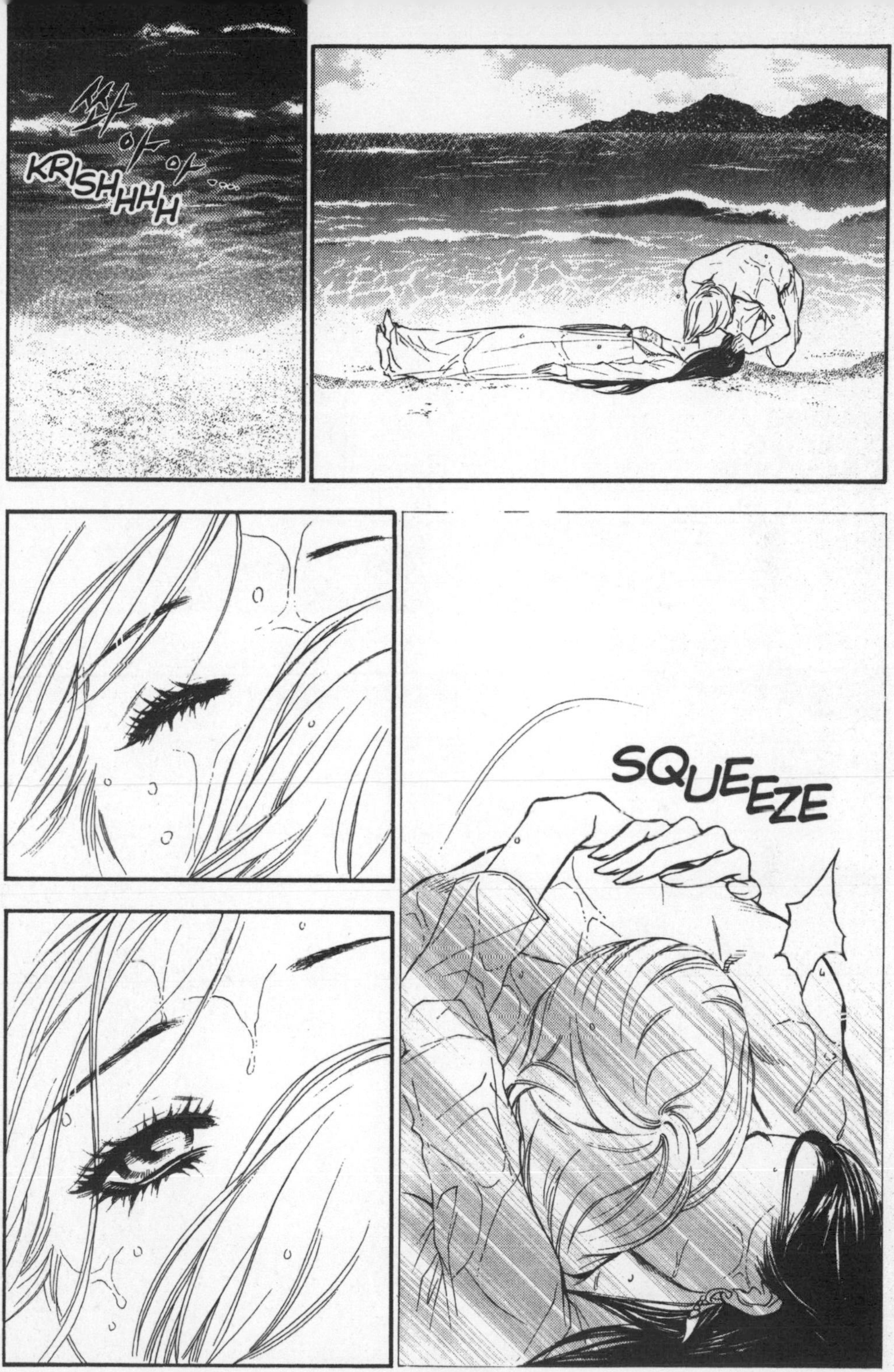
쏴아아…
KRISHHHH
SQUEEZE

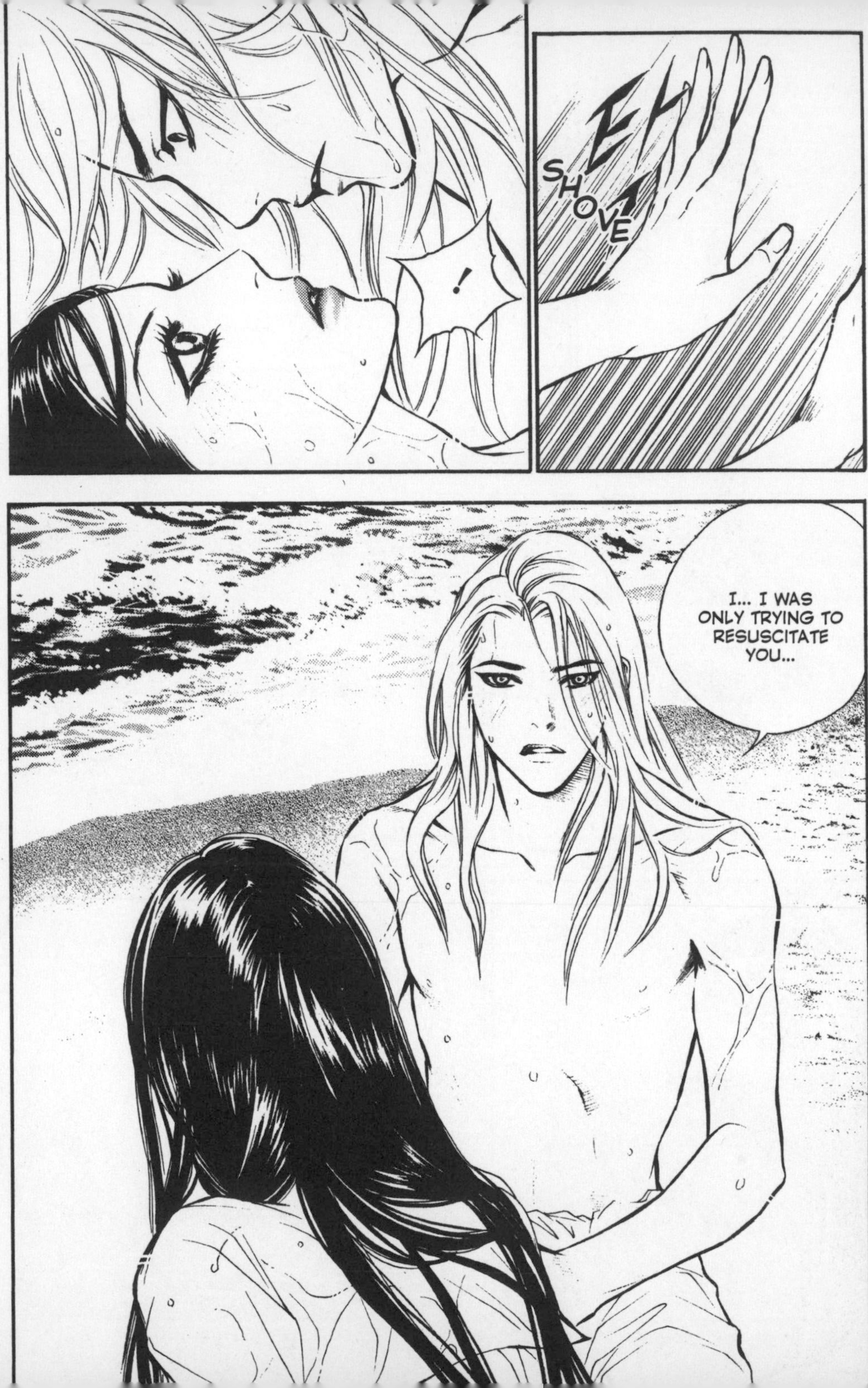
!
SHOVE
I... I WAS ONLY TRYING TO RESUSCITATE YOU...

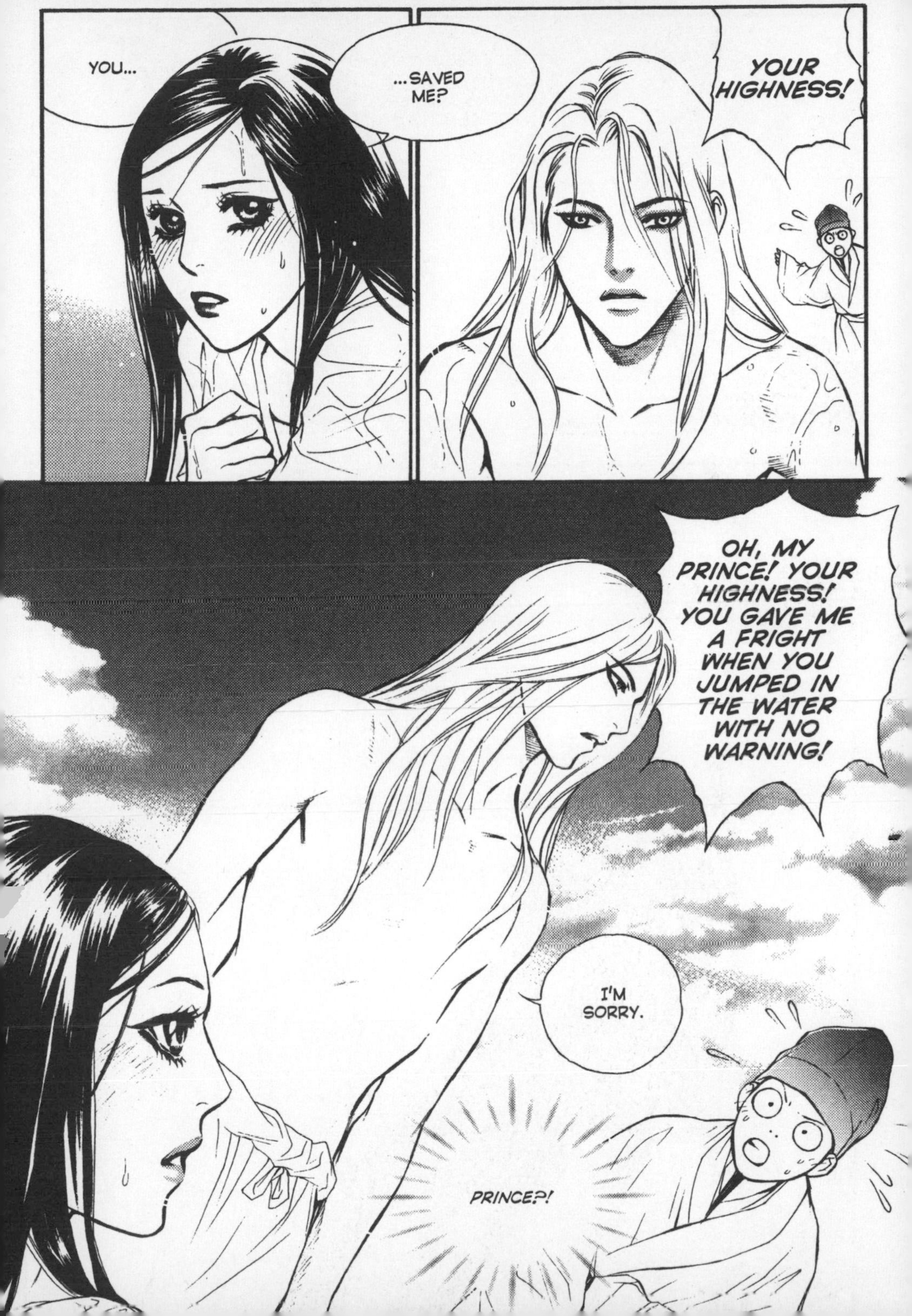
YOU...
...SAVED ME?
YOUR HIGHNESS!
OH, MY PRINCE! YOUR HIGHNESS! YOU GAVE ME A FRIGHT WHEN YOU JUMPED IN THE WATER WITH NO WARNING!
I'M SORRY.
PRINCE?!

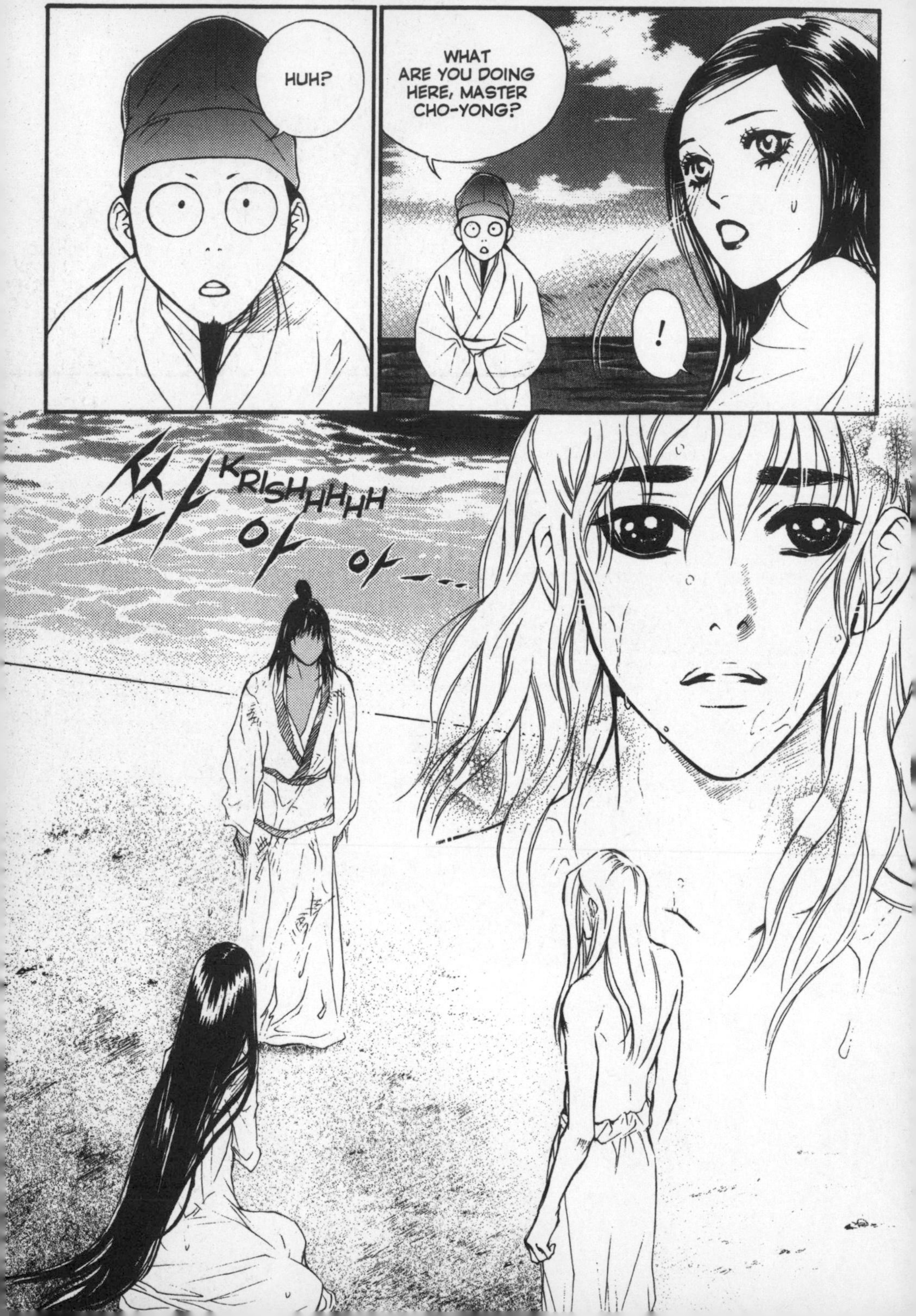
HUH?
WHAT ARE YOU DOING HERE, MASTER CHO-YONG?
!
KRISHHHHH
쏴아아

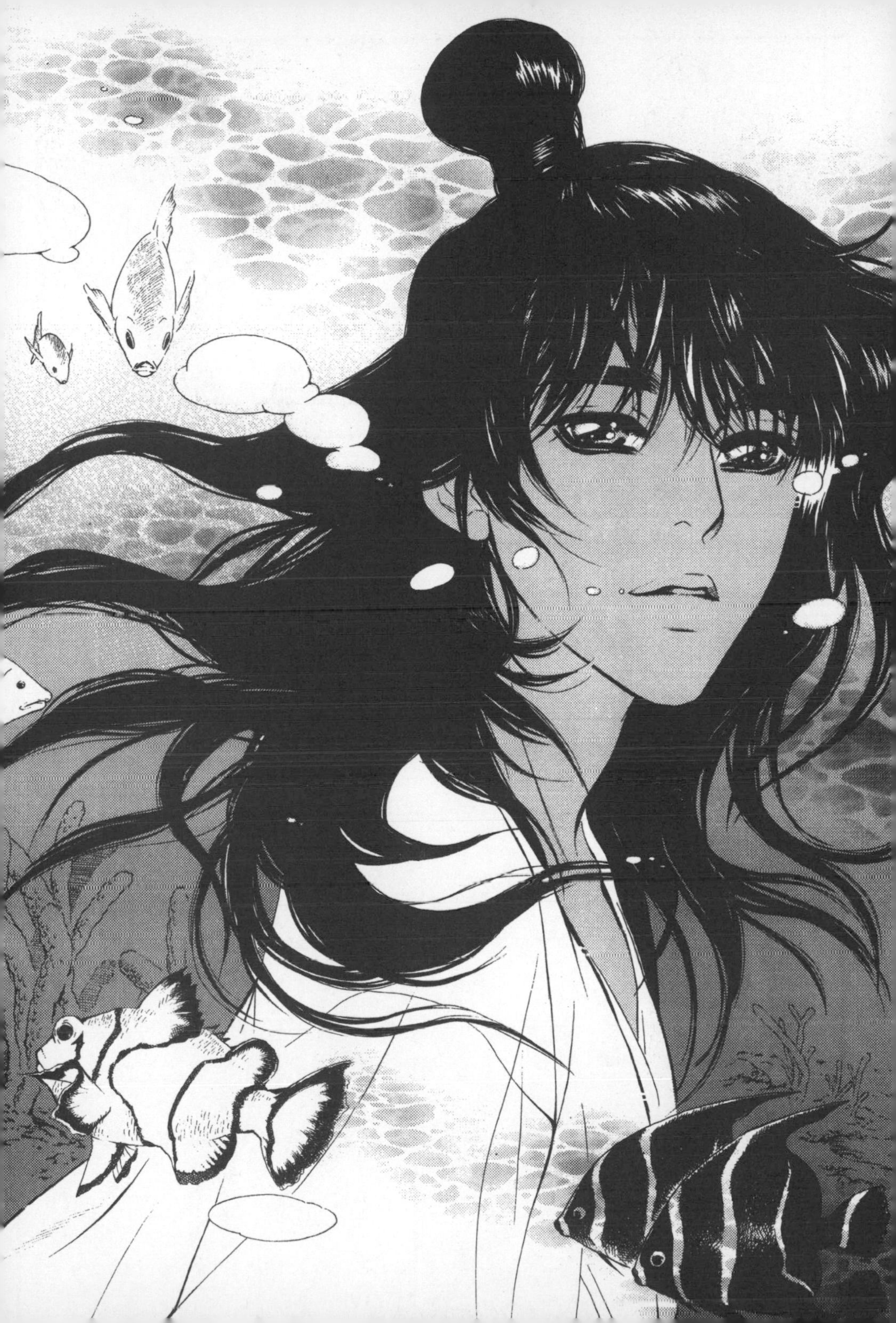

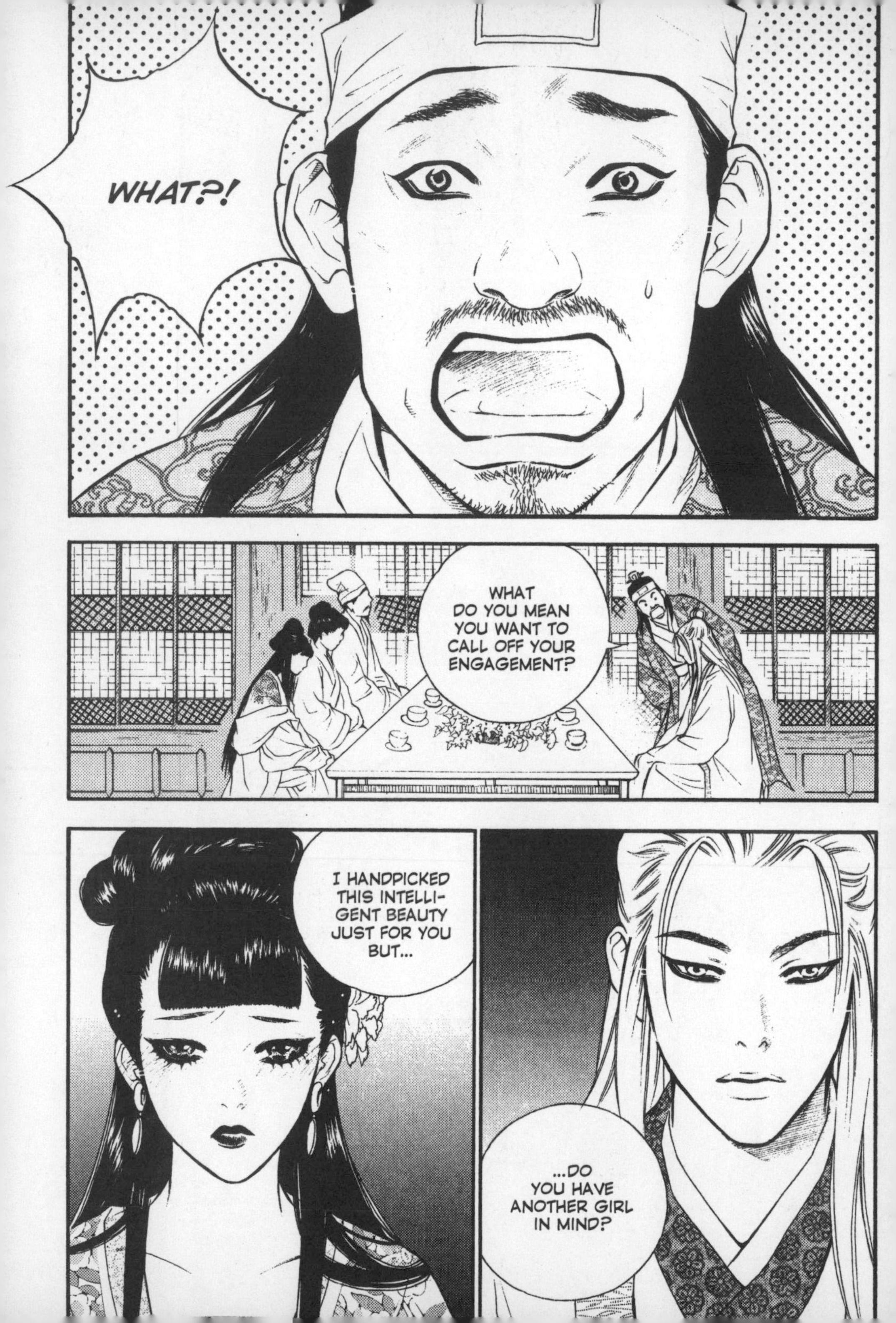
WHAT?!
WHAT DO YOU MEAN YOU WANT TO CALL OFF YOUR ENGAGEMENT?
I HANDPICKED THIS INTELLI-GENT BEAUTY JUST FOR YOU BUT...
...DO YOU HAVE ANOTHER GIRL IN MIND?

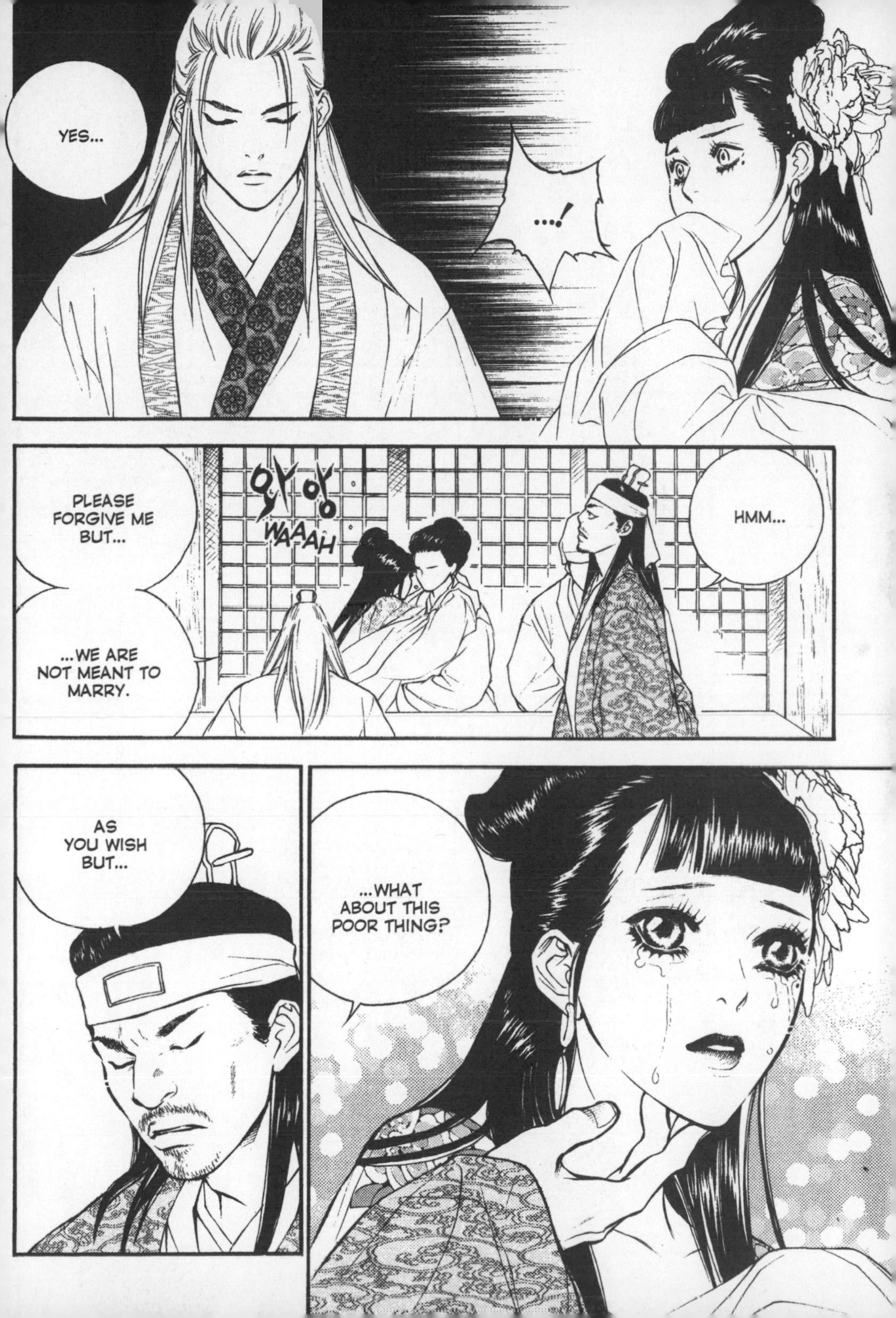
YES...
...!
PLEASE FORGIVE ME BUT...
...WE ARE NOT MEANT TO MARRY.
WAAAH
HMM...
AS YOU WISH BUT...
...WHAT ABOUT THIS POOR THING?

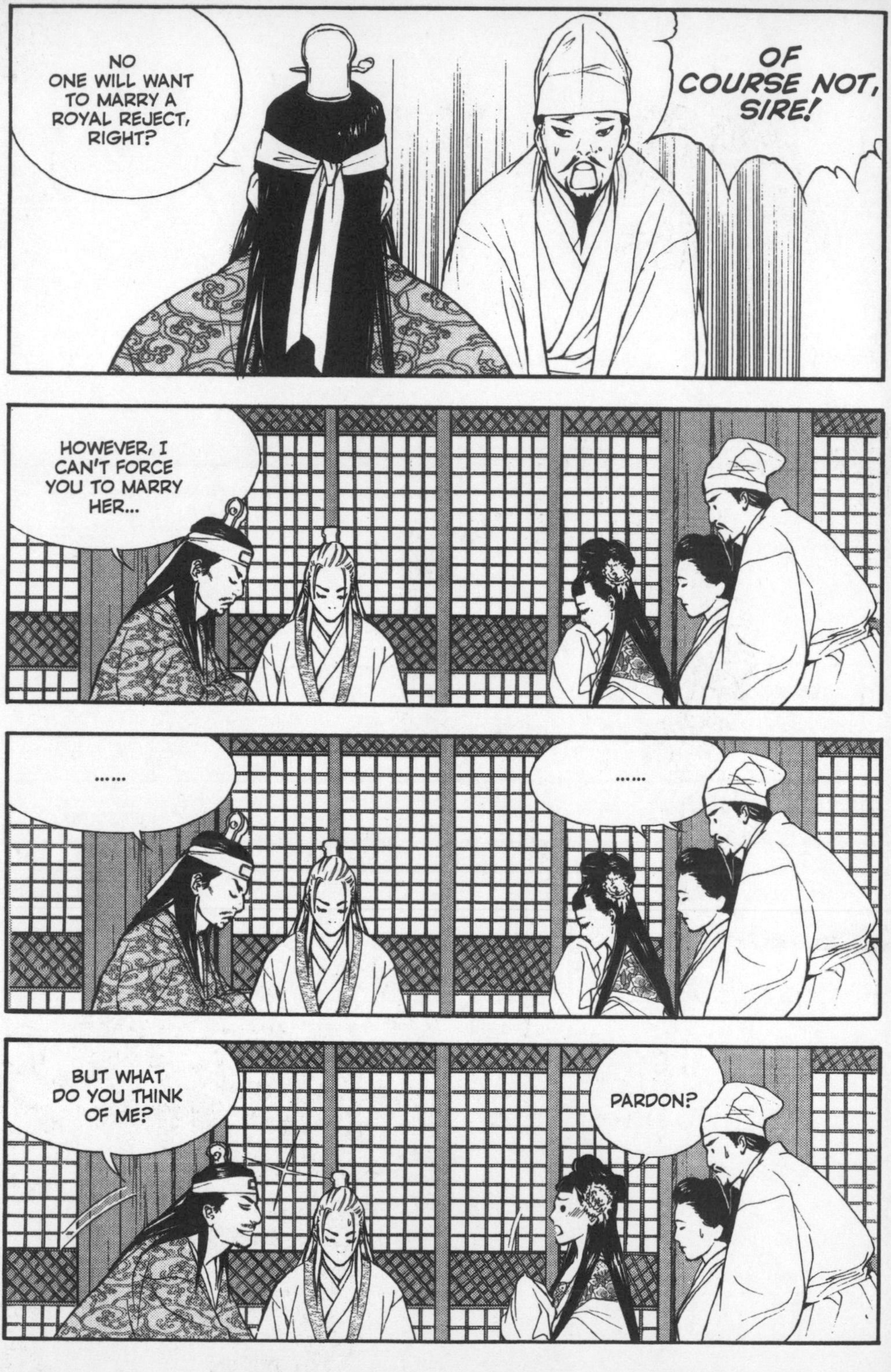
NO ONE WILL WANT TO MARRY A ROYAL REJECT, RIGHT?
OF COURSE NOT, SIRE!
HOWEVER, I CAN'T FORCE YOU TO MARRY HER...
......
......
BUT WHAT DO YOU THINK OF ME?
PARDON?

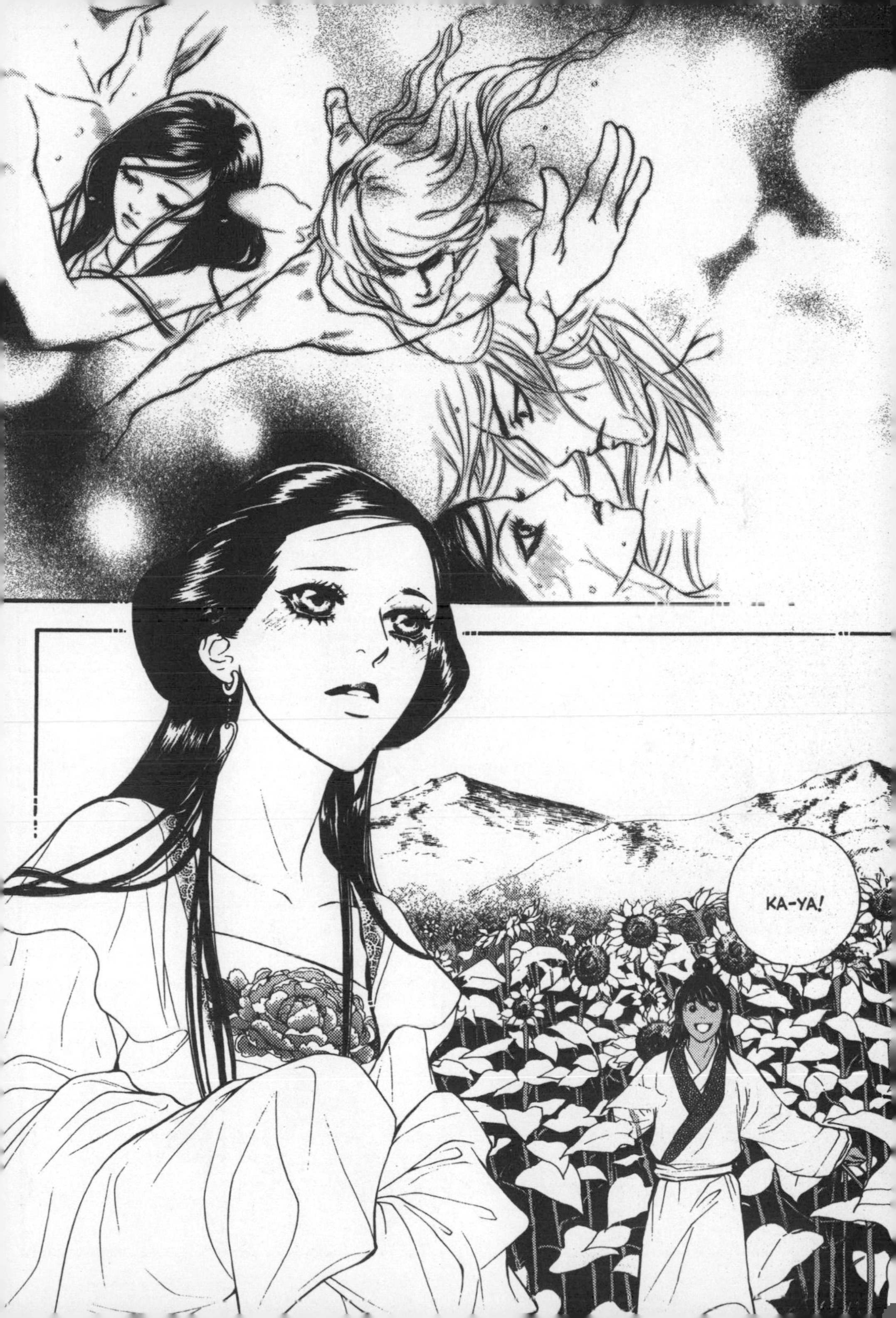
KA-YA!

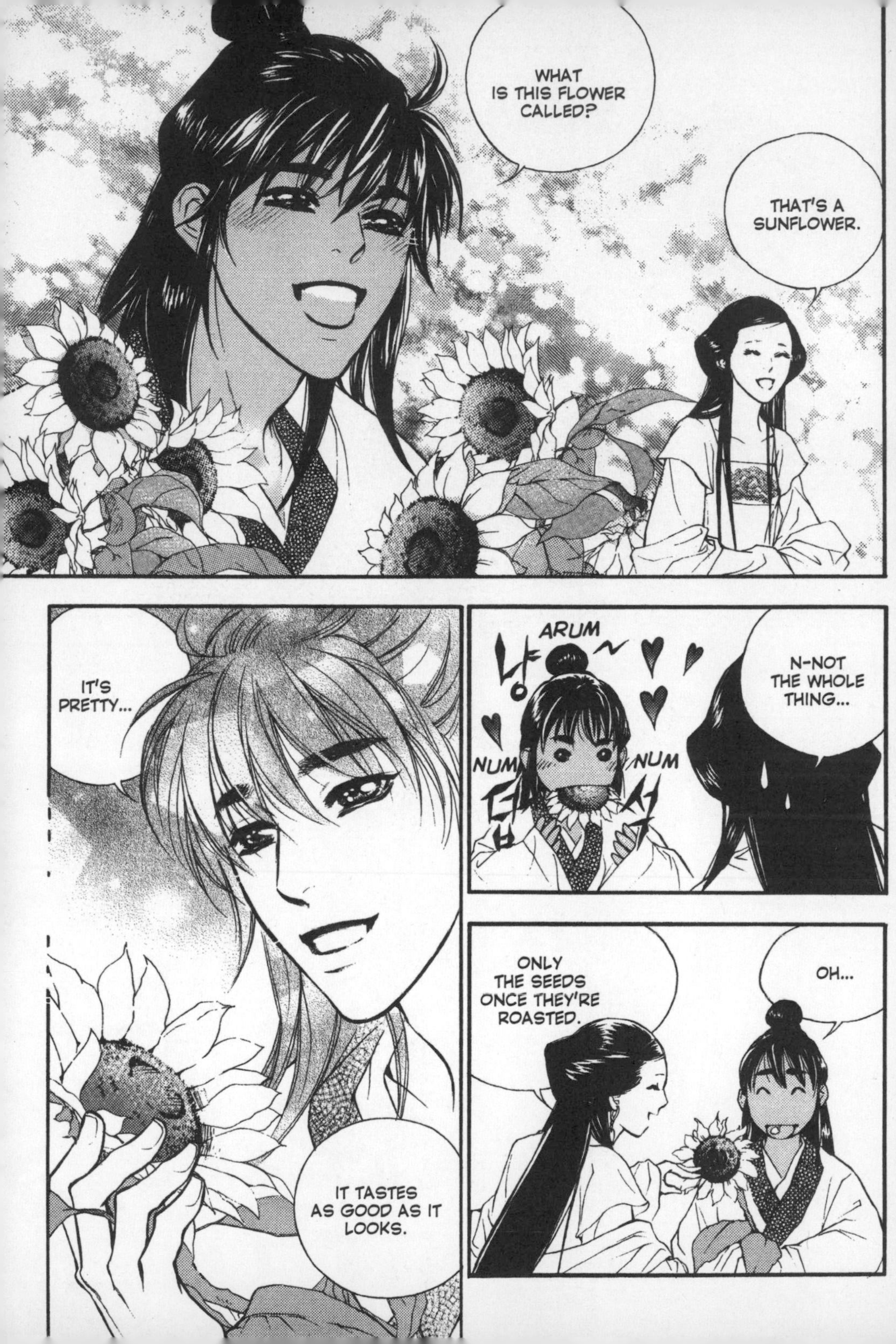
WHAT IS THIS FLOWER CALLED?
THAT'S A SUNFLOWER.
IT'S PRETTY...
IT TASTES AS GOOD AS IT LOOKS.
냠
ARUM
NUM
NUM
덥석
N-NOT THE WHOLE THING...
ONLY THE SEEDS ONCE THEY'RE ROASTED.
OH...

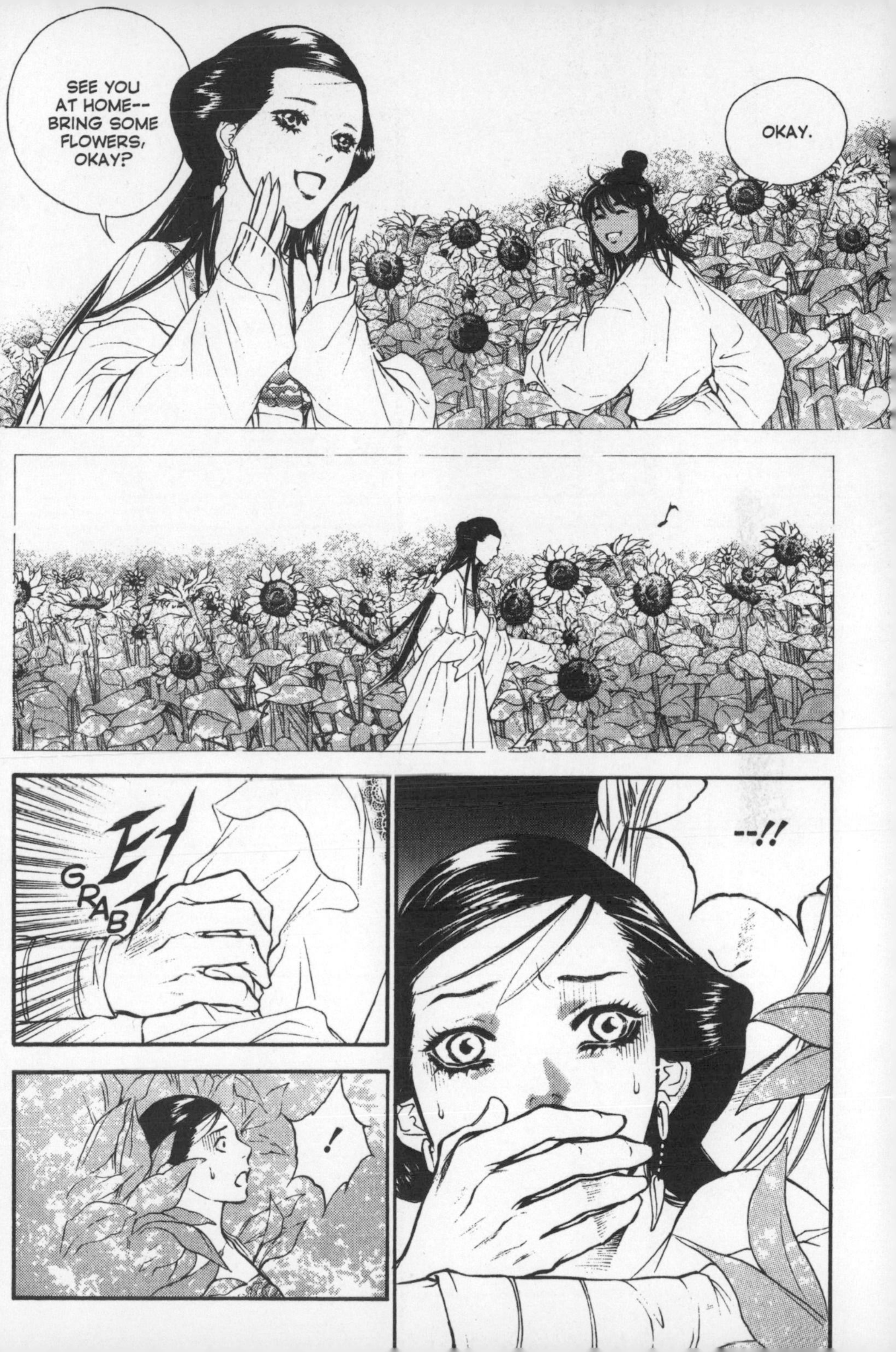
SEE YOU AT HOME-- BRING SOME FLOWERS, OKAY?
OKAY.
GRAB
!
--!!

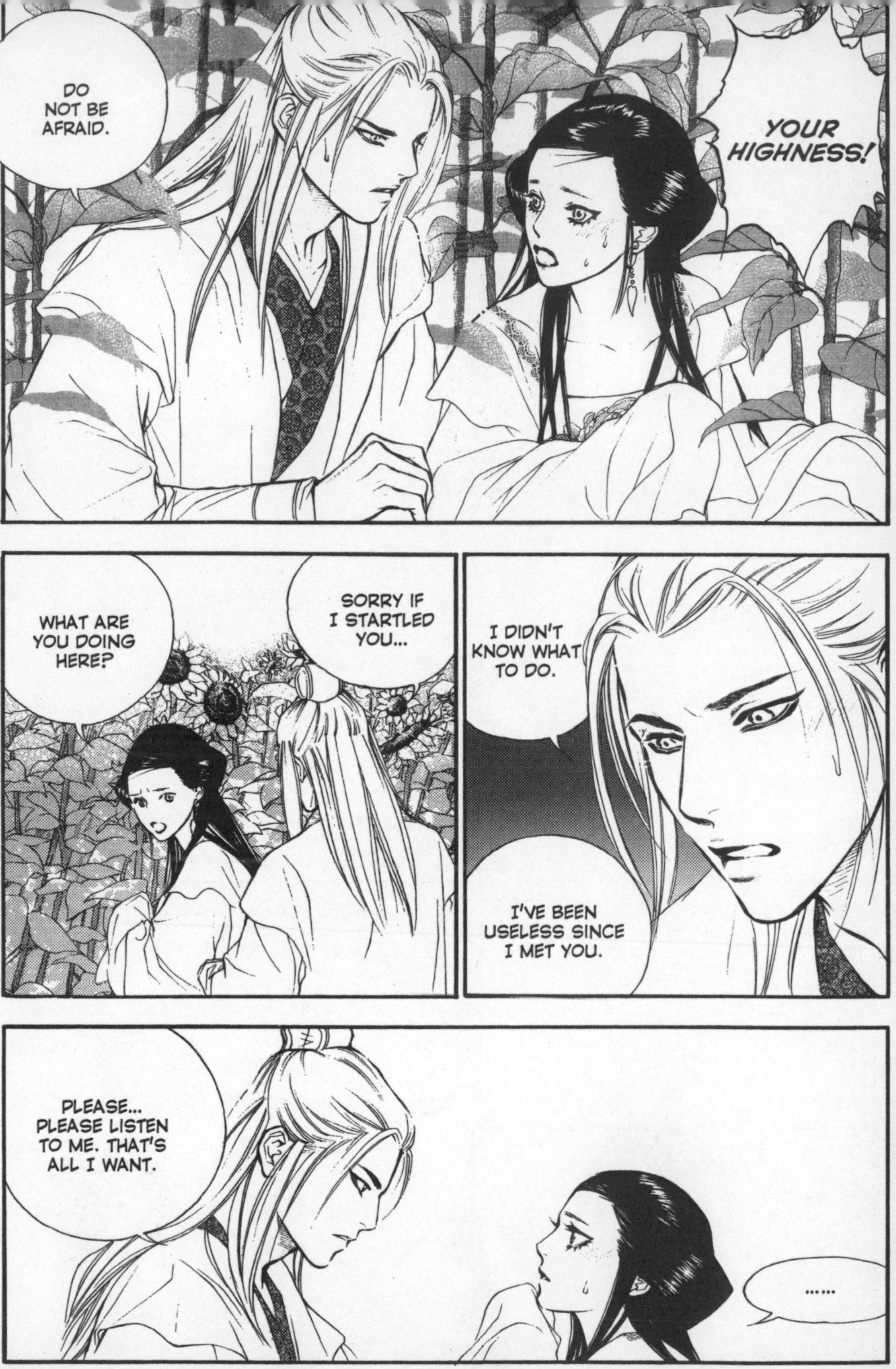
DO NOT BE AFRAID.
YOUR HIGHNESS!
WHAT ARE YOU DOING HERE?
SORRY IF I STARTLED YOU...
I DIDN'T KNOW WHAT TO DO.
I'VE BEEN USELESS SINCE I MET YOU.
PLEASE... PLEASE LISTEN TO ME. THAT'S ALL I WANT.
......

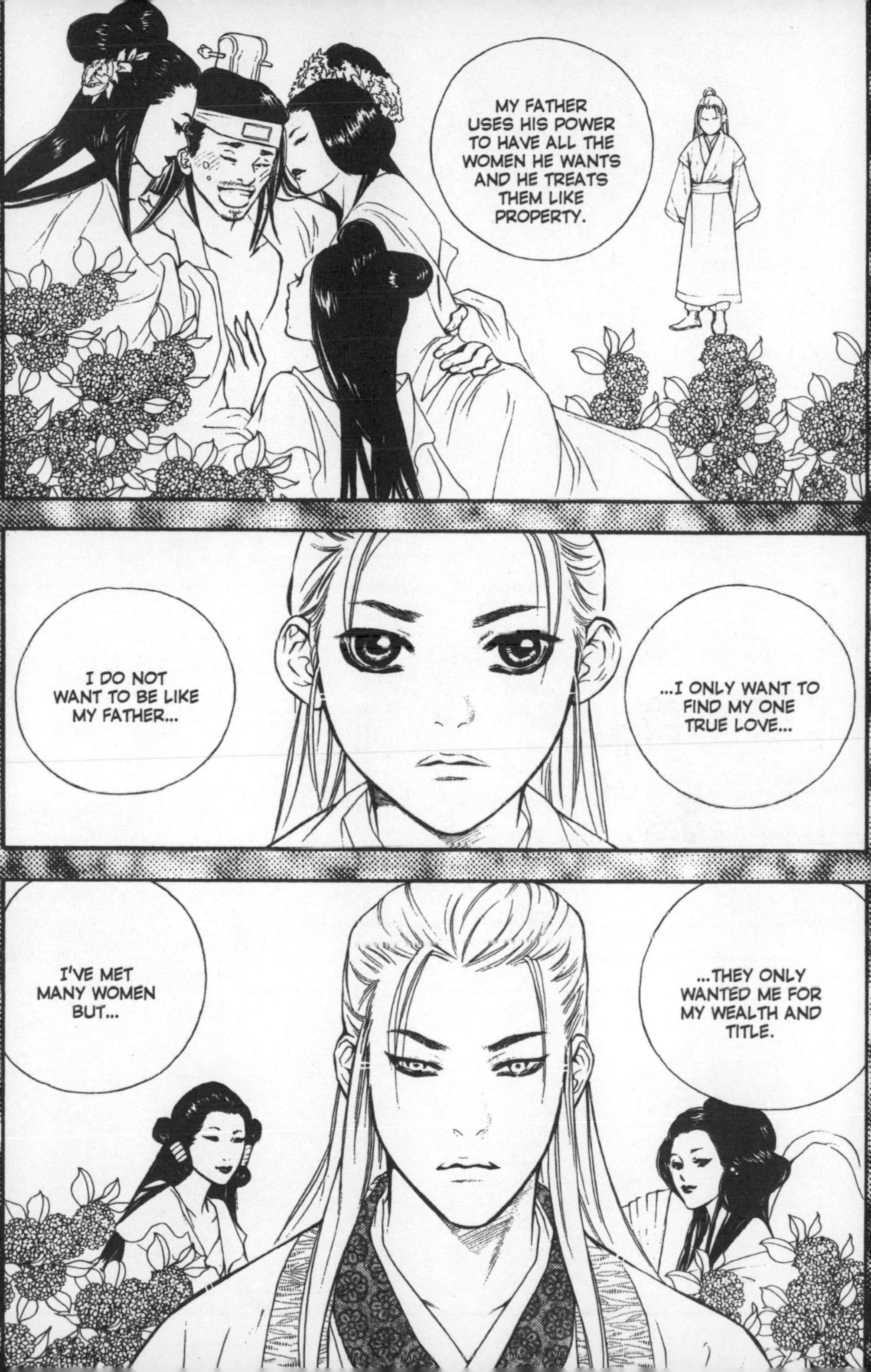
MY FATHER USES HIS POWER TO HAVE ALL THE WOMEN HE WANTS AND HE TREATS THEM LIKE PROPERTY.
I DO NOT WANT TO BE LIKE MY FATHER...
...I ONLY WANT TO FIND MY ONE TRUE LOVE...
I'VE MET MANY WOMEN BUT...
...THEY ONLY WANTED ME FOR MY WEALTH AND TITLE.

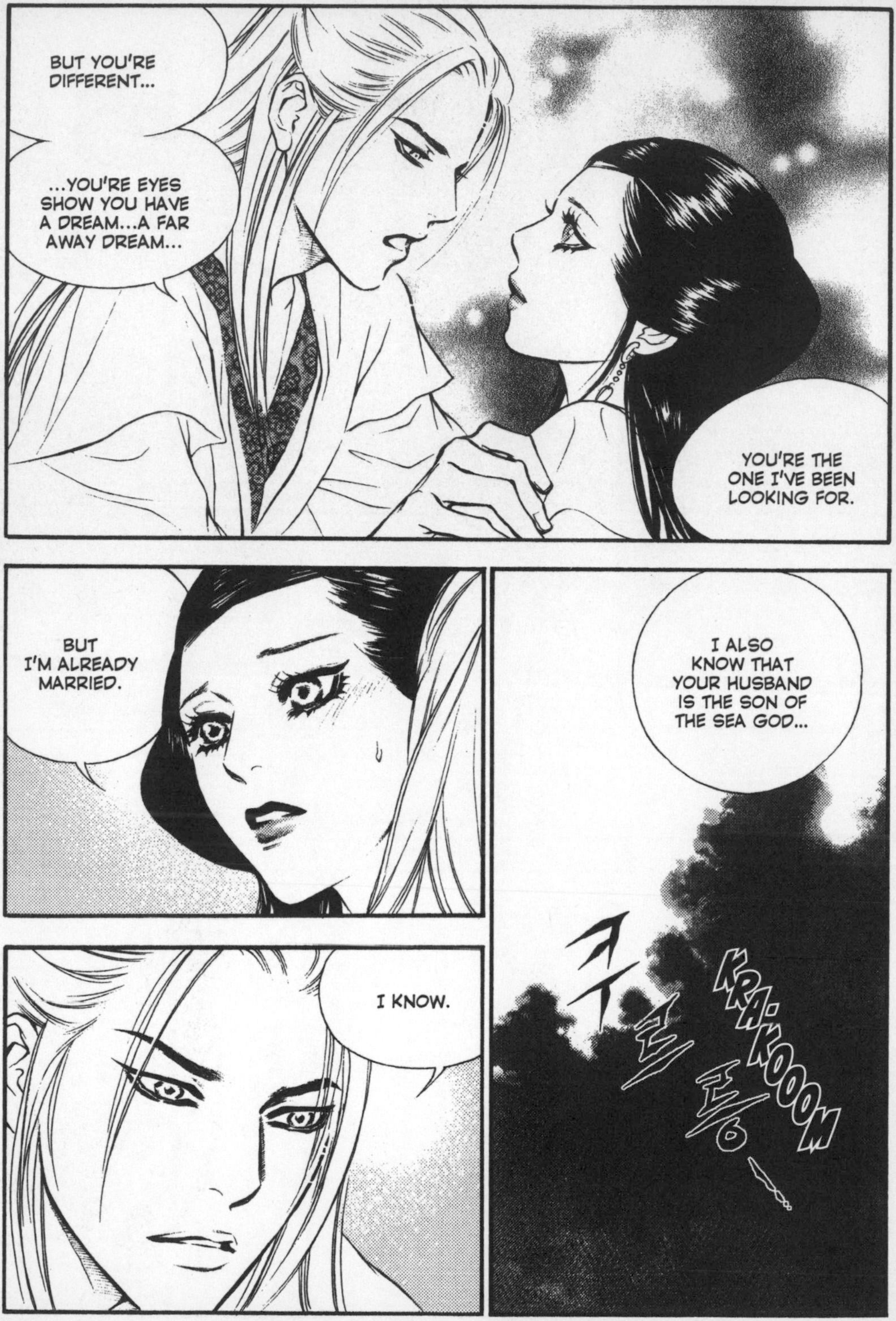
BUT YOU'RE DIFFERENT...
...YOU'RE EYES SHOW YOU HAVE A DREAM...A FAR AWAY DREAM...
YOU'RE THE ONE I'VE BEEN LOOKING FOR.
BUT I'M ALREADY MARRIED.
I KNOW.
I ALSO KNOW THAT YOUR HUSBAND IS THE SON OF THE SEA GOD...
KRA-KOOOM

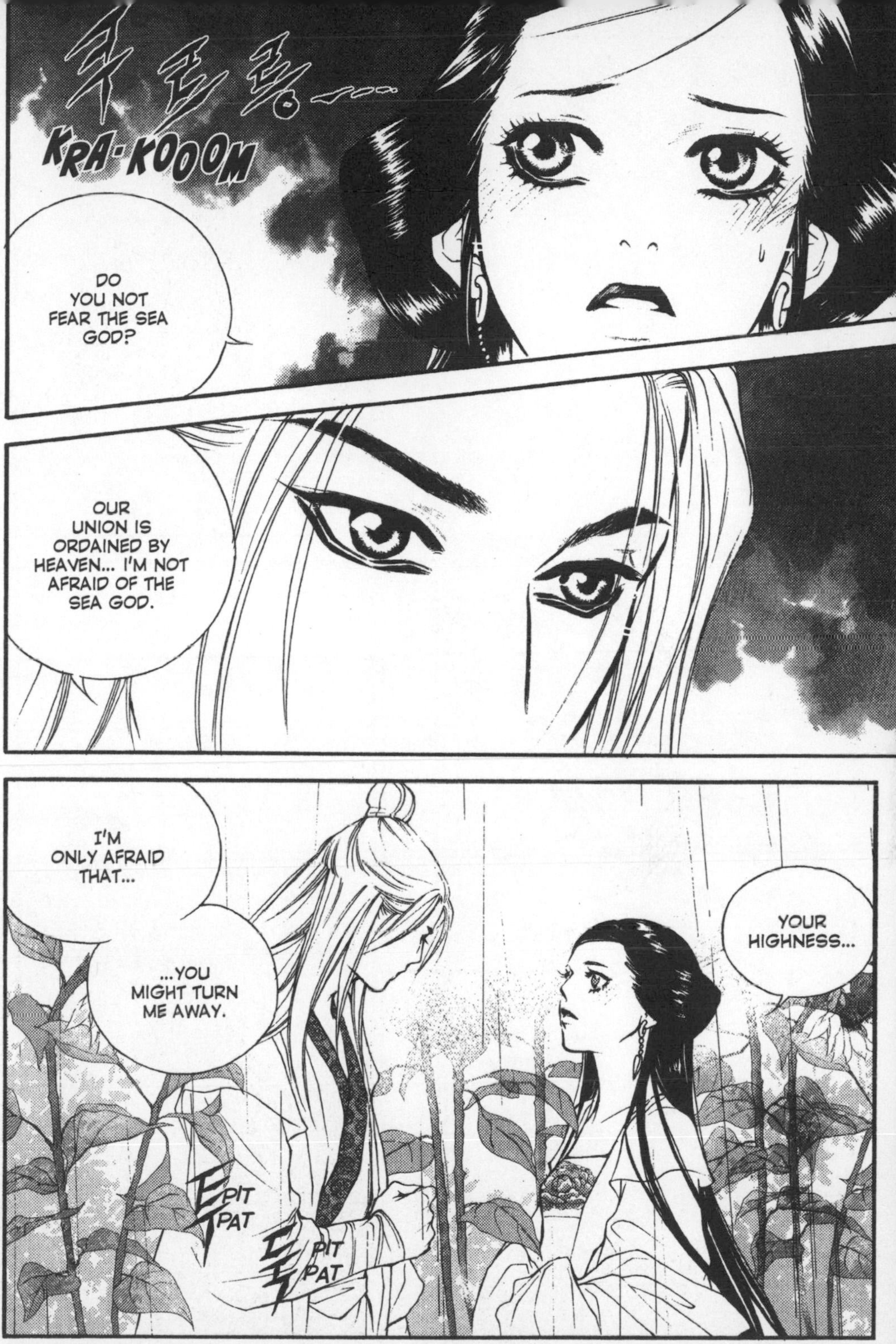
KRA-KOOOM
DO YOU NOT FEAR THE SEA GOD?
OUR UNION IS ORDAINED BY HEAVEN... I'M NOT AFRAID OF THE SEA GOD.
I'M ONLY AFRAID THAT...
...YOU MIGHT TURN ME AWAY.
PIT PAT
PIT PAT
YOUR HIGHNESS...

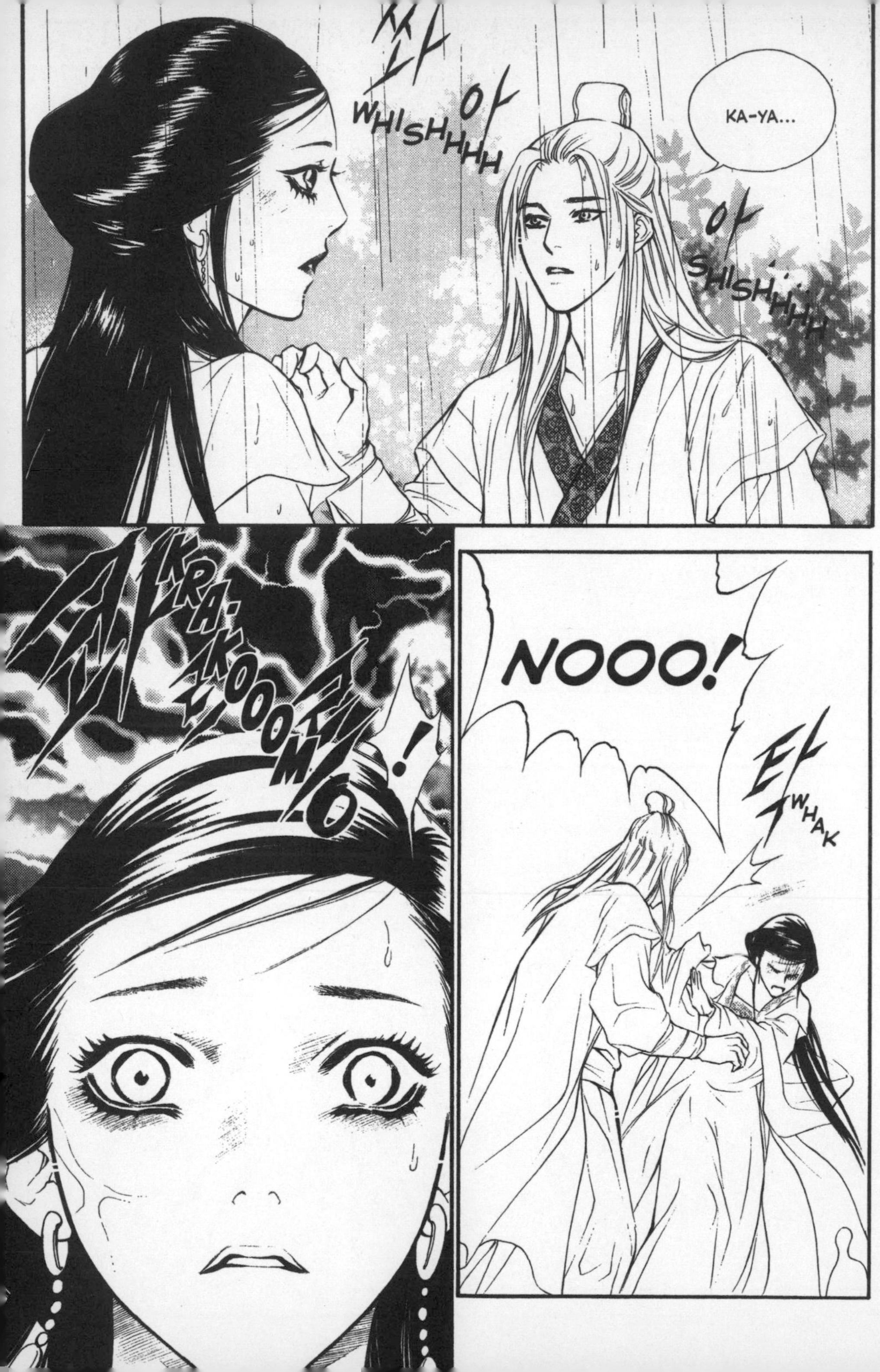
WHISHHHH
KA-YA...
SHISHHHH
KRA-KOOOOM
!
NOOO!
WHAK

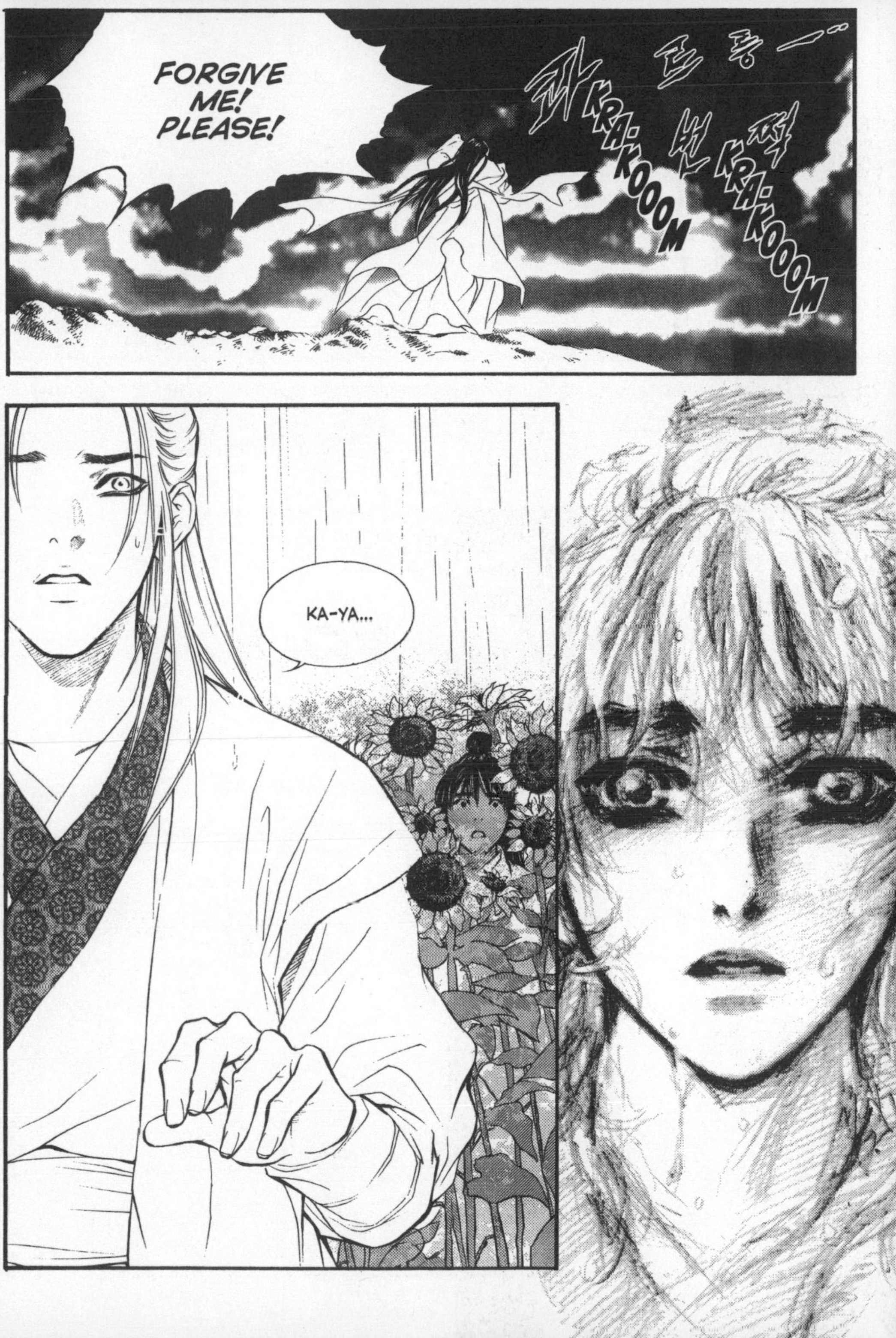
FORGIVE ME! PLEASE!
콰르릉ㅡ
KRA-KOOOM
번쩍
KRA-KOOOM
KA-YA...

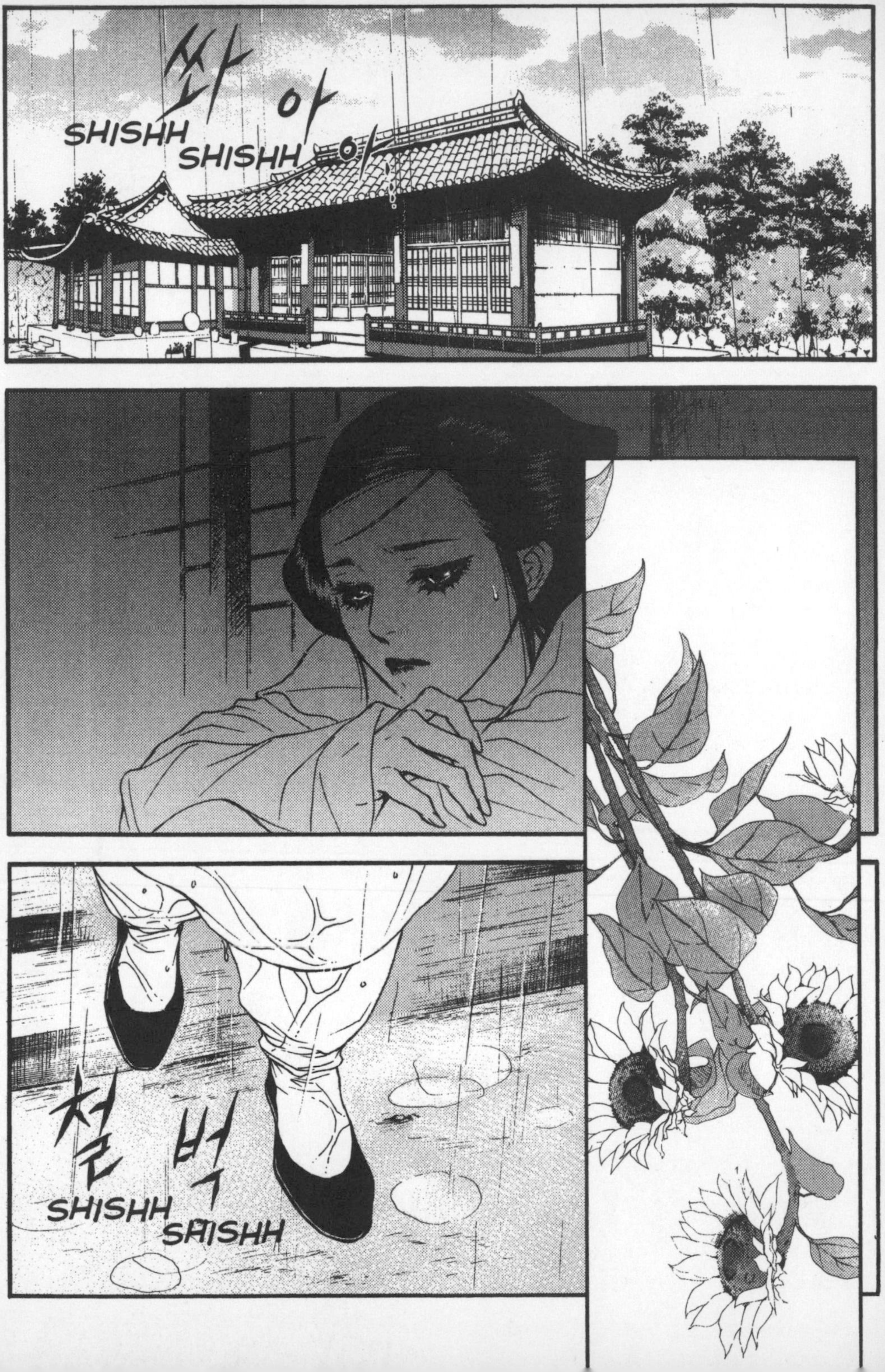
쏴아아
SHISHH
SHISHH
철벅
SHISHH
SHISHH

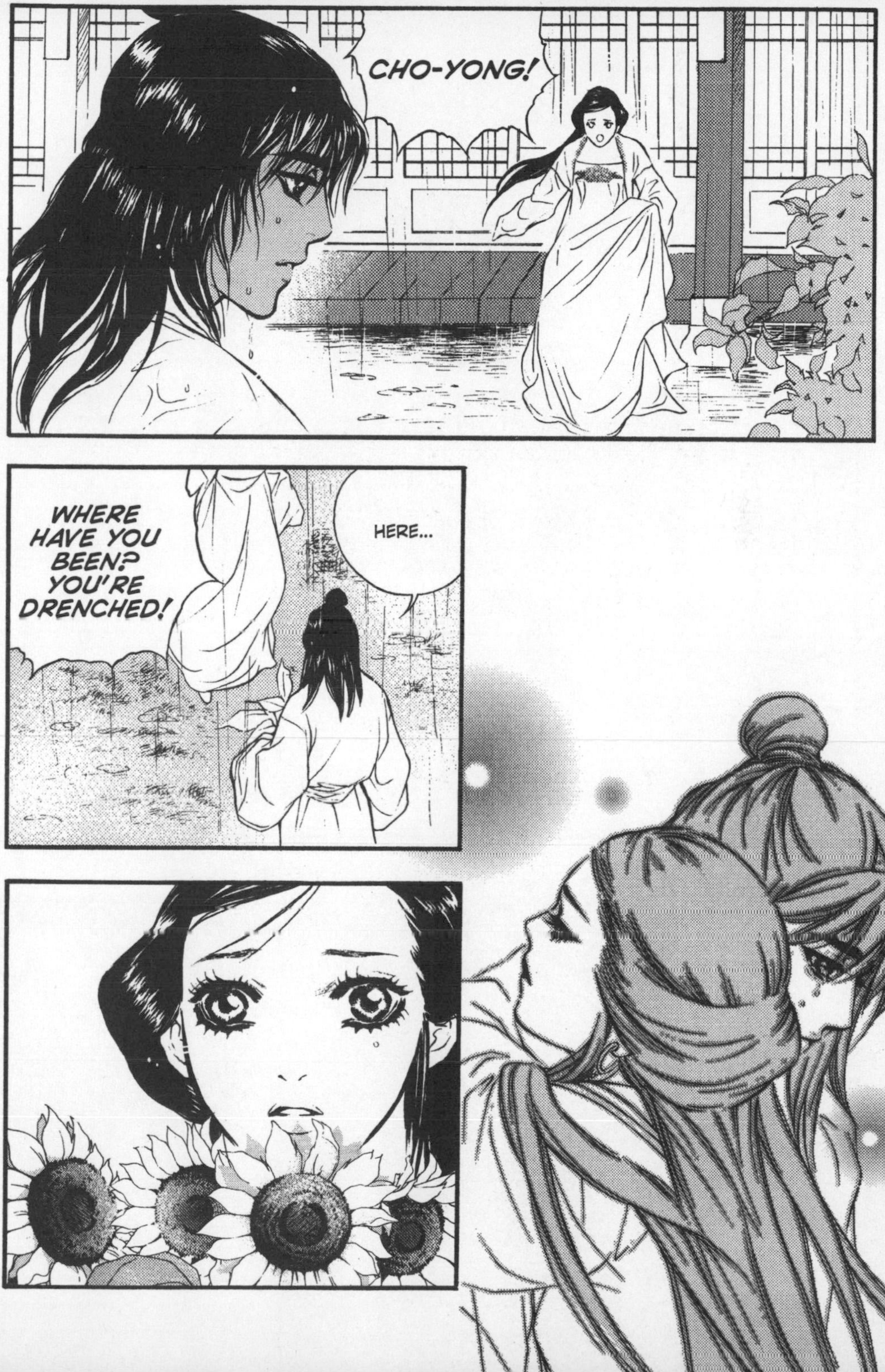
CHO-YONG!
WHERE HAVE YOU BEEN? YOU'RE DRENCHED!
HERE...

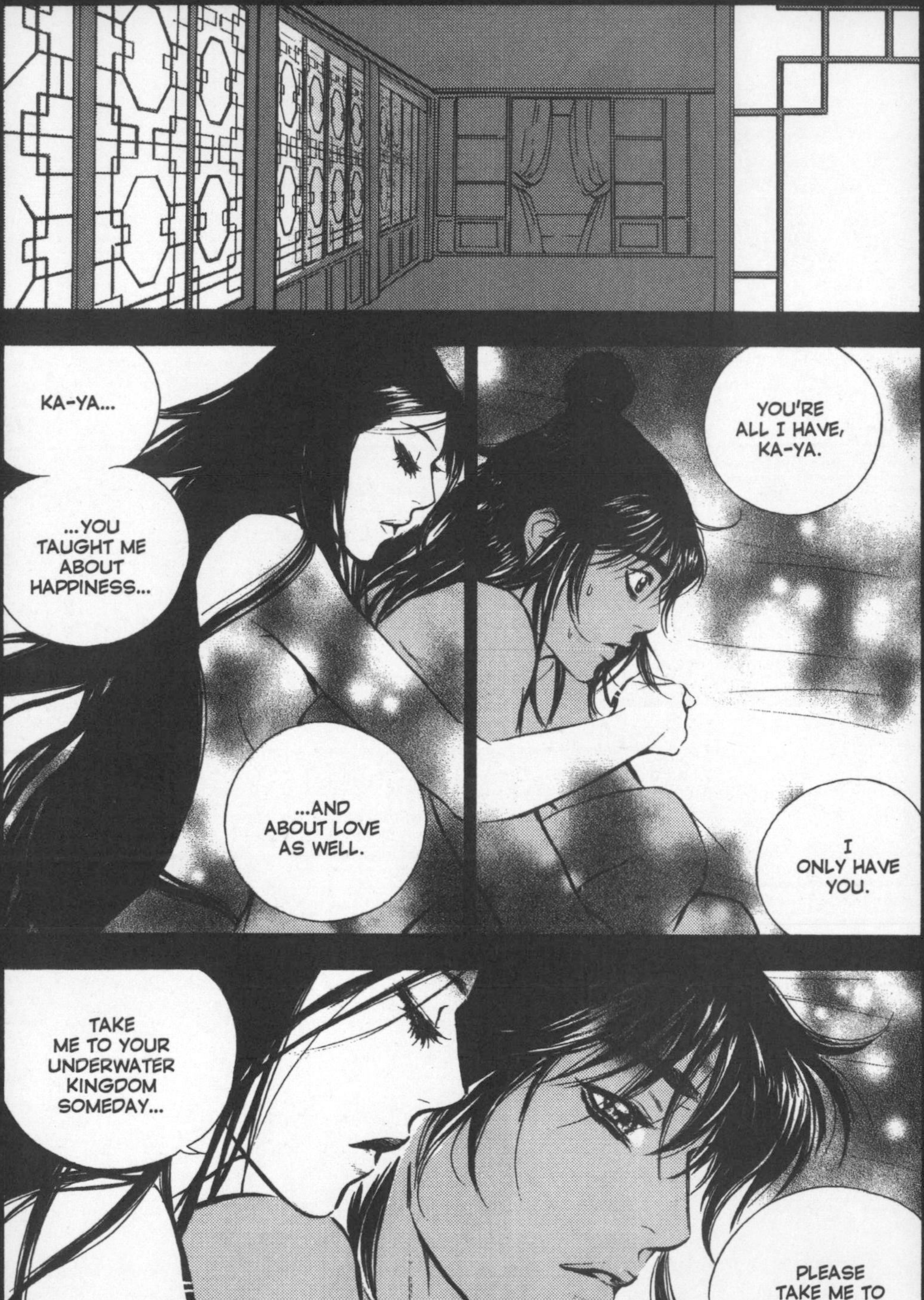
KA-YA...
...YOU TAUGHT ME ABOUT HAPPINESS...
...AND ABOUT LOVE AS WELL.
YOU'RE ALL I HAVE, KA-YA.
I ONLY HAVE YOU.
TAKE ME TO YOUR UNDERWATER KINGDOM SOMEDAY...
PLEASE TAKE ME TO YOUR PALACE...

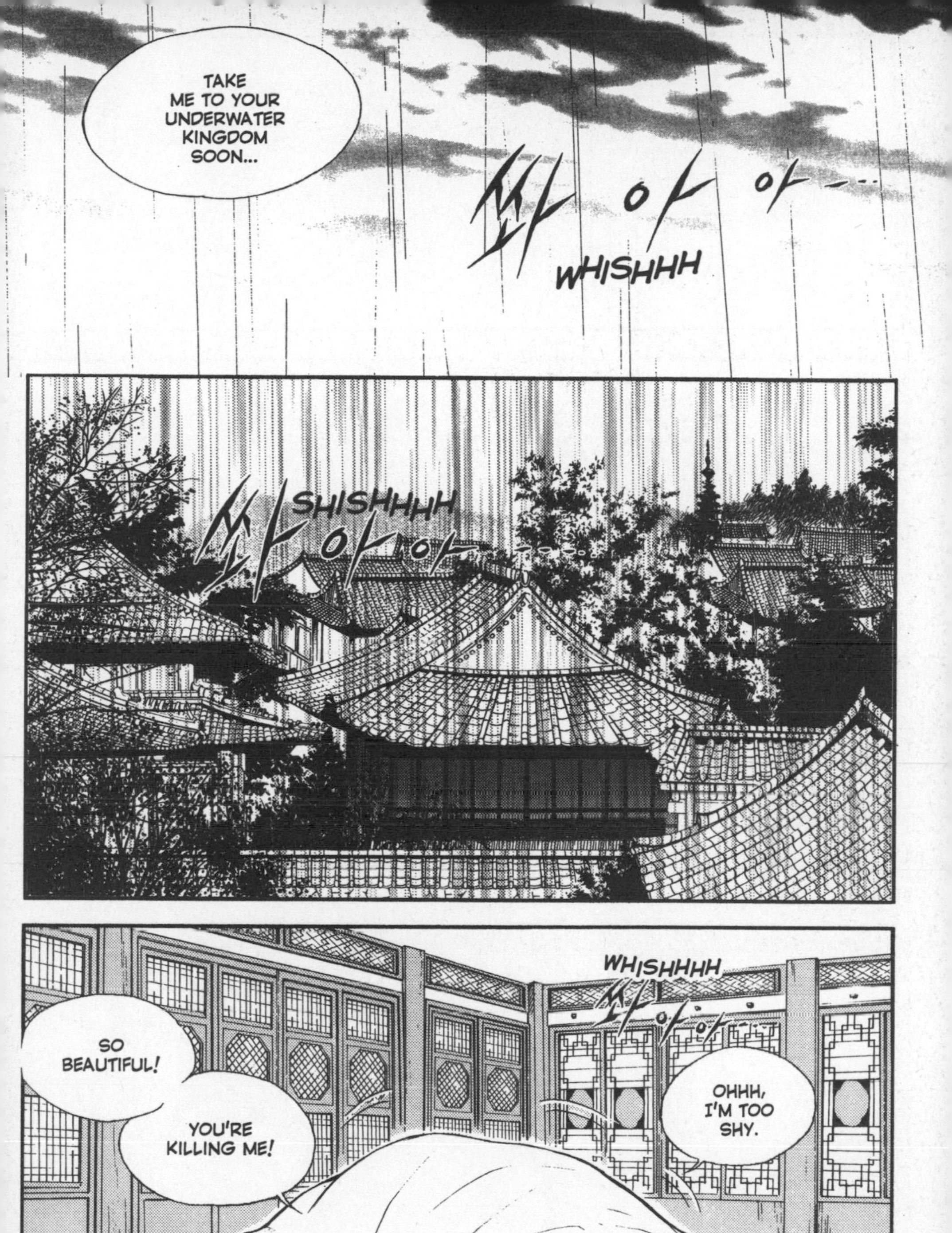
TAKE ME TO YOUR UNDERWATER KINGDOM SOON...
쏴아아-...
WHISHHH
쏴아아-...
SHISHHHH
WHISHHHH
쏴아아-...
SO BEAUTIFUL!
YOU'RE KILLING ME!
OHHH, I'M TOO SHY.

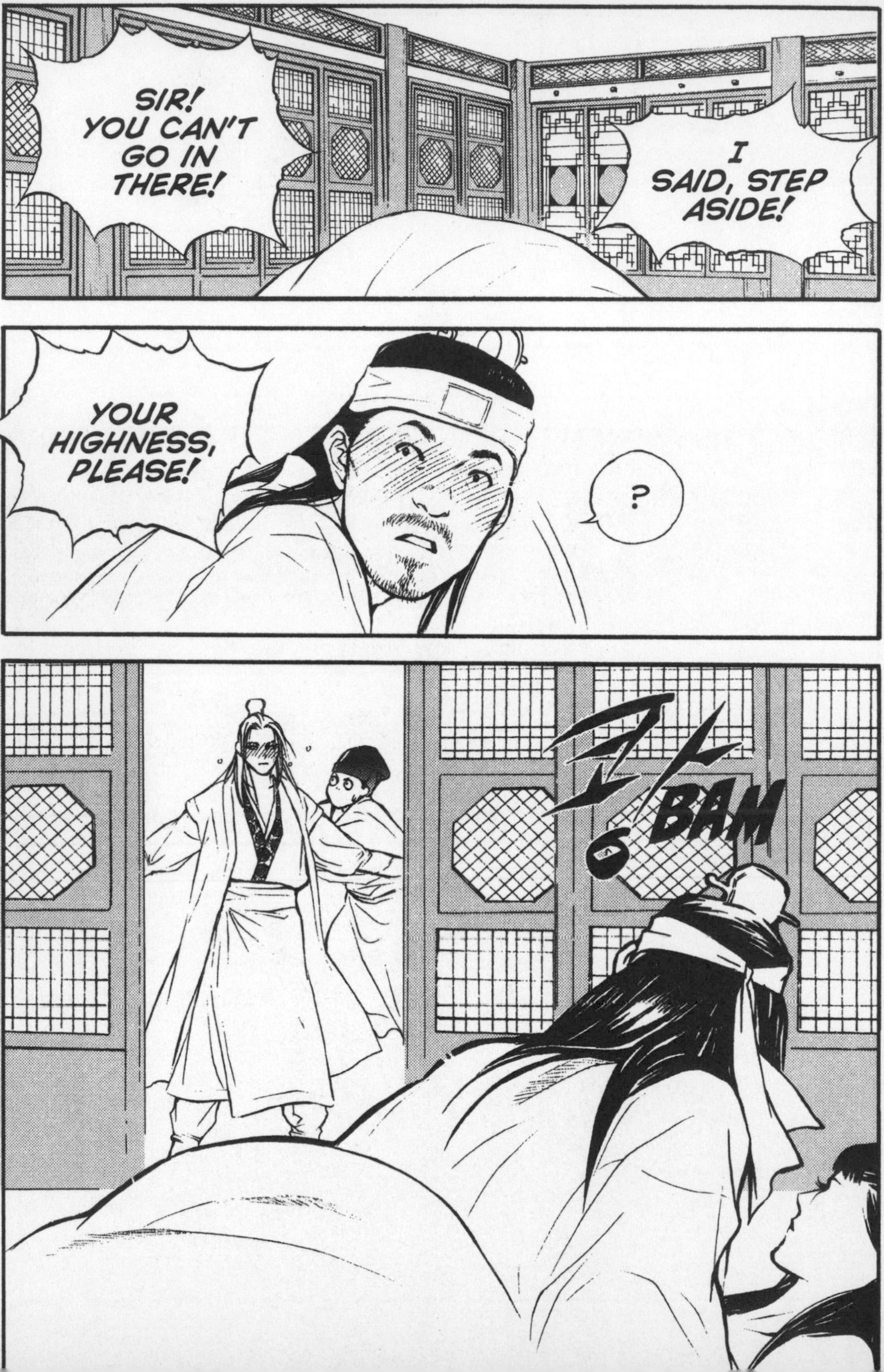
SIR! YOU CAN'T GO IN THERE!
I SAID, STEP ASIDE!
YOUR HIGHNESS, PLEASE!
?
BAM

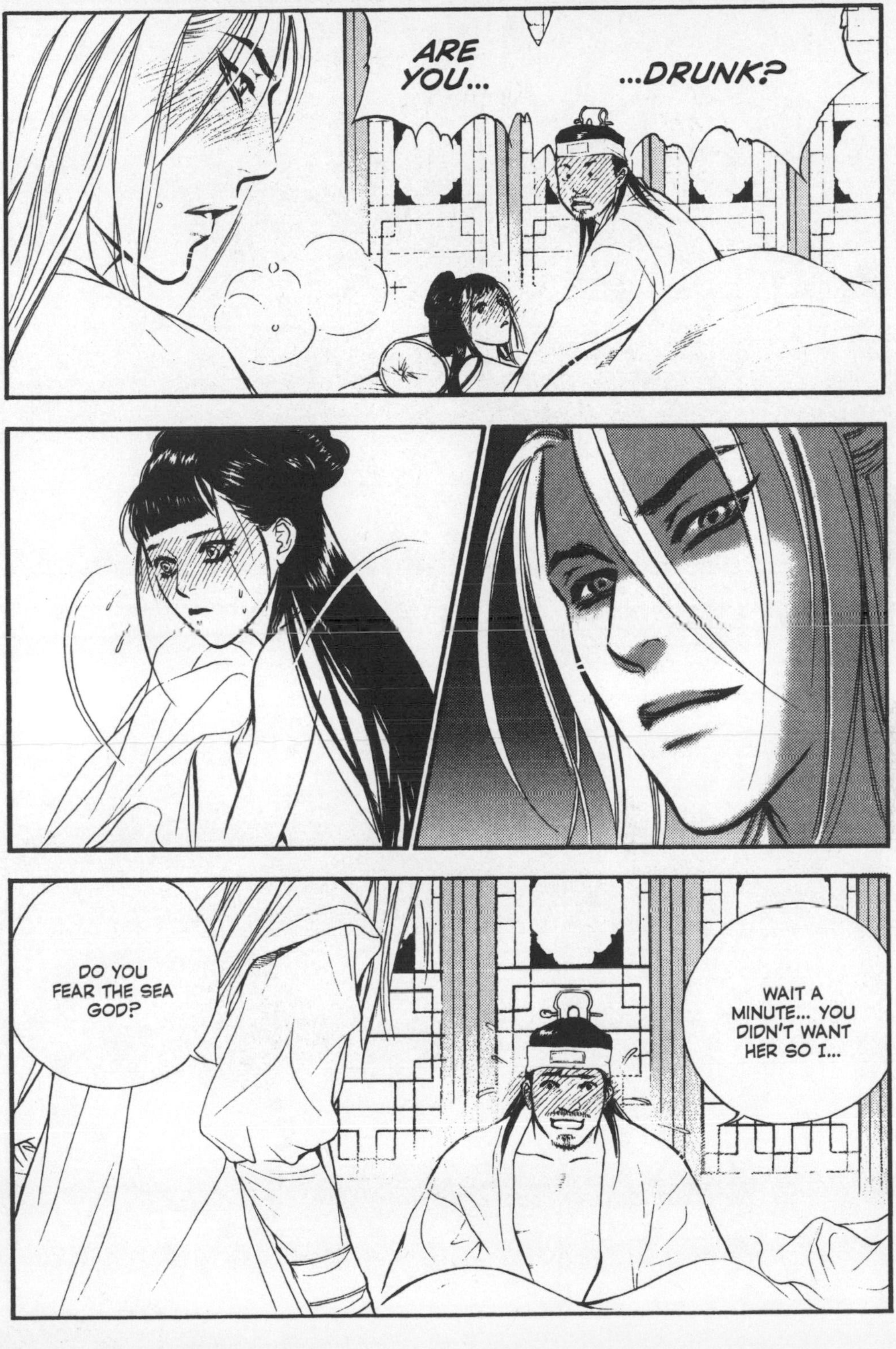
ARE YOU...
...DRUNK?
DO YOU FEAR THE SEA GOD?
WAIT A MINUTE... YOU DIDN'T WANT HER SO I...

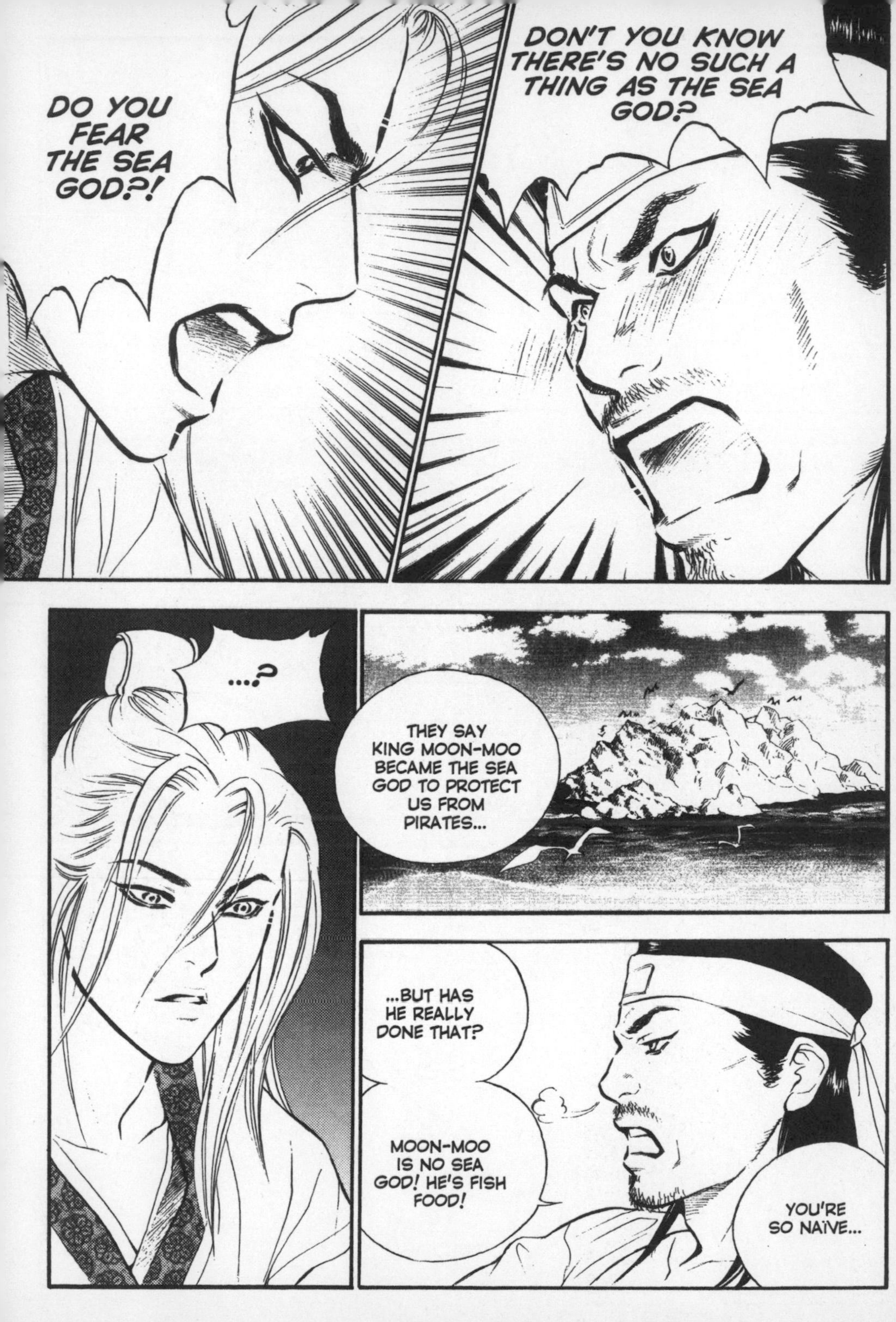
DO YOU FEAR THE SEA GOD?!
DON'T YOU KNOW THERE'S NO SUCH A THING AS THE SEA GOD?
...?
THEY SAY KING MOON-MOO BECAME THE SEA GOD TO PROTECT US FROM PIRATES...
...BUT HAS HE REALLY DONE THAT?
MOON-MOO IS NO SEA GOD! HE'S FISH FOOD!
YOU'RE SO NAÏVE...

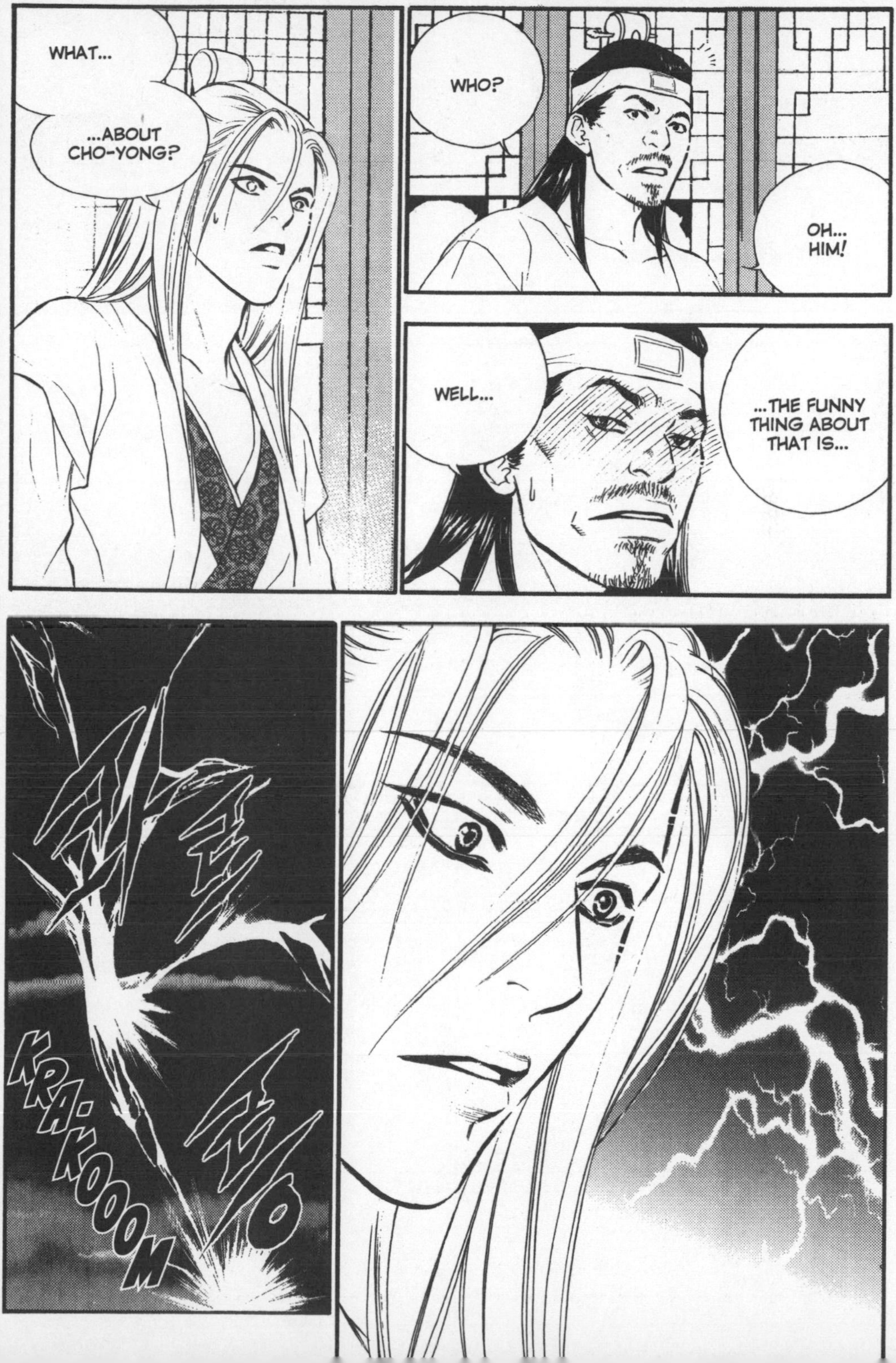
WHAT...
...ABOUT CHO-YONG?
WHO?
OH... HIM!
WELL...
...THE FUNNY THING ABOUT THAT IS...
KRA-KOOOM

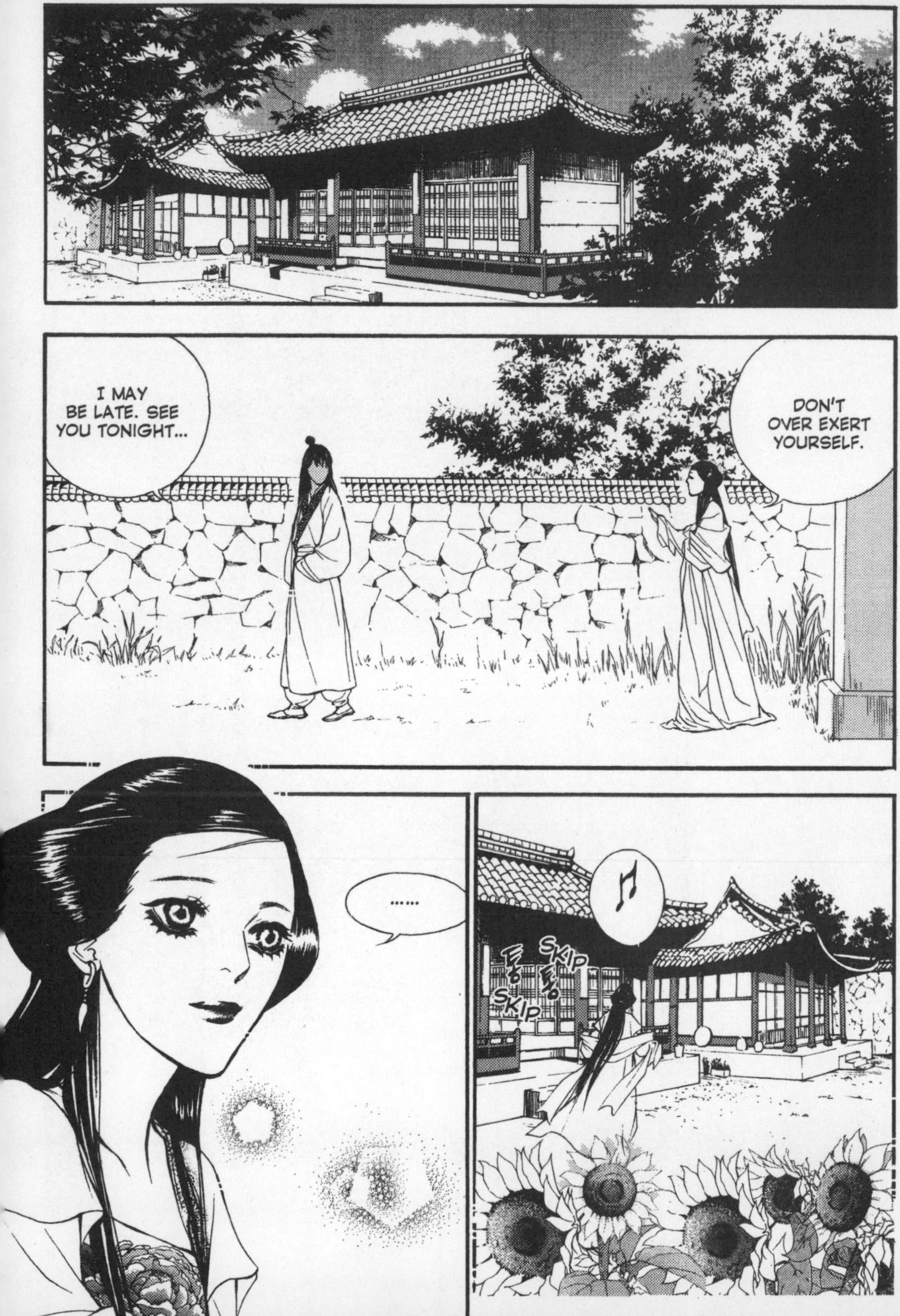
I MAY BE LATE. SEE YOU TONIGHT...
DON'T OVER EXERT YOURSELF.
......
SKIP
SKIP

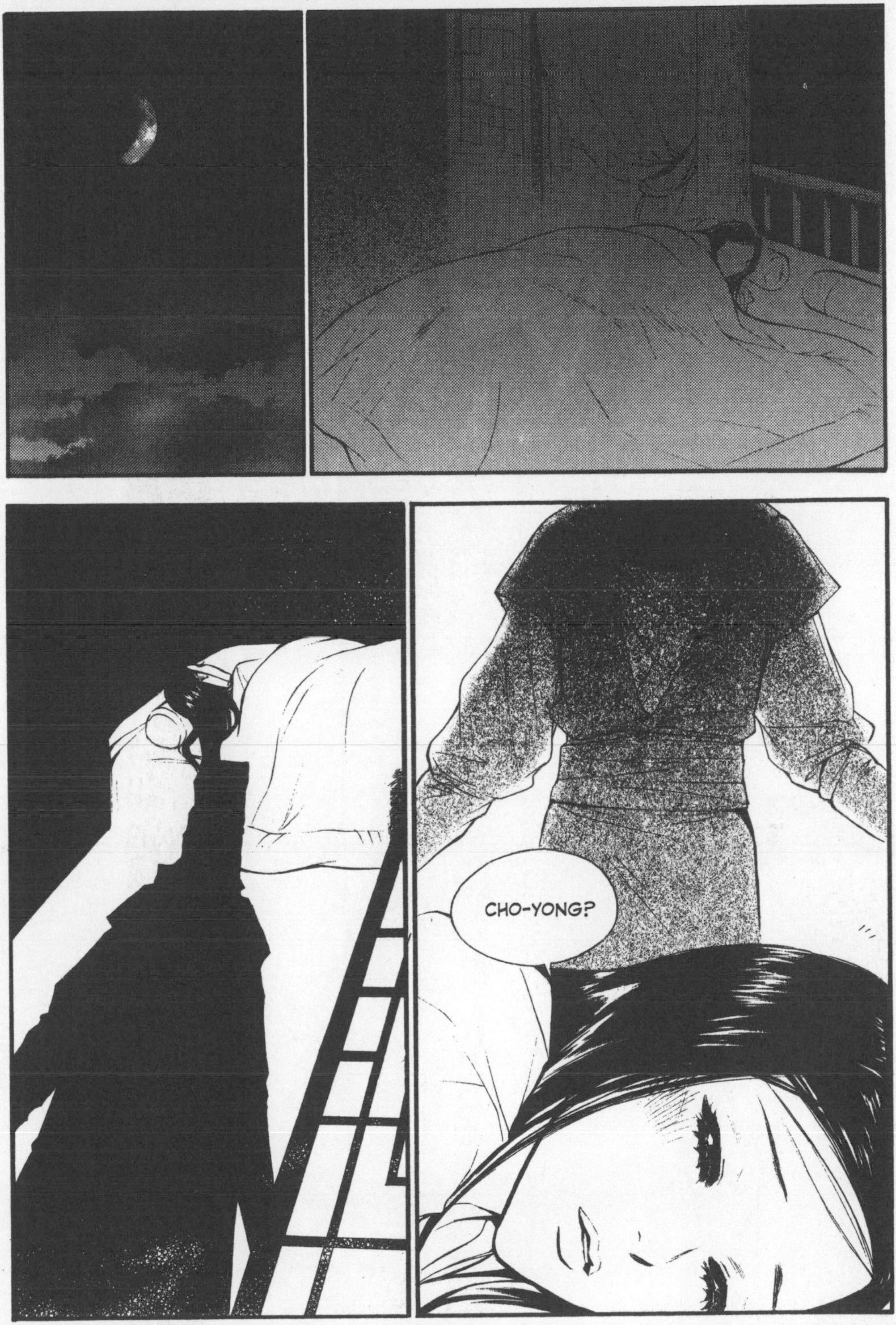
CHO-YONG?

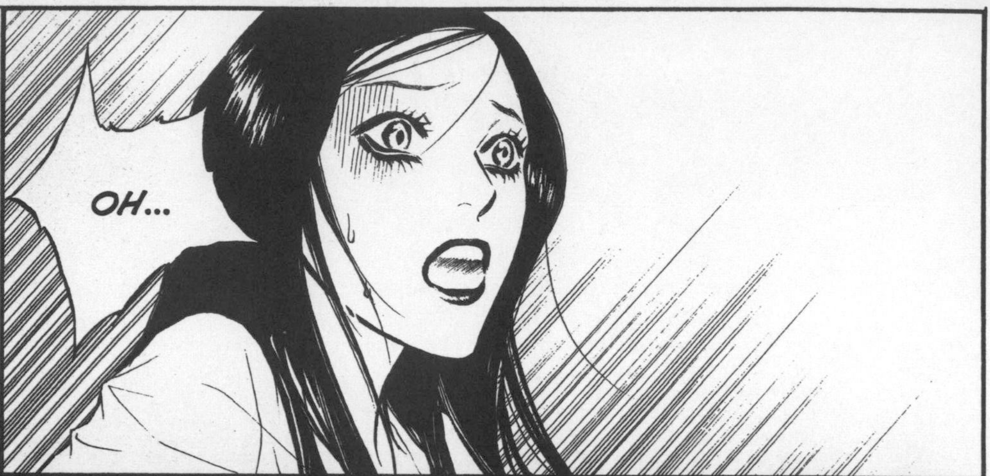
OH...

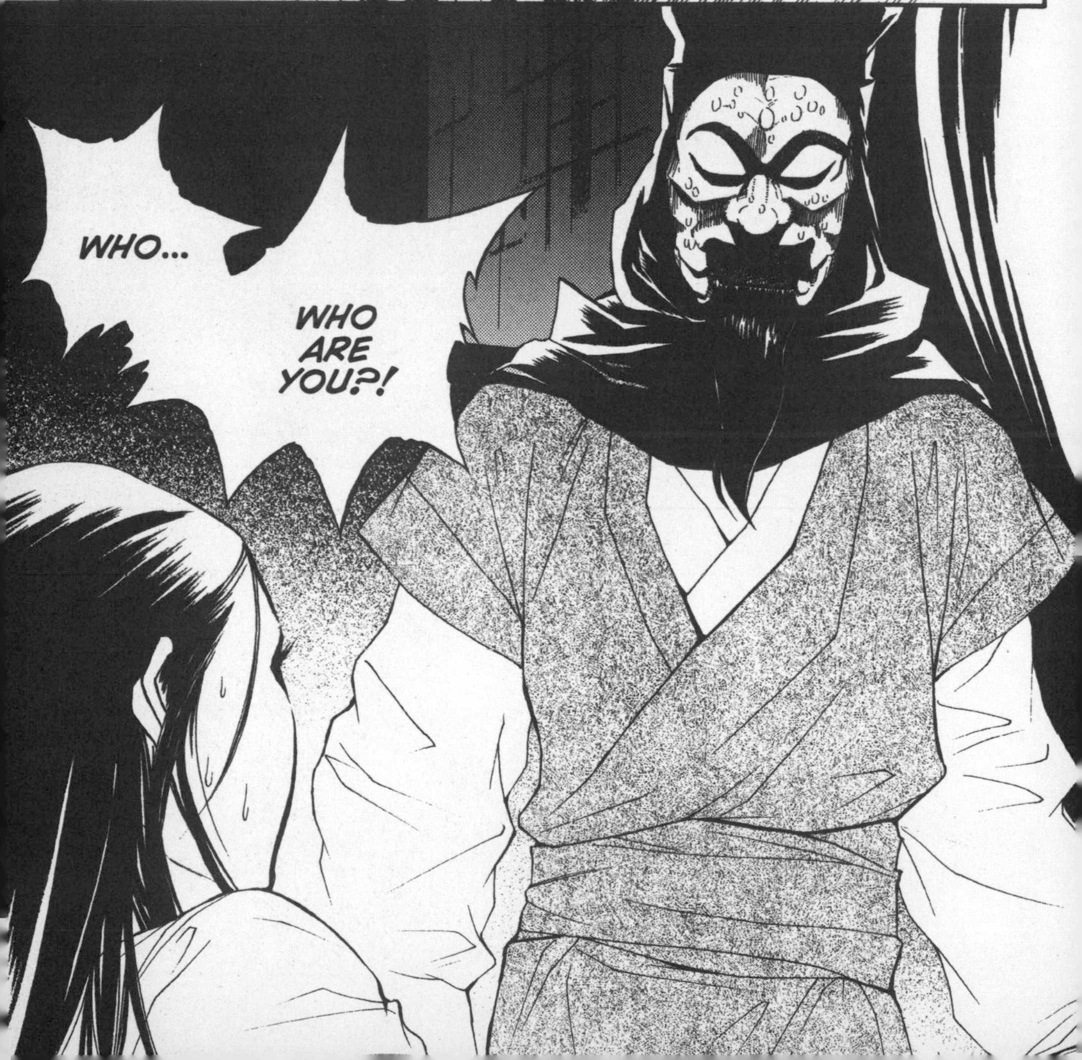
WHO...
WHO ARE YOU?!

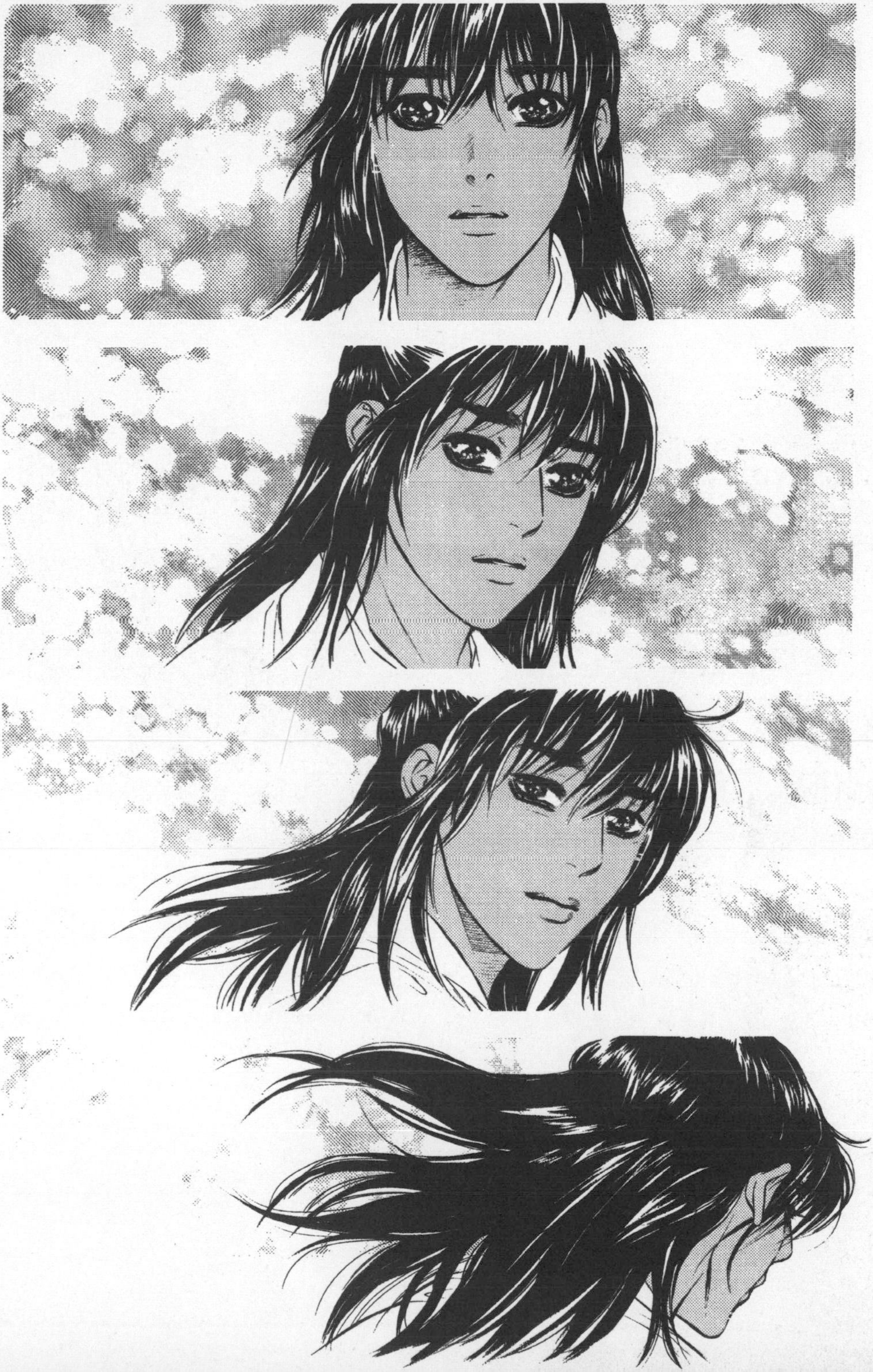

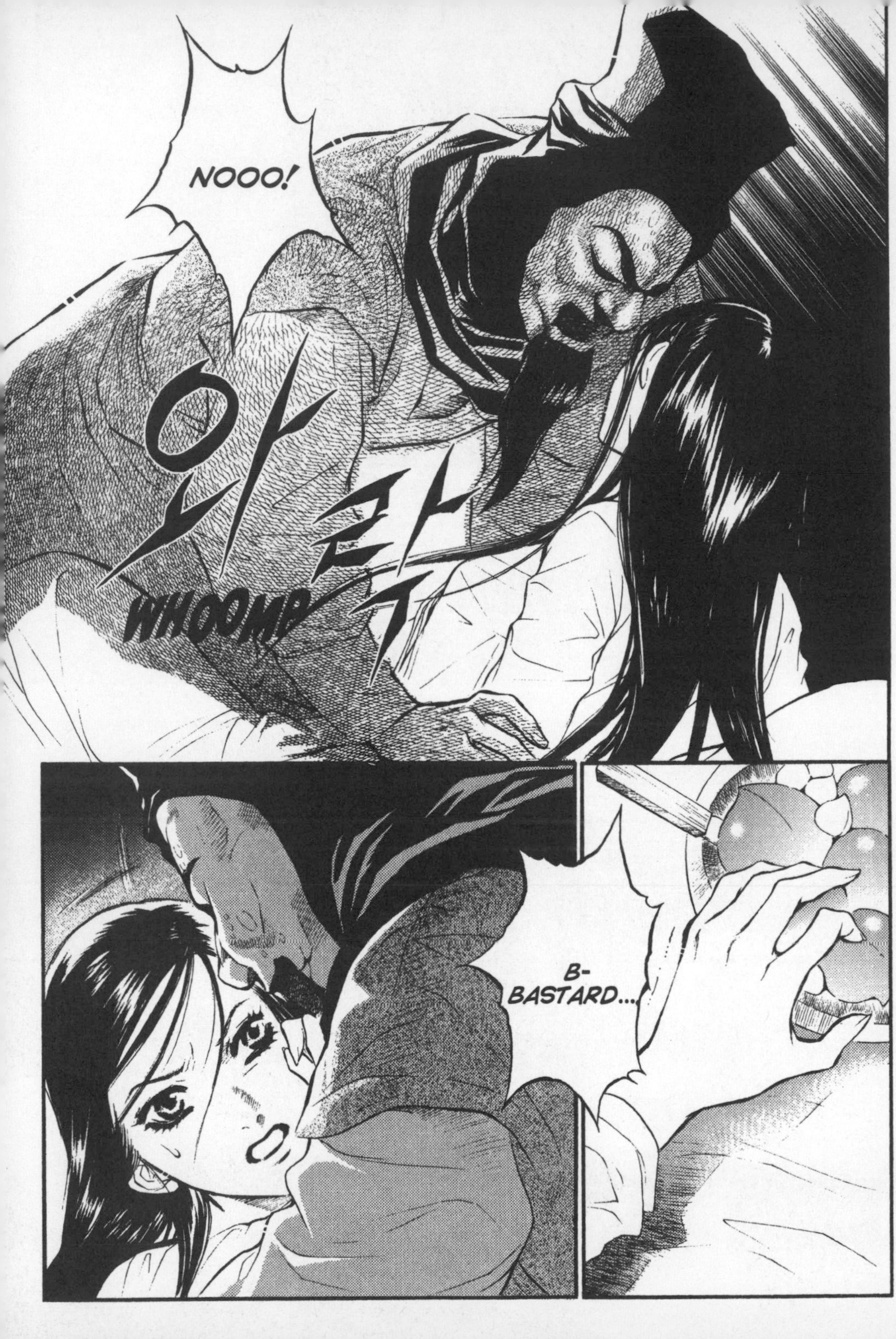
NOOO!
와락
WHOOMP
B- BASTARD...

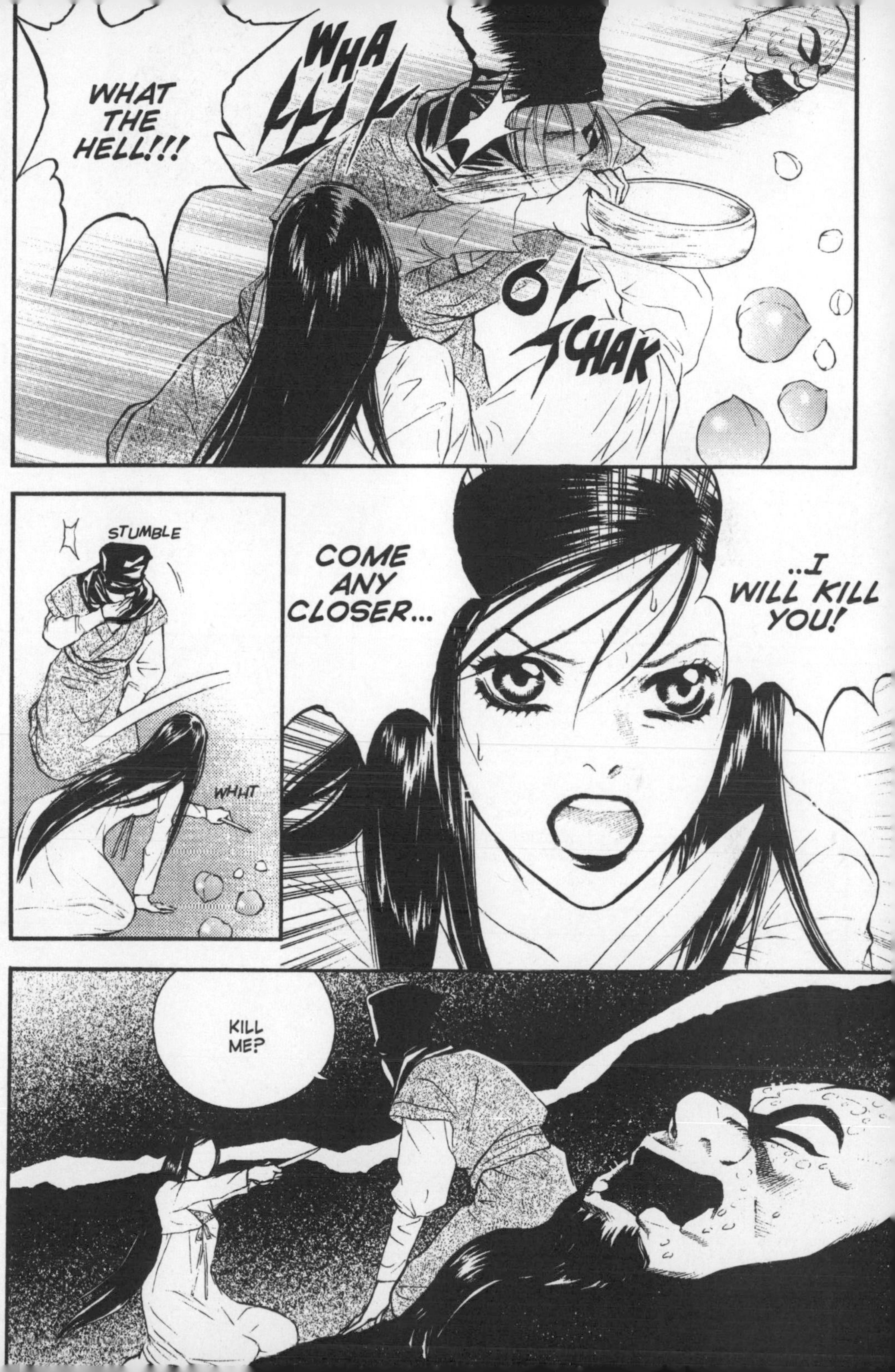
WHAT THE HELL!!!
WHA
CHAK
STUMBLE
WHHT
COME ANY CLOSER...
..I WILL KILL YOU!
KILL ME?

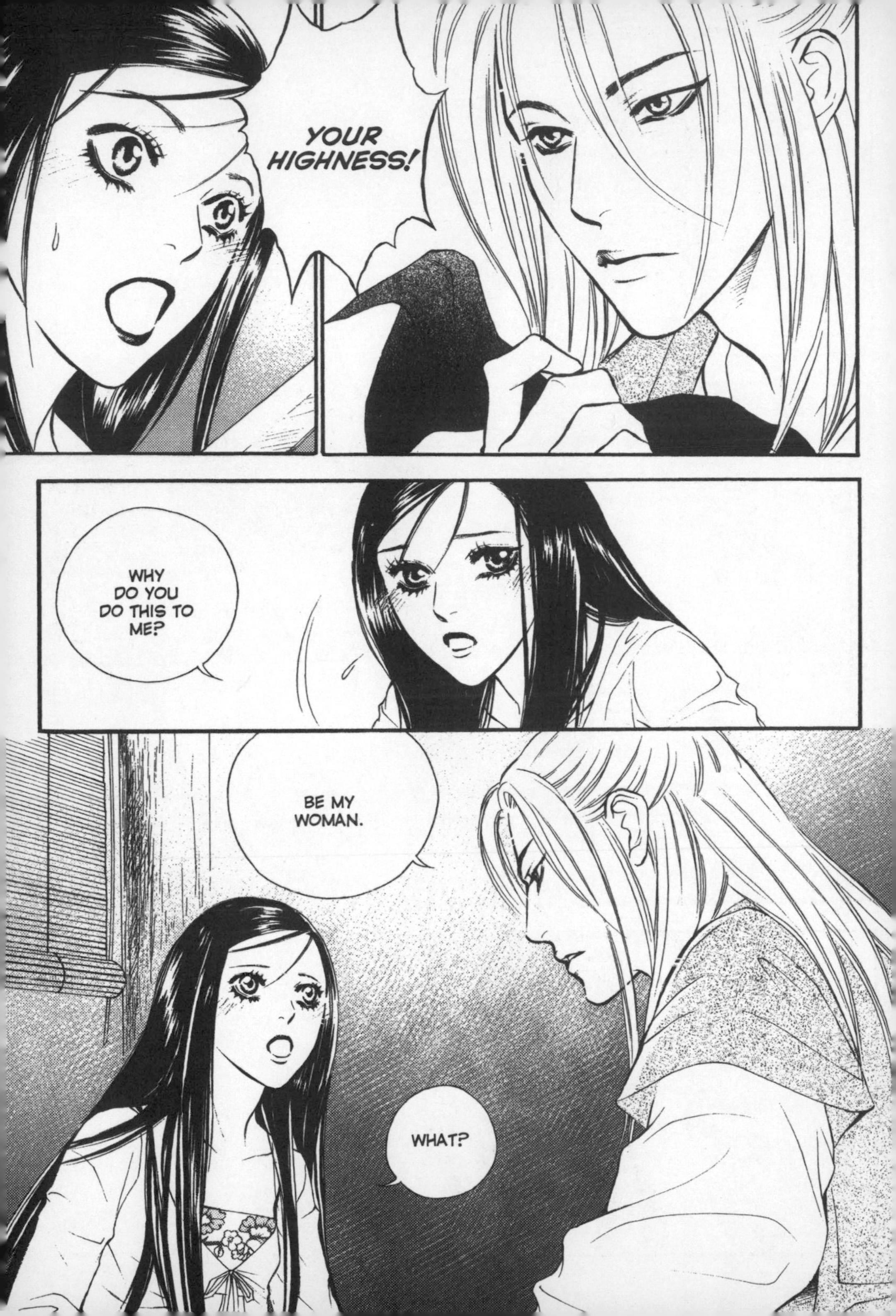
YOUR HIGHNESS!
WHY DO YOU DO THIS TO ME?
BE MY WOMAN.
WHAT?

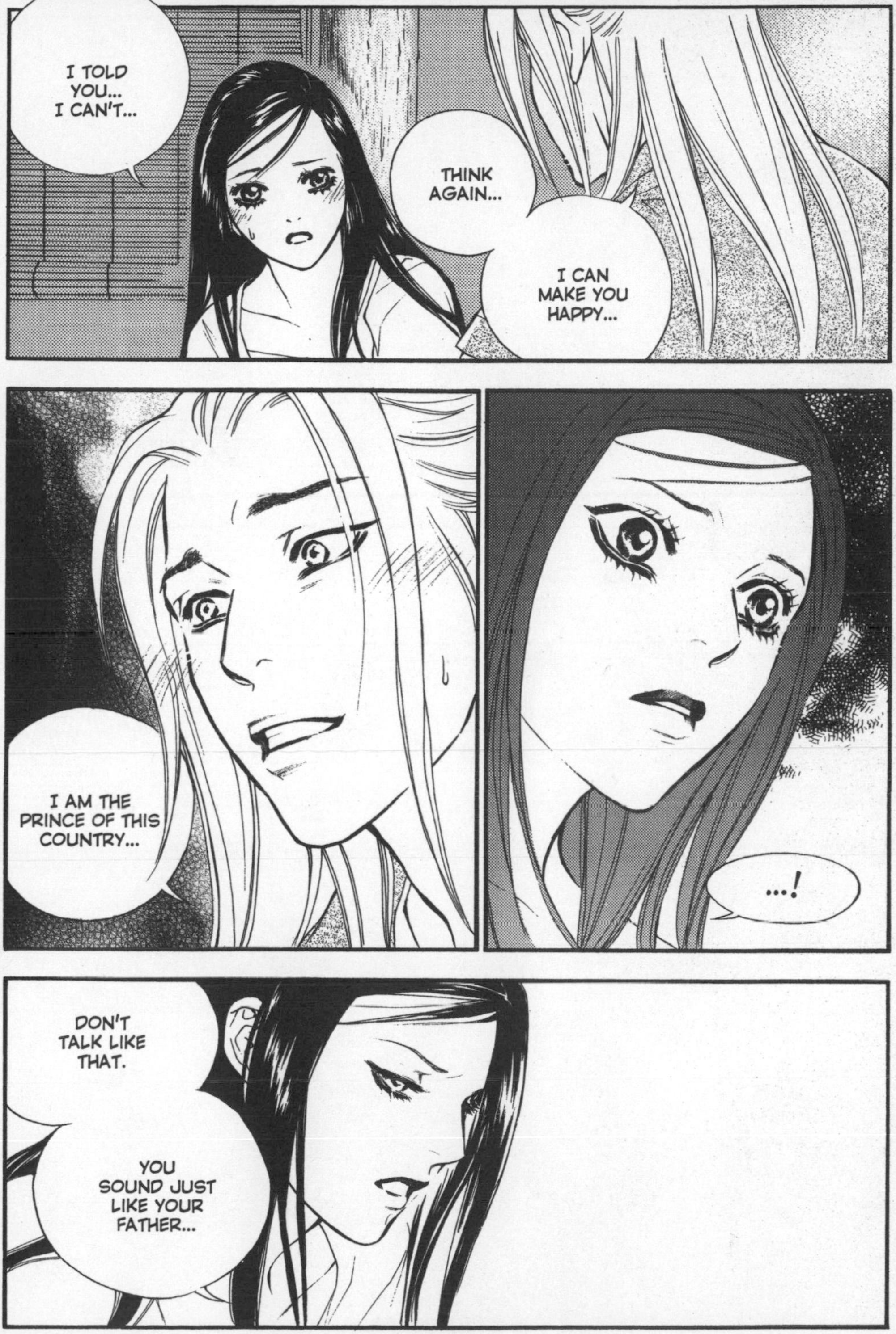
I TOLD YOU... I CAN'T...
THINK AGAIN...
I CAN MAKE YOU HAPPY...
I AM THE PRINCE OF THIS COUNTRY...
...!
DON'T TALK LIKE THAT.
YOU SOUND JUST LIKE YOUR FATHER...

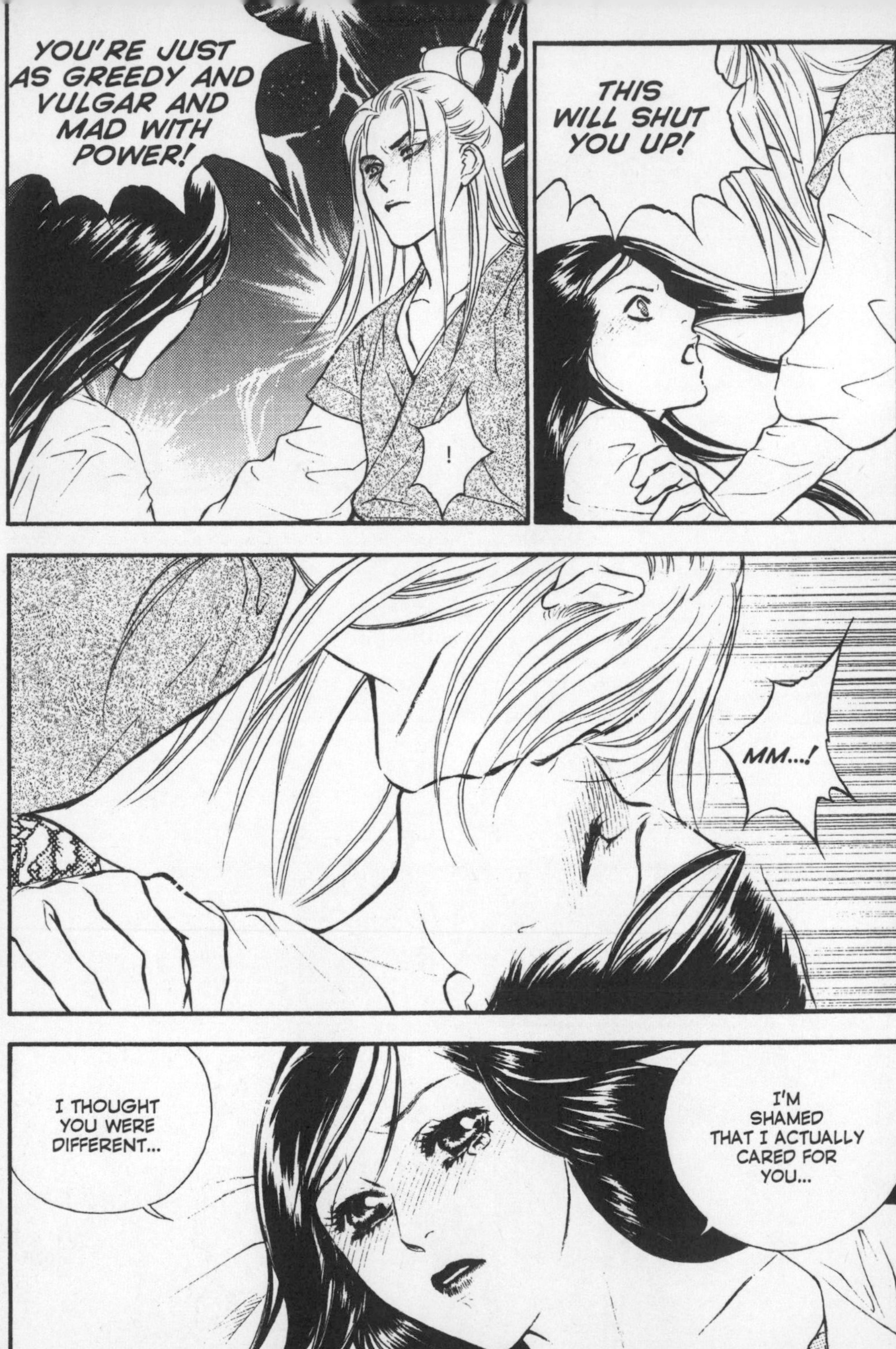
YOU'RE JUST AS GREEDY AND VULGAR AND MAD WITH POWER!
!
THIS WILL SHUT YOU UP!
MM...!
I THOUGHT YOU WERE DIFFERENT...
I'M SHAMED THAT I ACTUALLY CARED FOR YOU...

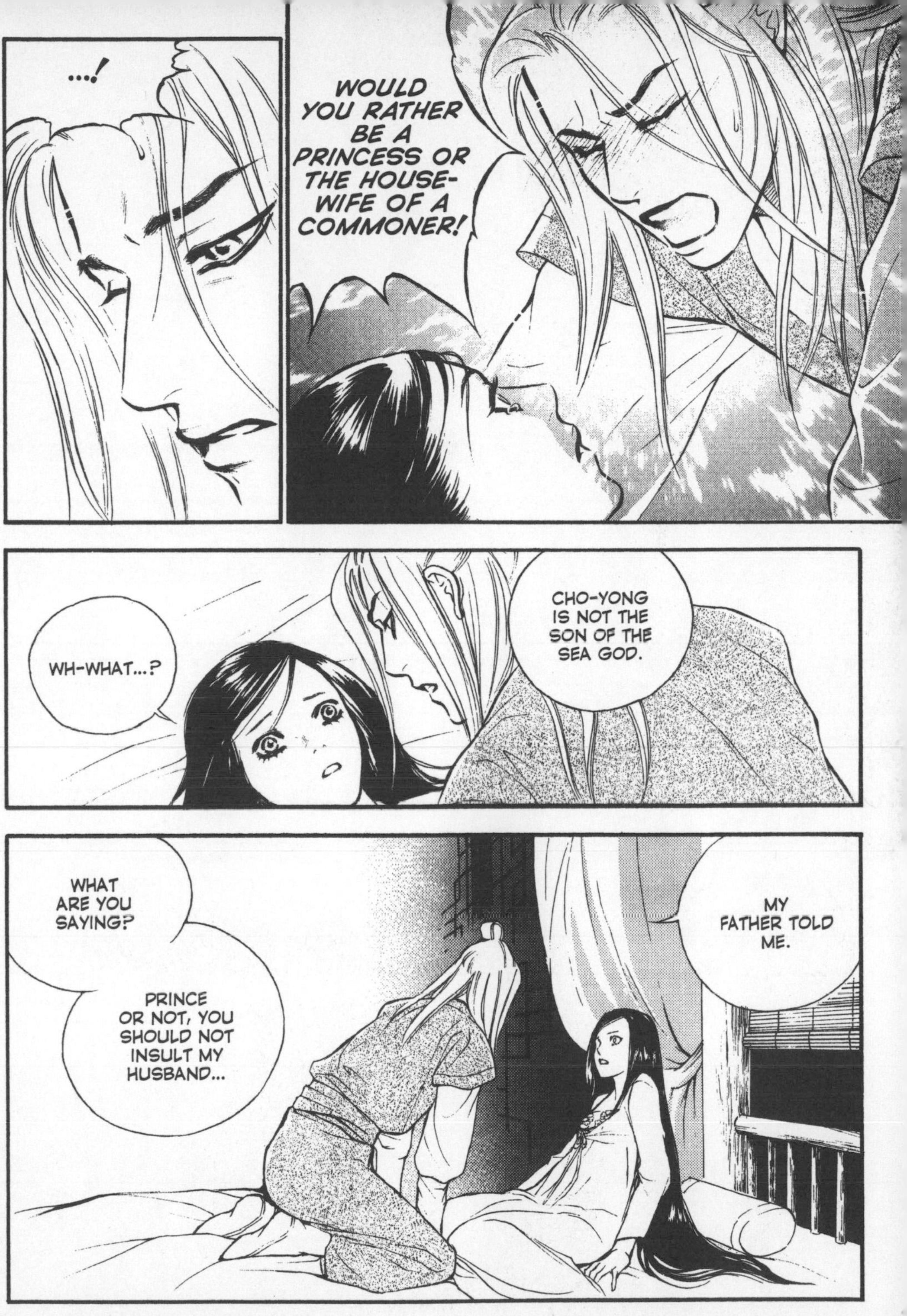
...!
WOULD YOU RATHER BE A PRINCESS OR THE HOUSE-WIFE OF A COMMONER!
WH-WHAT...?
CHO-YONG IS NOT THE SON OF THE SEA GOD.
WHAT ARE YOU SAYING?
PRINCE OR NOT, YOU SHOULD NOT INSULT MY HUSBAND...
MY FATHER TOLD ME.

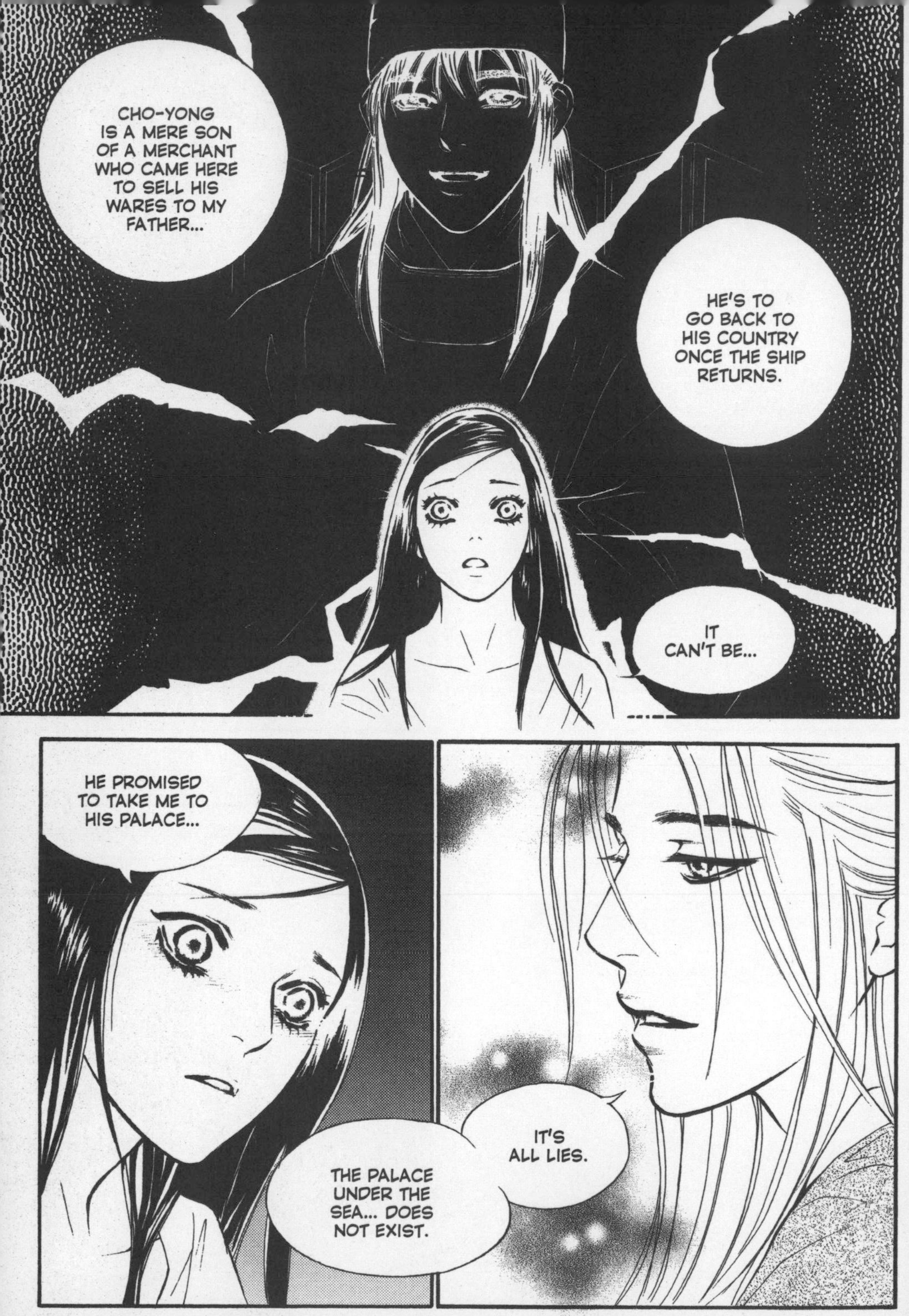
CHO-YONG IS A MERE SON OF A MERCHANT WHO CAME HERE TO SELL HIS WARES TO MY FATHER...
HE'S TO GO BACK TO HIS COUNTRY ONCE THE SHIP RETURNS.
IT CAN'T BE...
HE PROMISED TO TAKE ME TO HIS PALACE...
IT'S ALL LIES.
THE PALACE UNDER THE SEA... DOES NOT EXIST.

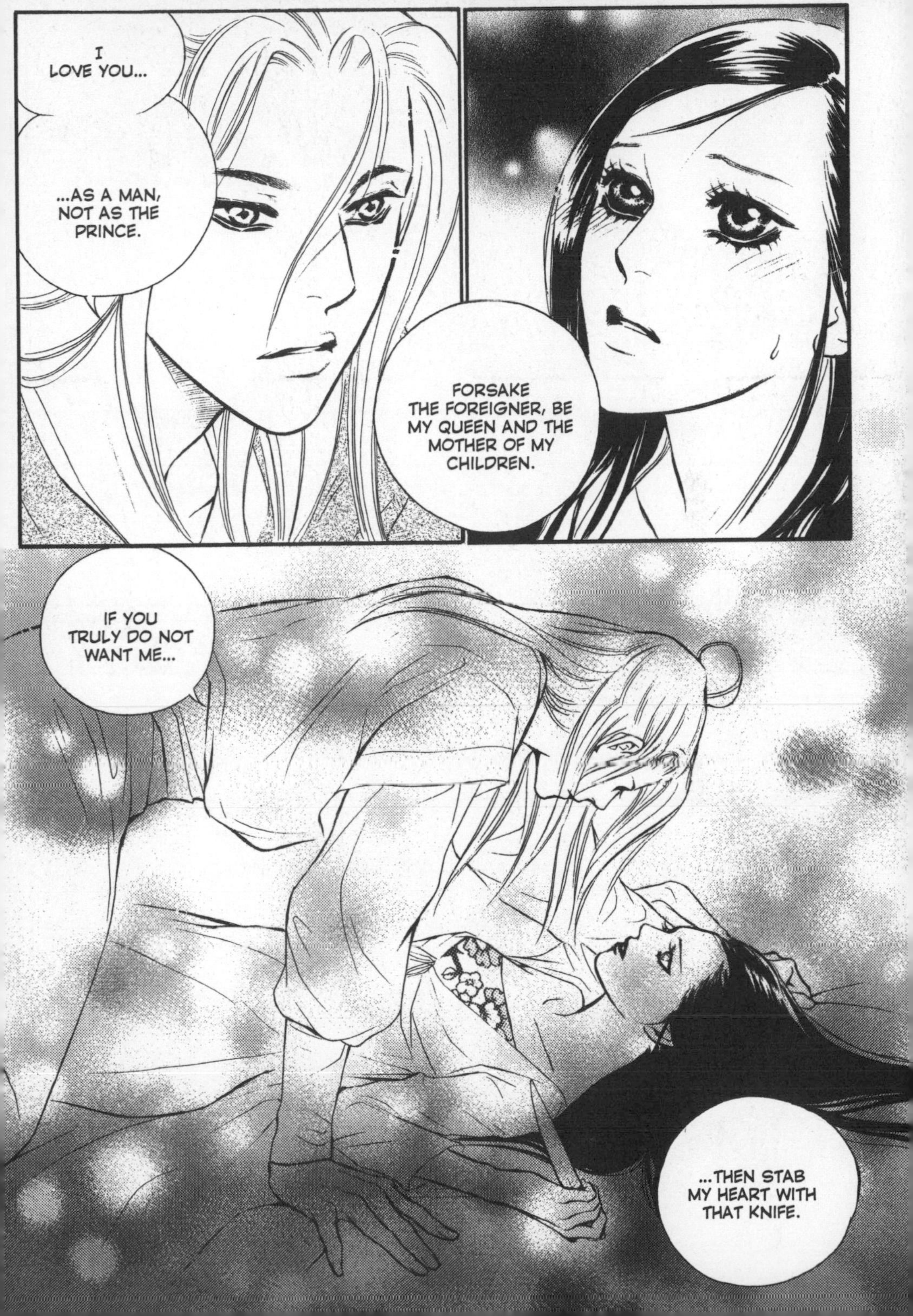
I LOVE YOU...
...AS A MAN, NOT AS THE PRINCE.
FORSAKE THE FOREIGNER, BE MY QUEEN AND THE MOTHER OF MY CHILDREN.
IF YOU TRULY DO NOT WANT ME...
...THEN STAB MY HEART WITH THAT KNIFE.

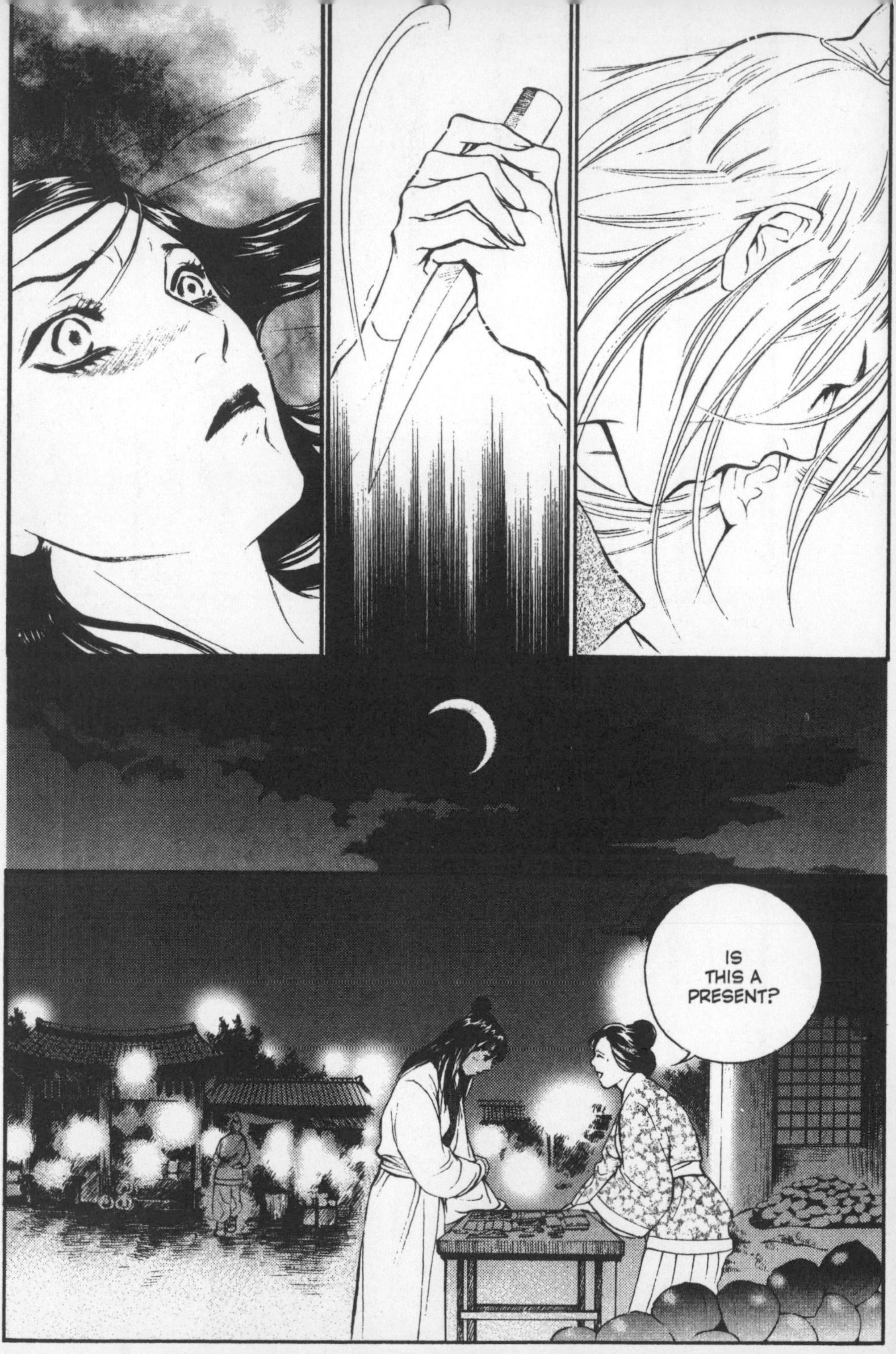
IS THIS A PRESENT?

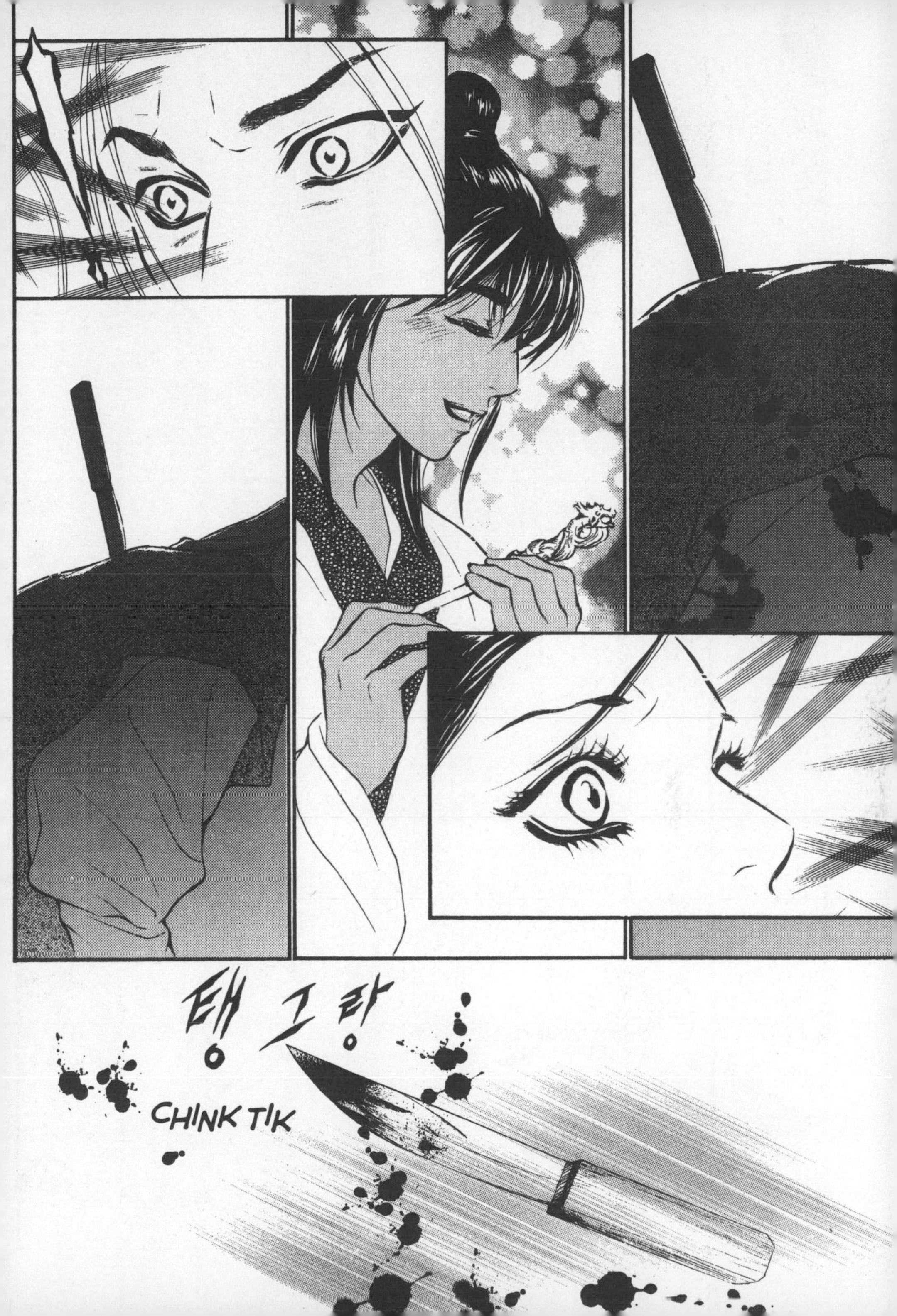

탱그랑
CHINK TIK

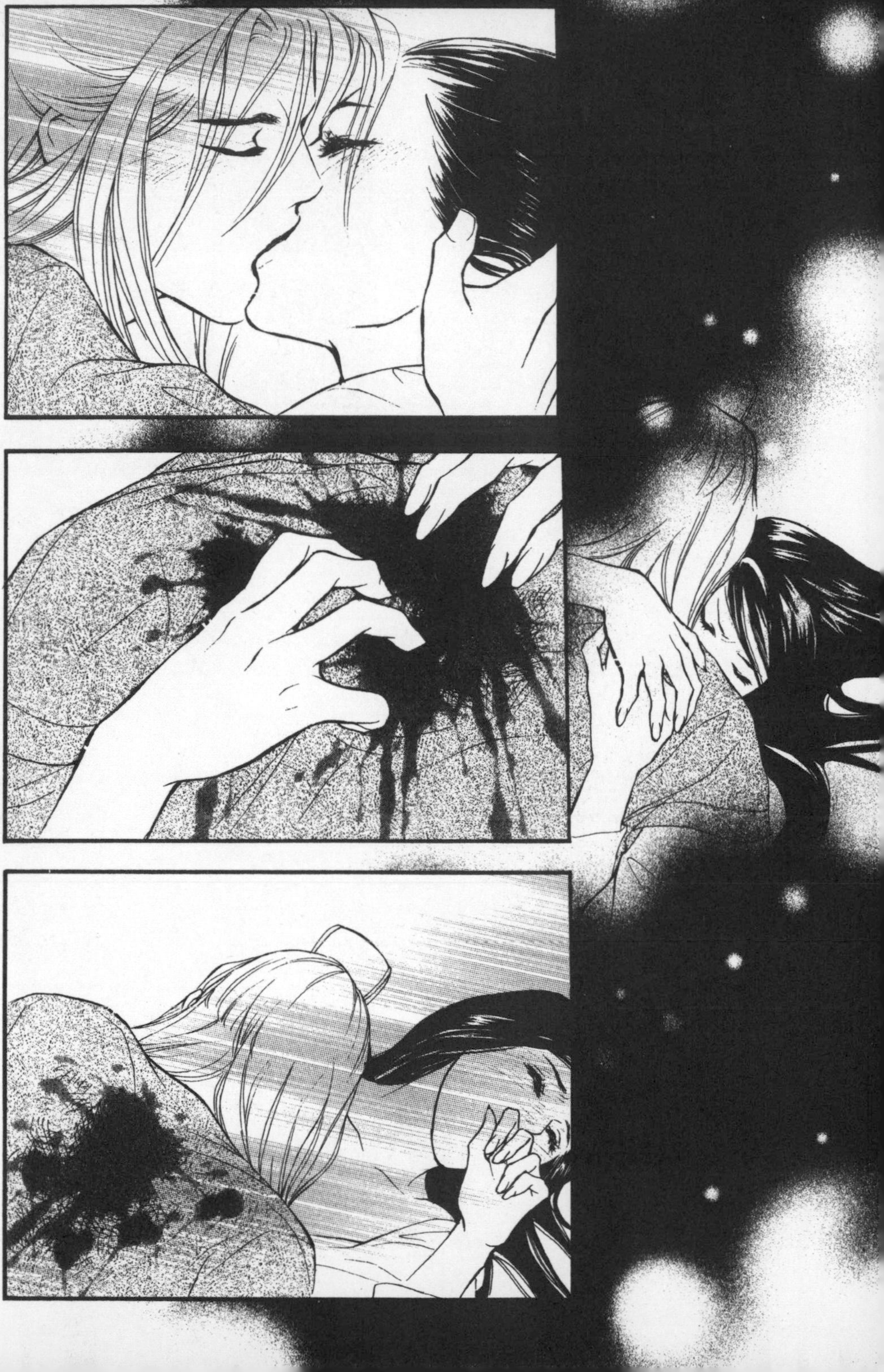

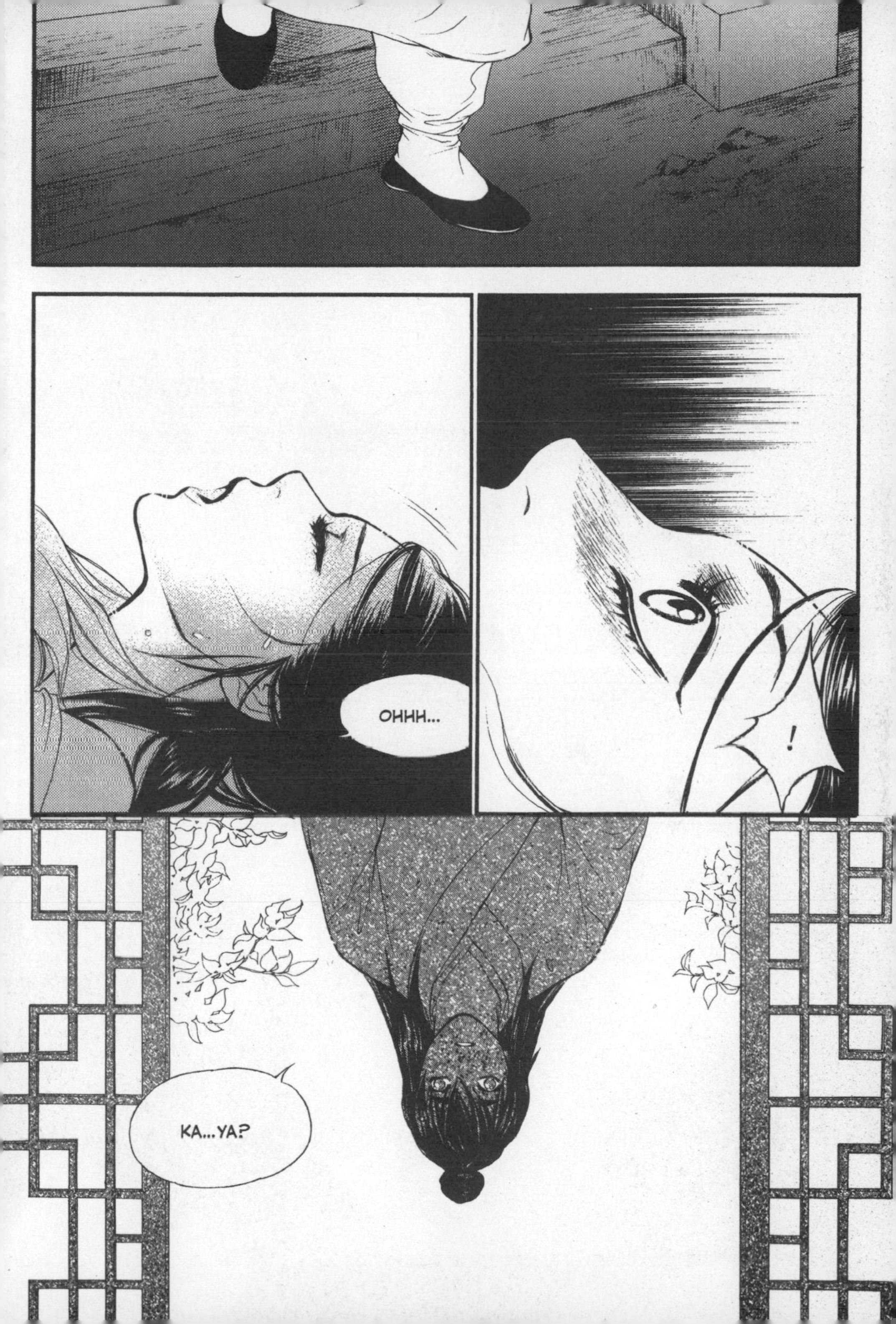
OHHH...
!
KA...YA?

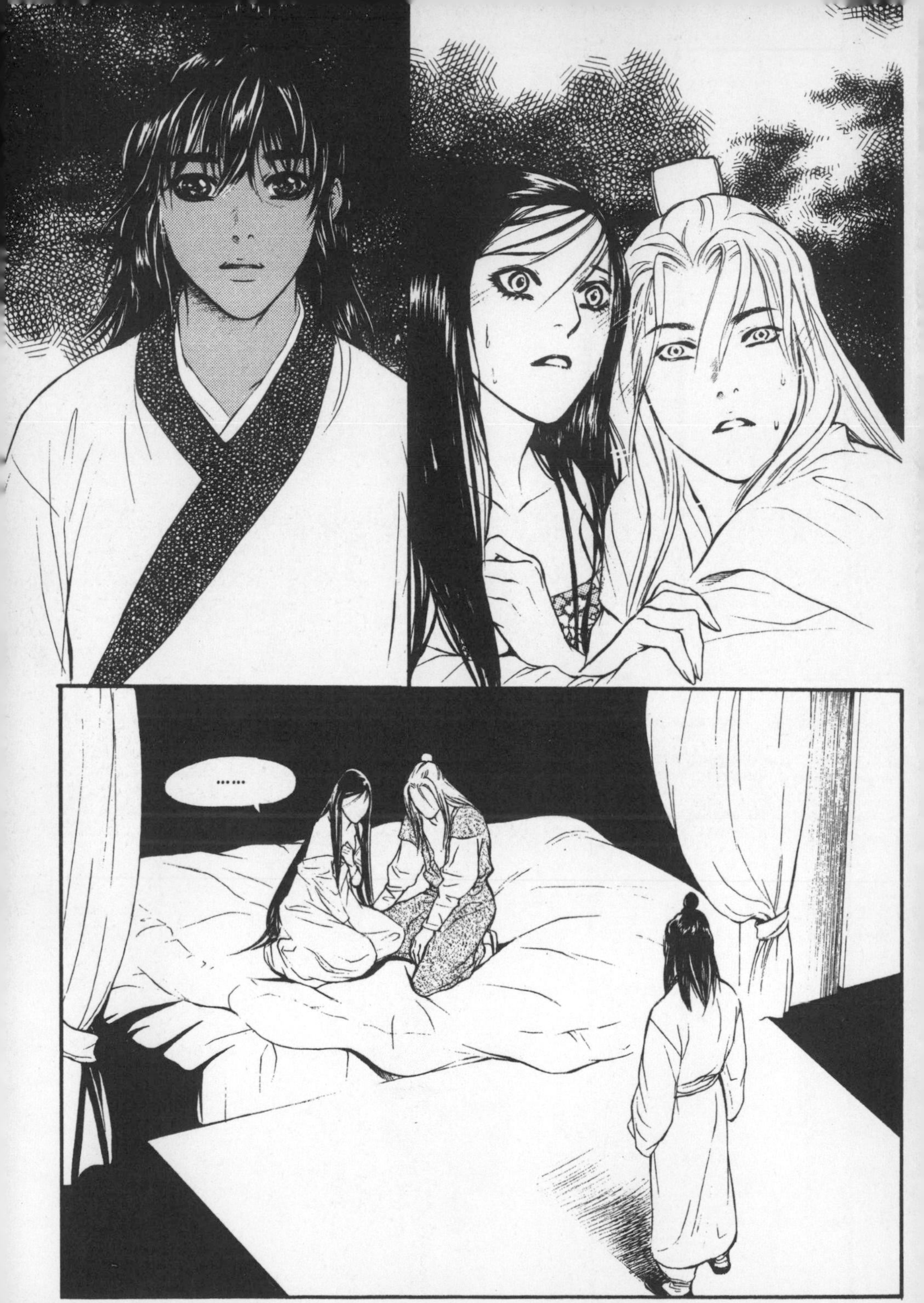
……

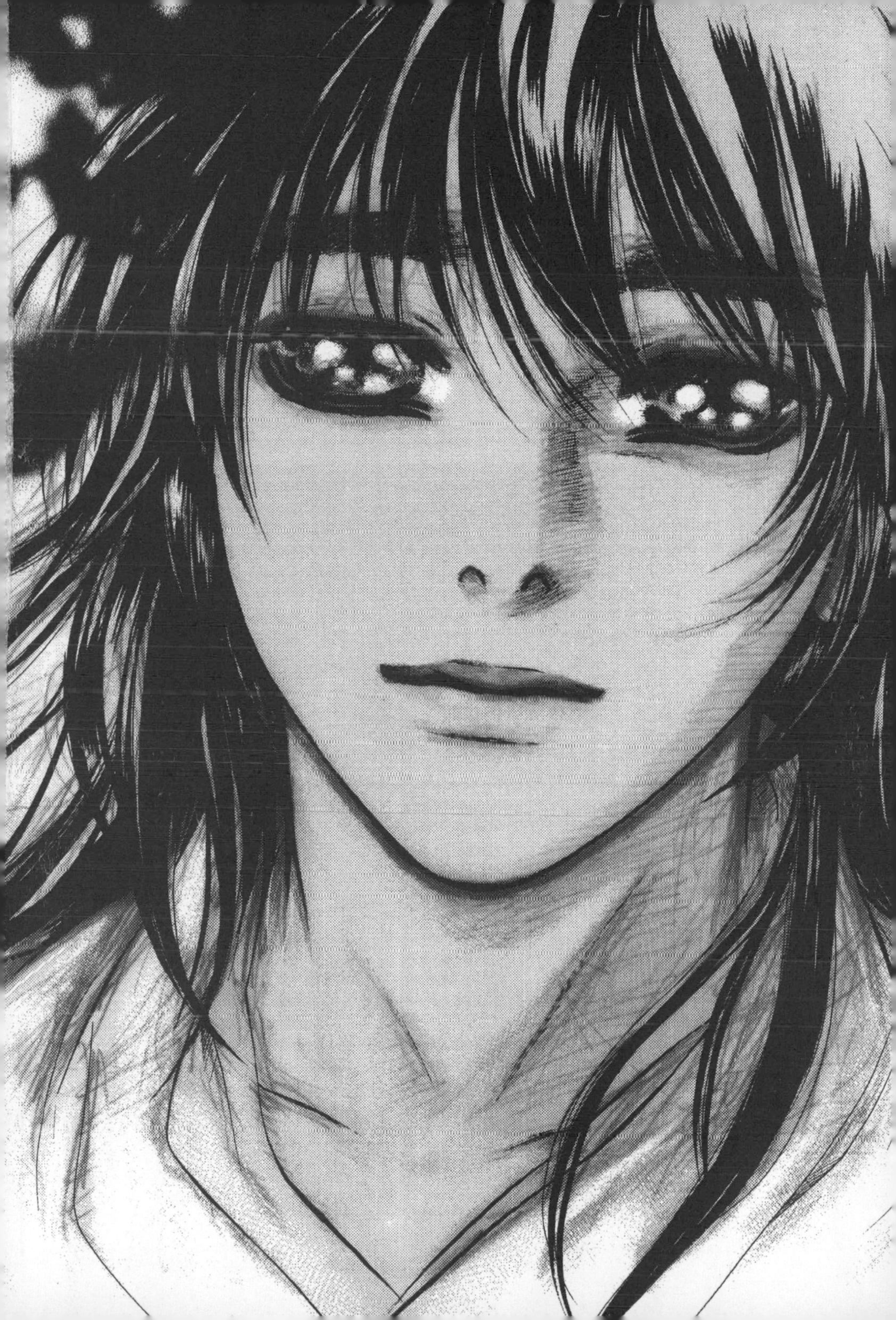

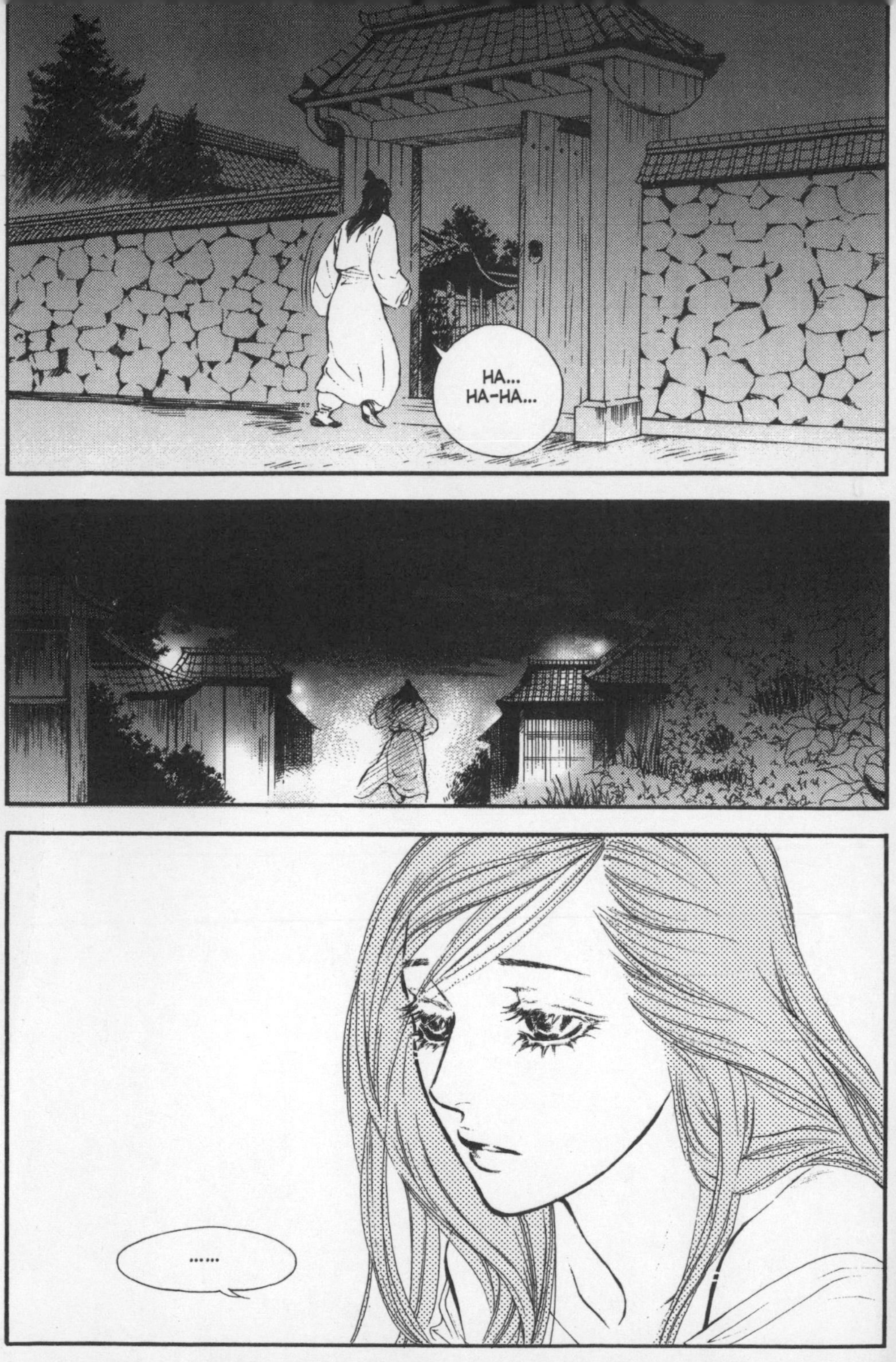
HA...
HA-HA...
......

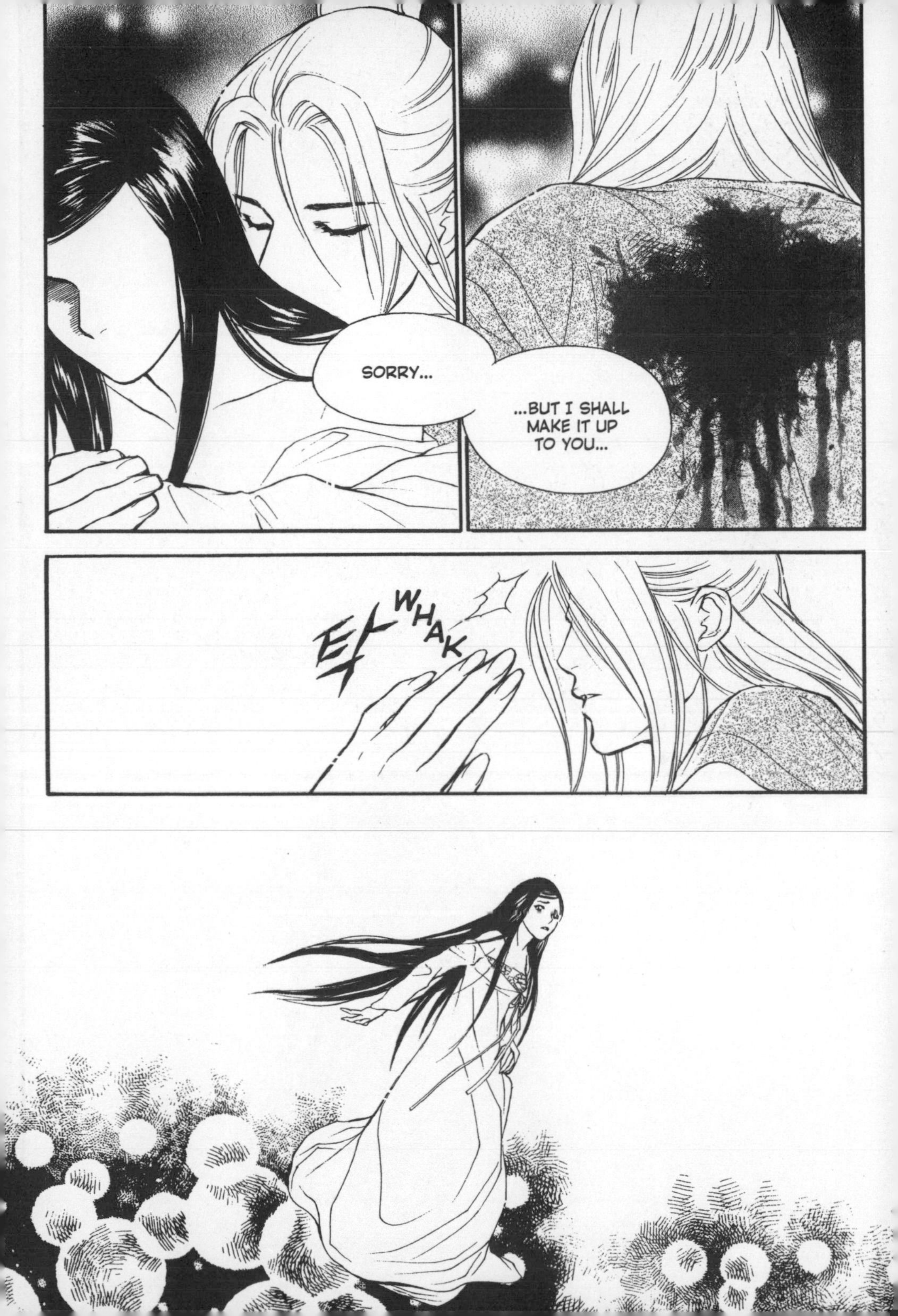
SORRY...
...BUT I SHALL MAKE IT UP TO YOU...
WHAK

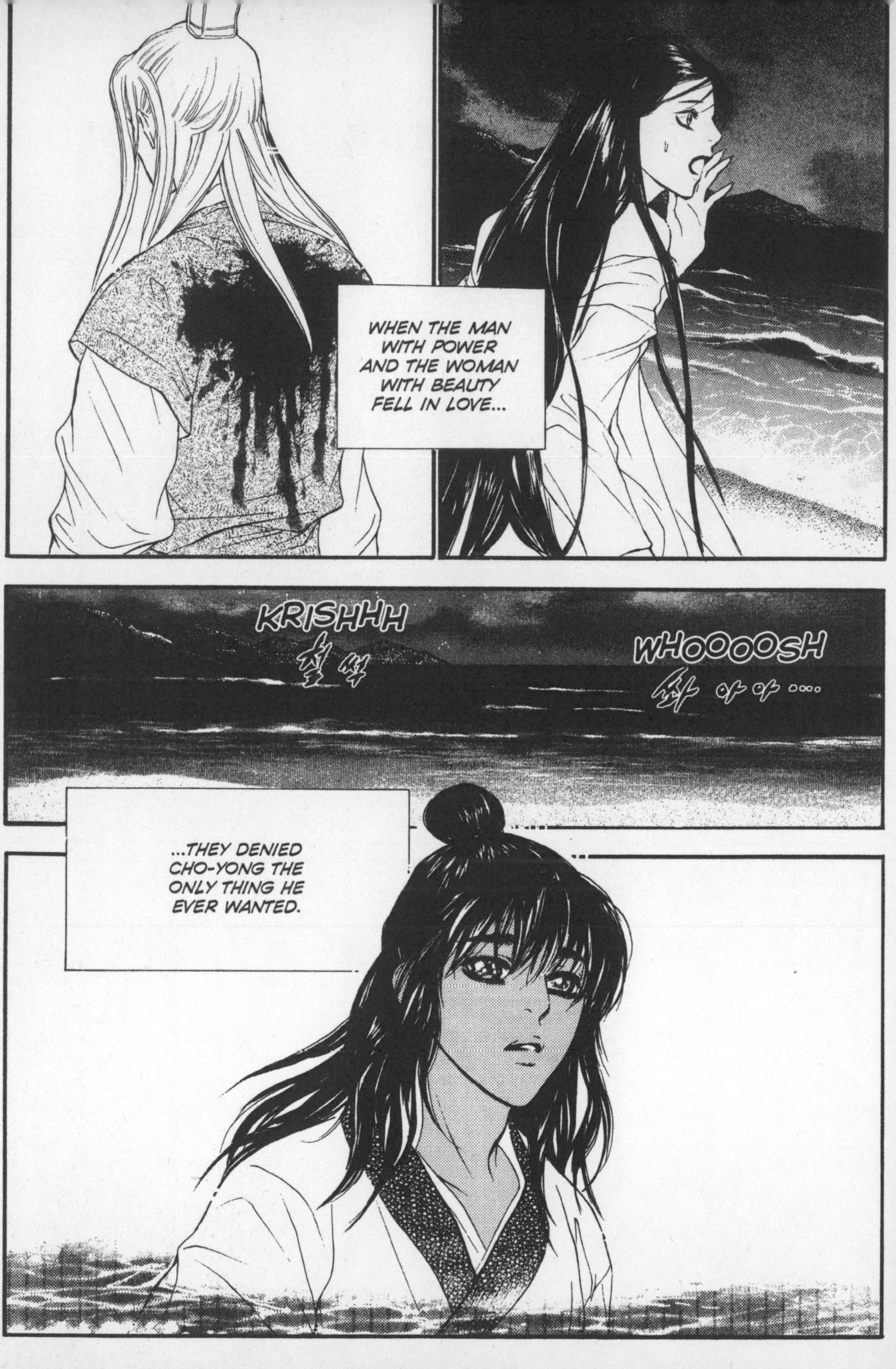
WHEN THE MAN WITH POWER AND THE WOMAN WITH BEAUTY FELL IN LOVE...
KRISHHH
철썩
WHOOOOSH
쏴아아....
...THEY DENIED CHO-YONG THE ONLY THING HE EVER WANTED.

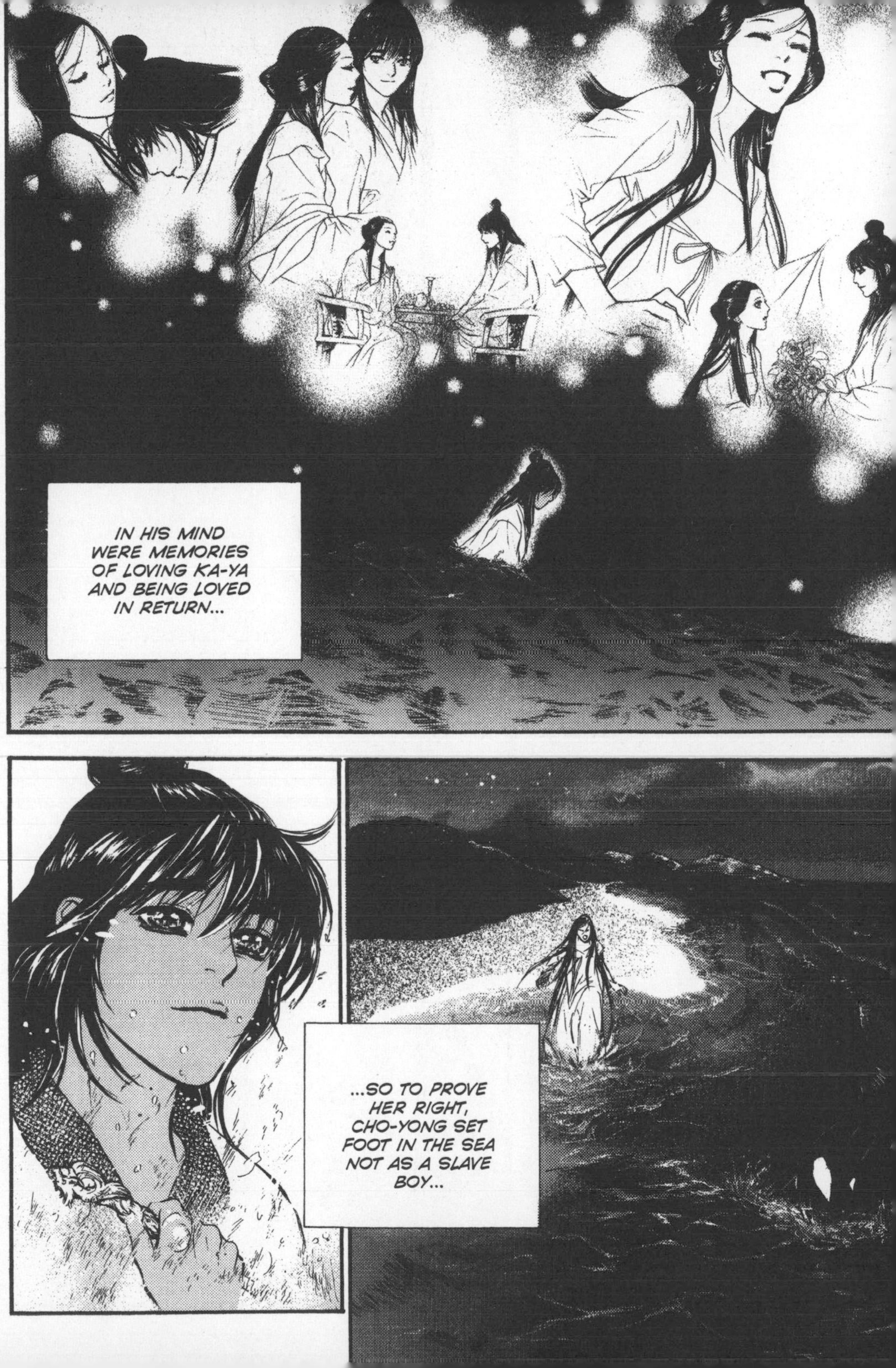
IN HIS MIND WERE MEMORIES OF LOVING KA-YA AND BEING LOVED IN RETURN...
...SO TO PROVE HER RIGHT, CHO-YONG SET FOOT IN THE SEA NOT AS A SLAVE BOY...

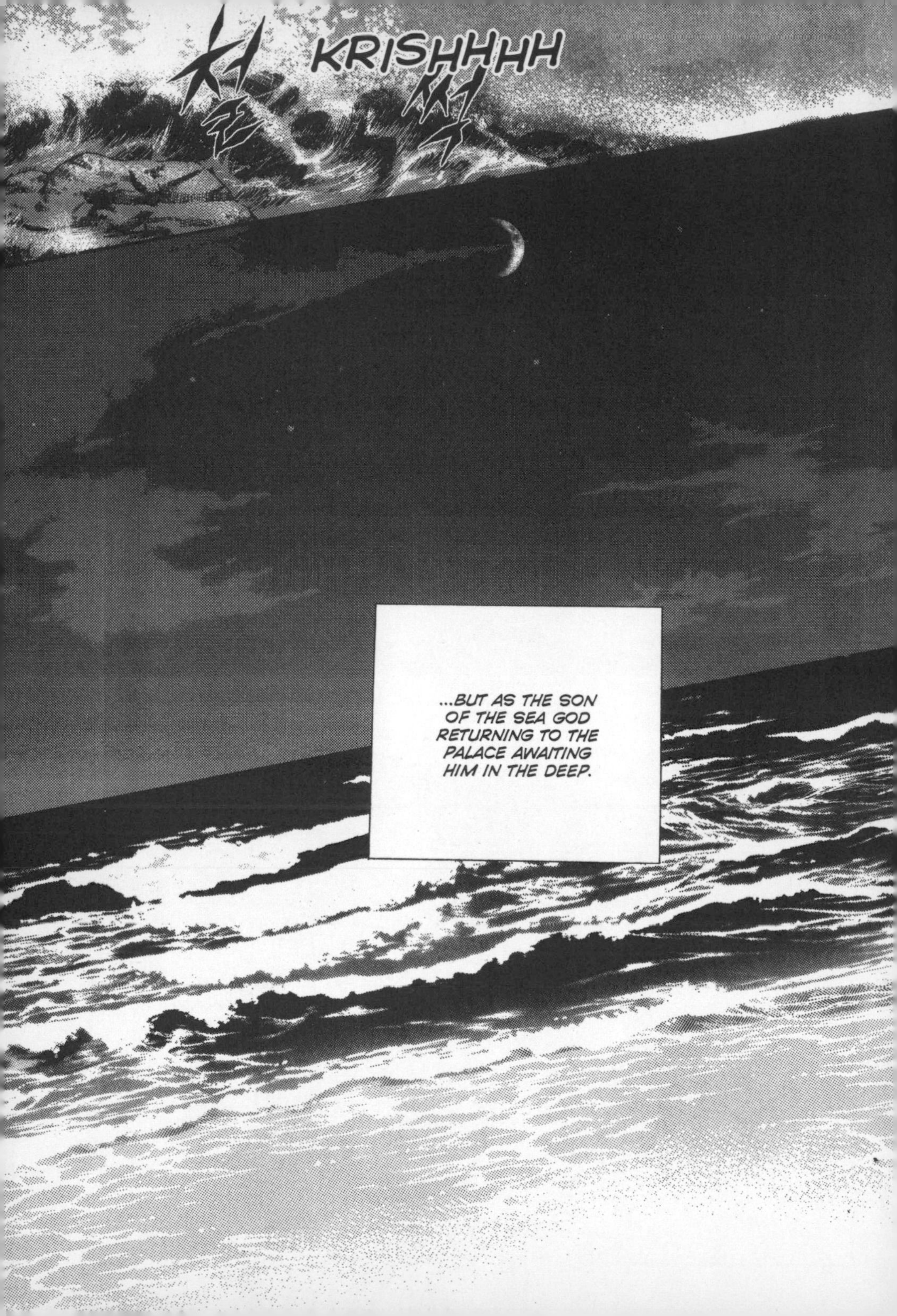
철썩
KRISHHHH
...BUT AS THE SON OF THE SEA GOD RETURNING TO THE PALACE AWAITING HIM IN THE DEEP.

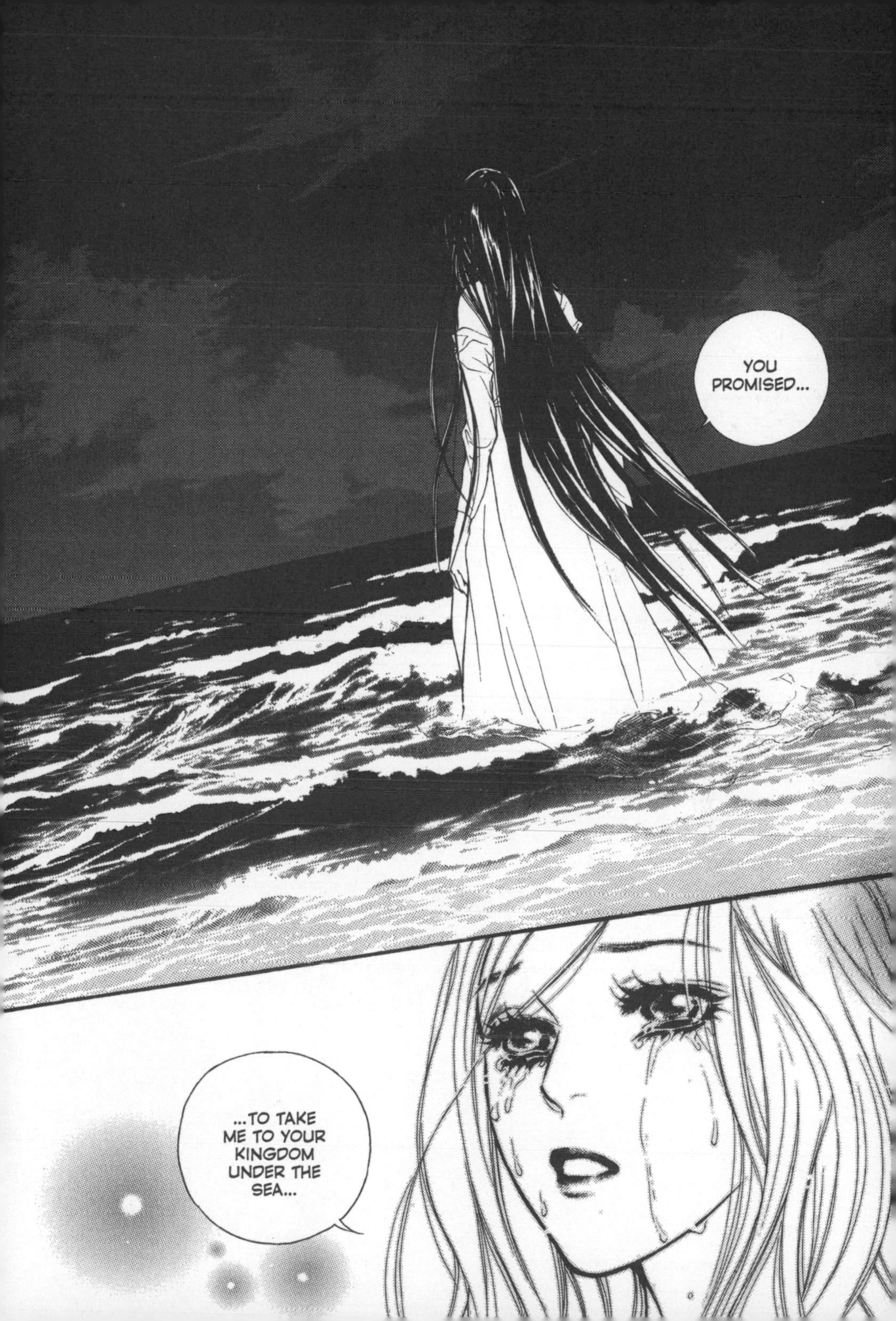
YOU PROMISED...
...TO TAKE ME TO YOUR KINGDOM UNDER THE SEA...

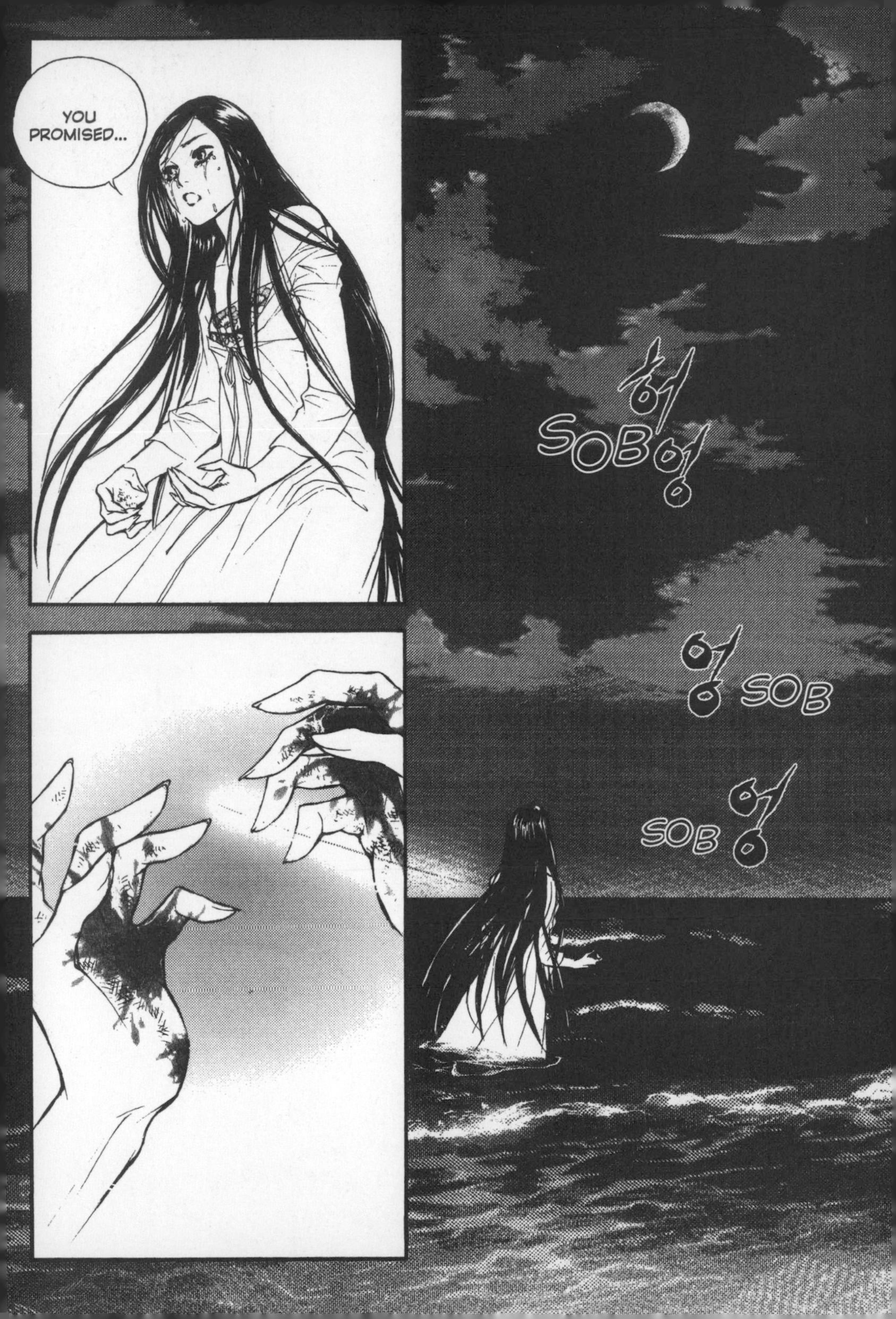
YOU PROMISED...
허엉 SOB
엉 SOB
SOB 엉

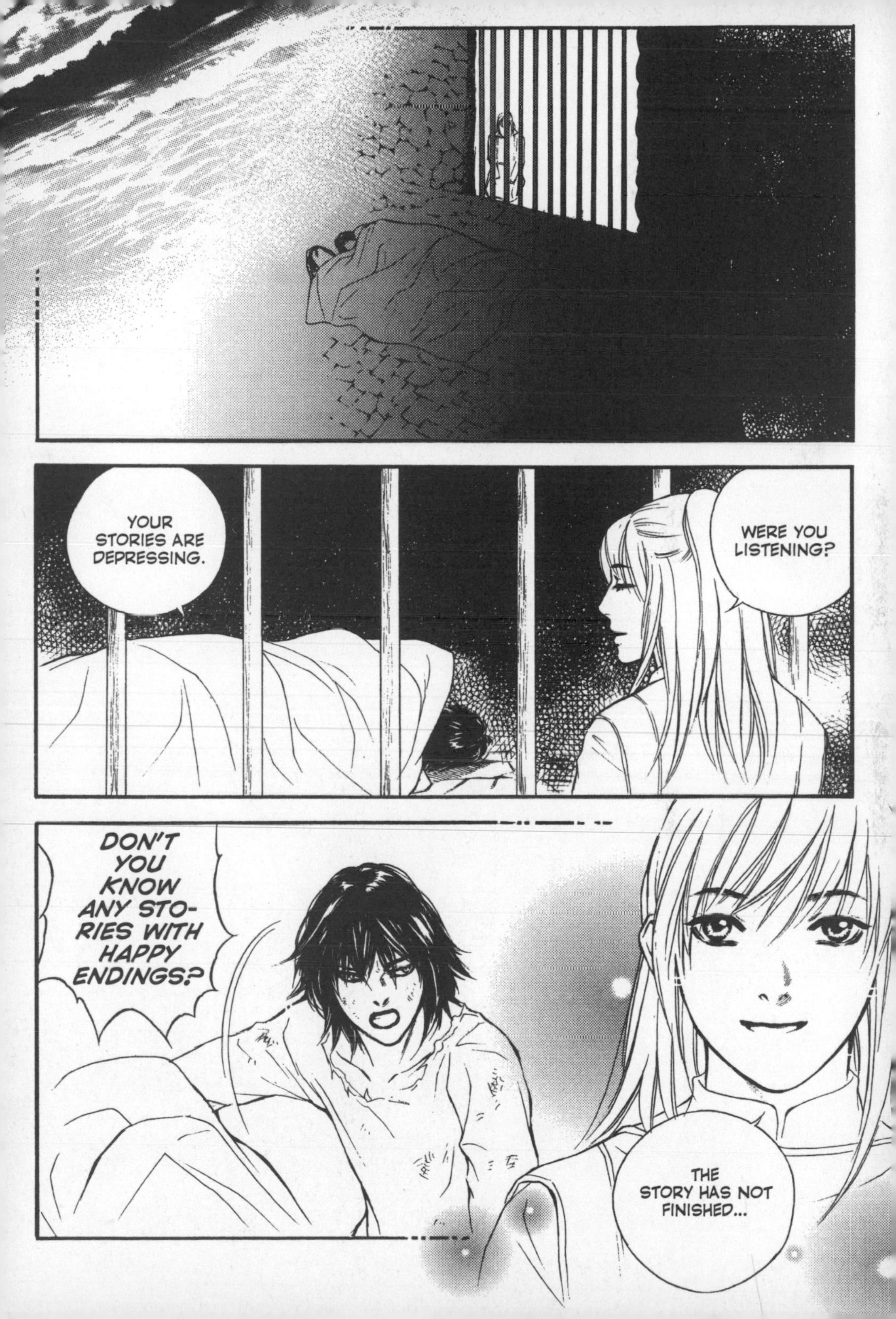
YOUR STORIES ARE DEPRESSING.
WERE YOU LISTENING?
DON'T YOU KNOW ANY STO-RIES WITH HAPPY ENDINGS?
THE STORY HAS NOT FINISHED...

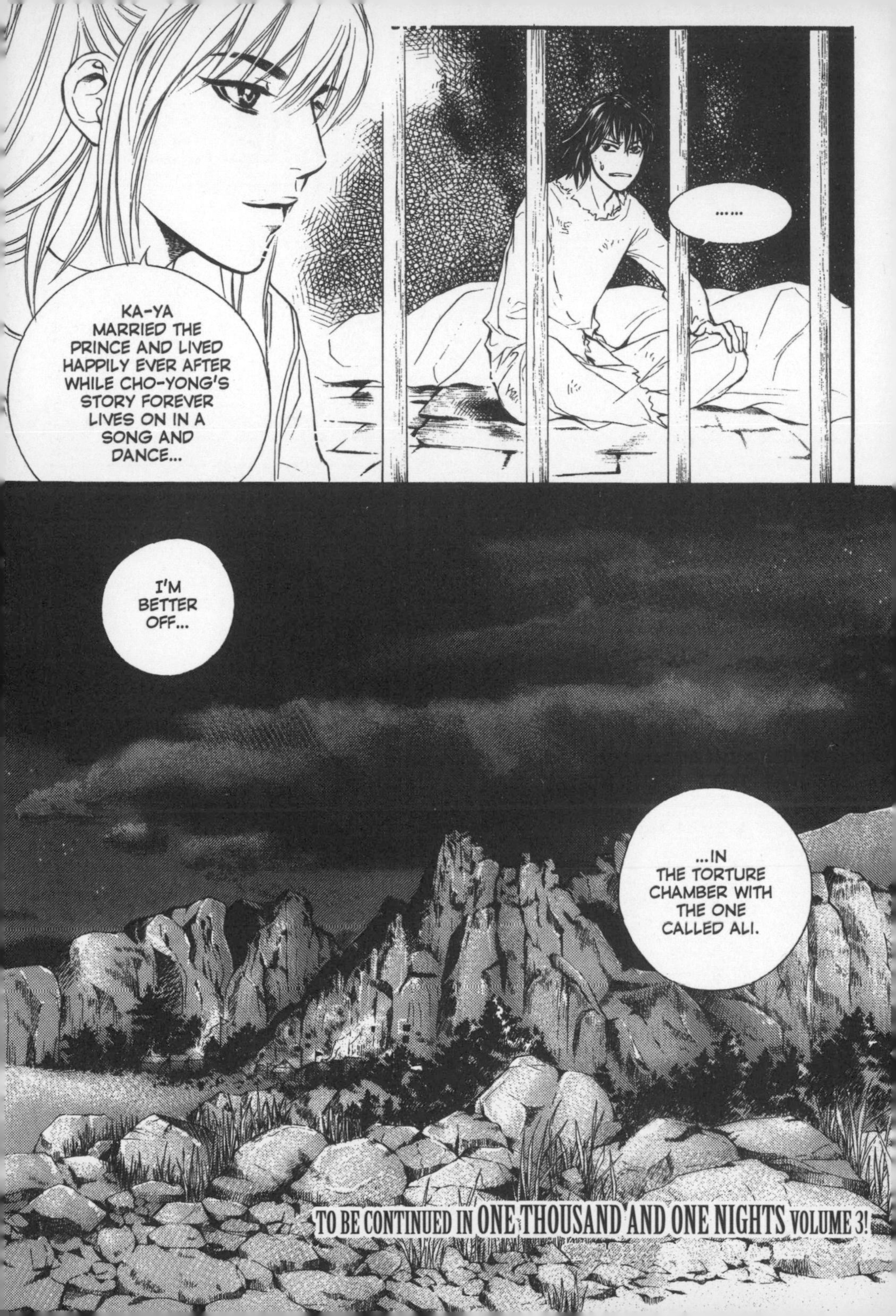
KA-YA MARRIED THE PRINCE AND LIVED HAPPILY EVER AFTER WHILE CHO-YONG'S STORY FOREVER LIVES ON IN A SONG AND DANCE...
......
I'M BETTER OFF...
...IN THE TORTURE CHAMBER WITH THE ONE CALLED ALI.
TO BE CONTINUED IN ONE THOUSAND AND ONE NIGHTS VOLUME 3!

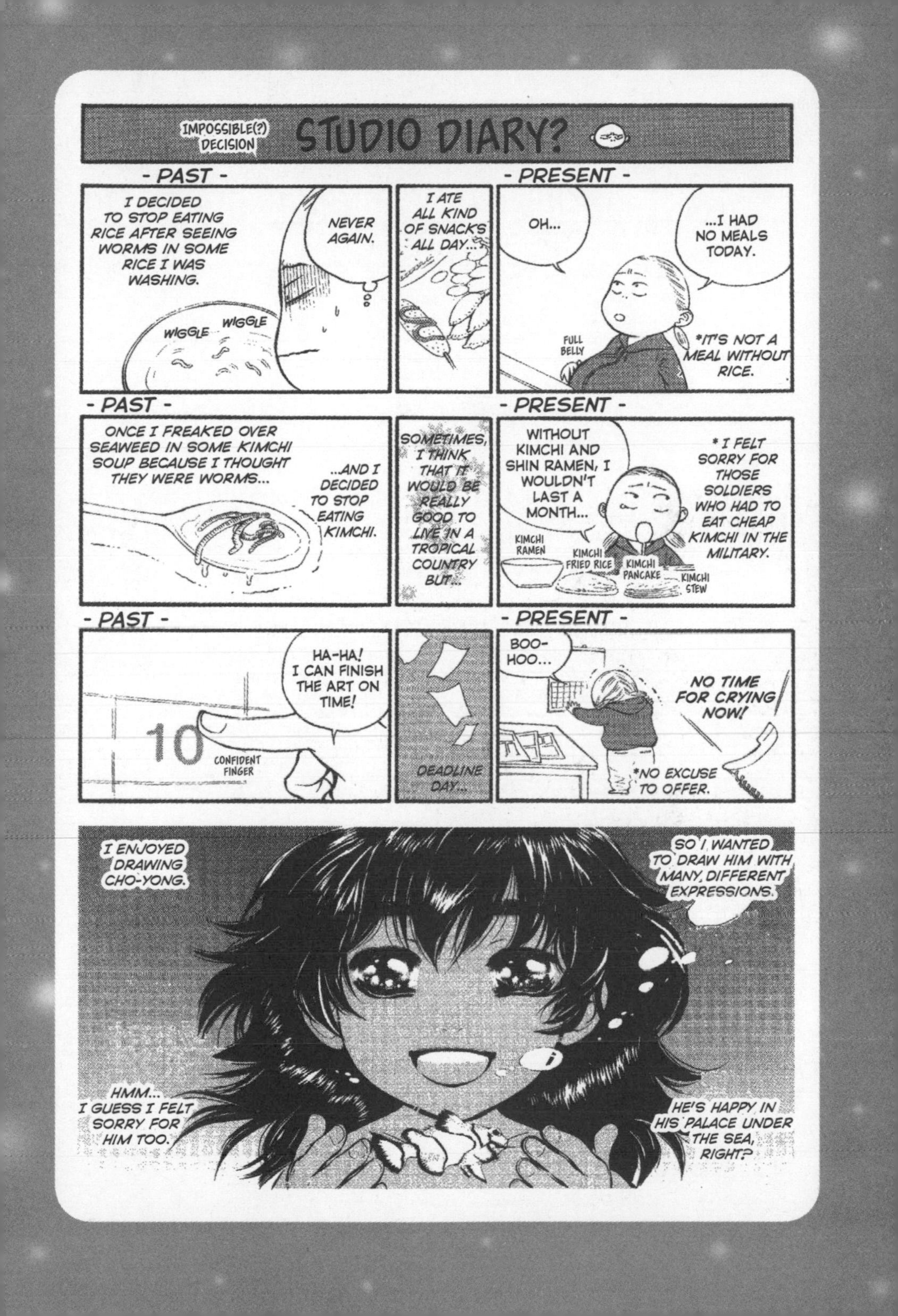
IMPOSSIBLE(?) DECISION
STUDIO DIARY?
- PAST -
I DECIDED TO STOP EATING RICE AFTER SEEING WORMS IN SOME RICE I WAS WASHING.
NEVER AGAIN.
WIGGLE WIGGLE
I ATE ALL KIND OF SNACKS ALL DAY...
- PRESENT -
OH...
...I HAD NO MEALS TODAY.
FULL BELLY
*IT'S NOT A MEAL WITHOUT RICE.
- PAST -
ONCE I FREAKED OVER SEAWEED IN SOME KIMCHI SOUP BECAUSE I THOUGHT THEY WERE WORMS...
...AND I DECIDED TO STOP EATING KIMCHI.
SOMETIMES, I THINK THAT IT WOULD BE REALLY GOOD TO LIVE IN A TROPICAL COUNTRY BUT...
- PRESENT -
WITHOUT KIMCHI AND SHIN RAMEN, I WOULDN'T LAST A MONTH...
* I FELT SORRY FOR THOSE SOLDIERS WHO HAD TO EAT CHEAP KIMCHI IN THE MILITARY.
KIMCHI RAMEN
KIMCHI FRIED RICE
KIMCHI PANCAKE
KIMCHI STEW
- PAST -
HA-HA! I CAN FINISH THE ART ON TIME!
10
CONFIDENT FINGER
DEADLINE DAY...
- PRESENT -
BOO-HOO...
NO TIME FOR CRYING NOW!
*NO EXCUSE TO OFFER.
I ENJOYED DRAWING CHO-YONG.
SO I WANTED TO DRAW HIM WITH MANY DIFFERENT EXPRESSIONS.
HMM... I GUESS I FELT SORRY FOR HIM TOO.
HE'S HAPPY IN HIS PALACE UNDER THE SEA, RIGHT?

Special Commentary
From The Writer Jin-seok Jeon

ONE

EXPLANATION FOR THE SAD STORIES

AFTER TWO SAD STORIES IN A ROW, I WAS ASKED WHY I DIDN'T TELL MORE HAPPY STORIES. (JUST LIKE SHAHRYAR COMPLAINING TO SEHARA.) ALLOW ME TO EXPLAIN SO THAT NO ONE THINKS I'M SOME SADIST TRYING TO BREAK READERS' HEARTS.

THERE WERE MORE SAD STORIES IN THE CHILDREN'S BOOKS I READ AS A KID. EVEN THOUGH SAD STORIES SUCH AS "THE LITTLE MERMAID", "THE BRAVE TIN SOLDIER", AND "THE HAPPY PRINCE" MADE ME SAD IN MY YOUTH, THEY LATER HELPED ME DEVELOP CERTAIN SENSIBILITIES.

HOWEVER, DURING THE 80S IT SEEMED THAT EVERYTHING HAD TO HAVE A HAPPY ENDING. IN WALT DISNEY'S "THE LITTLE MERMAID", THE RED-HAIRED TOMBOY WAS GRANTED TWO LEGS, GOT MARRIED TO THE PRINCE, AND LIVED HAPPILY EVER AFTER. THIS ENDING REALLY HURT MY FEELINGS. (I ADDRESSED A SIMILAR TOPIC IN VOLUME ONE AFTER TURANDOT'S STORY.) IT READ LIKE THE END OF A HEROINE'S STORY IN A CHEESY ACTION MOVIE. I DOUBT I WAS THE ONLY ONE WHO FELT THIS WAY AFTER WATCHING DISNEY'S "THE LITTLE MERMAID."

SOMETIMES, THE SAD ENDING IS MORE BEAUTIFUL. I'D RATHER BRING TEARS TO PEOPLE'S EYES THAN MAKE THEM LAUGH FOR SOME CHEESY REASON. I SOUND LIKE SEHARA. I HOPE YOU GUYS SEE ME EVOLVE AS A WRITER AS I WRITE <ONE THOUSAND AND ONE NIGHTS>.

TWO

AFTER CHO-YONG'S STORY

SEHARA'S SECOND STORY IS FINISHED. WHAT DID YOU THINK ABOUT CHO-YONG'S TRAGIC LOVE STORY? IT MIGHT COME AS A SURPRISE TO MANY PEOPLE THAT CHO-YONG'S STORY HERE IS DIFFERENT. TRADITIONALLY, CHO-YONG IS DEPICTED AS SOME KIND OF GOD WHO FORGAVE HIS CHEATING WIFE. HE IS LIKE A PERSON ABOVE FEELINGS LIKE LOVE, BETRAYAL, OR ANGER.

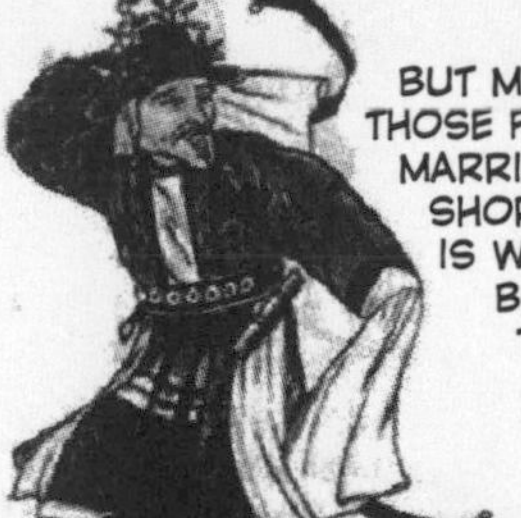

BUT MAYBE HE WAS ONLY UNABLE TO DO ANYTHING ABOUT THOSE FEELINGS! EVEN THOUGH CHO-YONG'S ROMANCE AND MARRIAGE AND TIME IN KING HUN-GANG'S KINGDOM WAS SHORT-LIVED, THE SONG AND DANCE TELLING HIS STORY IS WELL-KNOWN. CHO-YONG LOOKED DIFFERENT FROM US BUT HE HAD THE SAME FEELINGS KOREAN PEOPLE DO. THAT'S WHY OUR ANCESTORS WERE COMFORTED BY CHO-YONG'S STORY.

Preview

11th CAT

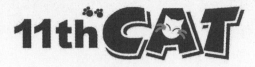

vol.3

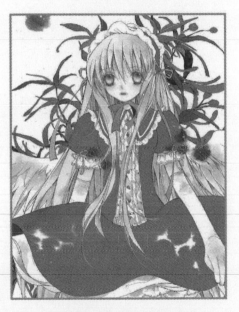

Kim MiKyung

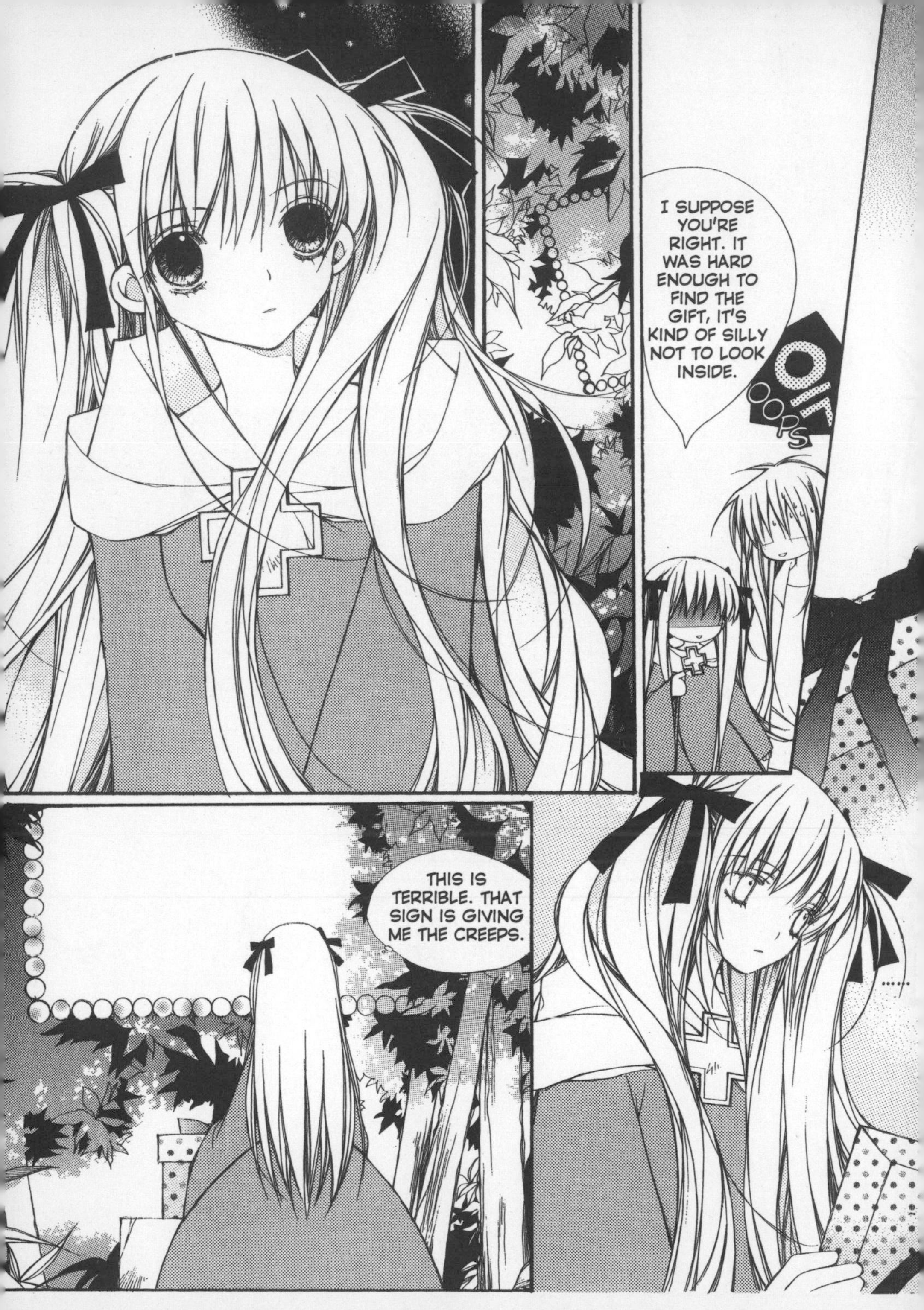
I SUPPOSE YOU'RE RIGHT. IT WAS HARD ENOUGH TO FIND THE GIFT, IT'S KIND OF SILLY NOT TO LOOK INSIDE.
OOPS
THIS IS TERRIBLE. THAT SIGN IS GIVING ME THE CREEPS.
......

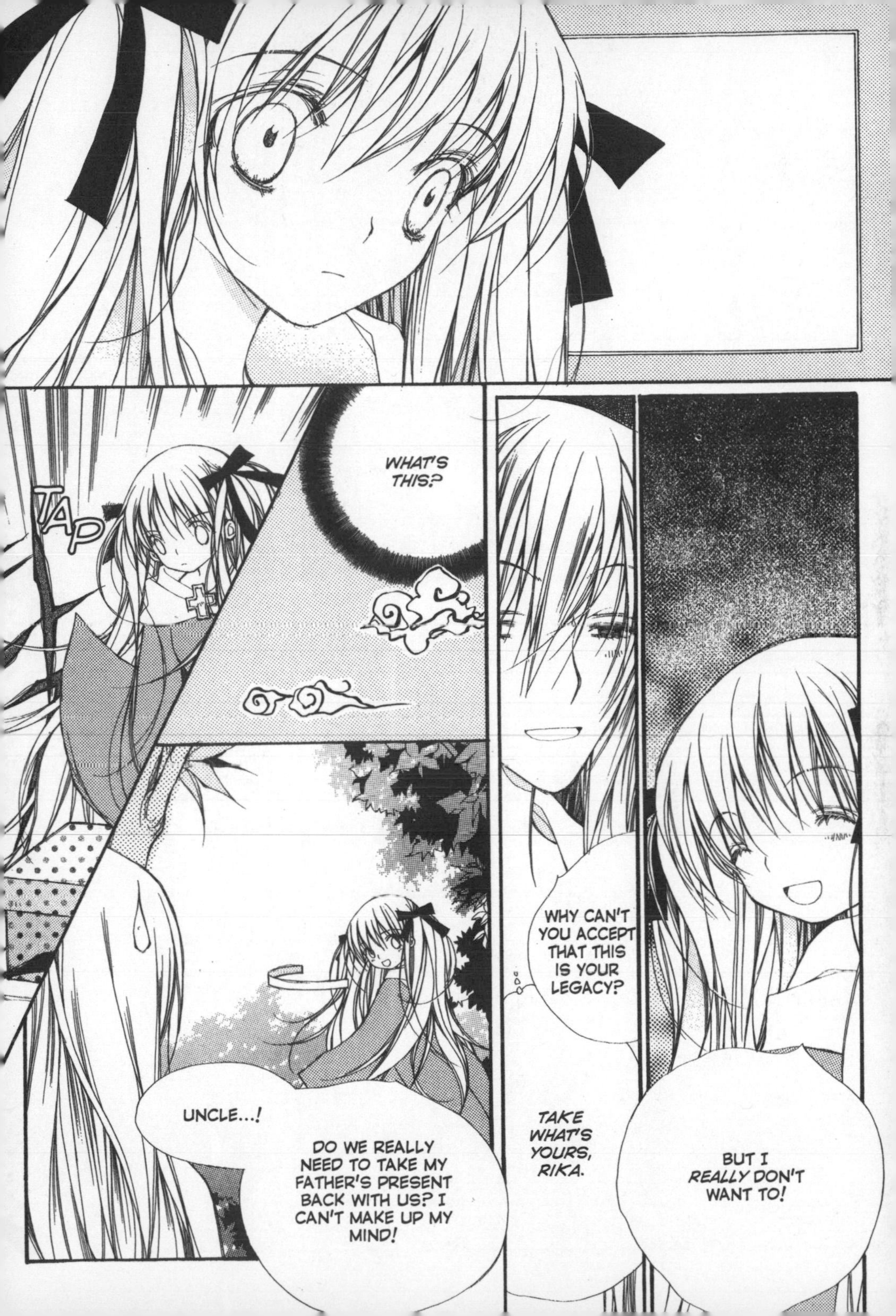
TAP
WHAT'S THIS?
UNCLE...!
DO WE REALLY NEED TO TAKE MY FATHER'S PRESENT BACK WITH US? I CAN'T MAKE UP MY MIND!
WHY CAN'T YOU ACCEPT THAT THIS IS YOUR LEGACY?
TAKE WHAT'S YOURS, RIKA.
BUT I REALLY DON'T WANT TO!

THE WAY YOU TALK, IT'S AS IF YOU'D SEEN IT BEFORE.

I REALIZE THAT IT MAY SEEM PRETTY STRANGE...

...BUT--HOW SHOULD I PUT THIS?-- PRECIOUS THINGS OFTEN DO.

IS THERE MAYBE A CHANCE THAT...THAT THE RED...?

OH, ARTHUR... WHAT WERE YOU THINKING? IF YOU WERE ALIVE, I'D SMACK YOU!

IF YOU REALLY FEEL IT'S THAT VALUABLE, UNCLE, THEN YOU SHOULD TAKE IT.

WHERE'RE YOU GOING?!

Bye~.

STRANGE I CAN HANDLE, BUT WEIRD IS A DIFFERENT STORY.

AND IT LOOKS REALLY WEIRD.

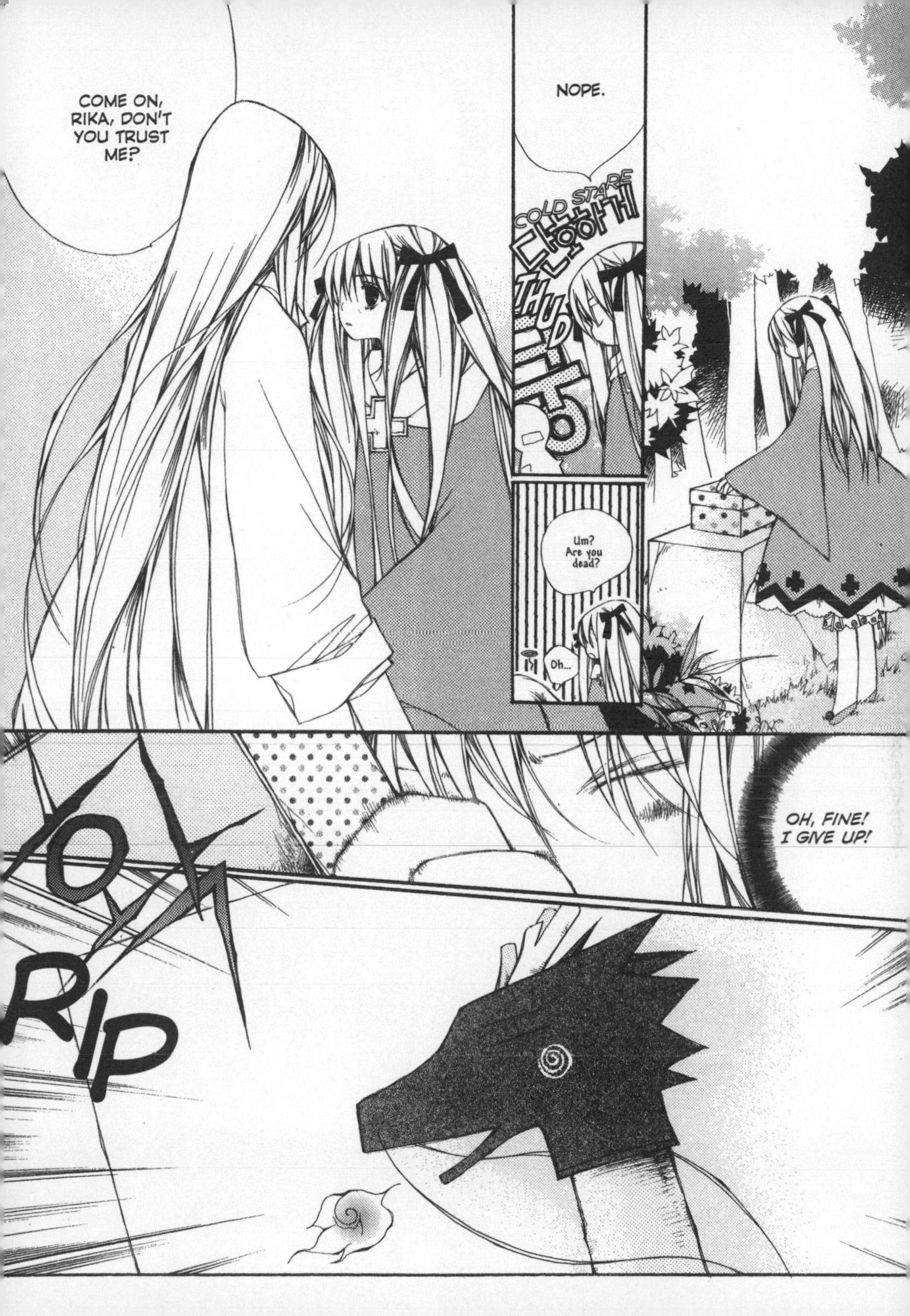
COME ON, RIKA, DON'T YOU TRUST ME?
NOPE.
COLD STARE
단호하게
THUD
Um? Are you dead?
Oh...
OH, FINE! I GIVE UP!
RIP

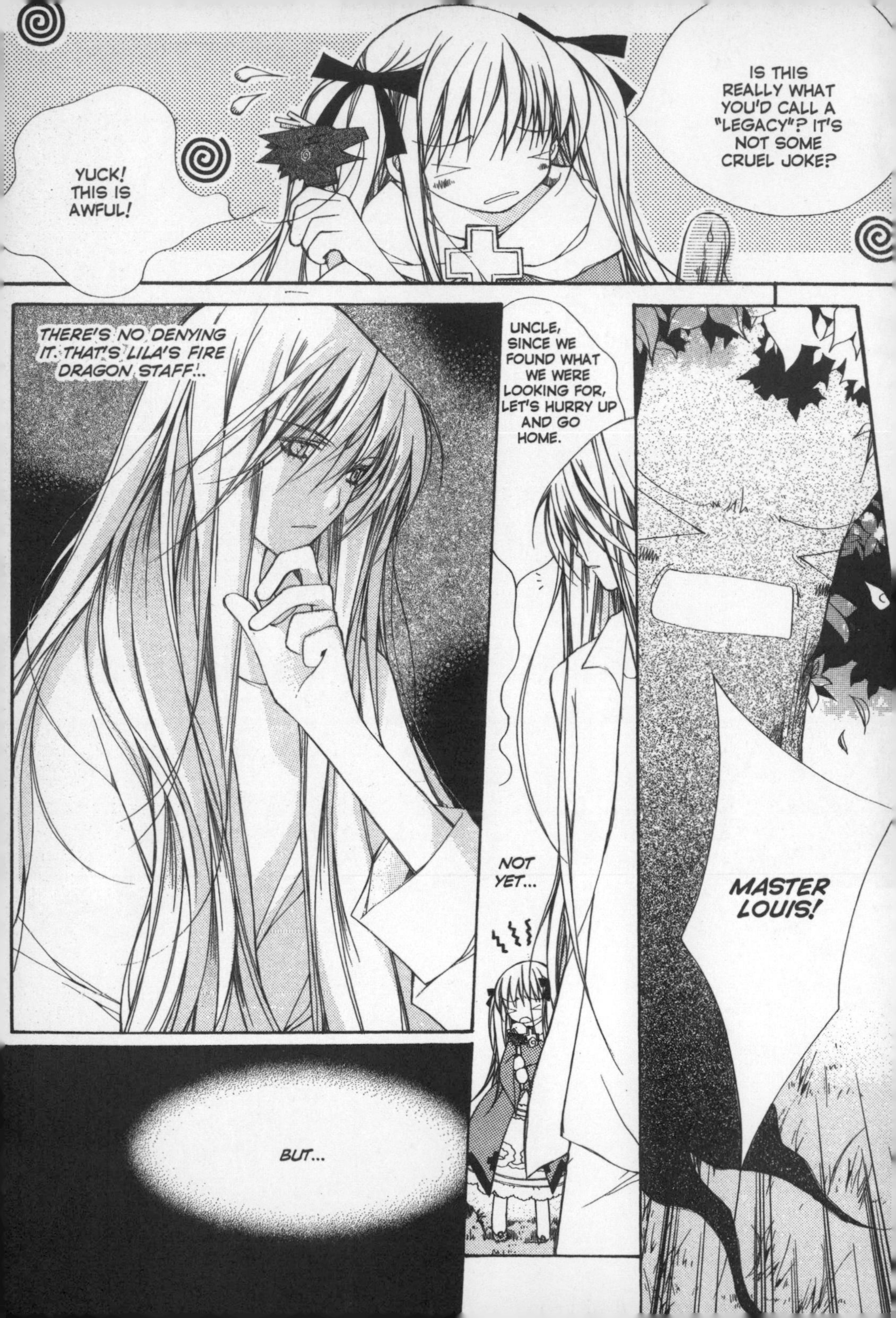
YUCK! THIS IS AWFUL!
IS THIS REALLY WHAT YOU'D CALL A "LEGACY"? IT'S NOT SOME CRUEL JOKE?
THERE'S NO DENYING IT. THAT'S LILA'S FIRE DRAGON STAFF...
BUT...
UNCLE, SINCE WE FOUND WHAT WE WERE LOOKING FOR, LET'S HURRY UP AND GO HOME.
NOT YET...
MASTER LOUIS!

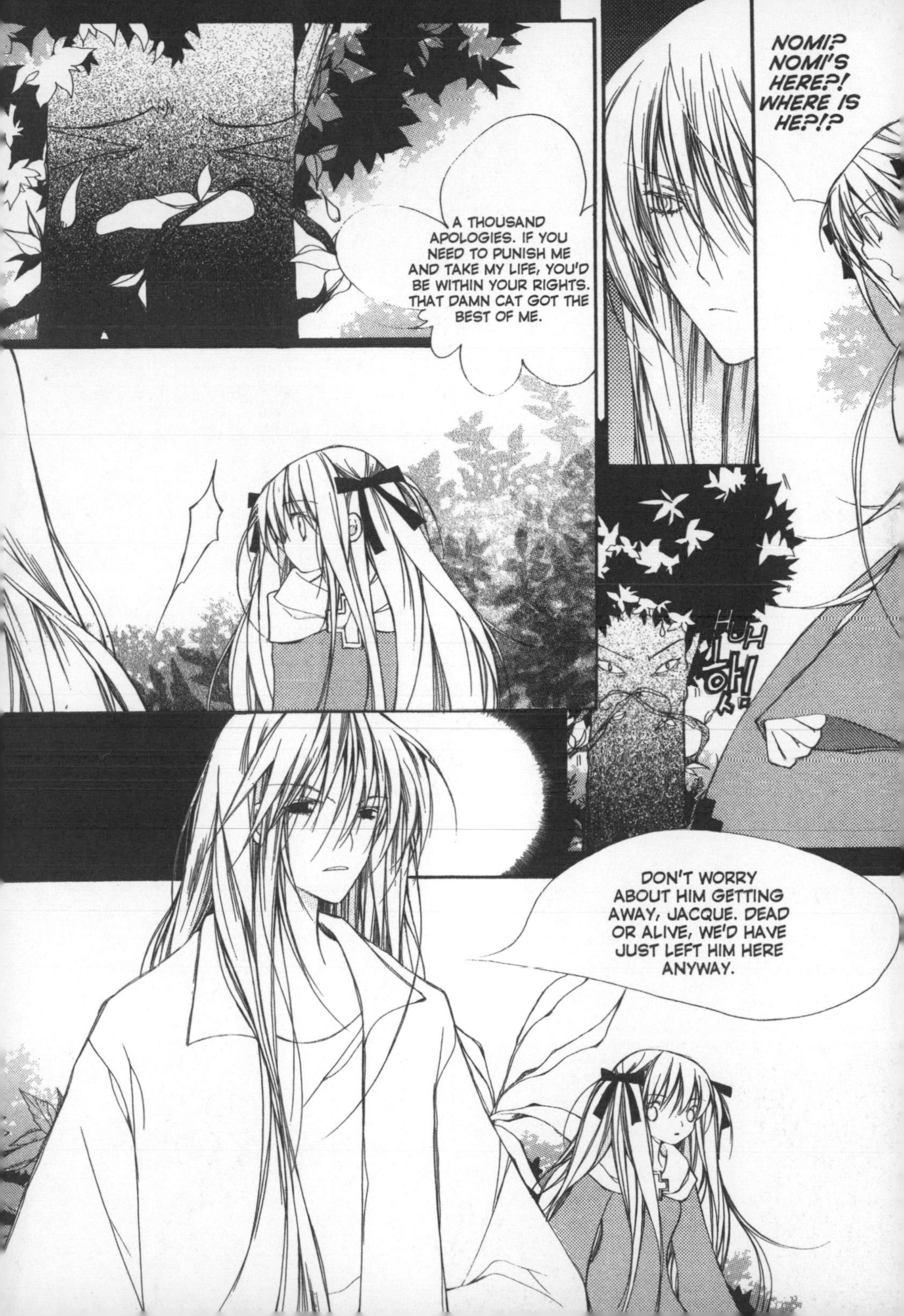

NOMI? NOMI'S HERE?! WHERE IS HE?!?
A THOUSAND APOLOGIES. IF YOU NEED TO PUNISH ME AND TAKE MY LIFE, YOU'D BE WITHIN YOUR RIGHTS. THAT DAMN CAT GOT THE BEST OF ME.
HUH
DON'T WORRY ABOUT HIM GETTING AWAY, JACQUE. DEAD OR ALIVE, WE'D HAVE JUST LEFT HIM HERE ANYWAY.

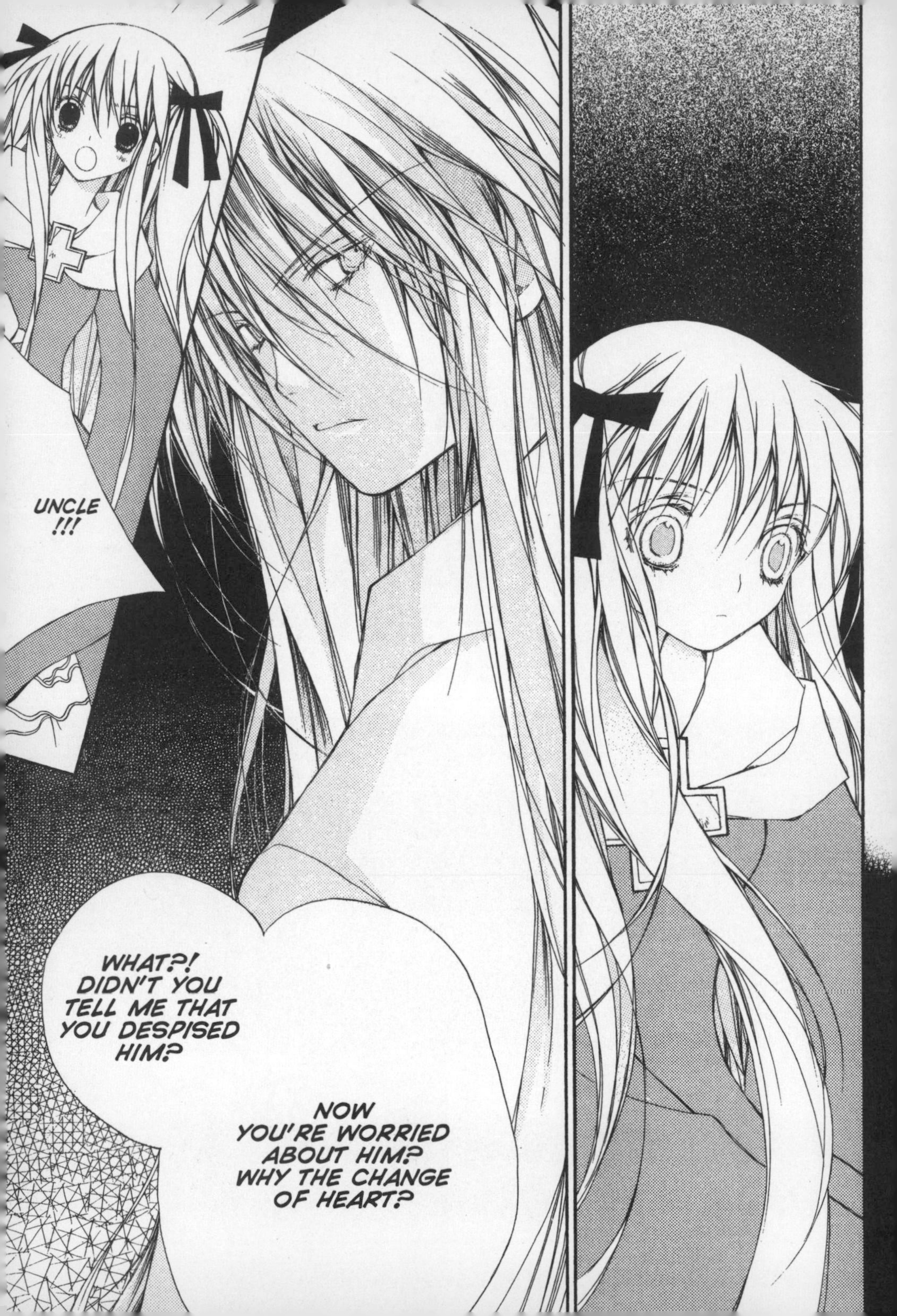
UNCLE !!!
WHAT?! DIDN'T YOU TELL ME THAT YOU DESPISED HIM?
NOW YOU'RE WORRIED ABOUT HIM? WHY THE CHANGE OF HEART?

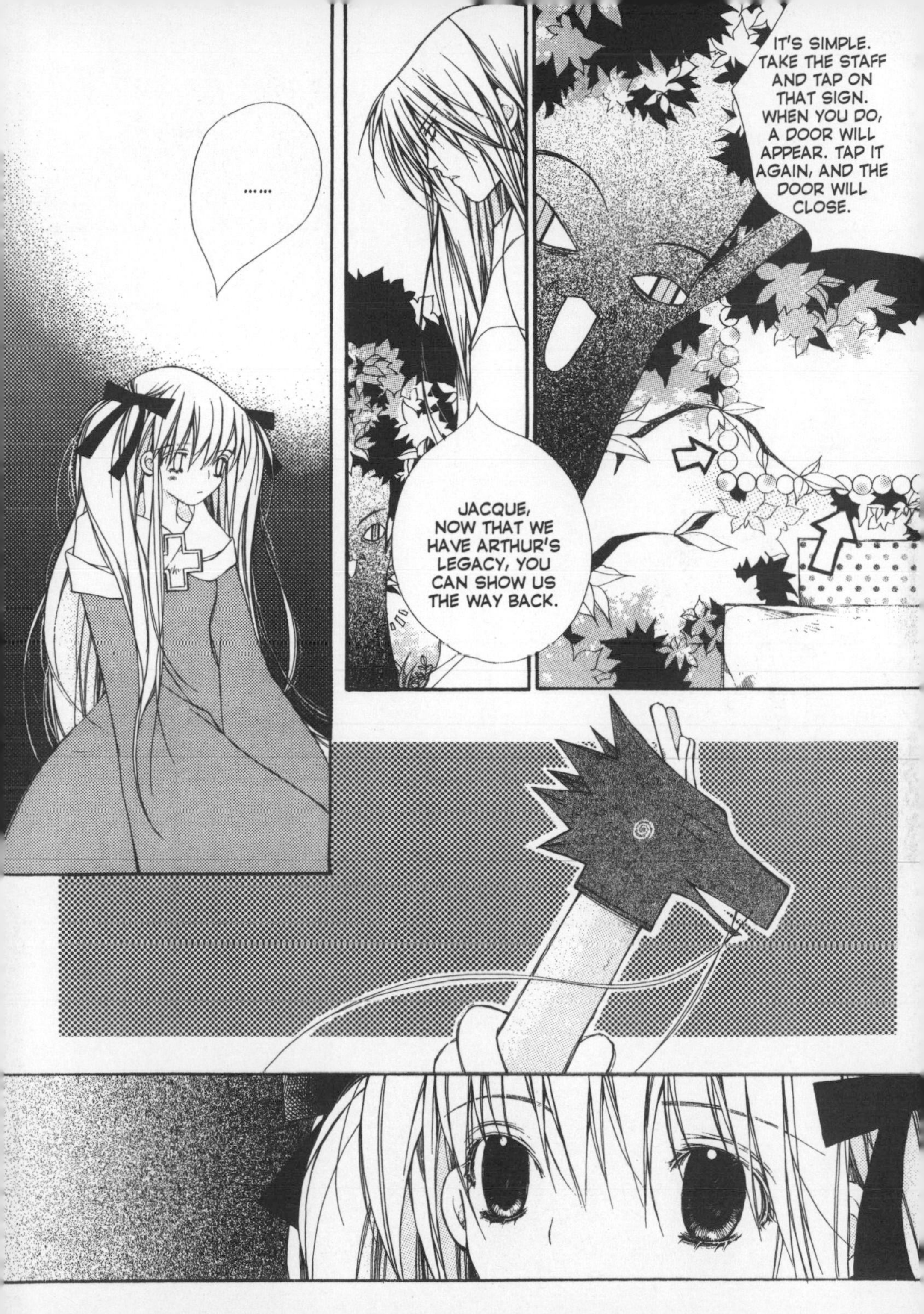
……
JACQUE, NOW THAT WE HAVE ARTHUR'S LEGACY, YOU CAN SHOW US THE WAY BACK.
IT'S SIMPLE. TAKE THE STAFF AND TAP ON THAT SIGN. WHEN YOU DO, A DOOR WILL APPEAR. TAP IT AGAIN, AND THE DOOR WILL CLOSE.

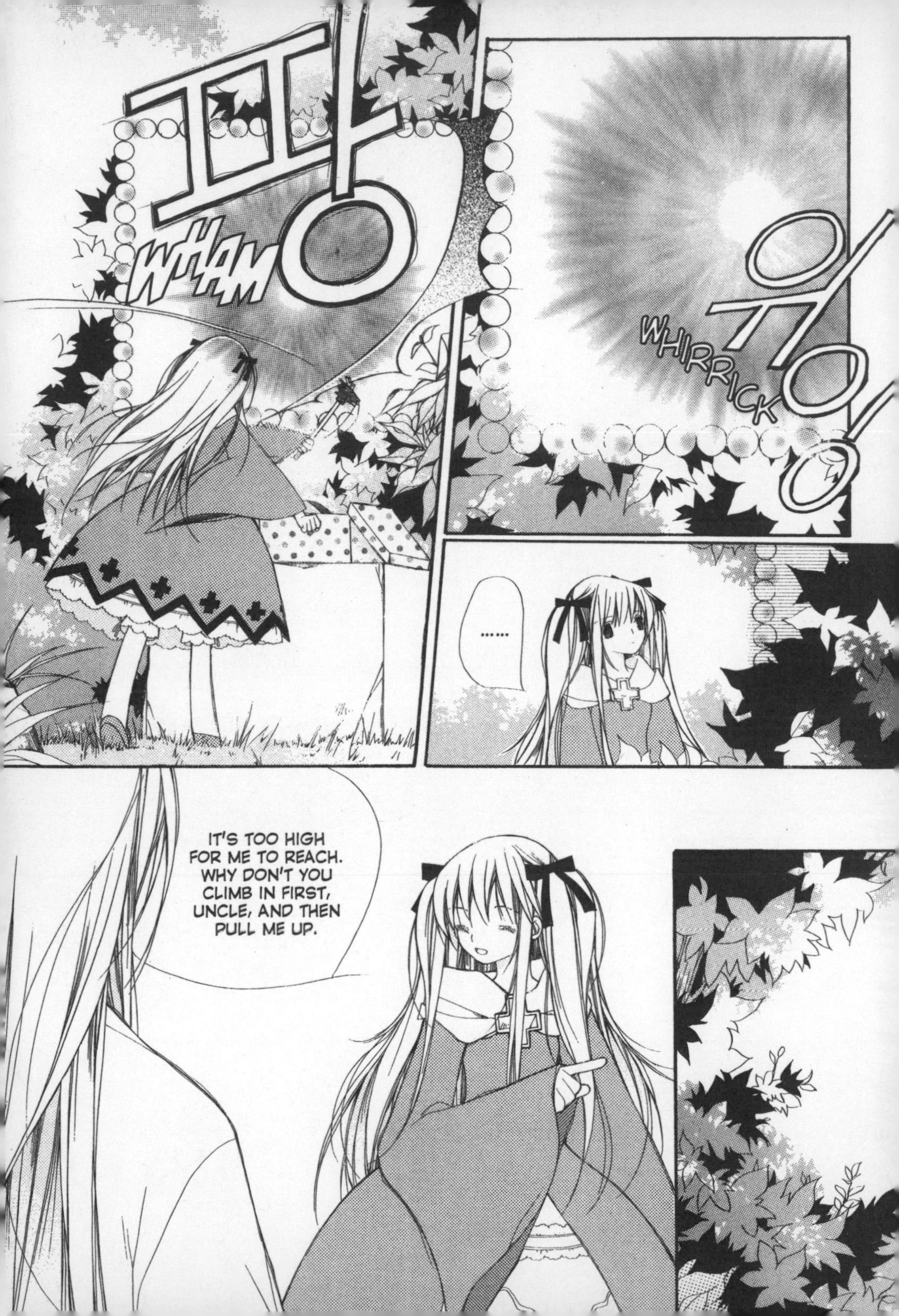
WHAM
WHIRRICK
......
IT'S TOO HIGH FOR ME TO REACH. WHY DON'T YOU CLIMB IN FIRST, UNCLE, AND THEN PULL ME UP.

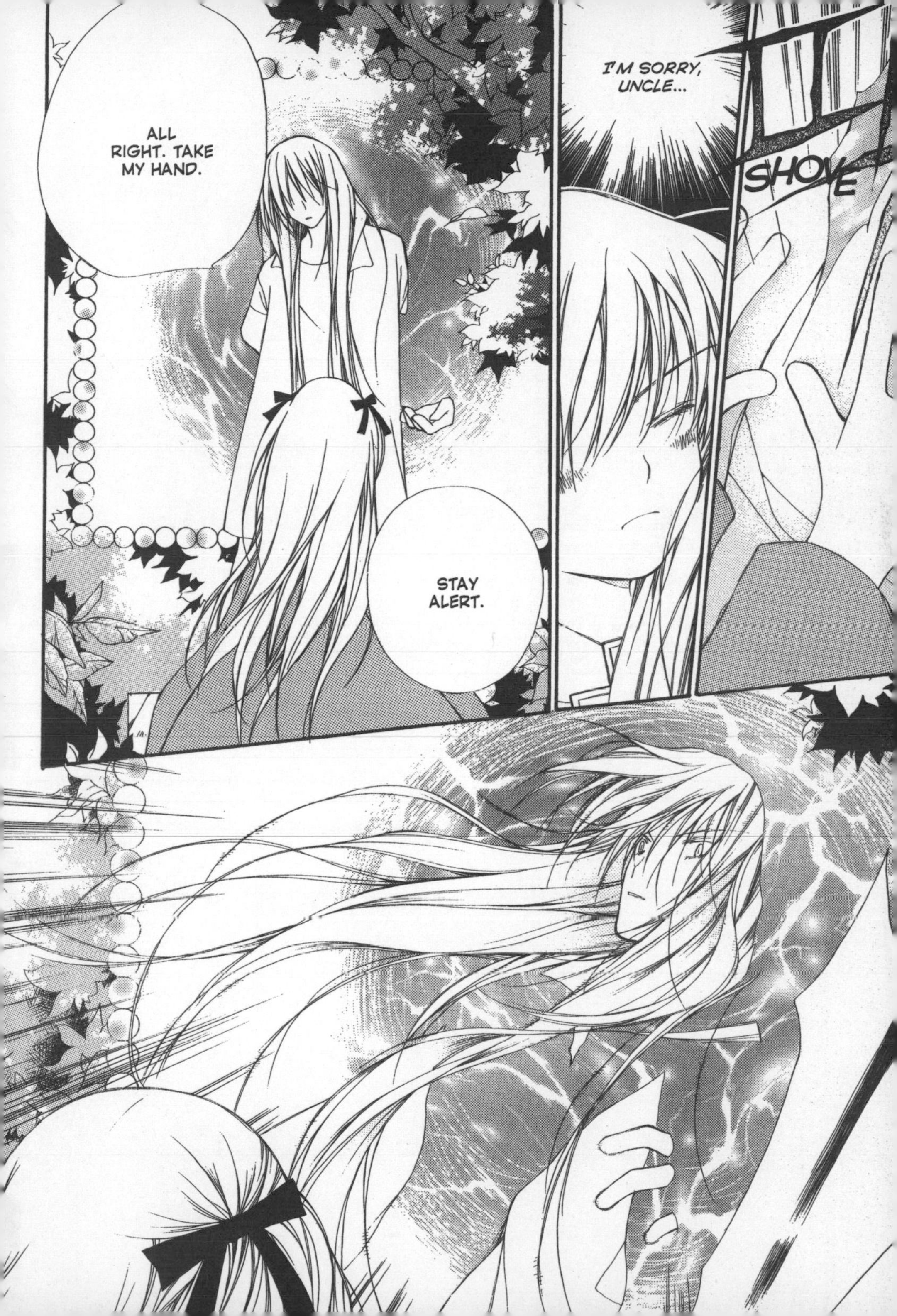
ALL RIGHT. TAKE MY HAND.
STAY ALERT.
I'M SORRY, UNCLE...
SHOVE

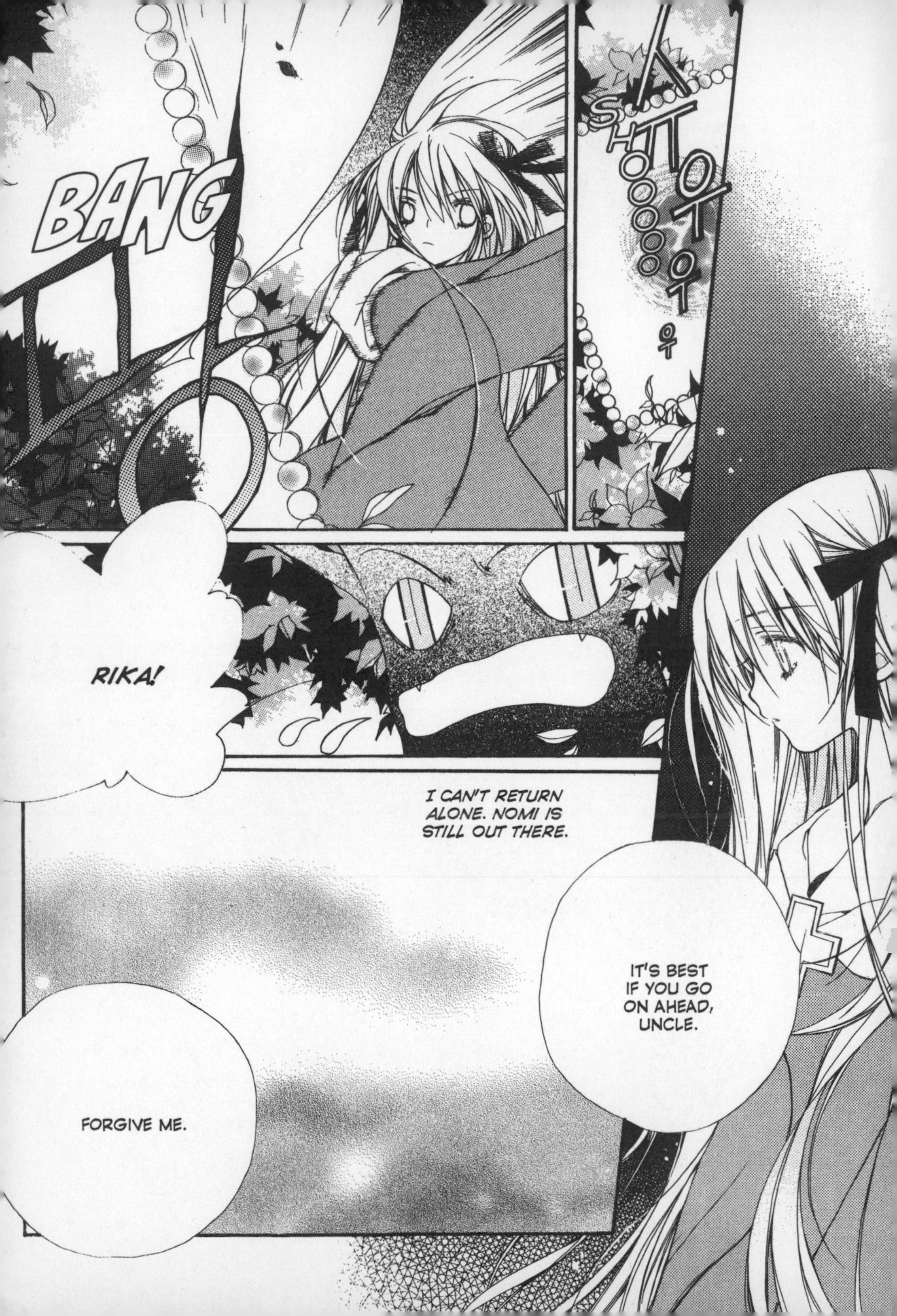
BANG
RIKA!
I CAN'T RETURN ALONE. NOMI IS STILL OUT THERE.
IT'S BEST IF YOU GO ON AHEAD, UNCLE.
FORGIVE ME.

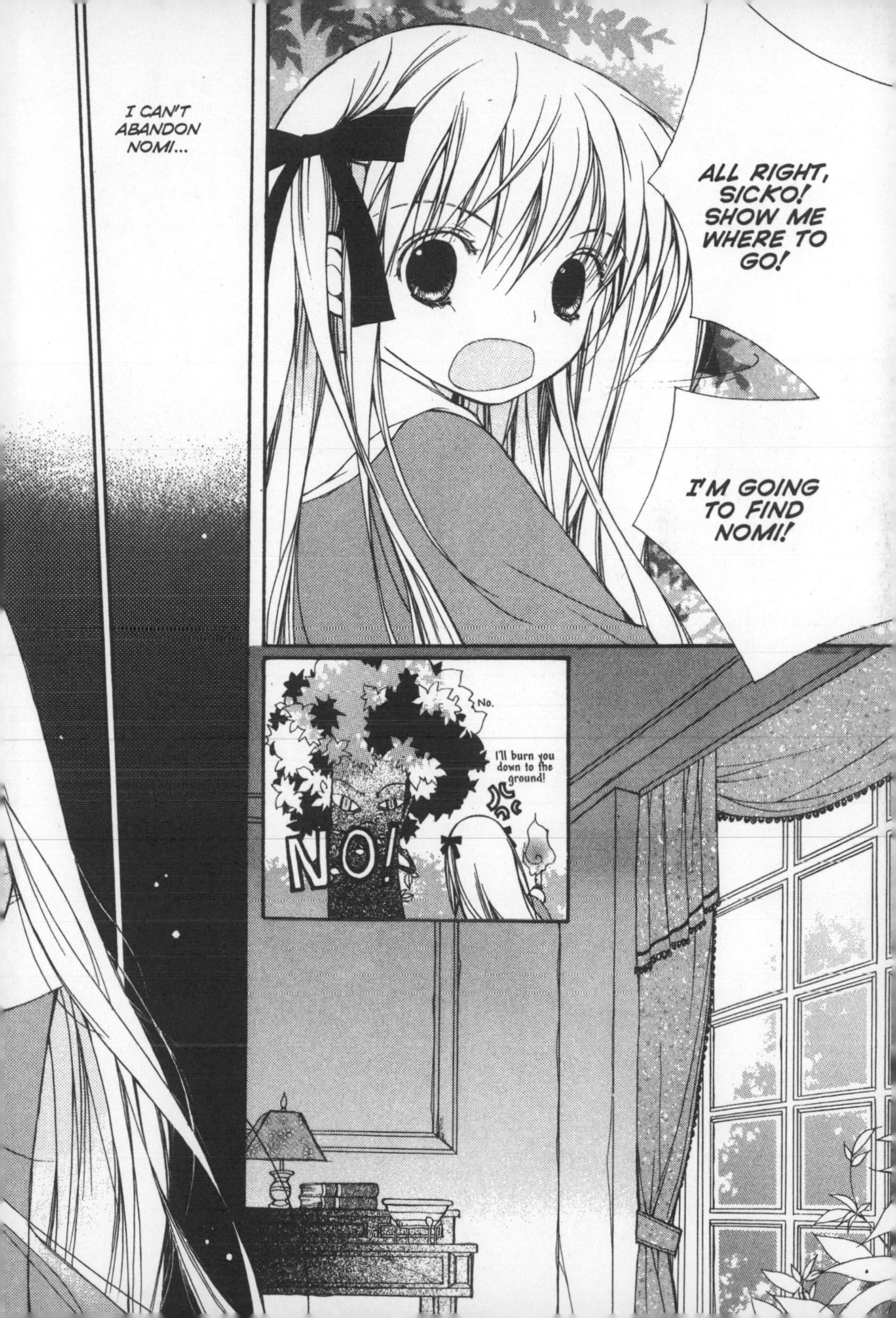
I CAN'T ABANDON NOMI...
ALL RIGHT, SICKO! SHOW ME WHERE TO GO!
I'M GOING TO FIND NOMI!
No.
I'll burn you down to the ground!
NO!

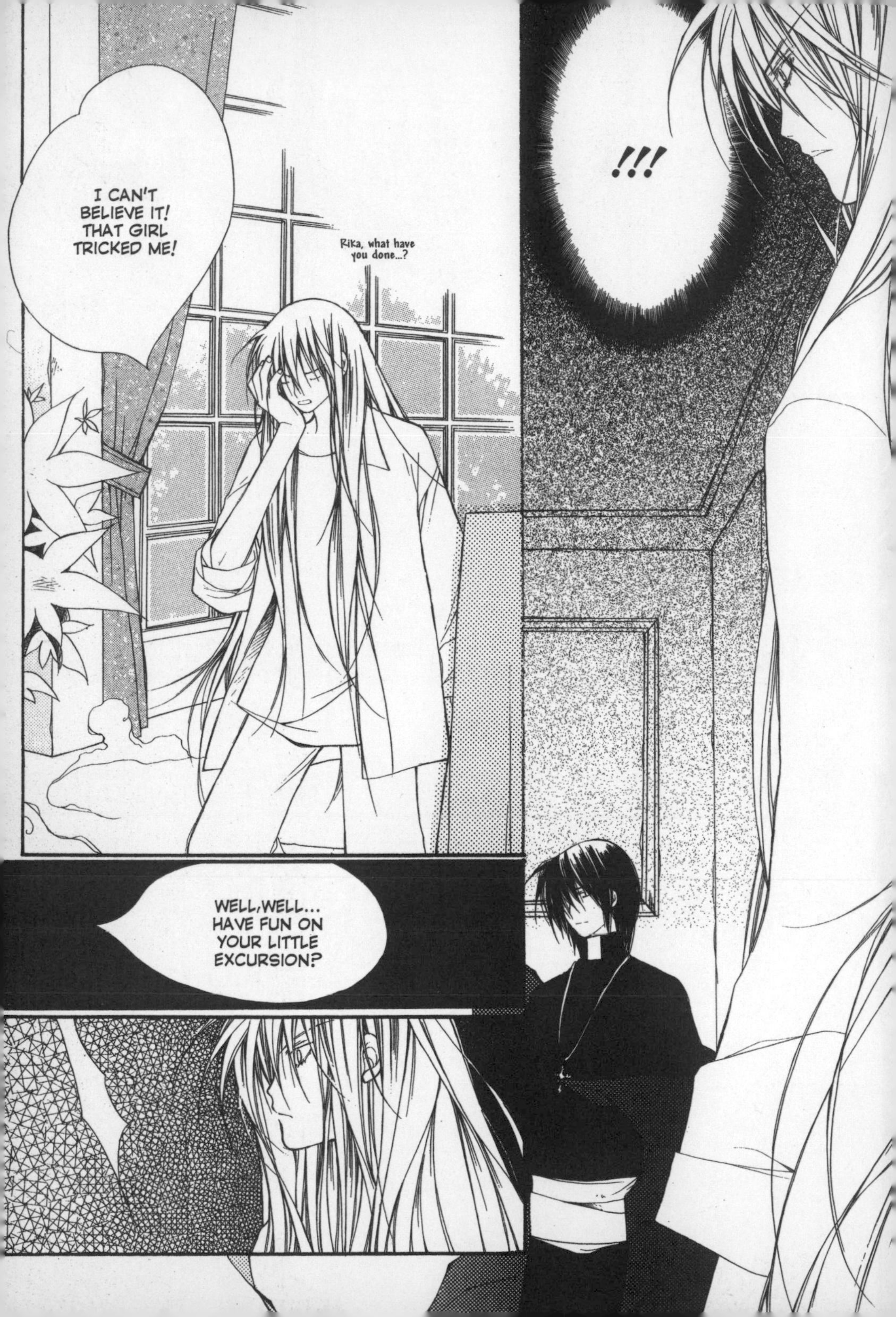
I CAN'T BELIEVE IT! THAT GIRL TRICKED ME!
Rika, what have you done...?
WELL,WELL... HAVE FUN ON YOUR LITTLE EXCURSION?
!!!

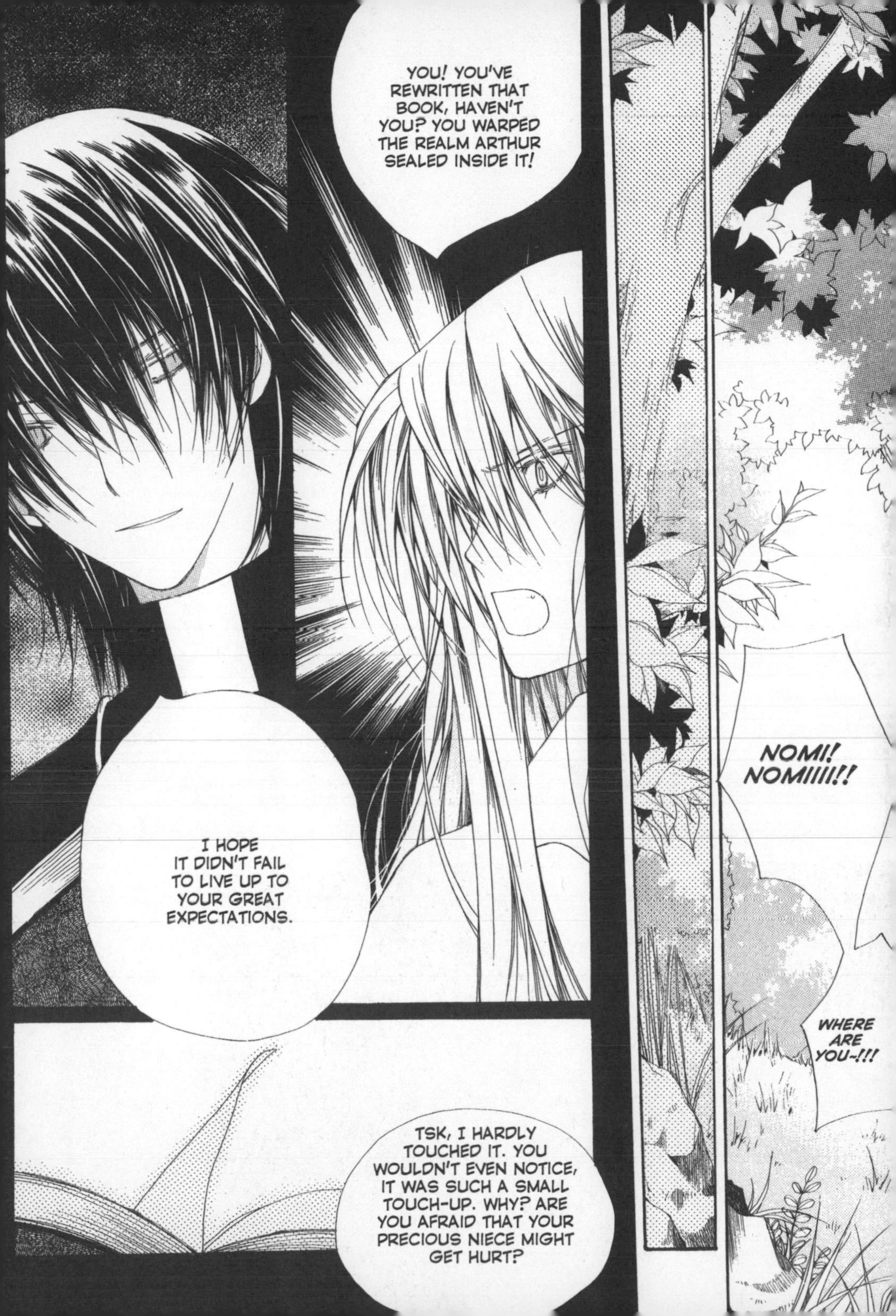
YOU! YOU'VE REWRITTEN THAT BOOK, HAVEN'T YOU? YOU WARPED THE REALM ARTHUR SEALED INSIDE IT!
I HOPE IT DIDN'T FAIL TO LIVE UP TO YOUR GREAT EXPECTATIONS.
TSK, I HARDLY TOUCHED IT. YOU WOULDN'T EVEN NOTICE, IT WAS SUCH A SMALL TOUCH-UP. WHY? ARE YOU AFRAID THAT YOUR PRECIOUS NIECE MIGHT GET HURT?
NOMI! NOMIIII!!
WHERE ARE YOU~!!!

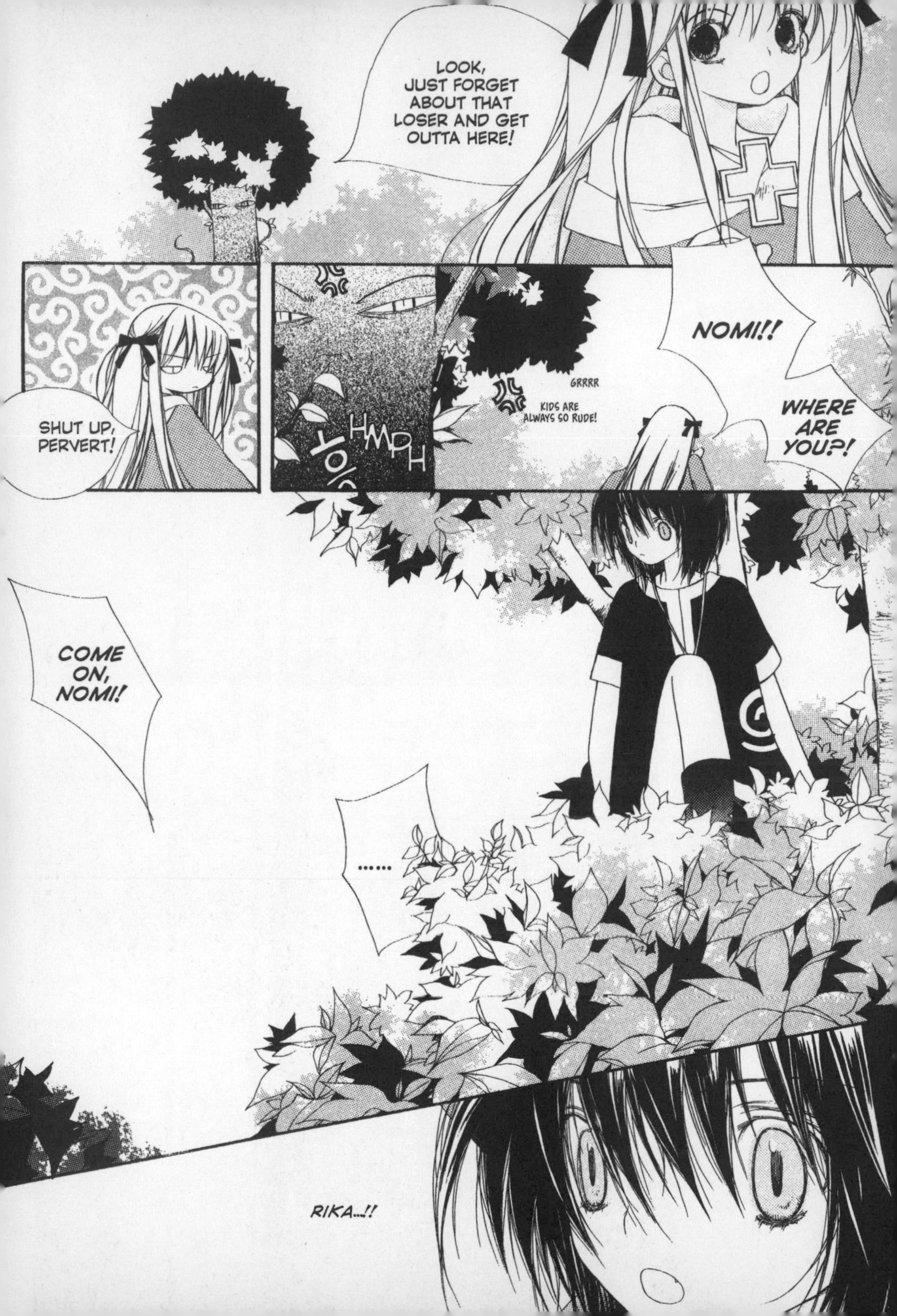
LOOK, JUST FORGET ABOUT THAT LOSER AND GET OUTTA HERE!
SHUT UP, PERVERT!
HMPH
GRRRR
KIDS ARE ALWAYS SO RUDE!
NOMI!!
WHERE ARE YOU?!
COME ON, NOMI!
......
RIKA...!!

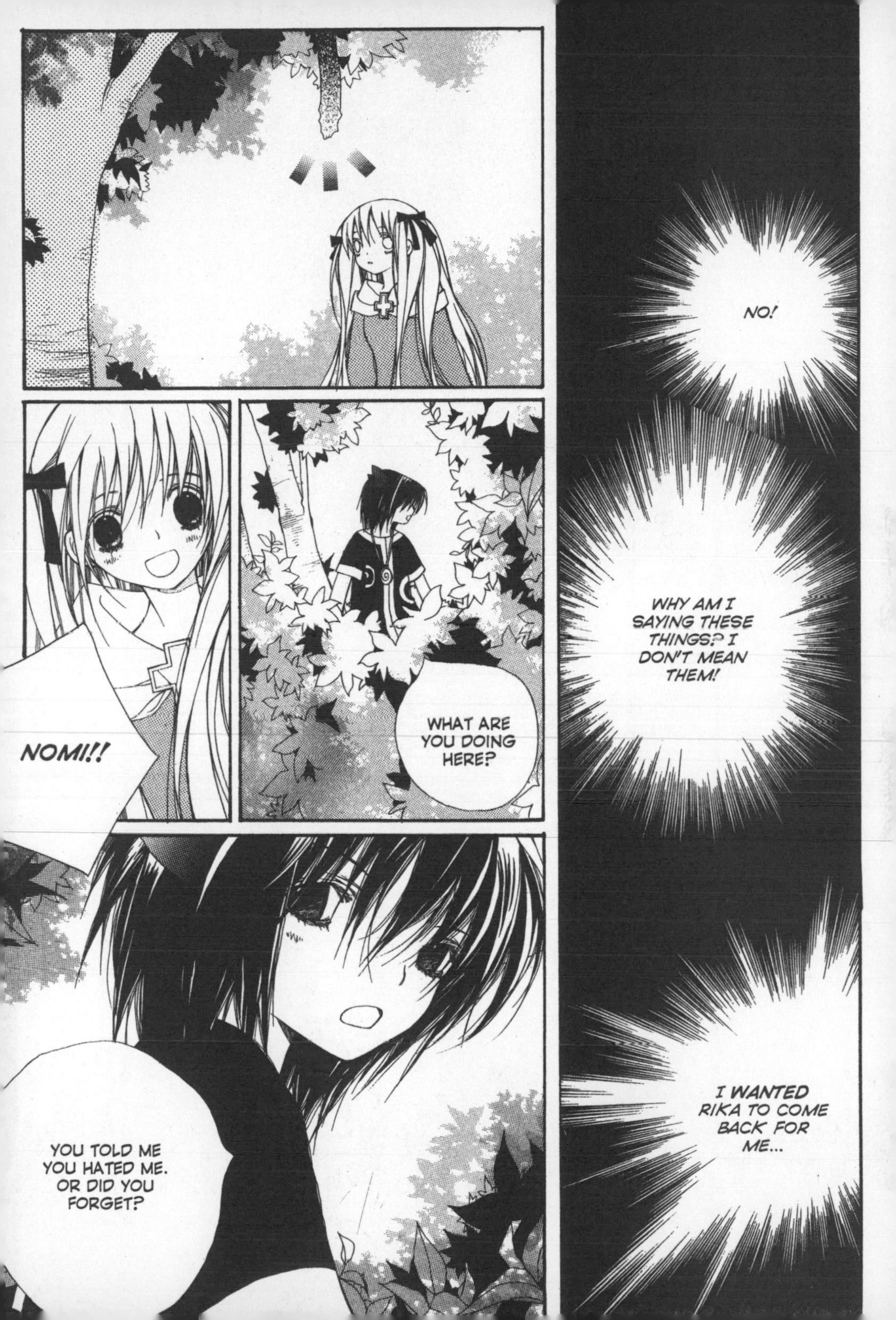
NOMI!!
WHAT ARE YOU DOING HERE?
YOU TOLD ME YOU HATED ME. OR DID YOU FORGET?
NO!
WHY AM I SAYING THESE THINGS? I DON'T MEAN THEM!
I WANTED RIKA TO COME BACK FOR ME...

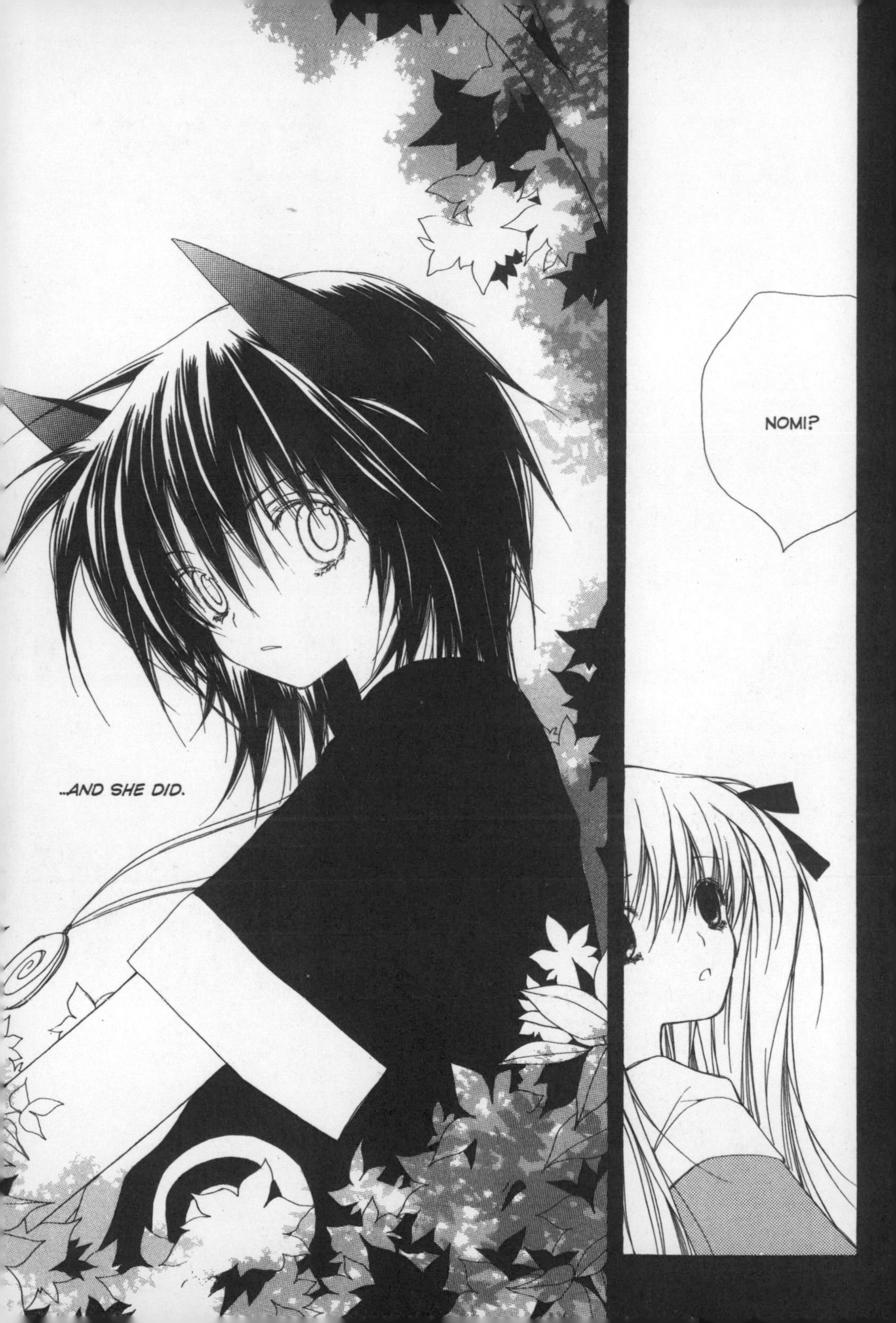
..AND SHE DID.
NOMI?

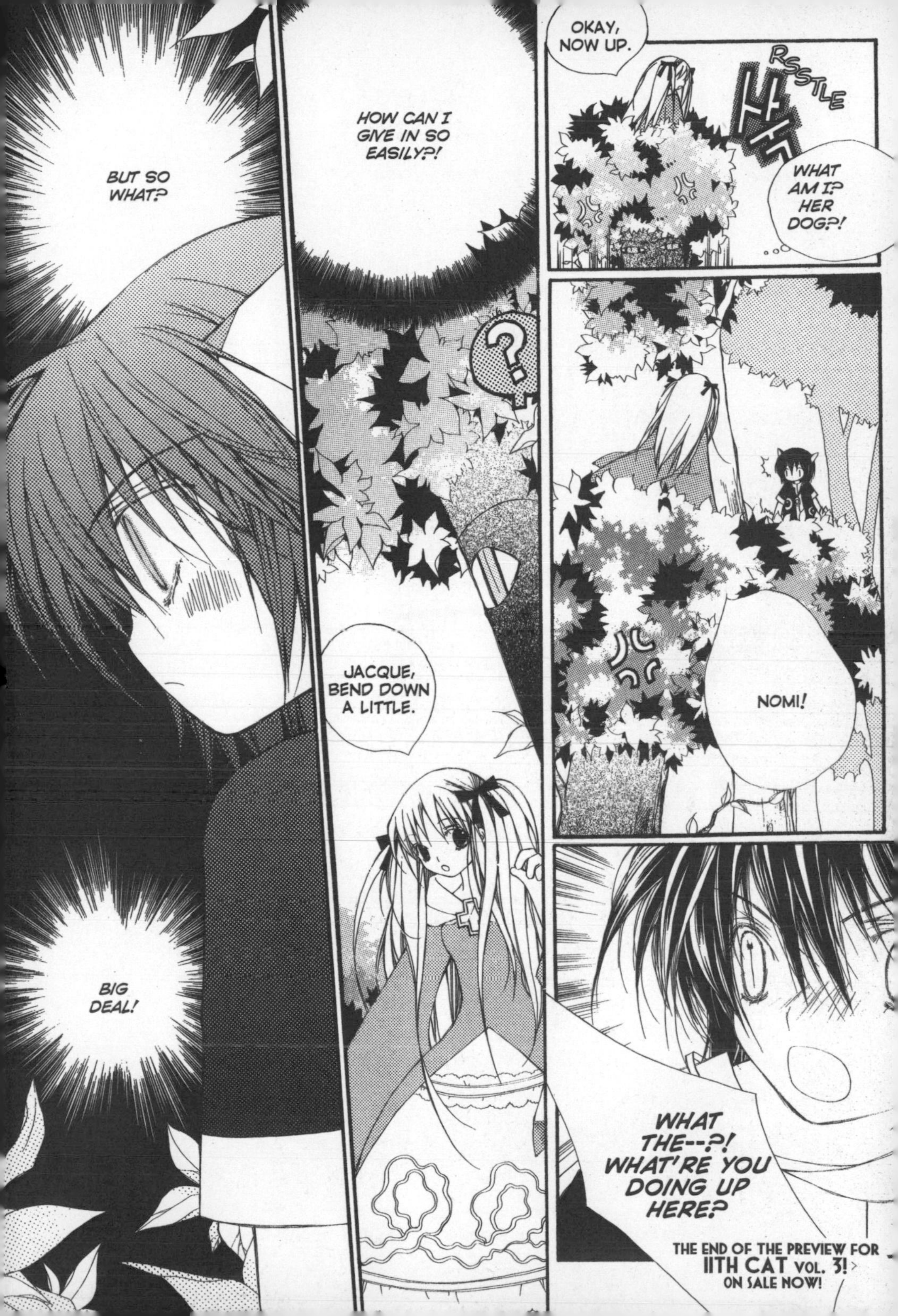

BUT SO WHAT?
BIG DEAL!
HOW CAN I GIVE IN SO EASILY?!
?
JACQUE, BEND DOWN A LITTLE.
OKAY, NOW UP.
RSSSTLE
WHAT AM I? HER DOG?!
NOMI!
WHAT THE--?! WHAT'RE YOU DOING UP HERE?
THE END OF THE PREVIEW FOR 11TH CAT VOL. 3! ON SALE NOW!

Danbi Original

One thousand and one nights vol.2

Story by JinSeok Jeon
Art by SeungHee Han

Translation HyeYoung Im
English Adaptation J. Torres
Touch-up and Lettering Terri Delgado · Marshall Dillon
Graphic Design EunKyung Kim

ICE Kunion

English Adaptation Editor HyeYoung Im · J. Torres
Managing Editor Marshall Dillon
Marketing Manager Erik Ko
Editor JuYoun Lee
Editor in Chief Eddie Yu
Editorial Director MoonJung Kim
Managing Director Jackie Lee
Publisher and C.E.O. JaeKook Chun

One thousand and one nights © 2005 SeungHee Han · JinSeok Jeon
First published in Korea in 2005 by SEOUL CULTURAL PUBLISHERS, Inc.
English text translation rights arranged by SEOUL CULTURAL PUBLISHERS, Inc.
English text © 2005 ICE KUNION

Published by ICE Kunion.
SIGONGSA 2F Yeil Bldg. 1619-4, Seocho-dong, Seocho-gu, Seoul, 137-878, Korea

ISBN : 89-527-4477-2

First printing, July 2006
10 9 8 7 6 5 4 3 2 1
Printed in Canada

www.icekunion.com/www.koreanmanhwa.com